Annual Report
of the
Adjutant General
of the
State of Illinois
1861-1862

Allen C. Fuller

HERITAGE BOOKS
2008

HERITAGE BOOKS
AN IMPRINT OF HERITAGE BOOKS, INC.

Books, CDs, and more—Worldwide

For our listing of thousands of titles see our website
at
www.HeritageBooks.com

Published 2008 by
HERITAGE BOOKS, INC.
Publishing Division
100 Railroad Ave. #104
Westminster, Maryland 21157

Copyright © 1863, 1995 Allen C. Fuller

All rights reserved. No part of this book may be reproduced or transmitted in any form or by any means, electronic or mechanical, including photocopying, recording or by any information storage and retrieval system without written permission from the author, except for the inclusion of brief quotations in a review.

International Standard Book Numbers
Paperbound: 978-0-7884-0228-9
Clothbound: 978-0-7884-7027-1

ANNUAL REPORT

OF THE

ADJUTANT GENERAL.

GENERAL HEAD QUARTERS, STATE OF ILLINOIS,
ADJUTANT GENERAL'S OFFICE,
Springfield, January 1, 1863.

To HIS EXCELLENCY, RICHARD YATES,
Governor of Illinois :

SIR:—I have the honor to submit herewith—

First—A statement—*Schedule A*—showing the number, name of commanding officer, date of organization or muster, and place of organization of Illinois regiments or independent corps, and the number of officers and enlisted men mustered into said regiments or corps at or since their organization, respectively.

Second—A statement—*Schedule B*—showing the number or letter of the command, the name of its commanding officer, and the date and place of organization or muster, as in schedule A, and the day on which they left for the field, arranged according to dates of such departure.

Third—A statement—*Schedule C*—showing the number and name of the officer of each regiment, when originally mustered, and the counties from which the same was principally recruited.

Fourth—A statement—*Schedule D*—showing the free white population in each county in the State, according to the census of 1860, the total number of able-bodied men between the ages of eighteen and forty-five, the number now in service, and those liable to military duty, (except two counties,) according to enrollment taken the past summer. This enrollment being taken before active enlistments for our new regiments ceased, the number of men in service is by very many thousand less than the number *now* in the service.

Fifth—A statement—*Schedule E*—Report of Board of Medical Examiners.

Sixth—A statement—*Schedule F*—showing the amount of salaries of officers and employees of the Adjutant General's office, from April 16, 1861, to January 1, 1863.

Seventh—A statement—*Schedule G*—showing the names of all commissioned officers of Illinois forces, including those who have resigned or been mustered out of service since the commencement of the present war.

It is but justice to myself here to state that it has been exceedingly inconvenient and difficult to prepare an accurate record of the organization and original strength of our old regiments, as stated in this report. The absence of any law requiring original muster-in-rolls or reports of regiments, after they left the State, to be filed in this department, as well as the unorganized condition of many of them when they received marching orders, have combined to make the labor of preparing a record of these forces expensive and perplexing. The imperfect condition of the records when I took possession, November 11, 1861—and I here refer to the subject by way of explanation only—I have endeavored to improve, by procuring the descriptive rolls of the most of the rank and file of our forces. I confess I have been ambitious to place among the permanent archives of the State the name, residence and description of every Illinois volunteer officer and private. This seemed to me due to the living, as well as to the memory of the heroic and lamented dead; and its importance to the people of the State was believed to outweigh all considerations of expense necessary to accomplish the object.

Prior to February 21, 1862, there was not even a regulation of the War Department which required copies of either muster or descriptive rolls to be filed in any of the State departments. In very many instances the United States mustering officers, sent here to muster into the service of the United States our volunteers, neglected, and in some cases positively refused, to file their rolls in this office.

Another source of difficulty and confusion, in this respect, grew out of the acceptance by the War Department of what were known as "independent regiments." In addition to the regiments authorized to be raised by the State, there were, during the year 1861, twenty-two regiments of infantry and four of cavalry authorized by the Secretary of War to be raised in this State. Their correspondence and reports were addressed to the War Department, instead of the State, and some of the persons who were engaged in recruiting these regiments, having been refused authority to raise regiments by you, were disinclined, for a time, to furnish copies of their rolls or give official information to you touching the condition of their commands.

To remedy evils growing out of this state of things, and to promote harmonious relations between the State and Federal authorities, the War Department, by General Order No. 18, promulgated February 21, 1862, provided as follows: "The Governors of states are legally the authorities for raising volunteer regiments and commissioning their officers. Accordingly, no independent organizations, as such, will be hereafter recognized in the United States service. Copies of the rolls of muster into service will be sent, as soon as practicable, to the Governors of the states to which they belong, by the commanders of all brigades, regiments, or corps, heretofore recognized as independent of state organizations;

and all vacancies of commissions in such regiments and corps will be hereafter filled by the respective Governors, according to law."

It will be observed that this order only applies to a particular class of regiments, and the difficulty, to some extent, for a time, continued. A rule was adopted to decline to deliver commissions until their rolls should be filed; but this rule could not, in all cases, be adhered to, for regiments would frequently be required to move before their rolls could be prepared. To supply these rolls and procure statistical information of the number of troops furnished by the State, as well as to ascertain the condition of our troops, in respect to their clothing, camp and garrison equipage and arms, agents, furnished with proper blanks, were dispatched to their camps, in November, 1861. These agents, in a few days, procured reports from most of the regiments; but, on account of active movements in the field, were unable to do so from all.

The same difficulty, although not to so great an extent, has been experienced during the present year, under the last calls for troops, although the rule of not delivering commissions until their muster-in-rolls were filed, has been rigidly adhered to. A reference to the dates of muster and the time when they left the State, will explain how difficult, indeed how impossible it was, in all cases, to procure their descriptive rolls before they moved. For the purpose, therefore, of obtaining the descriptive rolls of such old regiments as had not made their returns, an of such new regiments as were ordered away before theirs could be furnished, as well as to procure from all regiments lists of men joined companies subsequent to their original organization, list of casualties and effective strength of each regiment or corps, one clerk, in November last, was detailed to visit our forces in Missouri, one to Memphis, one to Helena, an agent to Kentucky and Eastern Tennessee, and my first assistant and one clerk to General Grant's department. As these parties were sent in November, I confidently expected to receive their full reports by this time, and be able to furnish a reliable exhibit of the precise strength and condition of all Illinois volunteers, and the names and residence of those who have fallen in battle, or died in hospitals, or been discharged from the service. In this, however, I have been painfully disappointed. Partial reports, only, have yet been received. The recent movement of troops and raids of the enemy, in the departments of the Cumberland and Mississippi, have cut off communications with them and the army. I have, however, prepared a statement of our forces, from the most reliable data in my possession. Its general accuracy is vouched for; but the strength therein stated is undoubtedly less, in some cases, than it should be. The force stated is intended to cover all who have at any time enlisted in our regiments, and includes all who have died or been discharged. As will be explained hereafter, recruiting for old regiments has not been conducted under orders from this department, since January 1, 1862. Those who have been enlisted, however, by the superintendent, and officially reported, are included in this statement. But several hundreds have, undoubtedly, joined these old regiments, who have not been officially reported to the superintendent. The estimate, therefore, is low, and considerably less than I think the balance of the returns, when received, will show. When the balance of the reports shall be received, if it is desired, a supplemental report of the names of all privates can be prepared, although it will make about one thousand pages.

THE SITUATION.

On the evening of April 15, 1861, the following dispatch was received:

"WASHINGTON, *April* 15, 1861.

HIS EXCELLENCY RICHARD YATES:

Call made on you by to-night's mail, for six regiments of militia, for immediate service.

SIMON CAMERON,
Secretary of War."

The great but humiliating event which immediately preceded this dispatch was the fall of Sumpter, at noon, on the 13th of that month, on which day, for the first time since the organization of our Government, our national ensign was struck to traitors. The event and dispatch found our State unprepared for war. Although secession ordinances had before then been passed by Southern states—although public property had been seized, in violation of law, and strange colors displayed over our Southern forts—although food and reinforcements for a beleaguered garrison had been driven back to sea, in January—yet our people could not easily realize that we were indeed in a state of civil war.

From a population, in 1850, of 851,470, we had increased to 1,711,951—more than doubling our population in one decade. Our real and personal property, in 1850, valued at $156,265,006, had, in 1860, increased to $871,860,282, being an increase of $715,595,276, or 457.93 per cent. Our improved lands, which, in 1850, was but 5,039,545 acres, with an estimated value of $96,133,290, had increased, in 1860, to 13,251,473 acres, with an estimated value of $432,531,072. The two principal staple products of our soil, wheat and corn, had increased in a similar ratio—the former from 9,414,575 bushels, in 1850, to 24,159,500, in 1860; and the latter, from 57,646,984, in 1850, to 115,296,779, in 1860. Our magnificent railways, which, in 1850, were only 110 miles, costing $1,440,507, had extended, in 1860, to 2867 miles, at a cost of $104,944,561. Nor had the progress of our people been confined to an increase of population and wealth. In every city and town had sprung up, as if by magic, the unmistakable evidences of progress in the arts and sciences. In fact, it could be truly said, that through the enlightened liberality of our citizens, the unfortunate, the poor, and the helpless, were provided for and educated, without money and without price.

These blessings—this advancement in greatness and power, were not confined to Illinois. Our sister states shared them with us, although not to such an unprecedented extent. North and south, east and west were all prosperous and happy. No nation on earth could show so bright a record—such a prosperous present or such a hopeful future as ours, up to the year 1860. And it was in the midst of such unexampled prosperity and individual and national happiness that gigantic conspiracies were matured to annul the Federal laws, to subvert the constitution, and overthrow the Government. So accustomed to the pursuits of peace, and so unaccustomed to war were our people, that, although there was little or no military organization in the State, yet, recognizing that all they had been, and all they were, and all they hoped to be, depended upon the maintenance of this Government, and laying aside recent party ties, forgetting for the time late partisan controversies, with an almost unanimous voice demanded the right of Illinois to do her full share in conquering, by force of arms, a peace.

On the twenty-eighth day of February, 1795, Congress had provided that, whenever the laws of the United States should be opposed, or the execution thereof obstructed, in any state, by combinations too powerful to be suppressed by the ordinary course of judicial proceedings, or by the powers vested in the marshal by that act, it should be lawful for the President of the United States " to call forth the militia " of such state or any other state or states, as might be necessary to suppress such combination and to cause the laws to be executed. It was further provided, that the militia employed in the service of the United States should be subject to the same rules and articles of war as the troops of the United States, and that no officer or private of the militia should be compelled to serve more than three months, after his arrival at the place of rendezvous, in any one year, nor more than his due rotation with every other able bodied man of the same rank in the battalion to which he belonged.

Our early statesmen, while guarding against standing armies, conferred upon the President, as Commander-in-chief of the army and navy, the right to call upon the militia, when necessary to uphold the Government and cause the laws to be executed; and that militia was declared to consist of every able bodied white male citizen between the ages of eighteen and forty-five, not specially exempted. The great source of military power in this country, then, is the militia. It may be drafted and compelled to serve a specified time. Its organization belongs to the states, respectively, and calls for it are made upon the states, not upon individuals. T encourage and maintain an organized militia is the duty of every state, since the maintenance of the supremacy of the laws of the United States, may, at any time, depend upon such organizations.

The call of April 15, was made upon you as the Commander-in-chief of the militia of the State, for six regiments. The President, on the same day, issued his Proclamation, and, after stating that the laws of the United States "were opposed" and the execution thereof "obstructed," called forth the militia of the several loyal states, to the aggregate number of seventy-five thousand. In the circular of the Secretary of War, of the same day, assigning the quotas to the several states under the call, required you to "detach from the militia" of this State 225 officers and 4458 men, being 4683. The call to "detach" these officers and men presupposed the existence of an efficient organized militia which could be immediately called into service.

Such, however, was not our condition. From papers turned over to me, November 23, 1862, by my predecessor, I find but twenty-five bonds for the return of arms issued to militia companies in 1857-8-9 and 60, and during the same time but thirty-seven certificates of the election of company officers. It will further appear, from the report of the Quartermaster General, who, until about the first of April, 1862, had charge of the Ordnance Department, there were but three hundred and sixty-two United States altered muskets—one hundred and five Harper's Ferry and Deniger's rifles—one hundred and thirty-three muskatoons and two hundred and ninety-seven horse pistols in the arsenal. A few hundred unserviceable arms and accoutrements were scattered through the State, principally in the possession of these militia companies. In fact, there were no available, efficient, armed and organized militia companies in the State, and it is doubted whether there were thirty companies with any regular organization. It is true there were in our principal cities and towns several independent militia companies, composed principally of active and enterprising young men, whose occasional meetings for drill were held more for exercise and amusement than from any sense of duty to the State. Many of these companies formed the nucleus of splendid companies, which came promptly forward, and who have rendered excellent service to their State and country.

Such then—a people literally loaded with bounties and blessings of long continued peace—of martial spirit but untried in war, and absolutely unarmed—was the *situation*.

SPECIAL SESSION—ORGANIZATION OF SIX REGIMENTS.

On the same day, April 15, 1861, your proclamation was issued, convening the Legislature on the 23d, and the subjects named for its consideration were, as follows: "The more perfect organization and equipment of the militia of the State and placing the same upon a war footing; and to render efficient assistance to the General Government in preserving the Union, enforcing the laws and protecting the property and rights of the people. And also to raise such money or other means as may be required to carry out the foregoing objects; and also to provide for the expenses of such session."

General Order, No. 1, from these headquarters was also issued, directing all commandants of divisions, brigades, regiments and companies to hold themselves in readiness for actual service, and on the 16th, General Order, No. 2, for the immediate organization of the six regiments.

In answer to this call, a prompt response was received from almost every part of the State. In ten days over ten thousand had tendered their services, and in addition to a part of the force sent to Cairo, more than our full quota was in camp at Springfield.

There being no serviceable arms in the arsenal at Springfield, an unsuccessful application was made to Brigadier General Harney, at the arsenal at St. Louis. Application was also made, on the 19th, at the arsenal in New York, and a messenger dispatched to Washington to obtain them. As these troops were to be mustered into the service of the United States, on the 19th, more than our full quota having been tendered, application was also made for a mustering officer, and, on the 22d, Captain Pope arrived to perform that service. There were volunteers enough and a surplus on that eventful 19th of April, 1861, but the want of arms had become painful and alarming. It was on that day that Union soldiers from a sister state, hastening to the defense of the national capital, were shot down in the streets of Baltimore; and on that and following days that your messenger, returning from that capital and bearing concealed orders from the President to the commanding officer at St. Louis for arms, was obliged to deny the principles of his manhood and avow disloyal sentiments, to escape the vengeance of an enfuriated mob of that city.

CAIRO EXPEDITION.

On the same day the following dispatch was received from the Secretary of War:

"WASHINGTON, *April* 19*th*, 1861.
GOVERNOR YATES:
As soon as enough of your troops is mustered into service, send a Brigadier General, with four regiments, at or near Grand Cairo.
SIMON CAMERON,
Secretary of War."

The importance of taking possession of this point was felt by all, and that too, without waiting the arrival and organization of a brigade. Accordingly, the following dispatch was sent to Brigadier General Swift, at Chicago:

"SPRINGFIELD, *April* 19, 1861.

GENERAL SWIFT:

As quick as possible have as strong a force as you can raise, armed and equipped with ammunition and accoutrements, and a company of artillery, ready to march at a moment's warning. A messenger will start to Chicago to-night.

RICHARD YATES,
Commander-in-chief."

At eleven (11) o'clock on the twenty-first, only forty-eight hours after this dispatch was delivered, General Swift left Chicago with a force of 595 men and four six pounder pieces of artillery. Capt. Houghtaling's battery, of Ottawa; Capt. Hawley's, of Lockport; Capt. McAllister's, of Plainfield, and Capt. Carr's, of Sandwich, did not arrive in Chicago in time to join the expedition, but followed it the next day. The expedition consisted of the following forces:

Brig. Gen. Swift and Staff	14
Chicago Light Artillery, Capt. Smith	150
Ottawa " " Capt. Houghtaling	86
Lockport " " Capt. Hawley	52
Plainfield " " Capt. McAllister	72
Co. A, Chicago Zouaves, Capt. Hayden	89
Co. B, " " Capt. Clyborne	83
Capt. Harding's company	80
Turner Union Cadets, Capt. Kowald	97
Lincoln Rifles, Capt. Mihalotzy	66
Sandwich company, Capt. Carr	102
Drum corps	17
Total	908

Captain Campbell's Ottawa Independent Artillery, with about twenty men and two six-pounder cannon, joined the force about the 28th April.

This expedition, indifferently armed with rifles, shot-guns, muskets and carbines, hastily gathered from stores and shops in Chicago, arrived at Big Muddy bridge, on the Illinois Central Railroad, at five o'clock, A. M., April 22d, and detaching Capt. Harding's company at that point, arrived at Cairo at eight o'clock the following morning. The batteries were unprovided , shell or canister, but slugs hurriedly prepared—and some of which were subsequently used at a critical time, and with terrible effect, by one of these batteries at Fort Donelson—answered the purpose of all.

This command was reinforced, on the twenty-fourth, by seven companies from Springfield, under the command of Col. Prentiss, who relieved Gen. Swift, except as to that portion—who did not desire to muster into the United States service—commanded by Captains Harding, Hayden and Clyborne, who returned to Springfield on the second of May, to join a regiment organizing here. These last companies, however, arrived too late, and were mustered out of the State service, with allowance of one month's pay, under an act of the Legislature then in session.

The importance of an early occupation, by our forces, of Cairo, was not over-estimated. Situated at the confluence of the Ohio and Mississippi rivers, and commanding the navigation of these waters, its possession in a strategical point of view, was absolutely necessary to our safety. The state governments of Missouri, Tennessee and Kentucky were controlled by disloyal men. Governor Magoffin had, on the 16th of April, said to the President, in reply to his call on that state for troops: "Your dispatch is received. In answer, I say emphatically, Kentucky will furnish no troops for the wicked purpose of subduing her sister Southern states." Governor Harris, of Tennessee, on the 18th, in reply to the call upon his state said, "Tennessee will not furnish a single man for coercion;" and on the same day Governor Jackson, of Missouri, said, "Requisition is illegal, unconstitutional, revolutionary, inhuman, diabolical, and cannot be complied with."

By taking possession of this point, at so early a date, our forces were enabled to prevent a traffic with the rebellious states in contraband property. This traffic was being actively carried on between Galena and St. Louis, with towns on the Mississippi below Cairo. The execution of the following telegraphic order was the first arrest made to this traffic:

"SPRINGFIELD, *April* 24, 1861.

COL. B. M. PRENTISS, *Cairo*:

The steamers C. E. Hillman and John D. Perry are about to leave St. Louis, with arms and munitions. Stop said boats, and sieze all the arms and munitions.

RICHARD YATES,
Commander-in-chief."

On the evening of the 24th and morning of the 25th, as these boats, bound for southern ports, neared Cairo, Col. Prentiss directed Captain Smith of the Chicago Light Artillery and Captain Scott of the Chicago Zouaves to board them and bring them to the wharf. His orders were executed, and large quantities of arms and munitions of war were seized and confiscated. Though this seizure was not expressly authorized by the War Department, the act of seizure and subsequent confiscation was approved. Further shipments were all forbidden, soon after, as appears from the following dispatch:

"WASHINGTON, *May* 7, 1861.

GOVERNOR YATES:

Circular has been sent to collectors forbidding shipments intended for ports under insurrectionary control. Stop such shipments from Cairo.

S. P. CHASE."

The Legislature having met on the 23d of April, proceeded at once to provide for the organization of these six regiments, and, on the 25th, an "act to organize six regiments of volunteers from the State of Illinois and provide for the election of regimental officers and of a Brigadier General," was approved and became a law. Under the old militia laws of the State a company of infantry consisted of one captain, one first, one second and one third lieutenant, four sergeants, four corporals, one drummer, one fifer, and not less than forty-six nor more than one hundred and sixteen rank and file. A regiment consisted of one Colonel, one, two or three Majors (as the case might be) the senior to be Lieutenant Colonel, with a regimental staff, to be appointed by the Colonel, to consist of one Adjutant, who should act as regimental judge advocate, one Quartermaster, one Paymaster, to rank as Captains, respectively; one Surgeon and Surgeon's Mate, one Sergeant Major, one Quartermaster Sergeant, one Drum Major and one Fife Major.

The regulations of the Secretary of War for organizing these regiments required each regiment to consist of one Colonel, one Lieutenant Colonel, one Major, one Adjutant, (a Lieutenant,) one regimental Quartermaster, (a Lieutenant,) one Surgeon, one Surgeon's Mate, one Sergeant Major; one Drum Major, one Fife Major, ten Captains, ten Lieutenants, ten Ensigns, forty Sergeants, forty Corporals, ten drummers, ten fifers and six hundred and forty privates.

The law provided that "in token of respect to the Illinois regiments in Mexico," these regiments should be numbered seven, eight, nine, ten, eleven, and twelve; and that when organized they should be known as the "First Brigade Illinois Volunteers." Under the provisions of this law they were organized and mustered into service and ordered to duty as follows:

The *Seventh*, Colonel Cook, was mustered at Springfield, April 25th, and ordered to Alton the 27th.

The *Eighth*, Colonel Oglesby, was mustered the same date, and ordered to Cairo the 27th.

The *Ninth*, Colonel Paine, was mustered at the same place, April 26th, and ordered to Cairo May 1st.

The *Tenth*, Colonel Prentiss, was, with a part of his command, ordered to Cairo, April 22d, and was, on the 29th, mustered at Cairo.

The *Eleventh*, Colonel Wallace, was mustered at Springfield, April 30th, and ordered to Villa Ridge May 5th.

The *Twelfth*, Colonel McArthur, was mustered at Springfield, May 2d, and ordered to Cairo, May 10th.

On the completion of the organization of these regiments several hundred volunteers were left unprovided for. Most of the companies arrived in camp with over one hundred men. Seven hundred and eighty, rank and file, was the maximum allowed by the War Department, and, among the most touching and painful incidents, indicating the patriotic fervor of our people at that time, noticed in the preparation of these troops for the field, was the rejecting from their companies these surplus volunteers. Strong men, who had left their homes at an hour's notice to enter the service of their country, wept at the disappointment of being refused admission to their companies on muster day. Provision was made of one month's pay for them, and they filed their rolls and were mustered out of the service of the State.

TEN REGIMENTS OF INFANTRY AND ONE OF CAVALRY.

In anticipation of a call for more troops by the General Government, and in addition to liberal appropriation bills to enable the State to be placed on a war footing, the Legislature, at the same session, authorized the acceptance, for State service, ten regiments of infantry, one regiment of cavalry and one battalion of light artillery.

The third section of that law provided that one of such regiments might be raised out of volunteer companies then in Springfield, and one regiment from each of the nine congressional districts theretofore established in this State. The fourth section provided that all persons voluntarily enlisting in said regiments or battalion, before being tendered or accepted as a company, or in regiments, should severally pledge themselves, if called upon, to tender their services to the General Government.

The fifth section provided that, as soon as arms could be provided, they should be put into encampments, by regiments, at their regimental headquarters, within the congressional district in which they were raised, and should be held in camp for thirty days, for the purpose of instruction and discipline, unless sooner demanded by the United States for actual duty.

The tenth section provided that, as soon as ten companies should be formed into a regiment, an election should be ordered for regimental officers.

This act took effect May 2d, and on the next day the President issued his proclamation, calling for 42,032 volunteers, to serve for three years, unless sooner discharged.

Over two hundred companies immediately tendered their services. The messenger, who had left Washington with an order for arms in the St. Louis arsenal had arrived, and, notwithstanding the arsenal was closely watched by secessionists in St. Louis, a *plan* was secretly adopted and executed, and on the morning of the 26th of April, a steamboat from St. Louis arrived at Alton, with about twenty-one thousand stand of arms on board, which were forwarded to Springfield the same day.

May 6th, controversies about tenders were settled and regiments ordered into camp. The regiment from the first congressional district was ordered to rendezvous at Freeport, May 11; the regiment from second, at Dixon, May 9; the regiment from third, at Joliet, May 11; the regiment from fourth, at Peoria, May 13; the regiment from fifth, at Quincy, May 9; the regiment from sixth, at Jacksonville, May 11; the regiment from seventh, at Mattoon, May 9; the regiment from eighth, at Belleville, May 11; and the regiment from the ninth, at Anna, May 16. The regiment from the State at large, composed in part of companies in Springfield, were, on the eleventh of June, ordered into camp at Chicago, on the thirteenth of June.

These ten regiments of infantry, and one of cavalry, and a battalion of artillery, were immediately tendered to the General Government. But on the third of May, the following reply was received, refusing to accept cavalry:

"WASHINGTON, *May* 3, 1861."

GOVERNOR YATES:

In reply to yours of the 2d, I am again obliged, at the solicitation of General Scott, to decline acceptance of cavalry. Adjutant General Thomas is clear in his opinion that they cannot be of service adequate to the expense incurred by accepting them.

SIMON CAMERON,
Secretary of War."

No decisive reply was received in relation to infantry until the 15th, when the following dispatch was received:

"WASHINGTON, *May* 15, 1861."

GOVERNOR YATES:

The quota of troops from your State, for three years or during the war, under the second call of the President, is six regiments. The plan of organization contained in Order No. 15, has already been forwarded you by mail. As soon as the regiments are ready the mustering officer sent to your State will muster them into service, who has already been instructed to do so.

SIMON CAMERON,
Secretary of War."

In a letter, dated the next day, the Secretary of War said:

"It is important to reduce rather than increase this number, and in no event, to exceed it. Let me earnestly recommend to you, therefore, to call for no more than twelve regiments, of which six only are to serve for three years or during the war, and if more are already called for, to reduce the number by discharge."

A messenger was immediately dispatched to Washington to urge upon the Secretary of War the importance of accepting the other four regiments—as they were all raised and the most of them actually in camp—and also to conclude an arrangement which had previously been suggested by the Secretary of War, of re-organizing the six three months' regiments for three years' service. The result was, that the other four regiments were accepted, and on the twenty-eighth of May an arrangement was made that the three months' regiments might be mustered into service for three years, immediately, provided four-fifths (4-5) of them were willing; and, if the remaining fifth declined, they were to be immediately mustered out of service. This proposition was declined at that time by the three months' regiments. A change of climate, bad water and poor clothing had sent many to the hospital, and the result was that out of 4680, who enlisted in the 7th, 8th, 9th, 10th, 11th and 12th regiments, but about 2000, subsequently re-enlisted, at the expiration of their term of service, in July following.

The 13th regiment was mustered at Dixon, July 24th, under Col. Wyman; the 14th, at Jacksonville, on the 25th, under Col. Palmer; the 15th, at Freeport, May 24th, under Col. Turner; the 16th, at Quincy, May 24th, under Col. Smith; the 17th, at Peoria, May 24th, under Col. Ross; the 18th, at Anna, May 28th, under Col. Lawler; the 19th, at Chicago, June 17th, under Col. Turchin; the 20th, at Joliet, June 13th, under Col. Marsh; the 21st, at Mattoon, June 15th, under Col. Grant; and the 22d, at Belleville, June 25th, under Col. Dougherty,

The refusal on the part of the Secretary of War to authorize you to accept more troops caused several thousand of our best and impatient volunteers to leave their State in May, June and July, and enlist elsewhere. Denied the privilege of serving their country in regiments from their own State they sought other fields of usefulness. Many whole companies entered Missouri regiments, and are now in the service. From correspondence with many of these so-called Missouri regiments, and from estimates made by those whose opinion is entitled to credit, I have no doubt more than ten thousand Illinoisans left their own State and enlisted in regiments of other states.

In several cases application has been made to you to have regiments, a large majority of which consisted of Illinoisans, recognized as Illinois regiments. To provide for these cases the War Department, on the 21st of February last, decided that "whenever a regiment is composed of companies from different states, it will be considered as belonging to the state from which the greatest number of companies was furnished for that regiment." Under this order the 59th regiment, formerly 9th Missouri, and the 66th, formerly known as "Birge's Sharp Shooters," have been reclaimed, and other similar applications are now pending.

The "*plan of organization*," referred to in the dispatch of the 15th, was promulgated in General Order, No. 15, of the War Department, May 15, 1861, and provided for raising thirty-nine additional regiments of infantry and one regiment of cavalry, making a minimum aggregate of 34,506 officers and enlisted men, and a maximum aggregate of 42,034 officers and enlisted men, as heretofore stated. Each regiment of infantry was to consist of one Colonel, one Lieutenant Colonel, one Major, one Adjutant, one Quartermaster, one Surgeon, one Assistant Surgeon, one Sergeant Major, one Quartermaster Sergeant, one Commissary Sergeant, one Hospital Steward, two principal Musicians and twenty-four Musicians for band. Each company to consist of one Captain, one First Lieutenant, one Second Lieutenant, one First Sergeant, four Sergeants, eight Corporals, two Musicians, one Wagoner and not less than sixty-four nor more than eighty-two privates—a minimum company being eighty-three, and maximum one hundred and one.

FIRST CAVALRY.

The cavalry regiment authorized by the law of the special session, May 3, 1861, was formed by the acceptance of companies as provided by the law.

The companies reported at Camp Yates previous to the passage of the law and known as the "Chicago Dragoons" and "Washington Light Cavalry," commanded, respectively, by Capts. Chas. W. Barker and Frederick Schambeck, were immediately organized and mustered into the State service; and subsequently, on the 10th day of May, three companies were accepted from that portion of the State lying south of the Ohio and Mississippi Railroad, viz: Captain Orlando Burrell, "White County Cavalry;" Captain James Foster's "Gallatin County Cavalry," and the "Centralia Cavalry," commanded by Captain R. D. Noleman.

In view of the great expense of this arm of the service, and the further fact, that the State did not need more than five companies for its own defense, your excellency declined organizing the full regiment until the services of the same should be required by the Government.

The five additional companies were, however, designated in compliance with law, and mentioned in special order, of May 16th, 1861, raised at points named, by the following officers: Capt. John McNulta, Bloomington; Capt. A. C. Harding, Monmouth; Capt. John Burnap, Springfield; Capt. J. B. Smith, Knoxville; Capt. Paul Walters, Hillsboro.

On the 21st day of June, 1861, the President accepted the services of ten companies of cavalry for three years' service, unless sooner discharged; and the companies previously accepted by your excellency were assigned to form the "First Regiment of Illinois Volunteer Cavalry," and under direction of the War Department were equipped and mustered into the United States service.

The Chicago Dragoons, Capt. Barker, were first ordered to Cairo, and thence, by order of General McClellan, transferred to his command in Western Virginia; but, upon declining to enter the three years' service, were ordered to Chicago, and mustered out of service, in the month of September, 1861.

Companies A, B, C, D, E, F, and G, commanded by Captains McNulta, Foster, Mitchell, Smith, Walters, Burnap and Palmer, were, with the 23d, Col. Mulligan, engaged at the siege of Lexington, Missouri, and, with other United States forces, taken prisoners of war, on the 20th of Sept., 1861.

By order of Major General John C. Fremont, then commanding Department of the West, the enlisted men of these seven companies were mustered out of service, on the 8th day of October, 1861; but, by order of the President, were reinstated and declared as continuously in service; and by order of War Department, dated 21st December, 1861, the regiment was reorganized at Benton Barracks, St. Louis, Missouri, during the month of December, 1861, but only continued in service a short time, because of difficulties arising in relation to large numbers of its members not having been properly exchanged.

Capt. Oscar Huntley's cavalry company, raised in Winnebago county, under authority of General Fremont, was assigned to this regiment at the time of its re-organization at Benton Barracks, but not mustered out of service, as it was not involved in the affair at Lexington.

The battalion of artillery, authorized by the law of May 2d, was not organized as such. Company "A," Chicago Artillery, Capt. Smith, (afterwards Capt. Willard's,) Capt. Houghtaling's Ottawa Artillery, and Capt. McAllister's Plainfield Artillery, formed a part of General Swift's expedition to Cairo, in April. Capt. Hopkins' Springfield Artillery was also ordered to Cairo, in April, and all remained in the service. They were first mustered into the three months' service, and afterwards into the three years' service. Capt. Houghtaling's battery was first mustered into the three months' service, as company "F," 10th regiment; Capt. McAllister's, as company "K," same regiment, three months' service, and Capt. Hopkins', as company "I," in same regiment. Company "B," Capt. Taylor, Chicago Artillery; Capt. Davidson, Peoria Artillery; Capt. Madison's battery, and company "A," Chicago Artillery, re-organized under Capt. Willard, were accepted under this law as batteries. These seven batteries and Capt. Campbell's Ottawa battery, were mustered into service, and their organization protected by an acceptance from the War Department of an additional battalion of artillery, in July.

INDEPENDENT REGIMENTS.

These regiments of infantry, to-wit: No. 7 to 22, inclusive, which you had been authorized to raise, were, in June, either full or nearly so. In May, June and July, the following regiments of infantry were authorized by the Secretary of War:

23d,	Colonel	Mulligan;	24th,	Colonel	Hecker;
25th,	"	Coler;	33d,	"	Hovey;
34th,	"	Kirk;	35th,	"	Smith;
36th,	"	Greusel;	37th,	"	White;
39th,	"	Light;	40th,	"	Hicks;
41st,	"	Pugh;	42d,	"	Webb;
44th,	"	Knobelsdorf;	45th,	"	Smith;
47th,	"	Bryner;	52d,	"	Wilson;
55th,	"	Stuart;	4th cavalry, Col. Dickey;		

8th cavalry, Col. Farnsworth; 9th cavalry, Col. Brackett, and the 11th cavalry, Col. Ingersoll, by General Fremont.

All these regiments were speedily filled, and, on the second of July, you were authorized to organize the Second Cavalry, Colonel Noble.

In answer to frequent applications to accept more troops from this State, the Secretary of War, on the 16th of July, returned the following answer:

"WAR DEPARTMENT, *July* 16, 1861.

SIR: No more troops will be accepted by this Department till authorized by Congress. Your offer will be filed, and receive attention at the proper time.

Yours, respectfully,

SIMON CAMERON,
Secretary of War.

Hon. RICHARD YATES, *Springfield.*"

NEW CALL—INFANTRY AND ARTILLERY.

On the 21st of July, the memorable battle of Bull Run was fought and lost, and on the next day Congress authorized the President to call into service five hundred thousand troops.

On the 23d, the following correspondence took place:

"HON. SIMON CAMERON,
Secretary of War.

SIR: Being advised that you are receiving tenders of additional troops, I desire to tender you, for Illinois, thirteen additional regiments of infantry, most of them now ready to rendezvous; three additional regiments of cavalry, and one additional battalion of light artillery. Illinois demands the right to do her full share in the work of preserving our glorious Union from the assaults of high handed rebellion, and I insist that you respond favorably to the tender I have made. RICHARD YATES."

"WAR DEPARTMENT, *July* 25, 1862.

GOVERNOR:

I have telegraphed to-day, accepting your patriotic offer of thirteen additional regiments of infantry, three additional regiments of cavalry, and one additional battery of artillery, advising you that, if you so desire, you can provide for and equip them, if you can do so with advantage, as respects economy and dispatch.

"It is absolutely necessary that the officers should be capable and reliable men; and to this end the Department wishes it distinctly understood that it will revoke the commissions of all officers who may be found incompetent for command.

"You will please telegraph immediately to the Adjutant General, at Washington, where and when these troops will be ready to be mustered into the service, in order that an officer may be detailed for that duty, without delay.

"I appreciate the patriotic spirit of your people, as evinced in your noble offer, and doubt not that they will prove equal to every demand that may be made upon them in behalf of the preservation of our glorious Union.

I am, Governor, with high respect,
Your obedient servant,
SIMON CAMERON,
Secretary of War."

Under this authority the 26th, Colonel Loomis; 27th, Colonel Buford; 28th, " Johnson; 29th, " Reardon; 30th, " Fouke; 31st " John Logan; 32d, " John A. Logan; 38th, " Carlin; 43d, " Raith; 46th, " Davis; 48th, " Haynie; 49th, " Morrison; 50th, " Bane, were raised. Also, the 3d cavalry, Colonel Carr; 7th cavalry, Colonel Kellogg, and the 6th cavalry, Colonel Cavanaugh.

GENERAL CALL—INFANTRY AND CAVALRY.

August 13, 1861, another application was made to the Secretary of War, to accept more troops, and, on the 14th, all restriction was removed, and all infantry regiments were authorized to be accepted, who were willing to enter the service.

On the 27th of the same month, authority was given to accept the 5th cavalry, Colonel Updegraff, and, on the fifth of September, to accept the tenth, Colonel Barrett.

On the 28th September, you were also authorized to accept the twelfth, Colonel Voss, and on the 27th November, the thirteenth, Colonel Bell. The last two regiments of cavalry were, however, limited to two battalions, of four companies each; and, in the latter case, a battalion, authorized some months before by the War Department, and raised by Lieutenant Colonel Hartman, was to constitute a part.

In addition to the thirteen regiments of cavalry, authorized in 1861, Captain Marx recruited a company, under the auspices of General Smith, for Thielman's battalion, and Major Thielman was commissioned as Major, with rank from November 1, 1861. His command, consisted of his company, nominally attached to the first cavalry, and now commanded by Captain Marshner, and Captain Marx's company.

Captain Warren Stewart also raised a company under authority of General Fremont, of August 3, 1861. Four companies were also raised in connection with the 27th, 29th 30th, and 31st regiments, (General McClernand's brigade), commanded by Captains Hutchens, Carmikel, O'Harnett, and Dollins. These four companies, and Captain Stewart's, were subsequently organized as a battalion, and Captain Stewart commissioned Major, with rank from February 1, 1862.

Another company was raised by Capt. Naughton, under authority from Gen. Fremont, to be attached to the 23d regiment, in September, 1861; but, after the battle of Lexington, was transferred, by the Governor of Missouri and attached to a Missouri regiment known as the "Curtis Horse," commanded by Col. Lowe.

A company, known as the Kane County Cavalry, Capt. Dodson, was also raised. This company was raised for the 2d cavalry, but was never assigned to it. It has recently been assigned to the 15th cavalry.

The company known as "Chicago Light Dragoons," commanded by Capt. Barker, was re-organized under the command of Capt. Shearer, and another company recruited, and have since been known as the "McClellan Dragoons." They were temporarily attached to a regiment of regulars. These companies have since been assigned to the 12th cavalry, Col. Voss.

Under the general permission of Secretary of War, of August 14, 1861, the following regiments of infantry were authorized: the 56th, Col. Kirkham; the 61st, Col. Fry; the 64th, Lieut. Col. Williams, being a battalion of six companies, known as "Yates' Sharp Shooters;" the 65th, Col. Cameron, verbally in November, and confirmed by War Department in December; 51st, Col. Cummings, September 20; the 53d, Col. Cushman, including squadron of cavalry and battery of artillery, September 16; the 58th, Col. Lynch, September 25th; the 57th, Col. Baldwin, August 14; the 54th, Col. Harris; the 60th, Col. Toler; 62d, Col. True, and the 63d, Col. Moro, known as the "Kentucky Brigade," were authorized by the War Department, subject to your approval, October 3, 1861.

In the summer of 1861, an informal permission had been given to raise an additional regiment of artillery. The most of the companies had been raised and the authority was formally recognized and approved by the Secretary of War, January 2, 1862.

RECRUITING AGAIN STOPPED.

On the third of December all recruiting, except for regiments then organizing and for old regiments, was suspended, by General Order No. 105, of War Department. Par. 1 and 2, of that order, is as follows:

HEADQUARTERS OF THE ARMY, ADJUTANT GENERAL'S OFFICE,
Washington, December 3, 1861.

"GENERAL ORDERS,}
"No. 105.   }

"The following orders have been received from the Secretary of War:

"I. No more regiments, batteries, or independent companies will be raised by the Governors of states, except upon the special requisition of the War Department.

"Those now forming in the various states will be completed, under direction of the respective Governors thereof, unless it be deemed more advantageous to the service to assign the men already raised to regiments, batteries or independent companies now in the field, in order to fill up their organizations to the maximum standard prescribed by law.

"II. The recruiting service in the various states for the volunteer forces already in service, and for those that may hereafter be received, is placed under charge of general superintendents for those states, respectively, with general depots for the collection and instruction of recruits."

At that time, beside the six regiments of three months' men, we had sent to the field over forty-three thousand (43,000,) men, and had then in camps of instruction, in the State, over seventeen thousand (17,000.)

During the month of December, 4160 more recruits were enlisted; all squads and parts of regiments were consolidated, and the 45th, 46th, 49th and 57th, were organized and mustered into service. The only incomplete regiments of infantry in the State, December 31st, were the 51st, Col Cummings, at Camp Douglas; the 53d, Col. Cushman, at Ottawa; the 58th, Col. Lynch, at Camp Douglas; the 23d, Col. Mulligan, at Camp Douglas, reorganizing, and four regiments at Jonesboro', 54th, 60th, 62d and 63d.

1862.

On the first of January, 1862, it seemed probable that Illinois, having at that time furnished about fifteen thousand more than her proportion of troops in the field, would not be called upon, or permitted to raise more, except to fill up the regiments last named, and such as might enlist in old regiments. The exciting scenes of the year just closed have taught us a sad experience, and show how unfounded were our expectations at its commencement. The State, instead of being able to rest with the satisfaction of having done her whole duty to the country, was soon called upon to redouble her energies for new and exciting and more eventful realities.

In January, the 32d regiment, Col. John Logan; the 45th regiment, Col. John E. Smith, and the 64th regiment, Lieut. Col. D. D. Williams, infantry, and the 10th cavalry regiment, Col. J. A. Barrett, were ordered to the field. In February, the 46th, Col. John A. Davis; 49th, Col. Wm. R. Morrison; 57th, Col. Silas D. Baldwin; 58th Col. Wm. F. Lynch, and 61st, Col. Jacob Fry, infantry; and 5th cavalry, Col. Wilson; 9th cavalry, Col. Brackett, and 13th cavalry, Col. Bell; and seven splendid batteries of light artillery followed, commanded by Captains Sparstrom, Stienbeck, Keith, Rogers, Waterhouse, Silversparre and Bouton. The most of these troops reached the field in time to join our old regiments, and with them, to participate in the battle of Fort Donelson, on the 15th and 16th of February.

Immediately after the battle of Fort Donelson over ten thousand prisoners of war were sent to Camp Douglas and Camp Butler, and the State was called upon to guard them with such troops as were then at these camps. The 23d and 65th regiments of infantry, and the 12th cavalry regiment, and two or three artillery companies were at Camp Douglas; the 53d infantry, at Ottawa, and two companies of artillery at Camp Butler. Neither of these regiments were full. The 12th cavalry was ordered to Camp Butler, and the 53d infantry to Camp Douglas.

In March, the 53d, 56th and 60th regiments of infantry, and three more batteries of artillery, commanded by Captains Bolton, Cheeney and Coggswell; and in April, the 62d and 63d infantry took the field, leaving in the State only the 65th, (fully organized); the 23d, (fully re-organized); Phillip's battery, and 12th cavalry; all doing guard duty at these camps.

RECRUITING FOR OLD REGIMENTS.

On the 3d of April, the War Department directed a discontinuance of the recruiting service, as established December 3d. The officers detached on that service were ordered to rejoin their regiments, and the superintendents directed to disband their recruiting parties and close their offices. The State having been directed, in December, to suspend recruiting, except to complete corps then commenced, and such corps having been filled, the entire recruiting in the State may be said to have closed on the 3d of April, 1862.

The system of recruiting for old regiments, under the State Superintendent, appointed by the War Department, was in operation during January, February and March; and with a large detail of recruiting officers, but three hundred and fifty-one recruits were enlisted. At first it was supposed that want of success was on account of recruits not being allowed to enlist for particular regiments; but this objection was removed on the 11th of January, and yet these officers met with little success.

On the 1st of May, the following order of the War Department was promulgated:

"WAR DEPARTMENT, ADJUTANT GENERAL'S OFFICE,
Washington, May 1, 1862.

"GENERAL ORDERS,}
No. 49. }

"Upon requisitions made by commanders of armies in the field, authority will be given by the War Department, to the Governors of the respective states, to recruit regiments now in service.

"By order of the Secretary of War,

"L. THOMAS,
Adjutant General."

On the next day, the following requisition was made for recruits to fill up old regiments:

"H'D. QR's., DEP'T. OF THE MISS.,
Pittsburg Landing, Tenn., May 2, 1862.

"HIS EXCELLENCY, RICH'D YATES,
Governor of Illinois, Springfield:

"GOVERNOR:

"I am authorized to call upon you for recruits to fill up the volunteer regiments from your State in this army.

"Many of them have been reduced, by disease and recent battles, very far below the minimum standard. A detail from such regiments will soon be sent to you for recruiting service, and it is hoped that you will give the matter your immediate attention.

"Very respectfully,
Your ob'dt serv't,
"H. W. HALLECK,
Major General Comm'dg."

On the 6th of June, however, the plan of December 3d was reinstated by the War Department, and invalid or disabled officers, necessarily absent from their regiments, were directed to be detailed for that duty whenever they were able to perform it.

A recent communication from Col. Morrison, Superintendent for this State, shows, that from the 5th of July to the 22d ultimo, two hundred and four officers had reported to him, and during that time 2,753 recruits had been enlisted and forwarded to their regiments, making an aggregate, from January 1st to December 22d, 1862, of 3,121. More than sixty per cent. of these recruits were enlisted during the excitement in August and September.

EXCITEMENT IN MAY.

On the 25th of May last the following dispatch was received from the Secretary of War:

"WASHINGTON, *May* 25, 1862.

GOVERNOR YATES:

Intelligence from various sources leaves no doubt that the enemy, in great force, are advancing on Washington. You will please organize and forward immediately all the volunteer and militia force in your State.

EDWIN M. STANTON,
Secretary of War."

In two weeks the 67th, Col. Hough, the 68th, Col. Stuart, the 69th, Col. Tucker, the 70th, Col. Reeves, the 71st, Col. Gilbert—infantry, for three months service, were in camp. The 23d, Col. Mulligan, and Rourke's Battery, left for Annapolis, June 12th; the 65th, Col. Cameron, June 21st; the 12th cavalry, June 27th; the

68th, July 6th; Phillips' Battery, July 12th, and the 71st, for Columbus, July 27th. The 67th, Col. Hough, and the 69th, Col. Tucker, were assigned to duty at Camp Douglas, and the 70th, Col. Reeves, at Camp Butler.

LAST CALLS

On the 17th of May a regiment was called for, for particular service, and on the 30th the Secretary of War informed you he would accept all three years' men who wished to enlist, and all volunteers and militia for three months who had before then offered their services, and who had so far perfected their organization as to be able to report for orders at certain places named, by the 10th of June.

On the 6th of July another call of three hundred thousand was made by the President. It was at first intended to credit on this call those states for any surplus which they had furnished. It was not known at the time what our surplus was. On the next day the Secretary of War called upon Illinois for nine more regiments, "being a part of your (our) quota under the call of the President." These regiments were immediately called for by General Order No. 42, from this department, and regulations prescribed for their rendezvous and organization. Before these regiments were filled, however, and on the 17th of July, Congress enacted that whenever the President should "call forth the militia of the states, to be employed in the service of the United States," he should specify in his call the period for which said service should be required, not exceeding nine months, and the militia so called should be mustered in and continue to serve during the period so specified. The fourth section of the act authorized the President, for the purpose of filling up old regiments, to accept the services of one hundred thousand volunteers, for a period not exceeding one year.

Three hundred thousand *militia*, to serve for a period of nine months, unless sooner discharged, were called for August 5th. The order of the Secretary of War, making the call upon this State, assumed that a draft would be necessary; and, in anticipation that the states would not be able to contribute their quotas of the call in July for three years' service, announced that if any state should not by the 18th of August furnish its quota of the three years' volunteers, the deficiency would be made up by a special draft from the militia. Two days after this order, to wit, August 7th, notice was given you that unless the enrollment of the militia had been commenced, to have it done immediately, at the expense of the General Government.

These vigorous measures gave hope of a speedy termination of this terrible war. The people of the State received the announcement with the wildest excitement and most unbounded satisfaction. Messengers and committees from every portion of the State hastened to the Capital, demanding that, as they were ready to perform their share of the work of saving the Government, that they should not be drafted so long as they were willing to volunteer. This condition of things was promptly communicated to the War Department, and the assignment of our quota, under both calls, urgently requested. The next day it was announced that our quota, under each call, would be 26,148, but as Illinois had furnished 16,978 in excess of her quota of those in the field, the total quotas under both calls was 35,320. Application was made hourly from the different counties in the State, to ascertain what their quota was, and immediately on ascertaining from the War Department what it was, the announcement was made through the public press. Still, in the minds of some, there appeared a question as to whether volunteers for three years would be accepted in lieu of militia. This was quickly settled, however, by a telegram on the 8th, from the War Department, that all volunteers would be accepted until the 15th of August, for new regiments, and all after that time for filling up old regiments, and that all volunteers enlisted before the draft, (August 18th,) would be credited on those calls.

On the 9th of August, from returns made to this department, I informed the public that there would not be a draft. This was upon the strength of the dispatch from Washington that our quota was 35,320. The records now on file show that the *announcement thus made was not premature*, and that the information thus communicated was correct. On the evening of that day, however, the Assistant Adjutant General telegraphed that it had been decided, in fixing the quota of volunteers, *not to regard those in the field before the call*, leaving our quota, under both calls, at 52,296, notwithstanding our previous excess of 16,978.

My dispatch of the 11th, urging continued efforts to fill our quotas was because of this change in our quotas, as well as the fact that many companies who had tendered their services were nine month's men.

To raise either 52,296, or 35,320 volunteers (with perhaps the exception of one thousand who had enlisted between July 7 and August 5,) *but thirteen days* were allowed. The floating population of the State who would enlist had already done so. These new volunteers must come, if come at all, from the farmers and mechanics of the State. Farmers were in the midst of their harvests, and it is no exaggeration to say, that inspired by a holy zeal, animated by a common purpose, and firmly resolved on rescuing this Government from the very brink of ruin, and restoring it to the condition our fathers left it, over fifty thousand of them left their harvests ungathered—their tools on their benches—the ploughs in the furrows and turned their backs upon home and loved ones, AND BEFORE ELEVEN DAYS EXPIRED THE DEMANDS OF THE COUNTRY WERE MET, AND BOTH QUOTAS WERE FILLED!! Proud indeed was the day to all Illinoisians when this extraordinary announcement was made that the enlistment rolls were full. And when the historian shall write the record of these eventful days of August, 1862, no prouder record can be erected to the honor and memory of a free people than a plain, full narrative of actual realities.

It is not my province, in this report, to bestow fulsome praise, or write glowing eulogies, but when I remember what we all witnessed in those days—when I remember the unselfish and patriotic impulse which animated every soul—and the universal liberality of those who were either too young or too old to enlist, to aid those who were eager to join their brethren in the field—when I remember the holy ardor which aged mothers and fair daughters infused into husbands, sons and brothers—I say when I remember these things I cannot but feel justified in departing from the dull routine of statistics, and bestow upon the subject this passing notice.

On the 14th of August the time was extended for filling up new regiments from the 18th to the 22d, and for old regiments to the first of September. The extension for this State was not necessary, for the muster rolls show that before the 19th of August our quotas, as last established, were filled. Yet on this same day, Aug. 14th, the War Department, by General Order No. 105, announced that unless old regiments should be filled by the 1st September a special draft would be ordered on that day, and you were informed that it required 34,719, to fill up those regiments. In view of this state of things it was determined that if the War Department should insist that Illinois should be required to raise this additional force of 34,719, to fill up old regiments, it would be useless to attempt to raise them by volunteer enlistments. On the 21st of August, therefore, General Militia Order No. 1, was issued from this Department, directing an enrollment of the entire militia of the State. This was deemed necessary to meet any contingencies that might arise, and be prepared for a draft in case one should be still demanded.

Immediately after the call for nine regiments, in July, nine camps were established, one in each of the old congressional districts of the State, for the temporary rendezvous of those regiments, but with the intention of removing them, as soon as they should be full, into the principal camps of instruction at Chicago and Springfield, for permanent organization and instruction.

There was, however, in the State, barely enough camp and garrison equipage for these regiments, and consequently an additional embarrassment presented itself to provide for those called August 5th. The State was soon full of volunteers. All had left their business and some of them were without homes. The General Government was unable to supply tents, and there was not time to erect barracks to accommodate half of them. Such, therefore, as were not supplied were directed to remain at home or seek temporary quarters, as best they could, and await orders.

And still another difficulty grew out of the want of clothing, and especially blankets. All the resources of the government were taxed to supply the immense army organizing throughout the country, and, considering the immense amount of supplies required, and the suddenness of the emergency which had called out these volunteers, their wants were met with very commendable promptness. In most of the counties of the State there were fair grounds at the county seats. In many counties the sheds on these county fair grounds were repaired and occupied by companies and regiments until quarters could be prepared for them at the general camps of instruction. Several regiments, however, who were unable to obtain quarters at the principal camps, moved from these neighborhood rendezvous directly to the field.

Six of these new regiments were organized, mustered, armed, and clothed, and sent into the field in August; twenty-two and Board of Trade Battery, Capt. Stokes, and Miller's Battery, in September; thirteen in October; fifteen, besides the Springfield Light Artillery, Capt. Vaughn, and Mercantile Battery, Capt. Cooley, in November, and three in December, making an aggregate of fifty-nine regiments of infantry and four batteries, consisting of fifty-three thousand eight hundred and nineteen (53,819) officers and enlisted men. Besides this, twenty-seven hundred and fifty-three (2753,) were, during about the same time, enlisted and sent to old regiments under the direction of Col. Morrison, State Superintendent. Add to these 1083, 14th cavalry, now organizing at Peoria; 386 in Camp Butler; 156, Elgin Battery, Capt. Renwick, at Camp Douglas, now under marching orders; 135, Henshaw's Battery, at Ottawa; and 83, Capt. Adams, cavalry company of the 15th regiment, makes the grand total under the last calls, fifty-eight thousand four hundred and sixteen (58,416,) or six thousand one hundred and nineteen (6119) more than our quotas under the last calls. The excess furnished by this State, as reported by the Secretary of War, August 8th, was sixteen thousand nine hundred and seventy-eight (16,978,) which, added to the surplus under the last calls of six thousand one hundred and nineteen (6119,) makes the total excess, as officially ascertained, *twenty-three thousand and ninety-seven* (23,097.) That the real excess is much greater there can be no doubt whatever. The reasons for this conclusion have heretofore been stated.

Since the call of August 5th, the Secretary of War has authorized the acceptance of several regiments of cavalry and six batteries of light artillery. But two of these regiments will probably be raised by enlistments, the 14th, Col. Capron, at Peoria, and the 16th, now known as the 17th, Col. Thieleman, at Camp Butler. The 15th, Col. Stewart, was organized on the 25th ultimo, by assigning to his battalion of six companies, two companies, Capts. Willis and Shearer, attached to the 36th infantry; one, Capt. Gilbert, formerly attached to the 52d, and afterwards nominally assigned to the 12th cavalry; one, Capt. Ford, attached to the 53d infantry; one, Capt. Huntley, formerly of the 1st cavalry; and one, Capt. Wilder, known as the "Kane County Cavalry."

Four of the six batteries have already been raised. Three of them—Board of Trade Battery, Capt. Stokes; Mercantile Battery, Capt. Cooley; and Springfield Battery, Capt. Vaughn—are in the field. The Elgin Battery, Capt. Renwick, is ready and under orders. Capt. Henshaw is nearly full, and Capt. Hawthorne will probably be full the present month.

MILITIA AND ENROLLMENT.

The second and third sections of article 1, of an act entitled "An act to amend chapter 70, Revised Statutes, entitled Militia," in force May 2, 1861, provided for the enrollment of the militia of the State, and the fourth section required returns to be made to this office, August 1, 1861, and annually thereafter.

Article 2 provided for a division of the militia into two classes, the *voluntary* and *reserve;* the first to consist of those who voluntarily organized themselves into companies of not less than fifty nor more than one hundred members each, and who shall have a uniform, and shall elect officers and assemble for drill and purposes of military discipline, not less than four days in each year, and *who shall be furnished with arms and equipments by the State*, and be first subject to call or draft into service, at the requisition of the Governor. The second to consist of all those who do not so organize, and also to be subject to draft.

Article 3 provides for the election of officers, authorizes the Governor to organize companies into regiments, and declares the term of service at six years.

Article 5, among other things, provides that there shall be kept in the Adjutant General's office a complete roll of the companies so organized—that the muster rolls of such companies shall be made annually by the officers of each company, and copies thereof kept on file in this office.

Section 4 provides that a record of the dates of all commissions granted under this act shall be kept, and that officers shall take rank from the date of their commissions.

In 1861, the enrollment was taken in most of the counties of the State and returned to this office, as contemplated by the law, but no "corrected lists" were returned on the first of August, 1862. On that day circulars were sent to all the county clerks, notifying them to immediately forward copies of such list, if possible, and in case the assessors had failed to file them in their offices to notify me of such failure. A few of these lists were received in August, but in most of the counties the failure was on the part of the assessors.

But little attention was paid to the organization of companies under this law. Only forty-two muster-rolls and twenty-nine certificates of election were filed and fifteen commissions issued in 1861.

On the 23d of August last, for the purpose of preparing the State for a draft to fill up old regiments in case it should be required, and in pursuance of an order of the War Department, the enrollment of the entire militia force of the State was ordered. An enrolling officer, a draft commissioner and surgeon were appointed in each county, as required by said order. The third paragraph of said order is as follows:

"*Third.* The Governors of the respective states will cause an enrollment to be made forthwith by the assessors of the several counties, or by any other officers, to be appointed by such Governers, of all able-bodied male citizens, between the ages of eighteen and forty-five, within the respective counties, giving the name, age and occupation of each, together with remarks showing whether he is in the service of the United States, and in what capacity, and any other facts which may determine his exemption from military duty.

All reasonable and proper expenses of such enrollment, and of the draft hereinafter provided, will be reimbursed by the United States, upon vouchers showing the detailed statement of service performed and expenses incurred, to be approved by such Governors."

To obtain the information required by this order, a new and full enrollment was indispensably necessary. The enrolling officers were furnished by this department with necessary blanks and instructions, and directed, if possible, to make returns by the 10th of September. It being impossible to do so, however, the time was afterwards extended.

Returns of the enrollment have been received from all but Saline and Warren counties. The number in service and liable to service in those counties are estimated from returns from other counties in that part of the State. An abstract of this enrollment will be found in schedule "D." A considerable portion of this enrollment was taken before active enlistments ceased. The returns show only 115,123 in service, whereas the number ascertained as actually on muster rolls is 135,440, as will be seen by schedule "A," being 20,317 more than returned by enrolling officers.

The returns show—
In service 115,123
Liable to service 276,196
                                                     ———————
                                                     391,319

Correcting these returns and adding 20,317 to 115,123 makes 135,440, according to schedule "A"; and deducting this 20,317 from 276,196, [stated in schedule "D," liable to service, leaves 255,879, still liable to service.

It further appears, from these returns and official reports, that .0794 of our population in 1860, or nearly 8 per cent. and 346.1000, or over one-third of all able-bodied male citizens, between 18 and 45 years, have already entered the service.

In September the draft commissioners were notified to await further orders before proceeding to investigate the cases of persons who claimed to be exempt from draft. In view of the probability that no draft would be required and to save expense this notice was given, but the enrolling officers who had not fully completed their returns were directed to do so. On the first of November, however, the following dispatch was received:

"WASHINGTON, *Oct.* 31, 1862.
GOVERNOR YATES:
Please send to me, as soon as possible: first—the number of men enrolled in your State for draft: Second—the number of men drafted: Third—the number of commissioners: Fourth—the number of surgeons to examine for exemption: Fifth—the number of camps of rendezvous: Sixth—the number of volunteers for nine months to

take the place of drafted men: Seventh—the number of drafted men who volunteered for three years.
By order of the Secretary of War.

C. P. BUCKINGHAM."

The following answer was returned:

BRIG. GEN. C. P. BUCKINGHAM, *Washington:*
"The enrollment of the militia of the State was suspended on Gov. Yates' return from Washington, on account of his being informed by the Secretary of War that no draft would probably be required in this State. Fifty-five thousand volunteers have enlisted in new regiments in this State under the last two calls. Shall the enrollment be completed?

ALLEN C. FULLER,
Adjutant General."

The following reply was received, November 4th:

"WASHINGTON, *Nov.* 3, 1862.
"ALLEN C. FULLER, *Adjutant General:*
It is not necessary to complete the enrollment, under the circumstances.

C. P. BUCKINGHAM."

On the 15th of September the enrollment and organization of two hundred companies of infantry were called for and the organization prescribed. An assurance was given that agents of the State had been sent to purchase arms for twenty regiments, and as soon as the same should be received they would be issued to regiments prepared to receive them. In fact every encouragement was given to the formation of volunteer militia companies, and *yet but very few muster rolls have been returned.*

The result of this last attempt to organize a volunteer militia force in this State, has confirmed me in the opinion long entertained, that an unpaid, uniformed, and unarmed militia organization cannot be secured. However sound the theory that a military education is desirable, or at least that all able-bodied male citizens should accustom themselves to the use of arms, and learn the rudiments of the art of war, yet our people of late years reject the theory as impracticable unless some inducement is offered by the State.

The theory is sound and may be reduced to practice. That our people are ready to fight is abundantly proven. That they quickly adapt themselves to a soldier's duties and a soldier's life is also well established. That they will not turn out on general militia muster day, without some more inducements from the State, I think is also true. Let the State uniform and arm and pay them for the time spent each year in company or battalion drill, and I think there will be no difficulty in having a reliable militia force, to meet any and every emergency. Until this is done, I think we shall be obliged to continue, as heretofore, and rely upon undisciplined volunteers, to take the field, and learn their duties as soldiers there.

PURCHASE OF ARMS.

Under the provision of the law of May 2, 1861, entitled, "An act to establish a magazine, to purchase efficient arms for the State militia, and for other purposes," commissioners were appointed, who visited eastern cities, in the summer of 1861, to negotiate a purchase of arms contemplated by that law. The extreme high price at which arms were then held in the market, as well as an urgent request from the General Government to states to withdraw from the market and prevent competition, induced the commissioners to make no further efforts to purchase.

During the present summer, I am informed, another effort was made to purchase arms for twenty regiments of infantry, but without success. They however, purchased, in 1861, nine hundred and ninety-nine Enfield rifles, five hundred Colt's revolvers, two hundred and fifty Whitney revolvers, nine hundred and forty cavalry sabers, and forty-two sets of artillery harness. This property, or the greater part, was immediately issued to Illinois volunteers, and the cost charged to the General Government.

REPORTS.

I regret to be unable, at this time, to communicate the reports of these commissioners, as well as the reports of the Quartermaster General, and Commissary General. The operations of the Quartermaster General's Department have been large. The reports of these officers are in course of preparation, and, I am assured, will be ready in a few days. The most of the business transacted by them was before I became connected with the military affairs of the State, and I am, therefore, unable to state the substance; but, as soon as their reports are received, they will be duly transmitted.

APPOINTMENTS AND PROMOTIONS.

The 10th section of the law of April 25, 1861, provides for the organization of the first six regiments, declares that, at all elections for company and regimental officers, every enrolled man of the company or regiment should be entitled to vote, and none others; and that at the election for Brigadier General for said brigade, all commissioned officers should be entitled to vote, and none others; and that all elections should be by written or printed ballots.

The 11th section declared that the provision of that act should only apply to the six regiments therein provided for.

These six regiments were organized and officers elected and commissioned, as therein provided. It was organized by the State and accepted by the General Government as an Illinois brigade. Col. Benjamin M. Prentiss was elected Brigadier General, commissioned by you, and mustered into the United States service, May 18, 1861, with rank from May 8, 1861.

The next ten regiments, which were accepted in pursuance of the act of the Legislature of May 2, were organized as therein directed. The 15th section of the act provided that as soon as ten companies should be formed in a regiment, the Adjutant General should order an election for regimental officers for the said regiments. These regiments were mustered into the service of the State for thirty days, as contemplated by that law; but before the expiration of that time they were called upon to enter the service of the United States, and were mustered into its service in the latter part of May and early in June.

The 2d section provided that the companies should be "officered in manner as should be provided by the general militia law of the State."

The law of May 3d, authorizing the acceptance of a regiment of cavalry, did not declare how the officers were to be selected. The line officers were elected and the field and staff officers were appointed.

With the exception of the first sixteen regiments of infantry, one of cavalry, and one battalion of artillery, authorized to be raised and organized by the several laws of this State, the volunteer forces of this State have been raised, either under authority directly from the War Department to individuals, or by you, under authority given you by the Secretary of War.

The 2d section of the law of Congress, approved July 22, 1861, declares that volunteers shall be subject to the rules and regulations governing the army of the United States, and that they should be "formed, by the President, into regiments," etc. The 4th section provides that the Governors of the states furnishing volunteers shall " commission the field, staff and company officers for the said volunteers;" but in cases where the State authorities refuse or omit to furnish volunteers at the call or on the proclamation of the President, and volunteers from such states offer their services, under such call or proclamation, the President may accept their services and commission the proper field, staff and company officers.

The 10th section of the act, however, provided that when vacancies should occur in any of the companies of volunteers, such vacancies should be filled by election, and that the person so elected should be commissioned by the Governors or President. This last provision concerning filling vacancies, was *repealed* by the 3d section of the act of Congress, approved August 6, 1861, and Governors required to fill such vacancies in the same manner as original appointments. General Order of the War Department, of May 2, 1861, heretofore referred to, is as follows:

"The commissioned officers of the company will be appointed by the Governor of the state furnishing it, and the non-commissioned officers, until the company shall be embodied in a regiment, will be appointed by the Captain—afterwards by the Colonel, on recommendation of the Captain."

Under these laws of Congress and regulations of the War Department, the *power* to appoint and commission field, staff and line officers of volunteer regiments, is vested in the Governors of states furnishing the regiments. The exercise of that power is full of embarrassments and difficulties. The power to appoint involves responsibility to the Government as well as the service, for the manner in which it is exercised. With the large army which Illinois has now in the field, including more than 5,000 commissioned officers, and being ten times greater than the regular army of the United States was a few years since, the labor and delicacy and anxiety of faithfully and impartially discharging such responsibilities cannot be over-estimated.

Original appointments of line officers have been made upon the recommendation of the company, or on account of service performed by those appointed in recruiting and bringing into camp the enlisted men; and in case of field officers upon the recommendation, or supposed recommendation, of the commissioned officers of the regiment. This has been the rule. There may have been occasional exceptions to it; but I know of but one, and that was the appointment of Major General Grant as Colonel of the 21st regiment. That a policy most liberal to the enlisted men of the commands has been adopted, as to original appointments, is undeniable. As to the appointment of field officers, the original policy was to procure the services of at least one army officer to each regiment; but frequent refusals of the War Department to grant a leave of absence to such officers, to accept commissions for field offices, made, to some extent, the practice finally adopted one of necessity.

In the organization of our new regiments every possible effort was made to obtain the consent of the War Department to allow officers who had served with distinction in our old regiments to accept commissions, by way of promotion, in our new regiments. These applications were at one time disposed of by the following order of the War Department, under date of Aug. 14:

"The exigencies of the service require that officers now in the field should remain with their commands; and no officer, now in the field in the regular or volunteer service, will, under any circumstances, be detailed to accept a new command."

Some days after this the application was renewed, and the following reply received:

"WASHINGTON, 12:30 P. M., 23d, 1862.

"GOVERNOR YATES:

"It is the anxious desire of the Department to give the new regiments the advantage of experienced officers of their own choice. I hope you understand that any delay or refusal arises from absolute military necessity. The regiments in the field and in the face of the enemy cannot safely nor justly be deprived of their officers, while in that condition. When relieved from it the Department will be disposed to sanction the appointments desired.

"EDWIN M. STANTON."

At length, after most of the regiments then forming were organized, the rule was relaxed, and on the recommendation of officers and men, in a few of our regiments, they were able to secure the services of such officers.

In relation to appointments to fill vacancies, it is evident that those *should be* promoted who render the best service in the field, and show the greatest capacity to command. But since it is impossible to know always who does so, some rule should exist which, on the one hand, holds out promotion as a reward for meritorious service, and on the other protects the officer or private in a vigorous discharge of duty, independent of the prejudices and caprices of the hour. It was believed that promotions by seniority, would best accomplish this object, and after much consultation and correspondence with both officers and privates, the following order was promulgated the 16th of last July:

"GENERAL HEADQUARTERS, STATE OF ILLINOIS,
"ADJUTANT GENERAL'S OFFICE,
"*Springfield, July* 16, 1862.

"GENERAL ORDER, No. 43.]

"The attention of commanding officer of Illinois forces in the field, is respectfully but earnestly called to the necessity of prompt action, on their part, in cases of vacancies in commissioned officers in their respective commands.

"To reward service in the field by prompt promotion, is one of the greatest incentives to individual action, as it is a special mark of personal merit, and to encourage the promotion of non-commissioned officers and privates to the vacancies in the corps and regiments from this State, promotions will be made to field officers *regimentally*, and to line officers *by companies.* In applying this principle, each company will be considered, with reference to promotion, a distinct body, and all vacancies will be filled, as far as practicable, from within the organization.

"In adopting this rule, the Governor is aware that it does not conform to the rules of the regular army. But the difference between the enlistments for the regular and volunteer service is believed to demand the application of a different rule in promotions.

"Although the act of Congress of July 22, 1861, confers upon the Governor the power to fill vacancies, which power *may* be exercised arbitrarily, yet he desires, in all cases, to consult the officers and the interests of the command, before ordering promotions, and, therefore, invites their recommendations.

"To the rule of promotion by seniority, there are some few cases which should be excepted. Instances have, and will occasionally arise, where, for great personal bravery in the field, or other distinguished meritorious services, a junior non-commissioned officer or private should be promoted, to the exclusion of a senior commissioned officer; and that, too, without an impeachment of the general merits of the latter. So, when an officer proves himself incompetent, a junior officer or private may justly be promoted over him. Such instances, however, are to be considered only as *exceptions* to the rule, and their existence *should be fully shown* before they will be recognized.

"In a communication, lately addressed to Governor Yates, by the Major General commanding this department, it is stated that commanding officers of divisions, regiments, and corps, will be directed to make recommendations for filling vacancies within their respective commands, stating the particular service and merit of the individuals recommended.

"Since that time, many recommendations for promotions, other than those by seniority, have been made, but have been unaccompanied by any statement of "particular service" or "merit," to justify their adoption. A decision upon such cases, has, therefore, been reserved until further advices.

"Frequent delays in issuing commissions are occasioned by a want of official information of the death of officers. To prevent this, in future, it is requested that commanding officers of regiments report to this department such deaths as soon as practicable.

"If frequent or occasional reports were made to this department of the sick and wounded sent to hospitals, it would greatly aid it in its correspondence with relatives and friends, who are constantly seeking information, as well as enable the State to render assistance to those of its citizens who are in the field.

"By order of his Excellency, Gov. Yates.
"ALLEN C. FULLER,
"*Adjutant General.*"

So far as is known, this order has given almost if not entire satisfaction both to rank and file. That injustice will occasionally be done, under this or any other rule, is not denied, for the commanding officers may recommend an undeserving officer for promotion. It is his duty, however, unless some valid reason exists, and that reason *stated upon his honor*, as an officer, to recommend promotions in the regular line. And it is also his duty to recommend, to the exclusion of the regular line, in cases of *special merit* of others. If he will always do his duty intelligently and impartially—if the captain will appoint the non-commissioned officers of his company, with reference to their relative merits, and by that means place the most meritorious privates in line of promotion, (although strictly there is no rank among the non-commissioned officers,) a favorable result will follow. Otherwise not. But no human foresight can provide against the partialities and prejudices of men.

MEDICAL DEPARTMENT.

The "plan of organization" for volunteer forces, as designated in General Order No. 15, of the War Department, was so far modified, on the 25th of May, 1861, as to allow one Surgeon and one Assistant Surgeon to be appointed by the Governors of the respective States, "after having passed an examination by a competent medical board, appointed by the Governors of the States."

In the organization of the "first brigade," the Legislature, in April, 1861, constituted a Medical Board, consisting of Drs. N. S. Davis, Chicago; Charles Ryan, of Sangamon county; George W. Stipp, of McLean county; William Chambers, of Coles county, and Dr. Carpenter, of St. Clair county. Surgeons and Assistant Surgeons were required to pass an examination by this board, and procure their certificates of qualification from said board before receiving an appointment as Surgeon or Assistant Surgeon in the regiments composing that brigade. But in case any portion of the troops should be ordered into active service before the session of the board, you were authorized temporarily to assign Surgeons or Assistant Surgeons, until permanent appointments could be made.

The board, thus constituted, continued to act until the 14th of June, when a new board, consisting of H. A. Johnson, Chicago; Henry Wing, Collinsville; Henry W. Davis, Paris; O. M. Bryan, Sycamore, and Robert Roscotton, Peoria, were appointed under General Order, No. 25. Dr. Davis was subsequently appointed Surgeon of the 18th regiment, and Dr. D. K. Green, of Salem, was appointed in his place; Dr. Bryan was subsequently promoted to Brigade Surgeon, and Dr. A. L. McArthur, of Ottawa, was appointed in his place; and, in October last, Dr. Daniel Brainard, of Chicago, was appointed to fill the vacancy occasioned by the resignation of Dr. Roscotton.

During that year the board consisted of three members, Drs. Johnson, Wing and Green. The increase of business the past few months required a full board and the number was increased, by the appointment of Drs. McArthur and Brainard.

A report from the board, made on the 13th of last month, shows that, since the 18th of June, 1861, seven hundred and ninety-three (793) candidates have registered their names for examination; 495

have been examined. Of these 159 have been recommended as Surgeons; 266 have been recommended as Assistant Surgeons, and 70 rejected. It further appears, from the report, that a considerable number, after being partially examined, withdrew from examination, with the consent of the board, with the privilege of a subsequent examination. As the report of these examinations is brief, and explains the extent of their labors, and the principles which have governed them in their examinations, I submit a copy, marked schedule E.

The duty of providing our regiments with good Surgeons and Assistant Surgeons is one of great importance. There no is branch of the service more so, and none that is at first less appreciated. Experience has shown that the health of our troops in the field does not depend so much upon a change of climate or exposure as upon the character of the Surgeon, whose duty it is to prevent sickness as well as cure disease.

The losses in battle is but a small per cent. of the mortality in the army. The sanitary condition of a regiment is what its Surgeons and commanding officers make it, and any man who takes upon himself the duties of a Surgeon, supposing his duties begin and end with treating surgical cases, is unfit for the place. To watch with paternal care over the soldier in health; to maintain rigid sanitary regulations in camp, and in sickness to minister to his wants with a sister's tenderness and a mother's love, is what our volunteers in the field and their relatives and friends at home have a right to demand. And I am rejoiced in believing that, as a rule, such treatment they receive at the hands of our Surgeons. To this there are, of course, exceptions; but the commanding officers of departments in which our forces are serving, have asserted that Illinois Surgeons have generally faithfully discharged their whole duties.

The want of additional Surgeons was a long time felt. After the battles of Fort Donelson and Shiloh a large number were temporarily appointed, and the War Department was applied to, to allow more Surgeons to accompany our regiments. The Secretary of War promptly conceded the necessity, but informed you there was no law allowing any more to be commissioned. On the 2d of July, however, Congress passed a law allowing an additional Assistant Surgeon to each regiment of infantry, and I believe a late law of Congress allows an additional Assistant Surgeon to cavalry regiments.

The new regiments were provided with these additional Assistant Surgeons. Many of the old regiments had Assistant Surgeons, who had served long and deserved promotion; and also acting Assistant Surgeons who could not obtain leave of absence to return to the State for examination. To afford such an opportunity of an examination in the field, last year the medical board went to the field and held sessions there. Dr. Johnson is now on duty at Memphis and Helena; Dr. Green at Holly Springs, and Dr. McArthur at Nashville, and are expected to return the present month.

EXPENSES OF ADJUTANT GENERAL'S OFFICE.

Under the law of May 2, 1861, the salary of the Adjutant General is fixed at seven dollars, the First Assistant at six, and Second Assistant at five dollars per day. No express authority was given the Adjutant General to employ clerks, but the law authorized you to employ such clerks, aids and messengers as the public interests might require, and allow them such reasonable compensation as in your judgment they should be entitled to.

When I took possession of the office, November 11, 1861, three clerks and a messenger boy were employed, beside the Adjutant General and his assistants. No injustice is done in saying that such had been the pressure of business upon the office that its affairs were very much behind hand. There were but few rolls on file and few permanent records.

Notwithstanding the great increase of business, I have endeavored to keep the expenses of the office to the very lowest possible figure, and in this I have had the generous co-operation of my assistants and clerks. The average number of hours which they have actually labored is not less than sixteen out of twenty-four. Under your direction they have been employed, and the average compensation has been a little less than three dollars per day. But it will be seen, by schedule F, that one hundred and sixty-one days have not been charged by both assistants, and their places to that extent has been supplied by these clerks.

It will also be seen that the number of days' service performed by clerks from April 16, 1861, to January 1, 1863, is 1,779, at a compensation of $5,261. The total amount of salaries and clerk hire during this period is $14,548. The total amount allowed to the Adjutant General and his two assistants, by law, for the same period, is $11,250, leaving $2,743, (beside one dollar a day for messenger boy,) for clerk hire, or at the rate of $2 20 per day for two clerks. This is explained by the additional fact that my salary rom November 11, 1861, to January 1, 1863, being 416 days, would amount to $2,912, whereas but $1,288, or pay from the first of July last is charged. The reason for this deduction is that until July last I held the office of Circuit Judge of the 13th Judicial Circuit, and I have not felt at liberty to draw salaries for two offices.

I trust I have kept the expenses of the Department, considering the amount of labor performed, within proper limits. The extent of that labor few can know as well as those who have performed it.

As the recruiting service is nearly closed, the expenses can be very much reduced, and I think, by an economical administration of affairs, they may be reduced at least one half the present year.

CONCLUSION.

Such is a brief history of the response which Illinois has made to aid the General Government in maintaining itself. Its military operations in sending her troops to the field have at times been embarrassed by refusals on the part of the War Department to accept her sons in the service. Impatient at the delay, and averse to a long war, they have at times manifested their discontent by murmurs of complaint. Not always appreciating the difficulty of quickly arming and supplying large armies, their confidence in the vigor of the Federal authorities has occasionally been shaken. Yet ever loyal, ever ready and ever obedient, they have quickly filled and more than filled every requisition of the General Government upon them.

The old regiments, which have served so long and so faithfully and bravely, have been reduced by sickness and casualties, but have won for themselves and the State immortal honors. No dishonor or disgrace has yet fallen upon either of them.

It will be seen by reference to schedule A, that one hundred and thirty-five thousand four hundred and forty have entered the service in our own organizations. Except those who have been honorably discharged or wasted away by disease or fallen in battle, they are there still; and there they will remain until an honorable peace or final success shall crown their arms and relieve them from the further duties of a soldier's life.

Southern and Central and Northern Illinois have vied with each other in the patriotic work of furnishing these troops, and the hearts and hopes of all loyal men and women are centered in their movements and final success.

Conscious of my own inexperience, but I trust not wholly unmindful of the responsibility of aiding you and your associates in preparing and sending so large an army to the field,

I have the honor to remain, very respectfully,
Your obedient servant,
ALLEN C. FULLER,
Adjutant General.

SCHEDULE "A,"

Showing the number, name of commanding officer, date of organization or muster, place of organization of Illinois regiments or independent corps, and the number of officers and enlisted men mustered in said regiments or corps at or since its organization, respectively.

No.	Colonel.	Date of organization or muster.	Place of organization.	Strength.
7*	John Cook	July 25, 1861	Cairo	869
8*	Richard J. Oglesby	" "	Cairo	967
9*	Eleazer A. Paine	" "	Cairo	1011
10*	James D. Morgan	" "	Cairo	844
11*	Wm. H. L. Wallace	" "	Cairo	801
12*	John McArthur	" "	Cairo	863
13	John B. Wyman	May 24, 1861	Dixon	1047
14	John M. Palmer	May 25, 1861	Jacksonville	984
15	Thomas J. Turner	May 24, 1861	Freeport	1057
16	Robert F. Smith	May 24, 1861	Quincy	1083
17	Leonard F. Ross	May 24, 1861	Peoria	1009
18	Michael K. Lawler	May 28, 1861	Anna	1071
19	John B. Turchin	June 17, 1861	Chicago	918
20	Charles C. Marsh	June 13, 1861	Joliet	924
21	Ulyses S. Grant	June 15, 1861	Mattoon	1020
22	Henry Dougherty	June 25, 1861	Belleville	1047
23	James A. Mulligan	June 18, 1861	Chicago	1060
24	Frederick Hecker	July 8, 1861	Chicago	812
25	William N. Coler	August 4. 1861	Danville	1007
26	John M. Loomis	October 31, 1861	Camp Butler	961
27	Nap. B. Buford	August, 1861	Camp Butler	949
28	Amory K. Johnson	August 3, 1861	Camp Butler	857
29	James S. Rearden	July 27, 1861	Camp Butler	1026
30	Philip B. Fouke	Sept. 30, 1861	Camp Butler	992
31	John A. Logan	August, 1861	Camp Butler	1134
32	John Logan	Dec. 31, 1862	Camp Butler	957
33	Charles E. Hovey	August 15, 1861	Camp Butler	1006
34	Edward N. Kirk	Sept. 7, 1861	Camp Butler	913
35	Gustavus A. Smith	July 3, 1861	Decatur	1045
36	Nicholas Greusel	Sept. 23, 1861	Aurora	1006
37	Julius White	Sept. 18, 1861	Chicago	1035
38	William P. Carlin	August 15, 1861	Camp Butler	890
39	Austin Light	December, 1861	Chicago	964
40	Stephen G. Hicks	August 10, 1861	Salem	923
41	Isaac C. Pugh	August 9, 1861	Decatur	973
42	William A. Webb	Sept. 17, 1861	Camp Douglas	1051
43	Julius Raith	Dec. 16, 1861	Camp Butler	844
44	Chas. Knobelsdorff	Sept. 13, 1861	Chicago	994
45	John E. Smith	Dec. 26, 1861	Galena and Chicago	957

* Mustered into three months' service, April, 1861, and remustered in July, 1861, for three years' service.

SCHEDULE A—Continued.

No.	Colonel.	Date of organization or muster.	Place of organization.	Strength.
46	John A. Davis	Dec. 28, 1861..	Camp Butler	906
47	John Bryner	Oct. 1, 1861 ...	Peoria	1059
48	Isham N. Haynie	Nov. 18, 1861..	Camp Butler.	852
49	William R. Morrison.	Dec. 31, 1861..	Camp Butler.	931
50	Moses M. Bane	Sept. 12, 1861..	Quincy	871
51	Gilbert W. Cumming.	Dec.'61&Feb.'62	Camp Douglas	678
52	Isaac G. Wilson	Nov. 19, 1861..	Geneva	1060
53	Wm. H. W. Cushman	March 1861....	Ottawa	655
54	Thomas W. Harris	Feb. 18, 1862..	Anna	907
55	David Stuart	Oct. 31, 1862 ..	Camp Douglas	999
56	Robert Kirkham	Feb. 27, 1862..	Shawneetown	885
57	Silas D. Baldwin	Dec. 26, 1862..	Camp Douglas	961
58	William F. Lynch	Dec. 20, 1861..	Camp Douglas	881
59	P. Sidney Post	Transf'd from Missouri 9th.	St. Louis	914
60	Silas C. Toler	Feb. 17, 1862 ..	Anna	935
61	Jacob Fry	March 7, 1862.	Carrollton	827
62	James M. True	April 10, 1862.	Anna	853
63	Francis Mora	April 10, 1862.	Anna	867
64	Lt. Col. D.D. Williams	Dec. 31, 1861..	Camp Butler	531
65	Daniel Cameron	May 15, 1862 ..	Camp Douglas	936
66	Patrick E. Burke	Transf'd from Missouri 14th.	St. Louis	1023
67*	Rosell M. Hough	June 13, 1862 .	Camp Douglas	979
68*	Elias Stuart	June 20, 1862..	Camp Butler	981
69*	Joseph H. Tucker	June 14, 1862..	Camp Douglas	994
70*	O. T. Reeves	July 4, 1862...	Camp Butler	1007
71*	Othniel Gilbert	July 26, 1862..	Camp Douglas	940
				61,303
72	Frederick A. Starring	Aug. 21, 1862..	Camp Douglas	920
73	James F. Jaquess	Aug. 21, 1862..	Camp Butler	806
74	Jason Marsh	Sept. 4, 1862..	Rockford	903
75	George Ryan	Sept. 2, 1862...	Dixon	812
76	A. W. Mack	Aug. 22, 1862..	Kankakee	989
77	David P. Grier	Sept. 2, 9 cos " 18, 1 co.	Peoria	837
78	W. II. Bennison	Sept. 1, 1862 ..	Quincy	861
79	Lyman Guinnip	Aug. 28, 1862..	Danville	905
80	Thomas G. Allen	Aug. 28, 1862..	Centralia	904
81	James J. Dollins	Aug. 26, 1862..	Anna	915
82	Frederick Hecker	Aug. 26, 1862..	Camp Butler	814
83	Abner C. Harding	Aug. 23, 2862..	Monmouth	938
84	Louis H. Waters	Sept. 1, 1862...	Quincy	887
85	Robert S. Moore	Aug. 27, 1862..	Peoria	907
86	David D. Irons	Aug. 27, 1862..	Peoria	865
87	John E. Whiting	Sept. 22, 1862..	Shawneetown	855
88	Francis T. Sherman	Aug. 27, 1862..	Camp Douglas	846
89	John Christopher	Aug. 25, 9 cos Oct. 13, 1 co.	Camp Douglas	881
90	Timothy O'Meara	Nov. 22, 1862..	Camp Douglas	883
91	Henry M. Day	Sept. 8, 1862...	Camp Butler	918
92	Smith D. Atkins	Sept. 4, 1862...	Rockford	889

* Three months' service. Mustered out.

SCHEDULE A—Continued.

No.	Colonel.	Date of organization or muster.	Place of organization.	Strength.
93	Holden Putnam	Oct. 13, 1862	Princeton and Chicago	915
94	William W. Orme	Aug. 20, 1862	Bloomington	907
95	Lawrence S. Church	Sept. 4, 1862	Rockford	930
96	Thomas E. Champion	Sept. 5, 1862	Rockford	917
97	Friend S. Rutherford	Sept. 8, 1862	Camp Butler	843
98	John J. Funkhouser	Sept. 3, 1862	Centralia	873
99	Geo. W. K. Bailey	Aug. 26, 1862	Florence, Pike county	827
100	Fred. A. Bartleson	Aug. 30, 1862	Joliet	851
101	Charles H. Fox	Sept. 2, 1862	Jacksonville	825
102	William McMurtry	Sept. 2, 1862	Knoxville	864
103	Amos C. Babcock	Oct. 2, 1862	Canton and Peoria	805
104	Absalom B. Moore	Aug. 27, 1862	Ottawa	875
105	Daniel Dustin	Sept. 2, 1862	Dixon and Chicago	907
106	Robert B. Latham	Sept. 17, 1862	Lincoln	835
107	Thomas Snell	Sept. 4, 1862	Camp Butler	869
108	John Warner	Aug. 28, 1862	Peoria	805
109	Alexander J. Nimmo	Sept. 17, 1862	Anna	865
110	Thomas S. Casey	Sept. 11, 1862	Anna	815
111	James S. Martin	Sept. 18, 1862	Salem	886
112	Thomas J. Henderson	Sept. 12, 1862	Peoria	912
113	George B. Hoge	Oct. 1, 1862	Camp Douglas	805
114	James W. Judy	Sept. 18, 1862	Camp Butler	845
115	Jesse H. Moore	Sept. 13, 1862	Camp Butler	817
116	Nathan H. Tupper	Sept. 30, 1862	Decatur	861
117	Risden M. Moore	Sept. 19, 1862	Camp Butler	834
118	John G. Fonda	Nov. 29, 1862	Camp Butler	813
119	Thomas J. Kinney	Oct. 7, 1862	Quincy	838
120	George W. McKeaig	Oct. 29, 1862	Camp Butler	802
121	Will not probably organize			
122	John J. Rinaker	Sept. 4, 1862	Carlinville	803
123	James Monroe	Sept. 6, 1862	Mattoon	876
124	Thomas J. Sloan	Sept. 10, 1862	Camp Butler	866
125	Oscar F. Harmon	Sept. 3, 1862	Danville	829
126	Jonathan Richmond	Sept. 4, 1862	Chicago	838
127	John Van Arman	Sept. 5, 9 co's, Oct. 22, 1 co	Camp Douglas	886
128	Robert M. Hundley	Dec. 18, 1862	Camp Butler	824
129	George P. Smith	Sept. 8, 1862	Pontiac	893
130	Nathaniel Niles	Oct. 25, 1862	Camp Butler	816
131	George W. Neeley	Nov. 13, 1862	Camp Massac	813

	New regiments—Enlisted men			50,920
	" " Commissioned officers			2,301
				53,221
	Old regiments			61,303
	Total infantry			114,524

SCHEDULE A—Continued.

CAVALRY.

No.	Colonel.	Date of organization.	Place of organization.	Strength.
1	T. A. Marshall......	....	Bloomington...............	994
2	Silas Noble.........	....	Camp Butler...............	1251
3	E. A. Carr..........	....	Camp Butler...............	1237
4	T. L. Dickey........	....	Ottawa....................	1140
5	John J. Updegraff...	....	Camp Butler...............	1081
6	T. H. Cavanaugh....	....	Camp Butler...............	1151
7	W. P. Kellogg.......	....	Camp Butler...............	1266
8	J. F. Farnsworth....	....	St. Charles................	1222
9	A. G. Brackett......	Oct. 26, 1861..	Camp Douglas..............	1159
10	J. A. Barrett........	....	Camp Butler...............	1114
11	R. G. Ingersoll......	....	Peoria.....................	1024
12	Arno Voss...........	....	Camp Butler...............	826
13	Joseph W. Bell......	....	Camp Douglas..............	674
14	Horace Capron......	....	....	1083
15	Warren Stewart.....	Dec. 25, 1862..	....	1114
				16,336

UNASSIGNED CAVALRY.

Thielman's Cavalry.	Capt. Marschner...		Chicago	78
	" M. Marx.....		Paducah.................	92
	" John Klein..		Camp Butler.............	96
	" E. M. Seibel.		Camp Butler.............103	
	" Schambeck..	July 6, 1861...	Camp Butler.............	99
	" " ..	In camp.......	Camp Butler.............	59
	McClernand Guards..	In camp.......	Camp Butler.............	26
	Capt. Fletcher......	In camp.......	Camp Butler.............	28	581
				16,917

FIRST REGIMENT ILLINOIS LIGHT ARTILLERY.

Letter.	Captain.	Date of organization or muster.	Place of organization.	Strength.
A	C. M. Willard.......			131
B	Ezra Taylor			100
C	C. Houghtaling....	Ap'l 29, '61, 3 m. Oct. 31, 1861...	Ottawa....	110
D	Edward McAllister..	Jan. 14, 1862...	Plainfield.................	127
E	Allen C. Waterhouse.	Dec. 19, 1861...	Chicago...................	142
F	John T. Cheney.....	Feb. 25, 1862...	Camp Butler...............	94
G	Arthur O'Leary.....	Feb. 28, 1862...	Cairo.....................	103
H	Axel Silversparre...	Feb. 20, 1862...	Chicago...................	107
I	Edward Bouton.....	Feb. 15, 1862...	Chicago...................	142
K	Angreau Franklin...	Jan. 9, 1862....	Shawneetown..............	91
L	John Rourke.......	Feb. 22, 1862...	Chicago...................	109
M	John B. Miller......	Aug. 12, 1862..	Chicago...................	150
				1,406
	Recruits......................................			128
	Field and Staff and Company officers..........			71
	Regimental strength...........................			1,605

Regiment organized under authority of War Department, January 2, 1862.

Schedule A — Continued.

SECOND REGIMENT ILLINOIS LIGHT ARTILLERY.

Letter.	Captain.	Date of organization or muster.	Place of organization.	Strength.
A	Peter Davidson	Aug. 17, 1861	St. Louis	116
B	Riley Madison	June 20, 1861	Springfield	127
C	Caleb Hopkins		Cairo	97
D	Jasper M. Dresser	Dec. 17, 1861	Cairo	117
E	Andolph Gumbert		Cairo	90
F	John W. Powell	Dec. 11, 1861	Cape Girardeau	154
G	Charles J. Stolbrand	Dec. 31, 1861	Camp Butler	104
H	Andrew Steinbeck	Dec. 31, 1861	Camp Butler	115
I	Charles W. Keith	Dec. 31, 1861	Camp Butler	103
K	Benjamin F. Rogers	Dec. 31, 1861	Camp Butler	78
	William H. Bolton	Feb. 28, 1862	Chicago	104
	John C. Phillips	June 6, 1862	Chicago	96
				1,301
	Recruits			81
	Field, Staff and Company officers			70
	Regimental strength			1,452

Regiment organized under authority of the War Department, January 2, 1862.

UNASSIGNED BATTERIES LIGHT ARTILLERY.

Name.	Captain.	Date of organization or muster.	Place of organization.	Strength.
"Stokes"	James S. Stokes	July 31, 1862	Chicago	161
"Springfield"	Thomas F. Vaughn	Aug. 21, 1862	Springfield	134
"Mercantile"	Charles G. Cooley	Aug. 29, 1862	Chicago	153
"Elgin"	George W. Renwick	Nov. 15, 1862	Elgin	156
"Attached to 53d infantry"	William Coggswell	Sept. 23, 1861	Camp Douglas	138
"Henshaw's"	Edward C. Henshaw		Ottawa	135
"Hawthorn's"				65
Total				942

RECAPITULATION.

Infantry—old regiments	61,303	
" new "	53,221	114,524
Cavalry—regiments	16,336	
" unassigned	581	16,917
Artillery—First regiment	1,605	
" Second "	1,452	
" Batteries	942	3,999
Total		135,440

SCHEDULE "B,"

Showing the number or letter of the command, the name of its commanding officer, and the date and place of organization or muster, as in schedule A, and the day on which they left for the field, arranged according to dates of such departure.

No.	Colonel.	Organized.	Place of organization	Departure for field.
7	John Cook.........	April 25, 1861..	Springfield.........	April 27, 1861 ....
8	Richard J. Oglesby...	" 25, " ..	"	" 27, " ....
9	Eleazer A. Paine....	" 26, " ..	"	May 1, " ....
10	Benjamin M. Prentiss.	" 29, " ..	Cairo............	April 27, " ....
11	Wm. H. L. Wallace..	" 30, " ..	Springfield.........	May 5, " ....
12	John McArthur......	May 2, " ..	"	" 10, " ....

The above were three months' men, and subsequently re-organized in the field under the same numbers.

No.	Colonel.	Organized.	Place of organization	Departure for field.
7	John Cook.........	} In the field	July 25, 1861.	
8	Richard J. Oglesby..			
9	Eleazer A. Paine....			
10	James D. Morgan....			
11	Wm. H. L. Wallace..			
12	John McArthur......			
16	Robert F. Smith.....	May 24, 1861..	Quincy............	June 11, 1861....
20	Charles C. Marsh....	June 13, "	Joliet.............	" 13 & 18, 1861
22	Henry Dougherty....	" 25, "	Belleville..........	" 13, 1861....
24	Frederick Hecker....	" "	Chicago...........	" 13, " ....
13	John B. Wyman.....	May 24, "	Dixon.............	" 16, " ....
17	Leonard F. Ross.....	" 24, "	Peoria.............	" 17, " ....
15	Thomas J. Turner....	" 24, "	Freeport...........	" 18, " ....
14	John M. Palmer.....	" 25, "	Jacksonville.......	" 19, " ....
18	Michael K. Lawler...	" 28, "	Anna..............	" 24, " ....
21	Ulyses S. Grant.....	June 15, "	Mattoon...........	July 3, " ....
19	John B. Turchin.....	" 17, "	Chicago...........	July 12, " ....
23	James A. Mulligan...	" 18, "	"	" 15, " ....
25	William N. Coler....	August "	Danville...........	July 31, Aug. 2, '61
35	Gustavus A. Smith...	July 3, "	Decatur...........	Aug. 2, " ....
41	Napoleon B. Buford..	Aug. 9, " ..	"	" 6, " ....
40	Amory K. Johnson...	" 10, " ..	Camp Butler.......	" 11, " ....
27	Isaac C. Pugh.......	" " ..	"	" 26, " ....
28	Stephen G. Hicks....	" 3, " ..	"	" 27, " ....
30	Phillip B. Fouke....		"	" 31, " ....
26	John M. Loomis....	{ Oct 31, '61, 7 cos Jan. 8, '62, 1 co. }	"	Sep. 1, " ....
31	John A. Logan......	August 1861..	Jacksonville.......	" 1, " ....
29	James S. Reardon....	July 27, " ..	Camp Butler.......	" 6, " ....
38	William P. Carlin...	Aug. 15, " ..	"	" 8, " ....
44	Charles Knoblesdorff.	Sep. 13, " ..	Chicago...........	" 15, " ....

SCHEDULE B—Continued.

No.	Colonel.	Organized.	Place of organization	Departure for field.
37	Julius White	Sep. 18, 1861	Chicago	Sept. 19, " ….
33	Charles E. Hovey	Aug. 15, "	Jacksonville	" 20, " ….
47	John Bryner	" " "	Peoria	" 21, " ….
36	Nicholas Greusel	Sep. 23, "	Aurora	" 24, " ….
34	Edward N. Kirk	Aug. 30, "	Sterling	Oct. 2, " ….
50	Moses M. Bane	Sep. 12, "	Quincy	" 3, " ….
42	William A. Webb	" 17, "	Camp Douglas	" 11, 1861 ….
33	Julius Raith	" " "	" Butler	" 13, " ….
39	Austin Light	" " "	Chicago	" 14, " ….
48	Isham N. Haynie	" " "	Camp Butler	Nov. 11, " ….
55	David Stuart	Oct. 31, "	" Douglas	Dec. 9, " ….
66	Patrick E. Burke	Tr'nf'd from Mo.	St. Louis	" 12, " ….
64	Lt. Col. D. D. Williams	Dec. 31, "	Camp Butler	Jan. 11, 1862 ….
45	John E. Smith	" 26, "	Galena and Chicago	" 14, " ….
32	John Logan	" 31, "	Jacksonville	" 31, " ….
49	William R. Morrison	" 31, "	Camp Butler	Feb. 3, " ….
57	Silas D. Baldwin	" 26, "	" Douglas	" 8, " ….
58	William F. Lynch	" 20, "	" "	" 11, " ….
46	John A. Davis	" 28, "	" Butler	" 11, " ….
51	Gilbert W. Cumming	Dec. '61, Feb. '62	" Douglas	" 14, " ….
54	Thomas W. Harris	Feb. 18, "	Anna	" 24, " ….
61	Jacob Fry	Mar. 7, "	Carrollton	" 25, " ….
60	Silas C. Toler	Feb. 17, "	Anna	Mar. " ….
53	Wm. H. W. Cushman	Mar. " "	Ottawa	" 17, " ….
56	Robert Kirkham	Feb. 27, "	Shawneetown	" 6, " ….
59	P. Sidney Post	Tr'nf'd from Mo.		" 9, " ….
52	Isaac G. Wilson	Nov. 19, 1861	Geneva	" 22, " ….
62	James M. True	Apr'l 10, 1862	Anna	April 19, " ….
63	Francis Mora	" "	"	" 28, " ….
65	Daniel Cameron	May 5, "	Camp Douglas	June 21, " ….
67	Rosell M. Hough	June 13, 1862	Camp Douglas	Guard to C. D. ….
68	Elias Stuart	" 20, "	" Butler	July 6, 1862 ….
69	Joseph H. Tucker	" 14, "	" Douglas	Guard to C. D. ….
70	O. T. Reeves	July 4, "	" Butler	Sep. 8, 1862 ….
71	Othniel Gilbert	" 26, "	" Douglas	July 27, " ….
87	John E. Whiting		Shawneetown	Aug. 12, 1862 ….
72	Frederick A. Starring		Camp Douglas	" 23, " ….
99	George W. K. Bailey		Florence	" 23, " ….
83	Abner C. Harding		Monmouth	" 25, " ….
94	William W. Orme		Bloomington	" 25, " ….
76	A. W. Mack		Kankakee	" 26, " ….
100	Fred'k A. Bartleson		Joliet	Sept. 3, " ….
79	Lyman Guinnip		Danville	" 4, " ….
80	Thomas J. Allen		Centralia	" 4, " ….
88	Francis T. Sherman		Camp Douglas	" 5, " ….
89	John Christopher		" "	" 5, " ….
104	Absalom B. Moore		Ottawa	" 6, " ….
81	James J. Dollins		Anna	" 7, " ….
85	R. S. Moore		Peoria	" 7, " ….
86	David D. Irons		Peoria	" 7, " ….
98	John J. Funkhouser		Centralia	" 8, " ….
	Stokes Board of Trade Battery		Camp Douglas	" 9, " ….
125	Oscar F. Harman		Danville	" 13, " ….
123	James Munroe		Mattoon	" 19, " ….
78	W. H. Benneson		Quincy	" 20, " ….
84	Louis H. Waters		Quincy	" 22, " ….

SCHEDULE B—Continued.

No.	Colonel.	Organized.	Place of organization	Departure for field.
129	George P. Smith....	....	Pontiac...........	Sept. 22, 1862.
110	Thomas S. Casey....	....	Anna.............	" 24, "
73	James F. Jaquess....	....	Camp Butler.......	" 27, "
75	George Ryan.......	....	Dixon.............	" 27, "
74	Jason Marsh.......	....	Rockford..........	" 28, 1862.
107	Thomas Snell.......	....	Camp Butler.......	" 29, "
102	William McMurtry...	....	Knoxville..........	" 30, "
105	David Dustin.......	....	Chicago...........	" 30, "
91	Henry M. Day......	....	Camp Butler.......	Oct. 1, "
97	Friend S. Rutherford.	....	" "	" 3, "
77	David P. Grier......	....	Peoria............	" 4, "
115	Jesse H. Moore.....	....	Camp Butler.......	" 5, "
101	Charles H. Fox.....	....	Jacksonville.......	" 6, "
108	John Warner.......	....	Peoria............	" 6, "
124	Thomas J. Sloan....	....	Camp Butler.......	" 6, "
96	Thomas E. Champion.	....	Rockford..........	" 8, "
112	Thomas J. Henderson	....	Peoria............	" 8, "
122	John J. Rinaker.....	....	Carlinville.........	" 8, "
92	Smith D. Atkins....	....	Rockford..........	" 10, "
109	Alex. J. Nimmo.....	....	Anna.............	" 19, "
103	Amos C. Babcock...	....	Peoria............	" 30, "
111	James S. Martin.....	....	Salem	Nov. 1, "
	Vaughn's Spring-field Battery C..	....	Camp Butler.......	" 2, "
119	Thomas J. Kinney...	....	Quincy............	" 2, "
82	Frederick Hecker...	....	Camp Butler.......	" 3, "
95	Lawrence S. Church.	....	Rockford..........	" 4, "
113	George B. Hoge.....	....	Camp Douglas.....	" 6, "
106	Robert B. Latham...	....	Lincoln............	" 7, "
93	Holden Putnam.....	....	Camp Douglas.....	" 8, "
114	James W. Judy.....	....	" Butler.......	" 8, "
116	Nathan H. Tupper...	....	Decatur...........	" 8, "
120	Geo. W. McKeaig...	....	Camp Butler	" 9, "
127	John Van Arman ...	....	" Douglas.....	" 9, "
	Cooley's Mercantile Battery........	....	" "	" 9, "
117	Risdon M. Moore....	....	" Butler.......	" 10, "
130	Nathaniel Niles.....	....	" "	" 13, "
126	Jonathan Richmond.	....	" Douglas.....	" 21, "
90	Timothy O'Meara....	....	" "	" 27, "
118	John G. Fonda	....	" Butler.......	Dec. 1, "
131	George W. Neeley...	....	" Massac......	" 2, "
128	Robert M. Hundley..	....	" Butler.......	" 25, "

SCHEDULE B—Continued.

ILLINOIS LIGHT ARTILLERY.
FIRST REGIMENT.

Letter.	Captain.	Date of organization.	Place of organization.	Departure for field.
A	C. M. Willard........	....	Chicago...........	April 21, 1861.
B	Ezra Taylor........	....	"	May "
C	Charles Houghtaling.	Oct. 31, 1861..	Ottawa...........	April 21, "
D	Edward McAllister..	Jan. 14, 1862..	Plainfield	" 21, "
E	A. C. Waterhouse...	Dec. 19, 1861..	Chicago...........	Feb. 9, 1862.
F	John T. Cheney.....	Feb. 25, 1862..	Camp Butler.......	March 13, "
G	Arthur O'Leary.....	" 28, " ..	Cairo	....
H	Axel Silversparre...	" 20, " ..	Camp Douglas ...	Feb. 27, "
I	Edward Bowton.....	" 15, " ..	" "	" 28, "
K	Angrean Franklin...	Jan. 9, " ..	Shawneetown	....
L	John Rourke.......	Feb. 22, " ..	Camp Douglas	June 12, "
M	John B. Miller......	Aug. 12, " ..	" "	Sept. 27, "

SECOND REGIMENT.

Letter.	Captain.	Date of organization.	Place of organization.	Departure for field.
A	Peter Davidson......	{May 23, '61} {Aug. 17, '67}	Peoria	July 1861.
B	Riley Madison	....	Springfield	....
C	Caleb Hopkins......	....	Cairo	....
D	Jasper M. Dresser...	Dec. 17, 1861..	"	....
E	Andolph Schwartz...	....	"	....
F	John W. Powell.....	Dec. 11, 1861..	Cape Girardeau....	....
G	Charles J. Stolbrand.	" 31, " ..	Camp Butler.......	Feb. 2, 1862.
H	Andrew Stienbeck ..	" 31, " ..	" "	" 7, "
I	Charles W. Keith...	" 31, " ..	" "	" 3, "
K	Benj. F. Rogers.....	" 31, " ..	" "	" 3, "
L	Wm. H. Bolton.....	Feb. 28, 1862..	" Douglas......	March 12, "
M	John C. Phillips	June 6, " ..	" Butler.......	July 12, "

INDEPENDENT BATTERIES.

	Captain.	Date of organization.	Place of organization.	Departure for field.
	James S. Stokes....	July 31, 1862..	Chicago...........	Sept. 9, 1862.
	Charles G. Cooley...	Aug. 29, " ..	Chicago...........	Nov. 9, "
	Thomas F. Vaughn..	" 21, " ..	Camp Butler.......	" 2, "
	William Coggswell..	" 23, " ..	" Douglas......	March 22, "
	Geo. W. Renwick...	Nov. 15, " ..	Elgin	....
	Edward C. Henshaw.	....	Ottawa	....

SCHEDULE B — Continued.

CAVALRY REGIMENTS.

No.	Colonel.	Organization.	Place of organization.	Departure for field.
1	Thomas A. Marshall.	....	Bloomington.......	June, 1861.
2	Silas Noble........	....	Camp Butler.......	Sept. 3, "
3	Eugene A. Carr.....	....	" "	" 25, "
4	T. Lyle Dickey.....	....	Ottawa............	Nov. 27, "
5	John J. Up degraff.	....	Camp Butler.......	Feb. 20, 1862.
6	Thos. H. Cavanaugh.	....	" "	Nov. 2, 1861.
7	Wm. Pitt Kellogg...	....	St. Charles........	Nov. 7, "
8	John F. Farnsworth.	....	Camp Douglas.....	Oct. "
9	Albert G. Brackett..	....	" "	Feb. 16, 1862.
10	James A. Barrett...	Oct. 26, 1861..	" Butler.......	Jan. 22, "
11	Robert G. Ingersoll..	....	Peoria............	Dec. 18, 1861.
12	Arno Voss.........	....	Camp Butler.......	June 27, 1862.
13	Joseph W. Bell.....	....	" Douglas......	Feb. 20, "
14	Horace Capron.....	....	Peoria............	....
15	Warren Stewart....	Dec. 25, 1862..	....	....

UNASSIGNED CAVALRY.

Captain.			
C. B. Dodson.......	....	Geneva............	....
P. Naughton........	....	St. Louis, Mo......	....
Albert Jenks.......	....	....	....
H. A. Smith........	....	....	....
William Ford.......	....	Chicago...........	March 22, 1862...
George W. Shears...	....	"	....
David C. Brown.....	....	"	....
F. Schambeck......	....	Springfield........	....
B. Marschner......	....	Chicago...........	....
Matthew Marx......	....	Paducah...........	....
Warren Stewart.....	....	Alexander co......	....
E. Carmichael......	....	Cairo.............	....
James J. Dollins....	....	Franklin co........	....
M. J. O'Harnett.....	....	Clinton co.........	....
Wm. D. Hutchens...	....	Jackson co........	....

SCHEDULE "C,"

Showing the number and name of the officer of each regiment when originally mustered, and the counties from which the same was principally recruited.

INFANTRY.

Seventh Regiment.
JOHN COOK, Colonel.
A—Kane ....
B—Coles ....
C—Kane, DuPage, Kendall.
D—Logan, Montgomery, Alexander ....
E—Logan ....
F—Macoupin ....
G—Sangamon, Fayette....
H—Logan ....
I—Sangamon ....
K—Macoupin ....

Eighth.
RICH'D J. OGLESBY.
A—Macon ....
B—Macon ....
C—Coles ....
D—Richland ....
E—Peoria, Fulton ....
F—Tazewell ....
G—Pike, Alexander ......
H—Fayette ....
I—Peoria ....
K—McLean ....

Ninth.
ELEAZER A. PAINE.
A—Madison ....
B—St. Clair ....
C—St. Clair ....
D—St. Clair ....
E—St. Clair, Mercer ......
F—St. Clair ....
G—Alexander ....
H—Montgomery ....
I—Madison ....
K—Pulaski ....

Tenth.
JAMES D. MORGAN.
A—Morgan ....
B—Morgan ....

C—Adams, Knox ....
D—Madison ....
E—Henderson ....
F—St. Louis, Mo. ....
G—Clark, Henderson.....
H—DeKalb ....
I—Randolph ....
K—Madison ....

Eleventh.
WM. H. L. WALLACE.
A—Stephenson ....
B—Marshall ....
C—Marion ....
D—Winnebago ....
E— ....
F—Jasper ....
G—Effingham ....
H—LaSalle ....
I—Marshall, LaSalle......
K—LaSalle ....

Twelfth.
JOHN McARTHUR.
A—Cook ....
B—LaSalle ....
C—Vermilion ....
D—Rock Island ....
E—Edgar ....
F—Jo Daviess ....
G— ....
H—Bureau ....
I—Bureau ....
K—Cook, Kankakee .....

Thirteenth.
JOHN B. WYMAN.
A—Lee ....
B—Whiteside ....
C—Lee ....
D—Rock Island, Cook ...
E—DeKalb ....
F—DeKalb ....
G—Whiteside ....

H—Kane ....
I—Cook ....
K—DuPage ....

Fourteenth.
JOHN M. PALMER.
A—Cass ....
B—Shelby ....
C—Macoupin ....
D—Greene ....
E—Morgan, Menard .....
F—Jersey ....
G—Sangamon ....
H—Christian ....
I—Morgan ....
K—Scott ....

Fifteenth.
THOMAS J. TURNER.
A—McHenry ....
B—Boone ....
C—Winnebago ....
D—McHenry ....
E—Jo Daviess ....
F—McHenry ....
G—Stephenson ....
H—Ogle ....
I—Lake ....
K—Carroll ....

Sixteenth.
ROBERT F. SMITH.
A—Adams, McDonough ...
B—McDonough ....
C—Adams, McDonough...
D—Hancock ....
E—Brown ....
F—Henderson ....
G—Adams, Schuyler......
H—Adams ....
I—Adams, Hancock .....
K—Pike ....

SCHEDULE C—Continued.

Seventeenth.	*Twenty-first.*	*Twenty-fifth.*
LEONARD F. ROSS.	ULYSSES S. GRANT.	WILLIAM N. COLER.
A—Peoria	A—Macon	A—Vermilion
B—Peoria	B—Cumberland	B—Vermilion
C—Fulton	C—Piatt	C—Champaign
D—Henry	D—Douglas	D—Vermilion
E—Knox	E—Moultrie	E—Coles
F—Warren	F—Edgar	F—Iroquois
G—Woodford	G—Clay	G—Champaign
H—Fulton	H—Clark	H—Douglas
I—Mercer	I—Crawford	I—Champaign
K—Mason	K—Jasper	K—Champaign

Eighteenth.	*Twenty-second.*	*Twenty-sixth.*
MICHAEL K. LAWLER.	HENRY DOUGHERTY.	JOHN M. LOOMIS.
A—Perry	A—Clinton	A—Effingham
B—Gallatin	B—Madison	B—Stephenson
C—Jackson	C—St. Clair	C—Bond
D—Alexander, Pulaski	D—Bond	D—Sangamon
E—Alexander	E—Bond	E—LaSalle
F—Wayne, Jefferson	F—Monroe	F—Champaign, Vermilion
G—Wayne	G—Marion	G—White
H—Pulaski	H—Randolph	H—State at large
I—Perry, Union	I—Randolph	I—Champaign
K—Jackson	K—St. Clair	K—McLean

Nineteenth.	*Twenty-third.*	*Twenty-seventh.*
JOHN B. TURCHIN.	JAMES A. MULLIGAN.	NAPOLEON B. BUFORD.
A—Cook	A—Wayne	A—Adams
B—	B—Cook	B—Scott
C—Lake	C—Cook	C—Pike
D—Cook	D—LaSalle	D—Madison, Jersey
E—Cook	E—Grundy	E—Mason
F—Cass	F—Cook	F—Macoupin
G—Cook	G—Cook	G—Mercer
H—	H—Cook	H—Jackson
I—Cook	I—Cook	I—Henry
K—Cook	K—Cook	K—Morgan

Twentieth.	*Twenty-fourth.*	*Twenty-eighth.*
CHARLES C. MARSH.	FREDERIC HECKER.	AMORY K. JOHNSON.
A—Champaign	A—Cook	A—Mason
B—Will	B—McLean	B—Pike
C—McLean	C—Cook	C—Scott
D—Livingston	D—Cook	D—McDonough
E—DeWitt	E—Cook	E—Pike
F—Will, Bureau	F—Cook	F—Menard
G—Kankakee	G—Cook	G—Schuyler
H—Putnam, LaSalle	H—Cook	H—Fulton
I—Iroquois	I—LaSalle	I—Pike
K—Kendall	K—State at large	K—Logan, Menard

Schedule C—Continued.

Twenty-ninth.
James S. Reardon.
- A—Hardin
- B—White, Alexander
- C—Gallatin
- D—Gallatin, White
- E—Saline
- F—Pope
- G—White
- H—Edgar
- I—Sangamon
- K—Massac

Thirtieth.
Philip B. Fouke.
- A—Mercer
- B—Sangamon
- C—Randolph
- D—Crawford
- E—Randolph
- F—Clark, Edgar
- G—Mercer
- H—Macoupin, Clinton
- I—Clinton, Bond
- K—Clinton

Thirty-first.
John A. Logan.
- A—Perry
- B—Saline
- C—Williamson
- D—Johnson, Pope
- E—Union
- F—Pulaski, Johnson, Williamson
- G—Saline
- H—Alexander, Jackson, Williamson
- I—Tazewell, Franklin
- K—Marion

Thirty-second.
John Logan.
- A—Macoupin
- B—Hancock, Logan
- C—Macoupin
- D—Greene
- E—Shelby, Greene, Fayette
- F—Madison
- G—St. Clair
- H—Morgan
- I—Macoupin, Peoria, Wabash
- K—Jasper

Thirty-third.
Charles E. Hovey.
- A—At large
- B—LaSalle, DuPage, Stark
- C—McLean
- D—Christian, Sangamon, Montgomery
- E—Bureau, Knox
- F—Scott, Morgan, Livingston
- G—McLean
- H—Knox
- I—Pike
- K—Cass, Menard, Morgan

Thirty-fourth.
Edward N. Kirk.
- A—Whiteside
- B—Whiteside
- C—Lee
- D—Lee
- E—Ogle
- F—Ogle
- G—Morgan, Randolph
- H—Ogle
- I—Carroll
- K—Edgar

Thirty-fifth.
Gustavus A. Smith.
- A—Piatt
- B—Christian, Shelby, Fayette
- C—Shelby
- D—Vermilion
- E—Vermilion
- F—Vermilion
- G—Fayette
- H—Fayette
- I—Vermilion
- K—Effingham, Fayette

Thirty-sixth.
Nicholas Greusel.
- A—Kane, McHenry
- B—Kane
- C—Warren
- D—Kendall
- E—Kendall
- F—Kendall
- G—Grundy
- H—McHenry
- I—Kendall
- K—DuPage

Thirty-seventh.
Julius White.
- A—Rock Island
- B—Stark
- C—Lake
- D—Cook, Michigan
- E—LaSalle
- F—Lake
- G—Cook
- H—Rock Island
- I—Cook, Boone
- K—Vermilion

Thirty-eighth.
William P. Carlin.
- A—
- B—Effingham
- C—Fayette, Champaign
- D—Crawford
- E—Coles
- F—Logan
- G—Mason, Tazewell
- H—Jasper
- I—
- K—Jasper

Thirty-ninth.
Austin Light.
- A—Will
- B—McLean
- C—Livingston
- D—Ogle
- E—Will
- F—Marion, Cook
- G—Cook, Will
- H—McLean
- I—McLean, DeWitt
- K—LaSalle

Fortieth.
Stephen G. Hicks.
- A—Hamilton
- B—Marion, Fayette
- C—White
- D—Wayne
- E—Wayne
- F—Franklin
- G—Wayne, Hamilton
- H—Marion, Fayette
- I—Wabash, Clay, Edwards
- K—Clay

SCHEDULE C—Continued.

Forty-first.
ISAAC C. PUGH.

A—Macon
B—Moultrie
C—DeWitt
D—Coles
E—Macon
F—DeWitt
G—Christian
H—Shelby
I—Christian
K—DeWitt

Forty-second.
WILLIAM A. WEBB.

A—Cook
B—Cook
C—Cook
D—Kankakee
E—Cook
F—Cook
G—Cook
H—Cook
I—Cook
K—Cook

Forty-third.
JULIUS RAITH.

A—St. Clair
B—St. Clair
C—Knox
D—Cook
E—Rock Island
F—Monroe
G—St. Clair
H—St. Clair
I—St. Clair
K—St. Clair

Forty-fourth.
CHARLES KNOBELSDORFF.

A—Tazewell
B—Michigan
C—Marshall, Livingston, Putnam
D—Ohio
E—Cook
F—Washington
G—Winnebago
H—Michigan
I—Jefferson
K—Cook and adjacent

Forty-fifth.
JOHN E. SMITH.

A—Carroll
B—Jo Daviess
C—Jo Daviess
D—Jo Daviess
E—Carroll, Jo Daviess
F—Winnebago, Brown
G—Winnebago
H—Rock Island
I—Grundy
K—Knox

Forty-sixth.
JOHN A. DAVIS.

A—Stephenson
B—Stephenson
C—Stephenson
D—Lee
E—Whiteside
F—Clay
G—Stephenson
H—Lee, Ogle
I—Will, Lee, Ogle
K—Stephenson

Forty-seventh.
JOHN BRYNER.

A—Peoria
B—Tazewell, Woodford
C—Peoria
D—Marshall
E—Tazewell
F—Peoria
G—Marshall
H—Bureau, Peoria
I—Woodford
K—Stark

Forty-Eighth.
ISHAM N. HAYNIE.

A—Pope
B—Clay
C—Hardin
D—Washington
E—Kentucky
F—Marion
G—Wabash
H—White
I—Wayne
K—Clay

Forty-ninth.
WILLIAM R. MORRISON.

A—Monroe
B—Monroe, Randolph
C—Washington
D—Marion
E | St. Clair, Macoupin
F—Washington
G—Madison
H—Monroe
I—Randolph, Washington
K—Jefferson

Fiftieth.
MOSES M. BANE.

A—Adams
B—Adams
C—Adams
D—Adams
E—Adams
F—Hancock
G—Hancock, Fulton
H—Brown
I—Warren
K—Clinton, Hancock

Fifty-first.
GILBERT W. CUMMING.

A—Cook
B—DuPage, Champaign
C—Iroquois
D—Woodford, McLean
E—Vermilion, Champaign
F—Mason
G—Lake
H—Rock Island
I—
K—Cook, Bureau, Knox

Fifty-second.
ISAAC G. WILSON.

A—Kane
B—Bureau
C—DeKalb
D—Kane
E—Winnebago
F—Whiteside
G—Kane
H—Kane
I—Kane
K—Kane

SCHEDULE C—Continued.

Fifty-third.
WM. W. H. CUSHMAN.

A—LaSalle.
B—LaSalle.
C—LaSalle.
D—LaSalle.
E—Kankakee.
F—LaSalle.
G—Livingston.
H—Marshall.
I—Mason.
K—LaSalle.

Fifty-fourth.
THOMAS W. HARRIS.

A—Christian.
B—Douglas.
C—Coles.
D—Effingham.
E—Jasper.
F—Edgar, Shelby.
G—Clark, Coles.
H—Shelby.
I—Effingham, Coles, Douglas.
K—Fayette, Edgar.

Fifty-fifth.
DAVID STUART.

A—Fulton.
B—Coles, DeKalb, Ogle, Cook.
C—Winnebago.
D—State at large.
E—Kane, DuPage.
F—McDonough.
G—McDonough, LaSalle.
H—Carroll.
I—LaSalle, Grundy.
K—Knox.

Fifty-sixth.
ROBERT KIRKHAM.

A—Massac.
B—White.
C—Hamilton, White, etc.
D—Gallatin, Saline, White.
E—Saline, Williamson.
F—Hamilton, Wabash.
G—Hamilton, White.
H—Saline, Gallatin.
I—Williamson, Franklin.
K—Pope, Saline.

Fifty-seventh.
SILAS D. BALDWIN.

A—LaSalle.
B—Bureau.
C—Cook.
D—Henry.
E—Cook.
F—Bureau.
G—Cook.
H—Bureau, Henry, Knox.
I—State at large.
K—Bureau.

Fifty-eighth.
WILLIAM F. LYNCH.

A—Kane, Cook.
B—Cook.
C—DeKalb.
D—Cook.
E—Cook, DeKalb.
F—Cook.
G—Knox, etc.
H—LaSalle, Cook.
I—Kane.
K—Rock Island.

Fifty-ninth.
P. SIDNEY POST.

A—Knox.
B—Warren, Henderson.
C—McDonough.
D—Madison.
E—St. Clair.
F—Cumberland.
G—Greene.
H—Edgar, Coles.
I—Macoupin.
K—Cook.

Sixtieth.
SILAS C. TOLER.

A—Union.
B—Union.
C—Jefferson.
D—Hamilton, Jefferson.
E—Williamson.
F—Richland, Union.
G—Hamilton.
H—Pope.
I—Jefferson.
K—Johnson.

Sixty-first.
JACOB FRY.

A—
B—
C—
D—
E—
F—
G—
H—Lawrence.
I—
K—

Sixty-second.
JAMES M. TRUE.

A—Lawrence.
B—Washington.
C—Clark.
D—White.
E—Fayette.
F—Crawford.
G—Marion.
H—McLean.
I—Union.
K—Coles.

Sixty-third.
FRANCIS MORA.

A—Richland.
B—Edwards.
C—Richland.
D—McLean.
E—Richland.
F—Franklin.
G—Crawford.
H—Macon.
I—Richland.
K—Coles.

Sixty-fourth.
LT. COL. D. D. WILLIAMS.

A—LaSalle.
B—
C—Sangamon.
D—Knox, McDonough.
E—Will.
F—Will, Kankakee.
G—
H—
I—
K—

SCHEDULE C—Continued.

Sixty-fifth.
DANIEL CAMERON.

A—Henderson, Stark, Ogle
B—Mercer
C—Marshall
D—Cook
E—Boone, McDonough
F—Lake
G—Will
H—Cook
I—State at large
K—Cook, Winnebago

Sixty-sixth.
PATRICK E. BURKE.

A—St. Louis, Mo
B—St. Louis, Mo
C—Logan, Bureau
D—Michigan
E—Edgar
F—St. Louis, Mo
G—Ohio
H—Ohio
I—Lawrence
K—Ohio

Sixty-seventh.
ROSELL M. HOUGH.

A—Winnebago
B—Cook
C—Winnebago
D—Cook
E—Cook
F—Fulton
G—Cook
H—Stephenson
I—Cook
K—Champaign

Sixty-eighth.
ELIAS STUART.

A—Morgan
B—Pike
C—Coles
D—Fayette
E—DeWitt
F—McLean
G—McLean
H—Logan
I—Macon
K—Tazewell

Sixty-ninth.
JOSEPH H. TUCKER.

A—Bureau
B—Kane
C—Cook, etc.
D—Henry
E—Cook
F—Rock Island
G—Livingston
H—Lee
I—Grundy
K—Ogle, Lee

Seventieth.
O. T. REEVES.

A—Douglas
B—Sangamon
C—Montgomery
D—Fulton
E—Sangamon
F—St. Clair
G—Edgar
H—McLean
I—Pike, Greene
K—Lawrence

Seventy-first.
OTHNIEL GILBERT.

A—Vermilion
B—Stephenson, Carroll
C—Champaign
D—Rock Island
E—Knox, Hancock, Peoria
F—Champaign
G—Menard
H—Champaign
I—Effingham
K—Hamilton, Franklin

Seventy-second.
FREDRICK A. STARRING.

A—Cook
B—Cook
C—Cook
D—Cook
E—Cook
F—Cook
G—Champaign, McDonough
H—Cook
I—Fulton
K—Cook

Seventy-third.
JAMES F. JAQUESS.

A—Sangamon
B—Tazewell
C—Vermilion
D—Piatt
E—Vermilion
F—Logan
G—Schuyler
H—Pike
I—Sangamon
K—Jackson

Seventy-fourth.
JASON MARSH.

A—Winnebago
B—Winnebago
C—Winnebago
D—Winnebago
E—Winnebago
F—Winnebago
G—Ogle
H—Winnebago
I—Stephenson
K—Winnebago

Seventy-fifth.
GEORGE RYAN.

A—Lee
B—Whiteside
C—Whiteside
D—Whiteside
E—Lee
F—Lee
G—Lee, Ogle
H—Whiteside
I—Whiteside
K—Lee

Seventy-sixth.
A. W. MACK.

A—Iroquois
B—Champaign
C—Grundy
D—Kankakee
E—Morgan
F—Kankakee
G—Champaign
H—Kankakee
I—Kankakee
K—Iroquois, Ford

SCHEDULE C—Continued.

Seventy-seventh.
DAVID P. GRIER.

A—Knox, Peoria..........
B—Putnam..............
C—Woodford............
D—Marshall.............
E—Peoria...............
F—Woodford, Peoria, etc..
G—Peoria...............
H—Woodford............
I—Peoria, Knox.........
K—Peoria...............

Seventy-eighth.
WM. H. BENNISON.

A—Schuyler.............
B—Adams...............
C—McDonough..........
D—Hancock.............
E—Adams...............
F—Adams...............
G—Adams...............
H—Hancock.............
I—McDonough..........
K—Adams, Clark........

Seventy-ninth.
LYMAN GUINNIP.

A—Edgar, Vermilion.....
B—Douglas.............
C—Edgar...............
D—Edgar...............
E—Douglas.............
F—Clark...............
G—Douglas.............
H—Edgar...............
I—Clark, Crawford.....
K—Douglas, Coles......

Eightieth.
THOMAS G. ALLEN.

A—Adams...............
B—Madison.............
C—Madison, St. Clair...
D—Randolph............
E—Jefferson............
F—Perry, Randolph.....
G—Randolph............
H—Marion..............
I—Washington, Marion..
K—Washington, Madison..

Eighty-fifth.
JAMES J. DOLLINS.

A—Perry...............
B—Jackson.............
C—Perry...............
D—Jackson.............
E—Williamson, Union...
F—Jackson.............
G—Williamson..........
H—Williamson..........
I—Pulaski.............
K—Perry...............

Eighty-second.
FREDERIC HECKER.

A—Cook................
B—Cook................
C—Cook................
D—Cook................
E—McLean, Peoria......
F—Cook, St. Clair.....
G—Cook, St. Clair.....
H—Cook, Madison.......
I—Cook................
K—Cook................

Eighty-third.
ABNER C. HARDING.

A—Warren..............
B—Warren..............
C—Warren..............
D—Mercer..............
E—Knox................
F—Warren..............
G—Knox................
H—Warren..............
I—Knox................
K—Knox................

Eighty-fourth.
LOUIS H. WATERS.

A—McDonough..........
B—Fulton..............
C—McDonough..........
D—Brown...............
E—Adams...............
F—Fulton, McDonough...
G—Henderson...........
H—Mercer..............
I—Adams...............
K—Henderson...........

Eighty-fifth.
ROBERT S. MOORE.

A—Mason, Tazewell.....
B—Fulton, Mason.......
C—Mason...............
D—Mason...............
E—Menard..............
F—Tazewell, Woodford...
G—Fulton, Schuyler....
H—Fulton..............
I—Fulton..., ...
K—Mason...............

Eighty-sixth.
DAVID D. IRONS.

A—Woodford............
B—Marshall............
C—Peoria..............
D—Peoria..............
E—Marshall............
F—Knox................
G—Tazewell............
H—Peoria..............
I—Peoria..............
K—Peoria..............

Eighty-seventh.
JOHN E. WHITING.

A—Hamilton............
B—White...............
C—
D—Wayne...............
E—Hamilton............
F—White...............
G—White...............
H—Edwards.............
I—White...............
K—White...............

Eighty-eighth.
FRANCIS T. SHERMAN.

A—Cook................
B—Cook................
C—Cook................
D—Cook................
E—Cook................
F—Cook................
G—Cook................
H—Cook................
I—Cook................
K—Cook................

SCHEDULE C—Continued.

Eighty-ninth.	*Ninety-third.*	*Ninety-seventh.*
JOHN CHRISTOPHER.	HOLDEN PUTNAM.	FRIEND S. RUTHERFORD.
A—Hancock, Henderson..	A—Rock Island..........	A—Macoupin............
B—Franklin	B—Bureau	B—Cumberland..........
C—Cook................	C—Bureau..............	C—Calhoun ....
D—Iroquois, Jackson.....	D—Stephenson	D—Cumberland ....
E—Kane, Knox..........	E—Bureau	E—Jasper..............
F—Rock Island	F—Whiteside...........	F—Fayette ....
G—Knox	G—Stephenson	G—Madison ....
H—Kendall	H—Bureau	H—Jersey ....
I—Lee	I—Bureau	I—Madison ....
K—Cook	K—Bureau	K—Jersey ....

Ninetieth.	*Ninety-fourth.*	*Ninety-eighth.*
TIMOTHY O'MEARA.	WILLIAM W. ORME.	JOHN J. FUNKHOUSER.
A—Winnebago	A—McLean	A—Clay ....
B—JoDaviess...........	B—McLean	B—Richland............
C—Will, Cook..........	C—McLean	C—Effingham..........
D—Will	D—McLean	D—Crawford ....
E—Cook	E—McLean	E—Crawford ....
F—Cook	F—McLean	F—Clay, White.........
G—Cook	G—McLean	G—Richland ....
H—Cook	H—McLean	H—Richland ....
I—Cook, Stephenson.....	I—McLean, Tazewell.....	I—Jasper..............
K—...................	K—McLean	K—Effingham ....

Ninety-first.	*Ninety-fifth.*	*Ninety-ninth.*
HENRY M. DAY.	LAWRENCE S. CHURCH.	GEORGE W. K. BAILEY.
A—Montgomery	A—McHenry	A—Pike ....
B—Henderson	B—Boone	B—Pike ....
C—Henderson	C—McHenry	C—Pike ....
D—Grundy	D—McHenry	D—Pike ....
E—Kendall	E—McHenry	E—Pike ....
F—Lawrence	F—McHenry	F—Pike ....
G—Greene	G—Boone	G—Pike ....
H—Will	H—McHenry	H—Pike ....
I—Greene	I—McHenry	I—Pike ....
K—Greene	K—Boone..............	K—Pike ....

Ninety-second.	*Ninety-sixth.*	*One hundredth.*
SMITH D. ATKINS.	THOMAS E. CHAMPION.	FREDERICK A. BARTLESON.
A—Stephenson	A—JoDaviess	A..Will ....
B—Ogle	B—Fulton	B..Will ....
C—Carroll	C—Lake	C..Will ....
D—Ogle	D—Lake	D..Will ....
E—Ogle	E—JoDaviess	E..Will ....
F—Stephenson..........	F—JoDaviess	F..Will...............
G—Stephenson	G—Lake	G..Will ....
H—Ogle	H—JoDaviess	H..Will ....
I—Carroll	I—JoDaviess..........	I—Will ....
K—Ogle	K—JoDaviess	K..Will ....

SCHEDULE C—Continued.

One hundred and first.

CHARLES H. FOX.

A..Morgan
B..Morgan
C..Morgan
D..Morgan
E..Morgan
F..Morgan
G..Morgan, Sangamon
H..Morgan
I...Morgan
K..Morgan

One hundred and second.

WILLIAM McMURTRY.

A..Knox
B........
C..Mercer, Rock Island
D..Knox
E..Mercer
F..Knox
G..Mercer
H..Knox
I..Knox
K..Mercer

One hundred and third.

AMOS C. BABCOCK.

A..Fulton
B..Lake
C..Fulton
D..Fulton
E..Fulton
F..Fulton
G..Fulton
H..Fulton
I..Fulton
K..Fulton

One hundred and fourth.

ABSALOM B. MOORE.

A..LaSalle
B..LaSalle
C..LaSalle
D..LaSalle
E..LaSalle
F..LaSalle
G..LaSalle
H..Franklin
I..Tazewell
K..LaSalle

One hundred and fifth.

DANIEL DUSTIN.

A..DeKalb
B..DuPage
C..DeKalb
D..DuPage
E..DeKalb
F..DuPage
G..DeKalb, Kane
H..DeKalb
I..DuPage
K..DeKalb

One hundred and sixth.

ROBERT B. LATHAM.

A..Sangamon
B..Logan
C..Logan
D..Logan
E..Logan
F..Logan
G..Logan
H..Logan
I..Logan
K..Menard

One hundred and seventh.

THOMAS SNELL.

A..DeWitt
B..DeWitt
C..Piatt
D..DeWitt
E..Piatt
F..DeWitt
G..Williamson
H..Piatt
I..DeWitt
K..Piatt, Sangamon

One hundred and eighth.

JOHN WARNER.

A..Tazewell
B..Tazewell
C..Peoria
D..Woodford
E..Woodford
F..Mason, Peoria
G..Peoria
H..Mason, Cass, Tazewell
I..Peoria
K..Peoria, Tazewell

One hundred and ninth.

ALEXANDER J. NIMMO.

A..Union
B..Alexander, Union, Jackson
C..Union
D..Union, Johnson
E..Union
F..Union
G..Union
H..Union
I..Union
K..Pulaski

One hundredth and tenth.

THOMAS S. CASEY.

A..Franklin
B..Jefferson
C..Williamson
D..Washington
E..Saline
F..Franklin
G..Wayne, Jefferson
H..Perry
I..Franklin
K..Hamilton

One hundred and eleventh.

JAMES S. MARTIN.

A..Marion
B..Washington
C..Clay
D..Marion
E..Logan
F..Marion
G..Marion
H..Marion
I..Clinton
K..Marion

One hundred and twelfth.

THOMAS J. HENDERSON.

A..Henry
B..Stark
C..Henry
D..Henry
E..Scott
F..Stark
G..Henry
H..Henry
I..Henry
K..Henry

SCHEDULE C—Continued.

One hundred and thirteenth.
GEORGE B. HOGE.

A..Cook
B..Kankakee, Iroquois
C..Cook
D..Iroquois
E..Cook
F..Iroquois
G..Cook
H..Kankakee
I..Iroquois
K..Kankakee

One hundred and fourteenth.
JAMES W. JUDY.

A..Cass
B..Sangamon
C..Sangamon
D..Cass
E..Sangamon
F..Menard, Cass, Sangamon
G..Sangamon
H..Sangamon
I..Sangamon
K..Menard

One hundred and fifteenth.
JESSE H. MOORE.

A..Christian
B..Shelby
C..Wabash
D..Schuyler
E..Christian, Macon
F..Shelby, Macon
G..Shelby
H..Tazewell
I..Morgan
K..Menard, Sangamon

One hundred and sixteenth.
NATHAN H. TUPPER.

A..Macon
B..Macon
C..Macon
D..Macon
E..Macon
F..McLean
G..Macon, Christian
H..Shelby, Christian
I..Macon
K..Macon

One hundred and seventeenth.
RISDON M. MOORE.

A..McLean
B..Montgomery
C..St. Clair
D..Madison
E..Clinton
F..Madison
G..Madison
H..St. Clair
I..St. Clair
K..St. Clair

One hundred and eighteenth.
JOHN G. FONDA.

A..Hancock
B..Hancock
C..Hancock
D..Adams
E..Hancock
F..Adams
G..Henderson, Hancock
H..Hancock
I..Hardin, Gallatin
K..Adams

One hundred and nineteenth.
THOMAS J. KINNEY.

A..Adams
B..Schuyler
C..Schuyler
D..Brown
E..Brown
F..Schuyler
G..Adams
H..McDonough
I..Adams, etc.
K..Adams

One hundred and twentieth.
GEORGE W. McKRAIG.

A..Pope
B..Johnson
C..Johnson
D..Gallatin
E..Pope
F..Saline
G..Williamson, Pope
H..White, Gallatin
I..Johnson
K..Johnson

One hundred and twenty-second.
JOHN J. RINAKER.

A..Macoupin
B..Macoupin
C..Greene
D..Macoupin
E..Macoupin
F..Macoupin, Montgomery
G..Macoupin
H..Macoupin
I..Macoupin
K..Macoupin

One hundred and twenty-third.
JAMES MONROE.

A..Coles
B..Cumberland
C..Coles
D..Coles
E..Putnam, Clark
F..Clark
G..Clark
H..Coles
L..Coles
K..Sangamon

One hundred and twenty-fourth.
THOMAS J. SLOAN.

A..Henry
B..Kane
C..Sangamon, Jersey
D..McDonough, Woodford
E..Kane
F..Henry
G..Mercer
H..Kane
I..McDonough, Sangamon
K..Sangamon, DuPage

One hundred and twenty-fifth.
OSCAR F. HARMON.

A..Vermilion
B..Vermilion
C..Vermilion
D..Vermilion
E..Champaign
F..Champaign
G..Champaign
H..Vermilion
I..Vermilion
K..Vermilion

SCHEDULE C—Continued.

One hundred and twenty-sixth.
JONATHAN RICHMOND.
- A..Moultrie
- B..Rock Island, Macon
- C..Moultrie
- D..Montgomery
- E..Rock Island
- F..Montgomery
- G..Rock Island
- H..Rock Island
- I...Rock Island
- K..Shelby

One hundred and twenty-seventh.
JOHN VAN ARMAN.
- A..Kendall
- B..Cook
- C..Kane
- D..Grundy
- E..Kane
- F..Kendall
- G..Cook
- H..Cook
- I...Kane
- K..Kendall

One hundred and twenty-eighth.
ROBERT M. HUNDLEY.
- A..Williamson, Franklin
- B..Williamson
- C..Williamson
- D..Williamson
- E..Williamson
- F..Williamson
- G..Williamson
- H..Williamson
- I...Williamson
- K..Saline

One hundred and twenty-ninth.
GEORGE P. SMITH.
- A..Livingston
- B..Livingston
- C..Livingston
- D..Scott
- E..Livingston
- F..Scott
- G..Livingston
- H..Scott
- I...Scott
- K..Rock Island

One hundred and thirtieth.
NATHANIEL NILES.
- A..Monroe
- B..Sangamon
- C..Alexander
- D..Christian
- E..Bond
- F..Bond
- G..Coles
- H..Richland
- I...Lawrence
- K..Clark, Edgar

One hundred and thirty-first.
GEORGE W. NEELEY.
- A..Massac
- B..Hardin
- C..Massac
- D..Massac
- E..Gallatin
- F..Hardin
- G..Gallatin
- H..Pope, Massac
- I...Hamilton
- K..Gallatin

CAVALRY.

First Regiment.
THOMAS A. MARSHALL.
- A..McLean, Pike
- B..Gallatin, Saline
- C..Coles
- D..Knox, Peoria, Marshall
- E..Montgomery
- F..Sangamon, Adams
- G..Warren, McDonough
- H..Marion
- I...White
- K..Winnebago
- L..
- M..

Second.
SILAS NOBLE.
- A..Ogle
- B..Logan
- C..Mason, Schuyler
- D..Madison, Jersey
- E..St. Clair
- F..Piatt, Macon, Douglas
- G..Hancock
- H..McDonough
- I...Champaign
- K..Pike
- L..Adams, Hancock
- M..Mason

Third.
EUGENE A. CARR.
- A..Sangamon
- B..Tazewell
- C..Cass
- D..Bond
- E..Saline
- F..Adams
- G..Brown
- H..Fulton
- I...McLean
- K..Livingston
- L..Macoupin
- M..Christian

Fourth.
T. LYLE DICKEY.
- A..Cook, LaSalle
- B..Cook, LaSalle
- C..Kendall
- D..Will
- E..Putnam
- F..Vermilion
- G..ElPasso, Woodford co.
- H..Logan
- I...LaSalle
- K..Kankakee
- L..McLean
- M..Rock Island

Fifth.
JOHN J. UPDEGRAFF.
- A..Cumberland
- B..Coles, Moultrie
- C..McLean
- D..Wayne

SCHEDULE C—Contnued.

E..Coles..................
F..Crawford..............
G..Pike, Shelby..........
H..Washington...........
I..Coles, Cumberland....
K..Randolph..............
L..Effingham.............
M..Wayne................

Sixth.

THOMAS H. CAVANAUGH.

A..Pope, Massac, Johnson.
B..Williamson, Johnson..
C..Scott, Morgan.........
D..Hamilton, Franklin....
E..Edwards, Richland...
F..Gallatin, Saline.......
G..Pope, Hardin..........
H..Hamilton.............
I...Perry, Jackson........
K..Hamilton, Saline......
L..Gallatin, Hardin, Pope.
M..Union, Alexander.....

Seventh.

WILLIAM P. KELLOGG.

A..Edgar................
B..Ogle, Carroll..........
C..Lee..................
D..Knox, Warren........
E..White................
F..Fayette..............
G..Randolph, Saline, Galla'n
H..Shelby, Christian.....
I..Macon................
K..Fulton...............
L..Knox, McDono'h, Fulton
M..Randolph............

Eighth.

JOHN F. FARNSWORTH.

A.....................
B.....................
C.....................
D.....................
E.....................
F.....................
G.....................
H.....................
I.....................
K.....................
L.....................
M.....................

Ninth.

ALBERT G. BRACKETT.

A..Rock Island.........
B..Henry...............
C..Henry...............
D..Cook................
E..Indiana.............
F..Cook................
G..Indiana.............
H..Henry...............
I..Boone...............
K...Bureau.............
L..Cook................
M..Iroquois............

Tenth.

JAMES A. BARRETT.

A..Menard, Sangamon....
B..Sangamon, Menard....
C..Kankakee............
D..Cook................
E..Madison.............
F..Madison.............
G..Sangamon............
H..Sangamon...........
I...Champaign..........
K..Brown...............
L..Sangamon............
M..Coles................

Eleventh.

ROBERT G. INGERSOLL.

A..Peoria...............
B..Fulton...............
C..Knox, Warren........
D..Peoria...............
E..Peoria...............
F..Peoria, Tazewell.....
G..Peoria, Fulton.......
H..Warren, McDonough, Henderson
I...McDonough..........
K..Warren..............
L..Peoria...............
M..Peoria...............

Twelfth.

ARNO VOSS.

A..Ogle, Winnebago, Cook
B..Jersey, Winnebago....
C..DuPage..............

D..Cook................
E..Kankakee............
F..Greene, Macoupin....
G..Hancock.............
H..Cook................
I..Cook................
K.....................
L.....................
M.....................

Thirteenth.

JOSEPH W. BELL.

A..Cook................
B..Cook................
C..Cook................
D..Cook................
E..Cook................
F..Will................
G..Warren.............
H..Kane, Kendall......
I.....................
K.....................
L.....................
M.....................

Fourteenth.

HORACE CAPRON.

A.....................
B.....................
C.....................
D.....................
E.....................
F.....................
G.....................
H.....................
I.....................
K.....................
L.....................
M.....................

Fifteenth.

WARREN STUART.

A..Alexander...........
B..Massac, Pope........
C..Franklin............
D..Clinton.............
E..Jackson.............
F..Franklin............
G..Kane, Fulton........
H..Kane...............
I..Kane................
K..Kane...............

SCHEDULE C—Continued.

L..LaSalle	G........................	C........................
M..Winnebago	H........................	D........................
	I........................	E........................
THIELEMAN'S CAVALRY.	K........................	F........................
	L........................	G........................
A..Cook	M........................	H........................
B..Cook...............		I........................
C........................	SCHAMBECK'S CAVALRY.	K........................
D........................		L........................
E........................	A........................	M........................
F........................	B........................	

FIRST REGIMENT ARTILLERY.

Capt. C. M. Willard, A Cook.	Capt. A. C. Waterhouse, E Cook, Winnebago.	Capt. Edward Bouton, I State at large.
Capt. Ezra Taylor, B Cook.	Capt. Jno. T. Cheney, F Ogle, DeKalb, Lee.	Capt. A. Franklin, K Johnson, Pope.
Capt. C. Houghtaling, C LaSalle.	Capt. Arthur O'Leary, G Alexander.	Capt. John Rourke, L Cook.
Capt. E. McAllister, D State at large.	Capt. A. Silversparre, H Cook, etc.	Capt. John B. Miller, M Cook, LaSalle, Lake.

SECOND ARTILLERY.

Capt. P. Davidson, A Peoria.	Capt. A. Gumbert, E State at large.	Capt. C. W. Keith, I Will, Peoria, Macon.
Capt. R. Madison, B Clark, Coles.	Capt. Jno. W. Powell, F Cape Girardeau.	Capt. Benj. F. Rogers, K Morgan, LaSalle.
Capt. C. Hopkins, C Sangamon, Alexander.	Capt. C. J. Stolbrand, G DeKalb, Ogle.	Capt. Wm. H. Bolton, L Cook, Ogle.
Capt. J. M. Dresser, D State at large.	Capt. A. Stienbeck, H Adams.	Capt. John C. Phillips, M Cook, Winnebago.

SCHEDULE C—Continued.

"Chicago Board of Trade Battery,"	Capt. Jas. S. Stokes	Cook.
"Springfield Light Artillery,"	Capt. Thos. F. Vaughn	Sangamon, Marshall, St. Clair.
"Chicago Mercantile Battery,"	Capt. Chas. G. Cooley	Cook.
"Elgin Battery,"	Capt. Geo. W. Renwick	Kane.
"Attached to 53d infantry,"	Capt. Wm. Coggswell	LaSalle.
"Henshaw's Battery,"	Capt. Edw. C. Henshaw	LaSalle.

SCHEDULE "D,"

Showing the free white population in each county in the State, according to the census of 1860, the total number of able-bodied men between the ages of eighteen and forty-five, the number now in service, and those liable to military duty, according to enrollment taken the past summer.

Counties.	Total enrollment. Population in 1860.		Number in service.	Liable to service.
Adams	41,144	9251	2293	6958
Alexander	4652	935	201	734
Bond	9767	2279	861	1418
Boone	11,670	2460	737	1723
Brown	9919	2152	686	1466
Bureau	26,415	6123	1994	4129
Calhoun	5143	1364	331	1033
Carroll	11,718	2968	645	2323
Cass	11,313	2459	690	1769
Champaign	14,581	3901	1533	2368
Christian	10,475	2795	642	2153
Clark	14,948	3006	916	2090
Clay	9309	2031	793	1238
Clinton	10,729	2709	665	2044
Coles	14,174	3146	171	2975
Cook	143,947	33,214	3677	29,537
Crawford	11,529	2614	644	1970
Cumberland	8309	1520	713	807
DeKalb	19,079	4823	1588	3235
DeWitt	10,814	2815	1334	1481
Douglas	7109	2079	836	1243
DuPage	14,696	2874	870	2004
Edgar	16,888	4697	1330	3367
Edwards	5379	1217	524	693
Effingham	7805	1479	498	981
Fayette	11,146	2716	857	1859
Ford	1979	512	144	368
Franklin	9367	1978	921	1057
Fulton	33,289	6460	2329	4131
Gallatin	7629	1714	773	941
Greene	16,067	3547	1123	2424
Grundy	10,372	2583	826	1757
Hamilton	9849	1897	917	990
Hancock	29,041	5857	1845	4012
Hardin	3704	791	332	459
Henderson	9499	1991	536	1455
Henry	20,658	7178	2130	5048
Iroquois	12,285	3339	1198	2141
Jackson	9560	2281	996	1285
Jasper	8350	1640	618	1022
Jefferson	12,931	2527	808	1719
Jersey	11,942	2722	738	1984

SCHEDULE D—Continued.

Counties.	Total enrollment. Population in 1860.		Number in service.	Liable to service.
JoDaviess	27,147	4816	1279	3537
Johnson	9306	1983	865	1118
Kane	30,024	6090	1987	4103
Kankakee	15,393	3420	1069	2351
Kendall	13,073	2846	1025	1821
Knox	28,512	7704	2719	4985
Lake	18,248	3542	1004	2538
LaSalle	48,272	12,304	2177	10,127
Lawrence	8976	1935	624	1311
Lee	17,643	4214	1476	2738
Livingston	11,632	3089	1010	2079
Logan	14,247	3554	1218	2326
Macon	13,555	4013	1716	2297
Macoupin	24,504	5973	1761	4212
Madison	30,689	7105	1164	5941
Marion	12,730	3056	1118	1938
Marshall	13,437	2947	786	2161
Mason	10,929	2816	1133	1683
Massac	6101	1245	505	740
McDonough	20,061	4880	1260	3620
McHenry	22,085	4605	1570	3035
McLean	28,580	6779	1370	5409
Menard	9577	2187	584	1603
Mercer	15,037	3452	1516	1936
Monroe	12,815	3787	441	3346
Montgomery	13,881	3135	953	2182
Morgan	21,937	5603	1882	3721
Moultrie	6384	1374	470	904
Ogle	22,863	5656	1972	3684
Peoria	36,475	7633	1958	5675
Perry	9508	2148	839	1309
Piatt	6124	1599	699	900
Pike	27,182	5571	2168	3403
Pope	6546	1735	651	1084
Pulaski	3904	1076	401	675
Putnam	5579	1236	331	905
Randolph	16,766	3674	922	2752
Richland	9709	2120	858	1262
Rock Island	20,981	4607	1863	2744
Saline	9161	1911	750	1161
Sangamon	31,963	7707	2186	5521
Schuyler	14,670	2939	1065	1874
Scott	9047	2076	764	1312
Shelby	14,590	3750	1122	2628
Stark	9003	2080	856	1224
St. Clair	37,169	8356	1371	6985
Stephenson	25,112	5359	1397	3962
Tazewell	21,427	4600	1423	3177
Union	11,145	2080	908	1172
Vermilion	19,779	4865	1813	3052
Wabash	7233	1334	423	911
Warren	18,293	4024	1422	2602
Washington	13,725	3012	749	2263
Wayne	12,222	2412	1048	1364

SCHEDULE D—Continued.

Counties.	Total enrollment. Population in 1860.		Number in service.	Liable to service.
White	12,274	2650	1194	1456
Whiteside	18,729	5062	1408	3654
Will	29,264	5848	1772	4076
Williamson	12,087	2238	1031	1207
Winnebago	24,457	5343	1630	3713
Woodford	13,281	3510	1184	2326
Total	1,704,323	391,319	115,123	276,196

NOTE.—Enrollment lists of the counties of SALINE and WARREN have not yet been received. The figures given opposite each are in the proportion returned from other counties of same population.

SCHEDULE "E."

Report of the Board of Medical Examiners.

To ALLEN C. FULLER,
    Adjutant General of the State of Illinois :

  The Board of Medical Examiners, appointed by the Governor of Illinois, in pursuance of General Order No. 25, of the Secretary of War, respectfully beg leave to report, that the Board convened in the city of Springfield, on the 18th day of June, 1861, and organized by the election of H. A. Johnson, President, and O. M. Bryan, Secretary. Subsequently, upon the resignation of Dr. Bryan, Dr. H. Wing was elected Secretary. Soon after their organization, they received a letter from the Secretary of War, instructing them to follow, as far as possible, the "army regulations; to investigate carefully, the physical ability, moral character, and professional attainments of each candidate, and to report favorably for appointment or promotion, in no case admitting of a reasonable doubt." The Board has endeavored to faithfully obey these instructions. In order to accommodate, as far as possible, the candidates, the sessions of the Board have been held at Springfield, Chicago, Cairo, Alton, and in the field.

  The whole number of candidates whose names have been registered on our books, is seven hundred and ninety-three (793.) The whole number examined, as reported in the list which accompanies this, is four hundred and ninety-five (495.) Of these, one hundred and fifty-nine (159) have been recommended for the office of Surgeon; two hundred and sixty-six (266) have been recommended for the office of Assistant Surgeon; and seventy (70) have been rejected.

  In addition to these cases reported, a very considerable number of candidates, after a partial examination, have become conscious of their deficiencies, and have requested permission to withdraw their application. This request has, we believe, in every case, been granted, with the understanding that it was not to be made a matter of record, and that they were in all respects to be considered as unexamined.

There is still another class of cases in which the examinations are not yet completed. Men of good moral character and with the ability to be useful, but who are deficient in some one department of medicine or surgery, have, in several instances, been advised to withdraw for a time, and to devote themselves to study with reference to a future examination. These cases are still unrecorded.

It is creditable alike to the patriotism and philanthropy of the profession of medicine, that one-third of all the physicians of our State have tendered to the Government their services, in this hour of national trial. They have come from the cities, from the villages, and from the broad prairies, often without stopping to ask themselves as to their qualification for the work, but anxious only to care for their friends, or to respond to the earnest appeals of those who have been the subjects of their ministrations, or who have witnessed their devotion to suffering humanity. They have come often from some quiet hamlet, where year after year they have treated *successfully*, diseases of similar character and of limited variety. It is not strange, then, that many of them, although good men and useful in their vocation, have been found sadly deficient or entirely wanting in qualification for the more extended field of professional labor of the military surgeon. For convenience, we may divide the candidates into three classes.

1st. Those whose studies and practice have made them familiar with the whole field of medicine and surgery. This class is necessarily very small, but the Board are happy to know that there are such men in the service.

2d. Those who, assuming the title of doctor, have never received the first rudiments of a medical or surgical education. As a general rule, we have found their ignorance only equaled by their impudence. It is unfortunate that these men have often gained the confidence of regiments and the nomination of colonels to the exclusion of better but more modest applicants.

3d. By far the larger proportion of those who have presented themselves, have been men of moderate attainments, capable of much usefulness in private practice, but unaccustomed to study, and able only with difficulty to express their ideas or demonstrate their knowledge.

In the examination of the first and second classes, but little time has been consumed; but in order to judge correctly of the third class, much patience has been necessary. The habits of mind, methods of reasoning, and probable action in any given case, have been the subjects of study, and the Board has often been compelled to form a judgment not so much upon the actual knowledge developed in the examination as upon the evidences of good sense, sound judgment, and adaptation to the service.

The examinations have consisted in an investigation—

1st. Of the moral character of the candidate.

2d. Of his professional character.
3d. His experience and adaptation to the work.
4th. His knowledge of his profession.

The strictly professional examination has consisted first, of oral questions and answers upon the following departments, to wit: Anatomy, Physiology, General Pathology, Materia Medica, Public Hygiene, Obstetrics, Practical Medicine and Practical Surgery. The Board has attached much importance to these personal and oral examinations, believing that by this method, they have been able to judge more correctly of the probable usefulness of the candidate. Second. Each candidate has been required to write a dissertation or essay upon some medical or surgical subject, designated at the time. In the preparation of this essay, he is not allowed to consult authorities.

The time consumed in the examination of each candidate has varied from two to six or even eight hours.

Throughout the sessions of the Board, daily reports have been made to the Adjutant General's office, of each day's work.

As the result of experience and observation, the following reflections suggest themselves to the Board:

1st. That the rank and pay of medical officers, in proportion to the responsibilities, are not such as to attract men of good qualifications.

2d. That if good men do accept the positions, they do so upon the solicitations of the regiments, and then reluctantly.

3d. That consequently the rejected men, with many others, who have not dared to present themselves for examination, would have been the Surgeons and Assistant Surgeons of our regiments, but for the existence and action of this Board.

4th. That the standard of qualifications adopted by the Board is as high as it is possible to place it and at the same time obtain a sufficient number to fill the positions.

5th. That however great may be the deficiencies of the medical staff, and we most certainly wish that they were less, the Surgeons and Assistant Surgeons of our volunteer regiments, are almost necessarily better qualified for the duties of their position than other volunteer officers.

All of which is respectfully submitted.

H. A. JOHNSON,
President Board Medical Examiners.

Springfield, Dec. 13, 1862.

SCHEDULE "F."

Statement of officers and employees of the Adjutant General's Department, with exhibit of salaries paid from April 16, 1861, to January 1, 1863.

Name.	Position.	From.	To.	No. of days.	Per diem.	Amount.
Thomas S. Mather	Adjutant General	April 16, 1861	November 11, 1861	209	$7 00	$1463 00
Allen C. Fuller	"	Nov. 11, 1861	January 1, 1863	416	7 00	1288 00
John B. Wyman	1st Assistant Adjutant General	April 19, 1861	June 21, 1861	55	6 00	330 00
John S. Loomis	2d " "	April 21, 1861	June 20, 1861	61	5 00	305 00
John S. Loomis	1st " "	June 21, 1861	January 1, 1863	416	6 00	2496 00
Daniel L. Gold	2d " "	August 17, 1861	January 1, 1863	492	5 00	2460 00
Charles H. Adams	Acting " "	April 17, 1861	April 21, 1861	5	6 00	30 00
Joseph H. Tucker	" " "	February 14, 1862	April 2, 1862	38	6 00	228 00
M. A. T. McHugh	" " "	April 19, 1861	May 27, 1861	38	6 00	82 00
John Belser	Clerk	May 6, 1861	August 11, 1861	98	4 00	392 00
Robert B. Nay	"	May 4, 1861	May 17, 1861	14	2 00	28 00
Chauncey Miller	"	April 20, 1861	May 27, 1861	38	3 3b	127 30
Benjamin F. Johnson	"	April 22, 1861	June 30, 1861	66	3 00	198 00
A. W. Kercheval	"	June 1, 1861	June 6, 1861	6	1 50	9 00
Louis D. Hubbard	"	June 6, 1461	August 18, 1861	96	3 00	288 00
John H. Barrett	"	July 22, 1861	October 30, 1861	100	3 00	300 00
Albert Pothoff	"	August 3, 1861	September 23, 1861	52	3 00	156 00
Thomas B. Paddock	"	November 12, 1861	November 26, 1861	15	3 00	45 00
Samuel F. True	"	November 12, 1861	November 27, 1861	16	3 00	48 00
James R. Loomis	"	November 21, 1861	June 2, 1862	246	3 00	738 00
Edward P. Niles	"	February 9, 1862	January 1, 1863	311	5–4–3	1057 00
Alfred Spink	"	April 9, 1862	April 17, 1862	7	5 00	35 00
John Brooks	"	September, 1862	September, 1862	9	3 00	27 00
Frank H. Walker	"	July 15, 1862	January 1, 1863	170	2 00	340 00
J. J. Richards	Acting Assistant Adjutant General	August 4, 1862	August 27, 1862	22	6 00	132 00
Morris B. Derrick	Clerk	September 4, 1862	January 1, 1863	118	3 00	354 00

Name	Role		Date	Date			
Enoch Howard	"		September 6, 1862	January 1, 1863	116	3 00	348 00
W. H. V. Raymond	"		August 22, 1862	January 1, 1863	132	3 00	396 00
James L. McNair	"		July 18, 1862	July 24, 1862	7	3 00	21 00
Joshua Rogers	"		August 30, 1862	December 7, 1862	100	2 00	200 00
Joshua Rogers	"		December 8, 1862	January 1, 1863	24	3 00	72 00
John Kiecher	Messenger		May 20, 1861	January 1, 1863	427	1 00	427 00
John Ellis	"		March 1, 1862	July 7, 1862	128	1 00	128 00
					4048		$14,548 30

SCHEDULE "G,"

Showing the names of all commissioned officers of Illinois forces, including those who have resigned or been mustered out of the service since the commencement of the present war.

Roster of Seventh Regiment Illinois (Three Months') Volunteers.

Field and Staff.		Rank.	Remarks.
Colonel	John Cook		
Lieut. Colonel	Wilford D. Wyatt	April 25, '61	
Major	Nicholas Greusel	April 25, '61	
Company A.			
Captain	Edward S. Joslyn	April 22, '61	
First Lieutenant	Reuben H. Adams	April 22, '61	
Second Lieutenant	James Davidson	April 22, '61	
B.			
Captain	James Monroe	April 24, '61	
First Lieutenant	Edmund W. True		
Second Lieutenant	Robt H. McFadden		
C.			
Captain	Nicholas Greusel		
"	Samuel E. Lawyer	April 29, '61	
First Lieutenant	Samuel E. Lawyer		
"	Silas Miller	April 29, '61	
Second Lieutenant	Silas Miller		
"	Rufus P. Pattison	April 29, '61	
D.			
Captain	Benjamin M. Munn		
First Lieutenant	Elizur Southworth		
Second Lieutenant	Mark P. Miller		
E.			
Captain	Wilford D. Wyatt	April 23, '61	Promoted
"	Geo. H. Estabrook	April 30, '61	
First Lieutenant	Geo. H. Estabrook	April 23, '61	Promoted
"	Otto Buzard	April 30, '61	
Second Lieutenant	Otto Buzard	April 23, '61	Promoted
"	H. C. Worthington	April 30, '61	
F.			
Captain	J. F. Cummings		
First Lieutenant	William O. Jenks		
Second Lieutenant	C. F. Adams		
G.			
Captain	William Sands	April 23, '61	
First Lieutenant	David L. Canfield	April 23, '61	
Second Lieutenant	W. G. Kercheval	April 23, '61	

SCHEDULE G—Continued.

		Rank.	Remarks.
H.			
Captain	Clifford W. Holden	May 15, '61	
First Lieutenant	Chris. C. Mason	May 15, '61	
Second Lieutenant	L. Wash. Myers	May 15, '61	
I.			
Captain	And. J. Babcock	April 27, '61	
First Lieutenant	Thos. G. Moffitt	April 27, '61	
Second Lieutenant	Noah E. Mendell	April 27, '61	
K.			
Captain	Richard Rowett	April 23, '61	
First Lieutenant	Manning Mayfield	April 23, '61	
Second Lieutenant	George Hunter	April 23, '61	

Schedule G—Continued.

Roster of Eighth Regiment Illinois (Three Months') Volunteers.

Field and Staff.		Rank.	Remarks.
Colonel	Richard J. Oglesby		
Lieut. Colonel	Frank L. Rhodes		
Major	John P. Post		

Company A.

Captain	Isaac C. Pugh	April 23, 1861	
First Lieutenant	Isaac Martin	April 23, 1861	
Second Lieutenant	George M. Bruce	April 23, 1861	

B.

Captain	H'y P. Westerfield	April 30, 1861	
"	John P. Post		Promoted
First Lieutenant	John M. Lowry		Resigned September 3, 1862.
Second Lieutenant	Thomas Goodman		Resigned July 25, 1861

C.

Captain	Jas. M. Ashmore	April 25, 1861	
First Lieutenant	James B. Hill	April 25, 1861	
Second Lieutenant	Daniel Sayer	April 25, 1861	

D.

Captain	John Lynch	April 25, 1861	Promoted
"	Wm. S. Marshall	May 27, 1861	
First Lieutenant	L. M. Startsman	April 25, 1861	
Second Lieutenant	John H. Roberts	April 25, 1861	

E.

Captain	Chas. E. Dennison	April 22, 1861	
First Lieutenant	John Wetzel	April 22, 1861	
Second Lieutenant	Charl's Prœbesting	April 22, 1861	

F.

Captain	Frank L. Rhodes	April 18, 1861	
"	Joseph M. Hauna	April 30, 1861	
First Lieutenant	Christ. C. Glass	April 18, 1861	
"	John M. Gill	May 20, 1861	
Second Lieutenant	Josiah A. Sheetz	April 18, 1861	

G.

Captain	John McWilliams		
First Lieutenant	James S. Bernard		
Second Lieutenant	Thomas Butler		

H.

Captain	A. J. McCraner	April 22, 1861	
First Lieutenant	R. H. Sturgess	April 22, 1861	
Second Lieutenant	John R. Mabry	April 22, 1861	

I.

Captain	Daniel Grass	April 25, 1861	
First Lieutenant	William C. Clark	April 22, 1861	
Second Lieutenant	Charles Fairbanks	April 25, 1861	

K.

Captain	Wm. H. Harvey	April 25, 1861	
First Lieutenant	Price Keith	April 25, 1861	
Second Lieutenant	Ab'm Vandenburg	April 25, 1861	

SCHEDULE G.—Continued.

Roster of Ninth Regiment Illinois (Three Months') Volunteers.

Field and Staff.		Rank.	Remarks.
Colonel..........	Eleazer A. Paine..		
Lieut. Colonel....	Augustus Mersey..		
Major..........	Jesse Philips....		
COMPANY A.			
Captain..........	Aug. S. Mersey...		
First Lieutenant..	Jacob Kœrcha...		
Second Lieutenant	Hugo Westerman..		
B.			
Captain..........	Rudolph Beckier..	May 10, '61.....	
First Lieutenant..	F'd. T. Ledergerber	May 10, '61.....	
Second Lieutenant	Henry C. Hay....	May 10, '61.....	
C.			
Captain..........	D. F. Tiedeman...	April 22, '61.....	
First Lieutenant..	Philip Conrad....	April 22, '61.....	
Second Lieutenant	Hamilton Leiber..	April 22, '61.....	
D.			
Captain..........	Alex. G. Hawes...	May 11, '61.....	
First Lieutenant..	Joseph A. Cox...	May 11, '61.....	
Second Lieutenant	Cassius F. Roman.	May 11, '61.....	
E.			
Captain..........	Otto Kochlein...	May 10, '61.....	
First Lieutenant..	William Scheittein	May 10, '61.....	
Second Lieutenant	S. Scheinminger..	April 25, '61.....	
F.			
Captain..........	Collins Van Cleve.	May 11, '61.....	
First Lieutenant..	Loren Webb.....	May 11, '61.....	
Second Lieutenant	George Adams...	May 11, '61.....	
G.			
Captain..........	Benj. W. Tucker..	April 18, '61.....	
First Lieutenant..	Cary H. H. Davis.	April 18, '61.....	
Second Lieutenant	Jared P. Ash.....	April 18, '61.....	
H.			
Captain..........	Jesse J. Phillips..	April 23, '61.....	Promoted........
"	John W. Kitchell.	April 23, '61.....	
First Lieutenant..	John W. Kitchell.	May 24, '61.....	Promoted........
" ...	James M. Munn..	May 25, '61.....	
Second Lieutenant	Wm. F. Armstrong	April 23, '61.....	
I.			
Captain..........	Jos. G. Robinson.	April 27, '61.....	
First Lieutenant..	Thos. J. Newsham.	April 27, '61.....	
Second Lieutenant	Gerhard Gerride..	April 27, '61.....	
K.			

Schedule G—Continued.

Roster of the Tenth Regiment Illinois (Three Months') Volunteers.

Field and Staff.		Rank.	Remarks.
Colonel	Benj. M. Prentiss.	May 8, 1861	Promoted to Brigadier General, May 17, 1861.
"	James D. Morgan.	May 20, 1860	
Lieut. Colonel	James D. Morgan.		Promoted Colonel.
"	Charles H. Adams		
Major	Charles H. Adams		Promoted Lieut. Colonel.
Adjutant			
Quartermaster			
Surgeon			
Assistant Surgeon	Daniel Stahl	May 18, 1861	

Company A.

Captain	John Tillson	April 23, 1861	Promoted.
"	John Wood, jr	June 11, 1861	
First Lieutenant	Jos. G. Rowland.	April 22, 1862	
Second Lieutenant	John Wood, jr	April 22, 1861	Promoted.
"	George A. Dills	June 11, 1861	

B.

Captain	Chas. H. Adams	April 29, 1861	Promoted
"	John W. King	June 1, 1861	
First Lieutenant	John W. King	April 29, 1861	Promoted.
"	Thomas W. Smith	June 1, 1861	
Second Lieutenant	Thomas W. Smith	April 29, 1861	Promoted.
"	John H. Burnett	June 1, 1861	

C.

Captain	Lindsey H. Carr	April 19, 1861	
First Lieutenant	Israel Jones	April 19, 1861	

D.

Captain	Francis A. Dallam	May 16, 1861	
First Lieutenant	Benjamin Edson	May 16, 1861	
Second Lieutenant	Samuel J. Wilson.	May 16, 1861	

E.

Captain	Benj. M. Prentiss.	April 22, 1861	Promoted.
"	Chas. S. Sheeley	May 15, 1861	
First Lieutenant	William H. Minter	April 22, 1861	
Second Lieutenant	Chas. Sheeley	April 22, 1861	Promoted.
"	James Short	May 15, 1861	Resigned.
"	R. C. Rutherford.	May 18, 1861	

F. (Artillery.)

Captain	Chas. Houghtaling	April 18, 1861	
First Lieutenant	Chas. C. Campbell	April 18, 1861	
Second Lieutenant	A. M. Wright	April 18, 1861	
Third Lieutenant	John W. Simmons	April 18, 1861	

G.

Captain	McLean F. Wood.	April 22, 1861	
First Lieutenant	James Mitchell	April 22, 1861	
Second Lieutenant	James F. Longley.	April 22, 1861	

SCHEDULE G—Continued.

		Rank.	Remarks.
H.			
Captain	Daniel H. Gilmer.	April 25, 1861	
First Lieutenant	George W. Olney.	April 25, 1861	
Second Lieutenant	James W. Harris.	April 25, 1861	
I. (Artillery.)			
Captain	Caleb Hopkins	April 22, 1861	
First Lieutenant	James A. Lott	April 22, 1861	
"	James P. Flood	April 22, 1861	
Second Lieutenant	James P. Flood	April 22, 1861	Promoted
"	Wells Bartram	April 22, 1861	
K. (Artillery.)			
Captain	E. ward McAlister	May 15, 1861	
First Lieutenant	George J. Wood	May 15, 1861	
Second Lieutenant	Wm. C. Chapman	May 15, 1861	

Schedule G—Continued.

Roster of Eleventh Regiment Illinois (Three Months') Volunteers.

Field and Staff.		Rank.	Remarks.
Colonel	W. H. L. Wallace.		
Lieut. Colonel	J. Warren Filler.		
Major	Thomas E. Ransom		

Company A.

Captain	Smith D. Atkins.	May 14, 1861	
First Lieutenant	M. E. Newcomer.	May 14, 1861	
Second Lieutenant	Silas W. Fields.	May 14, 1861	

B.

Captain	Fred. W. Shaw	April 22, 1861	
First Lieutenant	Greenbury L. Foot	April 22, 1861	
Second Lieutenant	J. M. McClanahan	April 22, 1861	

C.

Captain	A. L. Rockwood.	April 26, 1861	
First Lieutenant	S. P. Jones	April 26, 1861	
Second Lieutenant	J. C. Jewell	April 22, 1861	

D.

Captain	Garrett Nevius	May 14, 1861	
First Lieutenant	R. A. Bird	May 14, 1861	
Second Lieutenant	Wm. D. E. Andrus	May 14, 1861	

E.

Captain	T. E. G. Ransom.	April 26, 1861	Promoted Major.
First Lieutenant	Lloyd D. Waddell	April 26, 1861	
Second Lieutenant	Alvin H. Morey.	April 26, 1862	

F.

Captain	Wm. T. Hopkins.	May 14, 1861	
First Lieutenant	Samuel Elton	May 14, 1861	
Second Lieutenant	George S. Doane.	May 14, 1861	

G.

Captain	J. Warren Filler.	April 29, 1861	
First Lieutenant	John H. J. Lacy.	April 29, 1861	
Second Lieutenant	George W. Parks.	April 29, 1861	

H.

Captain	Theo. C. Gibson.	April 23, 1861	
First Lieutenant	Benj. F. Hotchkiss	April 23, 1861	Resigned, July 9, 1861
Second Lieutenant	Douglas Hasseman	April 23, 1861	

I.

Captain	Wm. L. Gibson.	April 24, 1861	
First Lieutenant	Joseph E. Skinner	April 24, 1861	
Second Lieutenant	E. A. Mullett	April 24, 1861	

K.

Captain	Henry H. Carter.	April 27, 1861	
First Lieutenant	John Dick	April 27, 1861	
Second Lieutenant	James Ireland	April 27, 1861	

SCHEDULE G — Continued.

Roster of Twelfth Regiment Illinois (Three Months') Volunteers.

Field and Staff.		Rank.	Remarks.
Colonel	John McArthur		
Lieut. Colonel	Aug. L. Chetlain		
Major	Wm. D. Williams		
COMPANY A.			
Captain	Joseph Kellogg	April 27, '61	
First Lieutenant	John Noyes, jr	April 27, '61	
Second Lieutenant	J. B. Rowland	April 27, '61	Commission returned
"	Arthur C. Ducat	May 11, '61	
B.			
Captain	Phineas B. Rust	April 29, '61	
First Lieutenant	Tyler Hale	April 29, '61	
Second Lieutenant	Henry Stephenson	April 29, '61	
C.			
Captain	Samuel Frazier	April 25, '61	
First Lieutenant	William Maum	April 25, '61	
Second Lieutenant	Joseph Kirkland	April 25, '61	
D.			
Captain	Wm. D. Williams	April 25, '61	
"	David Benson	May 11, '61	
First Lieutenant	David Benson	April 25, '61	
"	Leotus Dimock	May 11, '61	
Second Lieutenant	Quincy McNeill	April 25, '61	
"	David H. Hakes	May 11, '61	
E.			
Captain	Vincent Ridgely	April 25, '61	
First Lieutenant	John W. Fisher	April 25, '61	
Second Lieutenant	Nathaniel Sanford	April 25, '61	
F.			
Captain	Aug. L. Chetlain	April 27, '61	
"	Lucies M. Rose	May 11, '61	
First Lieutenant	Wallace Campbell	April 27, '61	
"	J. Bates Dickson	May 11, '61	
Second Lieutenant	J. Bates Dickson	April 27, '61	
"	G. S. Avery	May 11, '61	
G.			
Captain	Chas. H. Brookings	April 26, '61	
First Lieutenant	S. B. Whetmore	April 26, '61	
Second Lieutenant	Guy C. Ward	April 26, '61	
H.			
Captain	Wm. T. Swain	May 8, '61	
First Lieutenant	Thompson Gordon	May 8, '61	
Second Lieutenant	John M. Mills	May 8, '61	
I.			
Captain	Frank B. Ferris	April 29, '61	
First Lieutenant	Geo. L. Paddock	April 29, '61	
Second Lieutenant	G. Gilbert Gibon	April 29, '61	
K.			
Captain	Jas. R. Hugunin	April 25, '61	
First Lieutenant	Wm. E. Waite	April 25, '61	
Second Lieutenant	Eben Bacon	April 25, '61	

SCHEDULE G — Continued.

Roster of the Seventh Regiment Illinois Volunteers.

Field and Staff.		Rank.	Remarks.
Colonel	John Cook	April 25, 1861	Promoted Brig. Gen. March
"	A. J. Babcock	March 21, 1862	[21, 1862.
Lieut. Colonel	A. J. Babcock	July 25, 1861	Promoted
" "	Nicholas Greusel	July 24, 1861	Promoted Colonel 36th
" "	Richard Rowett	March 21, 1862	
Major	Nicholas Greusel	April 25, 1861	Promoted
"	Richard Rowett	July 25, 1861	Promoted
"	James Monroe	March 21, 1862	
Adjutant	Leroy R. Waller	July 25, 1861	Resigned Jan. 30, 1862
"	Benj. F. Smith	February 1, 1862	Promoted to Gen Cook's staff
"	Thomas N. Francis	March 21, 1862	Resigned Nov. 14, 1862
"	John S. Robinson	Nov. 14, 1862	
Quartermaster	Wm. Brown, jr.	Oct. 29, 1861	Died of wounds received at
"	Geo. M. Harrison	Oct. 9, 1862	Corinth, Oct. 9, 1862.
Surgeon	Rich. L. Metcalf	July 16, 1861	
1st Ass't Surgeon	James Hamilton	July 19, 1861	
2d " "			
Chaplain	Jesse P. Davis	July 25, 1861	

COMPANY A.

Captain	Samuel G. Ward	July 25, '61	Killed in battle
"	Geo. F. Wheeler	April 7, '62	
First Lieutenant	Jonathan Kimball	July 25, '61	Resigned Feb. 5, 1862
"	Mason M. Marsh	Aug. 26, '61	Not delivered
"	Thomas McGuire	June 21, '62	
Second Lieutenant	Wm. Renwick	July 25, '61	Resigned Jan. 30, '62
"	Thomas McGuire	Jan. 30, '62	Promoted
"	Benjamin Sweeny	June 21, '62	

B.

Captain	James Monroe	July 26, '61	Promoted
"	Hector Perrin	March 21, '62	
First Lieutenant	Hector Perrin	July 26, '61	Promoted
"	Orlando D. Ellis	March 21, '62	
Second Lieutenant	Orlando D. Ellis	July 26, '61	Promoted
"	Oscar Poole	March 21, '62	

C.

Captain	Samuel E. Lawyer	July 25, '61	
First Lieutenant	Leroy Walker	July 25, '61	Promoted to Adjutant
"	Ed. R. Roberts	Jan. 30, '62	
Second Lieutenant	Ed. R. Roberts	July 25, '61	Promoted
"	Alexander Adams	Sept. 6, '61	Resigned Jan. 14, '62
"	Wm. H. Ferguson	Jan. 30, '62	

D.

Captain	Benj. M. Munn	July 25, '61	Resigned Jan. 12, '62
"	Ira A. Church	Jan. 12, '62	Resigned Sept. 3, '62
"	H. N. Estabrook	Sept. 3, '62	Killed Oct. 4, '62
"	John K. Clark	Oct. 5, '62	
First Lieutenant	Ira A. Church	July 25, '61	Promoted
"	James M. Munn	Jan. 12, '62	Resigned May 30, '62
"	John K. Clark	June 1, '62	Promoted
"	Seth L. Raymond	Oct. 5, '62	
Second Lieutenant	James M. Munn	July 25, '61	Promoted

SCHEDULE G — Continued.

		Rank.	Remarks.
Second Lieutenant	John K. Clark....	Jan. 12, '62......	Promoted ....
"	Seth L. Raymond.	July 18, '62......	....
"	Michael McEvoy..	Oct. 5, '62......	....

E.

Captain.........	Geo. H. Estabrook	July 29, '61......	....
First Lieutenant..	John A. Smith...	July 29, '61......	....
Second Lieutenant	H. N. Estabrook.	July 29, '61......	Promoted Co. D..........
"	Wash. W. Judy..	Sept. 3, '62......	....

F.

Captain.........	Jas. T. Cummings.	July 25, '61......	Resigned April 7, '62......
"	William Mathie..	April 7, '62......	....
First Lieutenant..	William Mathie..	July 25, '61......	Promoted ....
" ..	A. D. Knowlton..	April 7, '62......	....
Second Lieutenant	A. D. Knowlton..	July 25, '61......	Promoted ....
"	Henry Apern ...	April 7, '62......	....

G.

Captain.........	Henry W. Allen..	July 25, '61......	....
First Lieutenant..	Geo. W. Tipton..	July 25, '61......	Resigned Sept. 3, '62....
" ..	Ferdinand Yeager	Sept. 11, '62......	....
Second Lieutenant	Adam E. Vrooman	July 25, '61......	Died April 7, '62..........
"	Ferdinand Yeager	April 7, '62......	Promoted ....
"	Paul J. B. Marion	Sept. 11, '62......	....

H.

Captain.........	Clifford W. Holden	April 25, '61......	Resigned Nov. 14, '62......
"	Jacob L. Ring ...	Nov. 14, '62......	....
First Lieutenant..	Leo W. Myers ...	July 25, '61......	Killed in battle............
" ..	Jacob L. Ring ...	April 7, '62......	Promoted ....
" ..	Thos. J. Pegram..	Nov. 14, '62......	....
Second Lieutenant	Jacob L. Ring....	July 25, '61......	Promoted ....
"	Thos. J. Pegram..	April 7, '62......	Promoted ....
"	Samuel E. Fergus.	Nov. 14, '62......	....

I.

Captain.........	Noah E. Mendell..	July 22, '61......	Killed at Ft. Donelson......
"	Ed. S. Johnson...	Feb. 15, '62......	....
First Lieutenant..	Ed. S. Johnson...	July 22, '61......	Promoted ....
" ..	Thomas N. Francis	Feb. 16, '62......	Promoted Adjutant........
" ..	John E. Sullivan.	March 21, '62......	....
Second Lieutenant	Newton Francis..	July 22, '61......	Promoted ....
"	John E. Sullivan.	Feb. 16, '62......	Promoted ....
"	Joseph S. Fisher·.	March 21, '62....	....

K.

Captain.........	Richard Rowett..	July 25, '61......	Promoted ....
"	George Hunter...	Aug. 27, '61......	....
First Lieutenant..	George Hunter...	July 25, '61......	Promoted ....
" ..	Joseph Rowett...	Aug. 27, '61......	....
Second Lieutenant	Thomas B. Rood..	July 25, '61......	Resigned Dec. 10, '61......
"	William Partridge	Dec. 10, '61......	....

SCHEDULE G.—Continued.

Roster of Eighth Regiment Illinois Volunteers.

Field and Staff.		Rank.	Remarks.
Colonel	Richard J. Oglesby	April 25, '61	Promoted Brig. General
"	Frank L. Rhoads	April 1, '62	Resigned October 7, 1862
"	John P. Post	October 7, '62	
Lieut. Colonel	Frank L. Rhoads	April 25, '61	Promoted
"	John P. Post	April 1, '62	Promoted
"	Rob't H. Sturgess	October 7, '62	
Major	John P. Post	April 25, '61	Promoted
"	Rob't H. Sturgess	April 1, '62	Promoted
"	Herman Lieb	October 7, '62	
Adjutant	William C. Clark	July 25, '61	Resigned June 25, 1862
"	Benj. F. Monroe	June 25, '62	
Quartermaster	Samuel Rhodes	July 25, '61	Resigned Dec. 9, 1861
"	Henry N. Pearse	Dec. 10, '61	
Surgeon	Silas T. Trowbridge	April 25, '61	
1st Asst. Surgeon	John M. Phipps	April 25, '61	
2d Asst. Surgeon	Charles N. Denison	Oct. 15, '62	
Chaplain	Samuel Day	Jan. 28, '62	

COMPANY A.

Captain	G. M. Bruce	July 25, '61	Resigned Feb. 5, 1862
"	Frank Leeper	Feb. 5, '62	
First Lieutenant	Frank Leeper	July 25, '61	Promoted
"	Walter J. Taylor	Feb. 5, '62	
Second Lieutenant	Walter J. Taylor	July 25, '61	Promoted
"	Benj. F. Monroe	Feb. 5, '62	Promoted
"	George S. Durfee	June 25, '62	

B.

Captain	Herman Lieb	July 25, '61	Promoted
"	Peter Schlosser	Oct. 7, '62	
First Lieutenant	Peter Schlosser	Sept. 3, '62	Promoted
"	Bernhard Zick	Oct. 7, '62	
Second Lieutenant	Henry J. Marsh	July 25, '61	Killed at Fort Donelson
"	Peter Schlosser	Feb. 15, '62	Promoted
"	Bernhard Zick	Sept. 3, '62	Promoted
"	John Collmer	Oct. 7, '62	

C.

Captain	James M. Ashmore	April 25, '61	Resigned May 15, '62
"	Daniel Sayers	May 15, '62	
First Lieutenant	Daniel Sayers	July 25, '61	Promoted
"	Aug. P. Whalen	May 15, '62	Resigned Sept. 29, '62
"	John F. Railsback	Sept. 29, '62	
Second Lieutenant	James S. Brown	July 25, '61	Resigned March 28, '62
"	Aug. P. Whalen	March 28, '62	Promoted
"	John F. Railsback	May 15, '62	Promoted
"	James J. C. Wilson	Sept. 29, '62	

D.

Captain	L. M. Startsman	July 25, '61	Resigned April 17, '62
"	Jos. W. Robards	April 17, '62	
First Lieutenant	Jos. W. Robards	July 25, '61	Promoted
"	Joseph E. Jones	April 17, '62	
Second Lieutenant	Joseph B. Jones	July 25, '61	Promoted
"	Aug. E. Barrett	April 17, '62	

SCHEDULE G.—Continued.

		Rank.	Remarks.

E.

Captain.........	John Wetzel.....	July 25, '61.....	Resigned March 25, 1862...
"	Lloyd Wheaton...	March 25, '62....	
First Lieutenant..	Lloyd Wheaton...	July 25, '61.....	Promoted ....
" ..	Samuel Caldwell..	March 25, '62....	
Second Lieutenant	Samuel Caldwell..	July 25, '61.....	Promoted ....
" ..	Frederick A. King.	March 25, '62....	

F.

Captain.........	Joseph M. Hanna.	April 30, '61.....	Killed at Fort Donelson....
"	Josiah A. Sheetz..	Feb. 22, '62.....	
First Lieutenant..	Josiah A. Sheetz..	July 25, '61.....	Promoted ....
" ..	Edwin L. Williams	Feb. 22, '62.....	
Second Lieutenant	Samuel Rhoads...	July 25, '61.....	Promoted Quartermaster....
" ..	Daniel A. Sheetz..	Sept. 1, '61.....	Killed in battle............
" ..	Jno. D. Handberry	Feb. 15, '62.....	Resigned Aug. 31, 1862....
" ..	Robert Brown ...	Sept. 1, '62.....	

G.

Captain.........	James S. Barnard.	July 25, '61.....	Resigned March 26, 1862...
"	Elihu Jones......	March 26, '62....	
First Lieutenant..	Elihu Jones......	Sept. 1, '61.....	Promoted ....
" ...	William P. Sitton.	March 26, '62....	
Second Lieutenant	William P. Sitton.	July 25, '61.....	Promoted ....
" ..	Charles Hurt.....	March 26, '62....	

H.

Captain.........	Rob't H. Sturgess.	July 25, '61.....	Promoted Major............
"	John L. Shaw...	April 1, '62.....	
First Lieutenant..	John L. Shaw...	July 25, '61.....	Promoted ....
" ..	Alva C. Bishop...	April 1, '62.....	
Second Lieutenant	Alva C. Bishop...	July 25, '61.....	Promoted ....
" ..	William W. Cover.	April 1, '62.....	

I.

Captain.........	Robert Wilson...	July 25, '61.....	Resigned Oct. 20, '62......
"	William Zeidler...	Oct. 20, '62.....	
First Lieutenant..	William Zeidler..	Sept. 1, '61.....	Promoted ....
" ..	Otto Brauns.....	Oct. 20, '62.....	
Second Lieutenant	William Zeidler..	July 25, '61.....	Promoted ....
" ..	Deitrich Smith...	Sept. 1, '61.....	Resigned Sept. 3, 1862.....
" ..	Otto Brauns......	Sept. 3, '62.....	Promoted ....
" ..	William Schlag ..	Oct. 20, '62	

K.

Captain.........	Wm. H. Harvey..	April 25, '61.....	Killed in battle............
"	Noah W. Dennison	April 7, '62.....	
First Lieutenant..	Joseph G. Howell.	July 25, '61.....	Killed at Fort Donelson.....
" ..	Noah W. Dennison	Feb. 15, '62.....	Promoted ....
" ..	Thos. J. McClung.	April 7, '62.....	
Second Lieutenant	Noah W. Dennison	July 25, '61.....	Promoted ....
" ..	Thos. J. McClung.	Feb. 15, '62.....	Promoted ....
" ..	Robert F. Mercer.	April 7, '62.....	

SCHEDULE G—Continued.

Roster of Ninth Regiment Illinois Volunteers.

Field and Staff.		Rank.	Remarks.
Colonel	Eleazer A. Paine..	July 26, 1861....	Pro. Brig. Gen'l Sept. 3, '61..
"	Augustus Mersey.	September 3, 1861	
Lieut. Colonel....	Augustus Mersey.	July 26, 1861....	Promoted
"	Jesse J. Phillips..	September 3, 1861	
Major	Jesse J. Phillips..	July 26, 1861....	Promoted
"	John H. Kuhn....	September 3, 1861	
Adjutant	Thos. J. Newsham	July 26, 1861....	Promoted to Gen. Paine's staff
"	Henry H. Klock..	October 3, 1861..	
Quartermaster	Wm. G. Pinckard.	August 21, 1861..	Promoted
"	Gustav Korn	June 30, 1862....	
Surgeon	Sam'l M. Hamilton	July 26, 1861....	Promoted
"	Emil Guilick	April 28, 1862....	
1st Ass't. Surgeon.	Emil Guilick	July 26, 1861....	Promoted
"	William D. Craig.	June 8, 1862.....	
2d Ass't. Surgeon.			
Chaplain	James J. Ferree...	July 26, 1861....	Resigned December 1, 1861.

COMPANY A.

Captain	John H. Kuhn....	July 26, 1861....	Promoted
"	Emil Adam	September 3, 1861	
First Lieutenant..	Emil Adam	July 26, 1861....	Promoted
"	Ernest J. Weiyrick	September 3, 1861	Resigned December 24, 1861
Second Lieutenant	Ernest J. Weiyrick	August 31, 1861..	Promoted
"	Fred'k E. Scheel..	September 3, 1861	

B.

Captain	Wm. C. Keeffner..	July 26, 1861....	
First Lieutenant..	Hamilton Leiber..	July 26, 1861....	
Second Lieutenant	Fred'k E. Vogeler	July 26, 1861....	Killed in battle.

C.

Captain	Deed'k F. Tedeman	July 26, 1861....	
First Lieutenant..	Oscar Rollman....	July 26, 1861....	
Second Lieutenant	Charles Scheve...	July 26, 1861 ...	

D.

Captain	Rudolphus Beckier	July 26, 1861....	
First Lieutenant..	Edward Krebs....	August 10, 1861..	
Second Lieutenant	William Bollen...	July 27, 1861....	
"	Theodore Gottlob.	January 30, 1862.	Resigned January 30, 1861..

E.

Captain	Alex'der G. Hawes	July 26, 1861....	
First Lieutenant..	William D. Craig.	August 6, 1861...	Promoted Assistant Surgeon
"	R. B. Patterson ..	June 8, 1862.....	
Second Lieutenant	R. B. Patterson ..	July 26, 1861....	Promoted
"	Chas. B. Fleming.	June 8, 1862.....	Canceled
"	Lewis C. Bornman	June 8, 1862.....	

F.

Captain	Loren Webb	July 26, 1861....	Resigned July 10, 1862.....
"	William Britt....	July 10, 1862....	
First Lieutenant..	William Britt....	July 26, 1861...	Promoted
"	G. W. Williford ..	July 10, 1862....	
Second Lieutenant	G. W. Williford ..	July 26, 1861....	Promoted
"	William C. Hawley	July 10, 1862....	

SCHEDULE G—Continued.

		Rank.	Remarks.
G			
Captain	Eager M. Lowe	July 26, 1861	
First Lieutenant	John S. Tutten	July 27, 1861	Resigned Septemb'r 13, 1862
"	Isaac Clements	Septem'er 13, 1862	
Second Lieutenant	Isaac Clements	July 27, 1861	Promoted
"	Nimrod G. Perrine	Septem'er 13, 1862	
H			
Captain	Wm. F. Armstrong	July 26, 1861	
First Lieutenant	Cyrus H. Gillmore	July 26, 1861	
Second Lieutenant	Alfred Cowgill	July 26, 1861	
I.			
Captain	Jos. G. Robinson	July 26, 1861	
First Lieutenant	Wm. H. Purviance	July 31, 1861	Hon'bly disch'g'd Aug. 16, '62
"	Samuel J. Hughes	August 16, 1862	
Second Lieutenant	Samuel J. Hughes	July 31, 1861	Promoted
"	Wm. Paden	August 16, 1862	
K.			
Captain	George B. Poor	July 26, 1861	Resigned December 10, 1861
"	Jas. C. McCleary	Decemb'r 10, 1861	Died of wounds July 9, 1862
"	Gilbert G. Low	July 9, 1862	
First Lieutenant	Jas. C. McCleary	October 2, 1861	Promoted
"	Gilbert G. Low	Decemb'r 10, 1861	Promoted
"	James Oates	July 9, 1862	
Second Lieutenant	Jas. C. McCleary	July 26, 1861	Promoted
"	Gilbert G. Low	October 2, 1861	Promoted
"	James Oates	Decemb'r 10, 1861	Promoted
"	Benjamin L. Ulm	July 9, 1862	

SCHEDULE G — Continued.

Roster of Tenth Regiment Illinois Volunteers.

Field and Staff.		Rank.	Remarks.
Colonel	James D. Morgan.		Promoted Brigadier General, [July 17, 1862.
"	John Tillson	June 13, 1862	
Lieut. Colonel	John Tillson	Sept. 9, 1861	Promoted
" "	McLain F. Wood.	June 23, 1862	
Major	John Tillson	May 27, 1861	Promoted
"	Francis A. Dallam	October 24, 1861	Resig'd Jan. 20, '62, for pro.
"	Joseph G. Rowland	February 11, 1862	Resigned June 23, 1862
"	Charles S. Cowan	June 23, 1862	
Adjutant	Joseph G. Rowland	April 29, 1861	Promoted
"	Theodore Wiseman	February 11, 1862	
Quartermaster	Oliver I. Pyatt	Sept. 20, 1861	
Surgeon	Henry R. Payne	November 4, 1861	
1st Assist. Surg'on	Daniel Stahl	May 18, 1861	Resigned Aug. 31, 1862
" "	Isaac H. Reeder	October 10, 1862	
2d Assist. Surgeon	John W. Craig	August 21, 1862	
Chaplain	William H. Collins	July 25, 1861	Resigned June 21, 1862
"	William B. Livell	December 16, 1862	

COMPANY A.

Captain	McLain F. Wood.	July 28, 1861	Promoted
"	James F. Longley.	June 13, 1862	Resigned December 31, 1862.
First Lieutenant	James F. Longley.	July 28, 1861	Promoted
" "	Charles Carpenter	June 13, 1862	
Second Lieutenant	Otho D. Critzer	July 28, 1861	Resigned June 17, 1862
" "	Henry McGrath	June 17, 1862	

B.

Captain	Thomas W. Smith	July 28, 1861	Resigned June 1, 1862
"	Chas. P. McEnally	June 3, 1862	
First Lieutenant	William D. Green	July 28, 1861	
Second Lieutenant	Chas. P. McEnally	July 28, 1861	Promoted
" "	John B. Tait	June 3, 1862	

C.

Captain	Charles S. Sheley	July 28, 1861	Resigned July 3, 1862
First Lieutenant	Andrew Wood	July 28, 1861	Resigned May 28, 1862
" "	John T. Boyle	May 28, 1862	
Second Lieutenant	William Morgan	July 28, 1861	Resigned May 30, 1862
" "	William H. Carr	August 20, 1862	

D

Captain	Samuel T. Mason.	July 28, 1861	
First Lieutenant	Harry M. Scaritt	July 28, 1861	
Second Lieutenant	Wm. G. Galion	July 28, 1861	

E

Captain	Charles S. Cowan	July 28, 1861	Promoted
"	Samuel I. Wilson.	June 23, 1862	
First Lieutenant	Samuel I. Wilson.	July 28, 1861	Promoted
" "	Colin McKinney	June 23, 1862	
Second Lieutenant	Colin McKinney	July 28, 1861	Promoted
" "	Lewis W. VanTuyl	June 23, 1862	

SCHEDULE G—Continued.

		Rank.	Remarks.
		F.	
Captain	George A. Race...	March 1, '62	
First Lieutenant	George A. Race...	March 13, '62	Promoted
"	Richm'd Wolcott.	March 1, '62	
Second Lieutenant	A. Neighmeyer...	Feb. 8, '62	
		G.	
Captain	John D. Mitchell..	March 1, '62	Resigned June 16, '62
"	David R. Waters..	June 16, '62	
First Lieutenant	John D. Mitchell..	Sept. 1, '61	Promoted
"	David R. Waters..	March 1, '62	Promoted
"	Guy W. Blanchard	June 16, '62	
Second Lieutenant	Guy W. Blanchard	March 1, '62	Promoted
"	Eph. A. Wilson ..	June 16, '62	
		H.	
Captain	Lindsay H. Carr..	July 28, '61	Died March 12, '62
"	Edward H. Sylla..	March 12, '62	Resigned June 16, '62
"	Daniel R. Ballen..	June 16, '62	
First Lieutenant	Edward H. Sylla..	July 28, '61	Promoted
"	Daniel B. Ballen..	March 12, '62	Promoted
"	F. A. Munson....	June 16, '62	
Second Lieutenant	J. B. Carpenter ..	July 28, '61	Resigned Feb. 13, '62
"	John Winsitt	March 1, '62	
		I.	
Captain	Morton S. McAtee	July 28, '61	Resigned June 14, '62
"	David Gillespie...	June 14, '62	
First Lieutenant	David Gillespie...	July 28, '61	Promoted
"	Jas. H. Rogerson .	June 14, '62	
Second Lieutenant	Robert H. Mann..	July 28, '61	
		K.	
Captain	George C. Lusk...	July 28, '61	
First Lieutenant	Godhold Girnt ...	July 28, '61	Resigned July 3, '62
"	James Rogers....	July 3, '62	
Second Lieutenant	Edward L. Friday.	July 28, '61	

SCHEDULE G — Continued.

Roster of Eleventh Regiment Illinois Volunteers.

Field and Staff.		Rank.	Remarks.
Colonel	W. H. L. Wallace.	May 1, '61	Promoted Brigadier General.
"	T. E. G. Ransom.	Feb. 15, '62	
Lieut Colonel	J. Warren Fillers.	May 1, '61	Resigned July 4, 1861.
"	T. E. G. Ransom.	July 30, '61	Promoted.
"	Garrett Nevius.	Feb. 15, '62	
Major	T. E. G. Ransom.	May 1, '61	Promoted.
"	Garrett Nevius.	July 30, '61	Promoted.
"	Smith D. Atkins.	Feb. 15, '62	Promoted Col. of 92d regi-
"	James H. Coates.	Sept. 4, '62	[ment infantry.
Adjutant	Cyrus E Dickey.	Aug. 3, '61	
Quartermaster	Guyan J. Davis.	Aug. 30, '61	
Surgeon	A. W. Heise.	Sept. 25, '61	Declined.
"	Owen M. Long.	Sept. 25, '61	
1st Ass't Surgeon.	Oliver G. Hunt.	Aug. 29, '61	
2d " "			
Chaplain	Ben. H. Pierson.	Oct. 12, '61	

COMPANY A.

Captain	Smith D. Atkins.	May 14, '61	Promoted.
"	Silas W. Field	Feb. 15, '62	Died May 9, '62.
"	Jas. O. Churchill	May 10, '62	
First Lieutenant.	Guyan J. Davis	Feb. 4, '61	Quartermaster.
"	Silas W. Field.	Feb. 30, '61	Promoted.
"	Jas. O. Churchill	Feb. 15, '62	Promoted.
"	Rich. W. Hurlbut.	May 10, '62	
Second Lieutenant	Jas. O. Churchill	Aug. 4, '61	Promoted.
"	Rich. W. Hurlbut.	Feb. 15, '62	Promoted.
"	Orten Ingersoll	May 10, '62	

B.

Captain	Fred. W. Shaw	April 22, '61	Killed in battle.
"	Harrison C. Vere.	Feb. 15, '62	
First Lieutenant.	Alfred R. Wilcox.	Feb. 30, '61	Killed in battle.
"	Samuel B. Dean	Feb. 15, '62	
Second Lieutenant	Samuel B. Dean	Sept. 1, '61	Promoted.
"	James D. Vernay	Feb. 15, '62	

C.

Captain	George C. McKee.	July 30, '61	
First Lieutenant.	George S. Doane.	July 30, '61	
Second Lieutenant	H. F. McWilliams.	July 30, '61	Resigned April 18, '62.
"	Robert Jehue	April 18, '62	

D.

Captain	Wm. D. E. Andrus	July 30, '61	
First Lieutenant.	Henry H. Deane	July 30, '61	
Second Lieutenant	Orrin C. Towne	July 30, '61	

E.

Captain	Lloyd D. Waddell.	July 30, '61	
First Lieutenant.	Harrison C. Vere.	July 30, '61	Promoted to company "B".
"	Solomon Bostwick	Feb. 15, '62	
Second Lieutenant	Samuel C. Moore.	July 30, '61	Resigned Nov. 27, '62.
"	Chas. A. Puronnet.	Nov. 27, '62	

SCHEDULE G—Continued.

		Rank.	Remarks.
		F.	
		G.	
First Lieutenant	Wm. J. Boyce	July 30, '61	Killed in battle
"	Wm. M. Murray	Feb. 15, '62	Resigned Nov. 22, '62
Second Lieutenant	Wm. M. Murray	July 30, '61	Promoted
"	Edward P. Thomas	Feb. 15, '62	
		H.	
Captain	James H. Coates	July 30, '61	Promoted
"	William Duncan	Sept. 4, '62	
First Lieutenant	William Duncan	July 30, '61	Promoted
Second Lieutenant	Douglas Hapeman	July 30, '61	Discharged for promotion
"	L. F. Alexander	Sept. 4, '62	
		I.	
Captain	Greenbury L. Fort	Sept. 1, 61	Resigned April 24, '62
"	John H. Widmer	April 24, '62	Discharged for promotion
"	Ben. F. Blackstone	Sept. 4, '62	
First Lieutenant	John H. Widmer	Sept. 1, '61	Promoted
"	Ben. F. Blackstone	April 24, '62	Promoted
"	Wm. W. Taggart	Sept. 4, '62	
Second Lieutenant	Ben. F. Blackstone	Sept. 1, '61	Promoted
"	Wm. W. Taggart	April 24, '62	Promoted
"	Thomas Alexander	Sept. 4, '62	
		K.	
Captain	Henry H. Carter	April 27, '61	Killed at Pittsburg Landing, [April 6, '62
"	Nath. C. Kenyan	April 6, '62	
First Lieutenant	Nath. C. Kenyan	July 30, '61	Promoted
"	Theo. H. Walrod	Feb. 15, '62	
Second Lieutenant	Theo. H. Walrod	July 30, '61	Promoted
"	Levi W. Locker	Feb. 15, 62	

SCHEDULE G—Continued.

Roster of Twelfth Regiment Illinois Volunteers.

Field and Staff.		Rank.	Remarks.
Colonel	John McArthur	May 3, '61	Promoted Brig. Gen. March
"	A. L. Chetlain	April 1, '62	.... [21, 1862.
Lieut. Colonel	A. L. Chetlain	May 3, '61	Promoted
"	Arthur C. Ducat	April 1, '62	
Major	Wm. D. Williams	May 3, '61	Resigned Oct. 2, 1861
"	Arthur C. Ducat	Sept. 24, '61	Promoted
"	James R. Hugunin	April 1, '62	
Adjutant	J. Bates Dickson	Aug. 1, '61	Promoted to staff
"	George Mason	May 22, '62	
Quartermaster	S. R. Wetmore	Aug. 1, '61	Resigned June 16, 1862
"	Duncan McLean	June 16, '62	Promoted Capt. Co. A
Surgeon	Horace Wardner	July 16, '61	Promoted to Brigade Surgeon
"	William F. Cady	May 1, '62	
1st Ass't Surgeon	James H. Farris	May 6, '61	
"	William F. Cady	Aug. 1, '61	Promoted
"	Samuel M. Swan	Oct. 6, '62	
2d Ass't Surgeon			
Chaplain	Joel Grant	Aug. 1, '61	

COMPANY A.

Captain	Arthur C. Ducat	Aug. 1, '61	Promoted
"	William Fisher	Oct. 15, '61	Resigned Sept. 3, 1862
"	Duncan McLean	Sept. 3, '62	
First Lieutenant	William Fisher	Aug. 1, '61	Promoted Quartermaster
"	Duncan McLean	Oct. 15, '61	
"	W. Van Horn	June 16, '62	
Second Lieutenant	Duncan McLean	Aug. 1, '61	Promoted
"	W. Van Horn	April 15, '62	Promoted
"	James B. Johnson	June 16, '62	

B.

Captain	John Tyler Hale	Aug. 1, '61	Killed in battle
"	H. S. Stephenson	Feb. 16, '62	
First Lieutenant	Henry Stephenson	Aug. 1, '61	Promoted
"	Justin D. Towner	Feb. 16, '62	
Second Lieutenant	Justin D. Towner	Aug. 1, '62	Promoted
"	David A. Cook	Feb. 16, '62	

C.

Captain	Wm. J. Allen	Sept. 12, '61	Resigned Nov. 13, '61
"	Rob't V. Chesley	Dec. 1, '61	Resigned May 26, '62
"	David C. Jones	May 26, '62	
First Lieutenant	Rob't V. Chesley	Aug. 3, '61	Promoted
"	Wright Seaman	Dec. 1, '61	Killed in Battle
"	O. L. Spaulding	May 26, '62	
Second Lieutenant	David Jones	Sept. 12, '61	Promoted
"	Perry F. Miller	May 26, '62	

D.

Captain	Robert H. Lackey	Aug. 1, '61	Dismissed
"	John W. Fisher	March 3, '62	Resigned July 2, '62
"	Robert Koehler	July 2, '62	
First Lieutenant	Robert Koehler	Aug. 1, '61	Promoted
"	Wm. F. Jobe	July 2, '62	
Second Lieutenant	Wm. F. Jobe	Aug. 1, '61	Promoted
"	Charles M. Barry	July 2, '62	

SCHEDULE G—Continued.

		Rank.	Remarks.
E.			
Captain	Vincent Ridgely..	Aug. 1, '61	Resigned Oct. 2, '61
"	Henry V. Sellar..	Oct. 18, '61	
First Lieutenant..	John W. Fisher.	Aug. 1, '61	Promoted to Co. D
"	Wm. C. Magner ..	March 3, '62	
Second Lieutenant	Henry V. Sellan..	Aug. 1, '61	Promoted
"	Wm. C. Magner..	Oct. 18, '61	Promoted
"	John A. Korgle..	March 3, '62	Deceased
"	Wm. H. Bowser..	May 22, '62	
F.			
Captain	Wallace Campbell	Aug. 1, '61	
First Lieutenant..	J. Bates Dickson .	Aug. 1, '61	Promoted Adjutant
"	R. K. Randolph ..	Oct. 18, '61	
Second Lieutenant	Nicholas Roth ...	Aug. 1, '61	Resigned June 20, '62
"	Charles Farr.....	June 20, '62	
G.			
Captain	Guy C. Ward	Aug. 1, '61	Died Oct. 4, '62
"	J. M. McArthur..	Oct. 4, '62	
First Lieutenant..	J. M. McArthur..	Aug. 1, '61	Promoted
"	John Hall	Oct. 4, '62	
Second Lieutenant	John F. Watkins.	Aug. 1, '61	Resigned Sept. 16, '62
"	John Hall	Sept. 16, '62	Promoted
"	Jason J. Sanborn.	Oct. 4, '62	
H.			
Captain	Wm. T. Swain ...	Aug. 1, '61	Died of wounds April 18, '62.
"	John M. Mills...	April 19, '62	Resigned Sept. 3, '62
"	W. S. Merriman..	Sept. 3, '62	
First Lieutenant..	John M. Mills....	Aug. 1, '61	Promoted
"	W. S. Merriman..	April 19, '62	Promoted
"	Alex. Branden...	Sept. 3, '62	
Second Lieutenant	W. S. Merriman..	Aug. 1, '61	Promoted
"	Quincy J. Drake..	April 19, '62	
I.			
Captain	Frank B. Farris ..	Aug. 1, '61	Killed at Pittsburg
"	Geo. L. Paddock .	April 7, '62	Declined
"	Wm. D. Mills ...	April 17, '62	
First Lieutenant..	Geo. L. Paddock.	Aug. 1, '61	Resigned June 16, '62
"	Wm. D. Mills....	April 7, '62	Promoted
"	A. A. Jackson ...	June 17, '62	
Second Lieutenant	Wm. D. Mills....	Aug. 1, '61	Promoted
"	Geo. W. Garwood	April 7, '62	
K.			
Captain	Jas. R. Hugunin..	Aug. 1, '61	Promoted Major
"	Wm. E. Waite...	April 1, '62	
First Lieutenant..	Wm. E. Waite...	Aug. 1, '61	Promoted
"	C. E. Beaumont..	April 1, '62	Resigned July 14, '62
"	Henry B. Wager..	July 14, '62	
Second Lieutenant	Eben Bacon	Aug. 1, '61	Resigned Nov. 24, '61
"	C. E. Beaumont..	Jan. 1, '62	Promoted
"	Henry B. Wager..	April 1, '62	Promoted
"	Leroy Clark	July 14, '62	Died Aug. 30, '62
"	Francis Rutger...	Aug. 30, '62	

Schedule G—Continued.

Roster of Thirteenth Regiment Illinois Volunteers.

Field and Staff.		Rank.	Remarks.
Colonel	John B. Wyman	May 24, 1861	
Lieut. Colonol	Benjamin F. Parks	May 9, 1861	Resigned June 24, 1861
"	Adam B. Gorgas	June 25, 1861	
Major	F. W. Partridge	June 25, 1861	
Adjutant	Henry T. Porter	May 24, 1861	
Quartermaster	Wm. C. Henderson	May 13, 1861	
Surgeon	Sam'l C. Plummer	November 7, 1862	
1st Asst. Surgeon	Sam'l C. Plummer	Septemb'r 9, 1861	Promoted
"	Chas. A. Thompson	December 18, 1862	
2d Asst. Surgeon	David H. Law	September 9, 1861	Resigned Nov. 15, 1862
Chaplain	Joseph C. Miller	May 9, 1861	

Company A.

Captain	Adam B. Gorgas		Promoted June 25, 1861
"	Henry T. Noble		
First Lieutenant	Henry T. Noble		Promoted
"	Henry D. Dement	May 24, 1861	
Second Lieutenant	Henry D. Dement		Promoted
"	Benjamin Gilman	May 24, 1861	Resigned October 1, 1861
"	George L. Acken	March 1, 1862	

B.

Captain	Doug. R. Bushnell		
First Lieutenant	H. Cooper Berry		
"	George P. Brown		
Second Lieutenant	Wm. W. Kilgour		Resigned February 3, 1862
"	Jos. M. Patterson	February 3, 1862	

C.

Captain	Henry M. Messinger		
First Lieutenant	Nathaniel Neff	April 27, 1861	Resigned November 15, 1862
"	George B. Sage	Novemb'r 15, 1862	
Second Lieutenant	George B. Sage		Promoted
"	Simon T. Joslyn	Novemb'r 15, 1862	

D.

Captain	Quincy McNiel		Promoted Major 2d Cavalry
"	James M. Beardsley	August 10, 1861	
First Lieutenant	James M. Beardsley		Promoted
"	Albert T. Higby	August 10, 1861	
Second Lieutenant	Albert T. Higby		Promoted
"	George G. Knox	August 10, 1861	Promoted 1st Artillery
"	Elisha J. Beardsley	March 16, 1862	

E.

Captain	Fred. W. Partridge		Promoted
"	A. J. Brinkerhoff	June 25, 1861	
First Lieutenant	A. J. Brinkerhoff		Promoted
"	Geo. B. Devoll	June 25, 1861	Resigned March 31, 1862
"	Geo. H. Carpenter	March 31, 1862	
Second Lieutenant	Geo. B. Devoll		Promoted
"	Henry T. Porter	June 25, 1861	Promoted Adjutant
"	Geo. H. Carpenter	January 29, 1862	Promoted
"	William Wallace	March 31, 1862	

SCHEDULE G — Continued.

	Rank.		Remarks.
F.			
Captain	Zelotes B. Maya		Resigned July 25, 1861
"	Everett F. Dutton		Discharged for promotion
"	Richard A. Smith	Sept. 22, 1862	
First Lieutenant	Everett F. Dutton		Promoted
"	Richard A. Smith	August 6, 1861	Promoted
"	Azro A. Buck	Sept. 22, 1862	
Second Lieutenant	Richard A. Smith		Promoted
"	Azro A. Buck	August 6, 1861	Promoted
"	Theodore Loring	Sept. 22, 1862	
G.			
Captain	George M. Cole		
First Lieutenant	William M. Jenks		
Second Lieutenant	Silas M. Jackson		
H.			
Captain	Benjamin F. Parks		Promoted Lieut. Colonel
"	Geo. H. Gardner		Dismissed with loss of pay,
First Lieutenant	Geo. H. Gardner,		Promoted.... [Sept. 3, '62
"	Edwin Went		
Second Lieutenant	Edwin Went		Promoted
"	Ethan A. Pritchard		
I.			
Captain	S. W. Wadsworth		
First Lieutenant	James G. Everest	May 3, 1861	
Second Lieutenant	Isaiah H. Williams	May 23, 1861	Resigned March 31, 1862
"	Geo. E. Hinmon	March 31, 1862	Resigned November 10, 1862
"	Hyacinth Cuniffe	November 10, 1862	
K.			
Captain	Walter Blanchard		
First Lieutenant	Merritt S. Hobson		Resigned January 22, 1862
"	Jordan J. Cole	January 22, 1862	
Second Lieutenant	Jordon J. Cole		Promoted
"	Geo. A. Napier	January 22, 1862	

Schedule G.— Continued.

Roster of Fourteenth Regiment Illinois Volunteers.

Field and Staff.		Rank.	Remarks.
Colonel..........	John M. Palmer..	May 13, 1861....	Promoted Brig. General, Dec.
"	Cyrus Hall	Feb. 1, 1862.....	[20, 1861
Lieut. Colonel ...	Amory K. Johnson	May 13, 1861....	Promoted, Colonel, 28th Inf'y
" ..	William Cam.....	Nov. 25, 1861....	....
Major.........	Jonathan Morris..	May 13, 1861....	Resigned, Sept. 3, 1862.....
" "	John F. Nolte....	Sept. 3, 1862....	....
Adjutant........	Rob't P. McKnight	Jan. 20, 1862....	....
Quartermaster ...	John F. Nolte....	May 25, 1861....	Resigned, Feb. 1, 1862.....
"	Jac'b R. Muhleman	Feb. 1, 1862....	....
Surgeon	George T. Allen..	Aug. 28, 1861....	Promoted to Brigade Surgeon
"	Benj. F. Stephenson	April 7, 1862....	....
1st. Ass't. Surgeon	Fred'k W. Kersting	Sept. 5, 1861....	Resigned, June 6, 1862.....
"	N. F. Chafer.....	Oct. 28, 1862....	....
2d Asst. Surgeon.	....	....	....
Chaplain........	Wm. J. Rutledge.	May 25, 1861....	....
	Company A		
Captain	Thos. M. Thompson	May 3, 1861.....	Resigned Dec. 7, 1861......
"	John F. Nolte....	Feb. 1, 1862....	Promoted ....
"	Charles Opitz ...	Sept. 3, 1862....	....
First Lieutenant..	John F. Nolte....	May 3, 1861.....	Promoted ....
" ..	Henry Rodecker..	May 25, 1861....	Resigned Sept. 3, 1862.....
"	Charles Opitz....	Sept. 3, 1862....	Promoted ....
"	Louis P. Bourquinn	Sept. 3, 1862....	....
Second Lieutenant	Henry Rodecker..	May 3, 1861.....	Promoted ....
"	Charles Opitz....	May 25, 1861....	Promoted ....
"	Louis P. Bourquinn	Sept. 3, 1862....	Promoted ....
"	Augustine A. Snow	Sept. 3, 1862....	....
	B		
Captain........	Cyrus Hall......	April 22, 1861....	Promoted ....
"	Dudley C. Smith..	Sept. 21, 1861....	....
First Lieutenant..	Dudley C. Smith..	April 22, 1861....	Promoted ....
" ..	George A. Poteet.	Sept. 21, 1861....	Promoted Major 115th.....
"	George Wright...	Sept. 13, 1862....	....
Second Lieutenant	Milton L. Webster	April 22, 1861....	Transferred to 7th Cavalry..
"	George Wright...	Sept. 21, 1861....	Promoted ....
"	Malc. H. Copeland	Sept. 13, 1862....	....
	C		
Captain	Aug. H. Cornman	May 10, 1861....	....
First Lieutenant..	Wm. E. Eastham	May 10, 1861....	....
Second Lieutenant	David N. Hamilton	May 10, 1861....	....
	D		
Captain	Thomas J. Bryant	May 3, 1861.....	Resigned Oct. 5, 1862......
"	James E. Williams	Oct. 5, 1862....	....
First Lieutenant..	Robt. P McKnight	May 3, 1861.....	Adjutant ....
"	James E. Williams	Jan. 20, 1862....	Promoted ....
"	Carlos C. Cox....	Oct. 5, 1862....	....
Second Lieutenant	James E. Williams	May 3, 1861.....	Promoted ....
"	Carlos C. Cox....	Jan. 20, 1862....	Promoted ....
"	Geo. W. Bates....	Oct. 5, 1862....	....

SCHEDULE G—Continued.

		Rank.	Remarks.
E			
Captain	Amory K. Johnson	April 22, 1861	Promoted Lieut. Colonel.
"	Frederick Mead	May 17, 1861	
First Lieutenant	Jacob M. Early	April 22, 1861	Resigned Jan. 13, 1862.
"	Ethan A. Norton	Jan. 13, 1862	
Second Lieutenant	Ethan A. Norton	April 22, 1861	Promoted
"	Alonzo J. Gillespie	Jan. 13, 1862	
F			
Captain	Milt. S. Littlefield	April 20, 1861	
First Lieutenant	Wm. H. Scott	April 20, 1861	
"	Thos. H. Simmons	May 25, 1861	
Second Lieutenant	Thos. H. Simmons	April 20, 1861	Promoted
"	John D. Moore	May 25, 1861	
G			
Captain	Lewis C. Reiner	April 20, 1861	
First Lieutenant	Fritz Fetzer	April 20, 1861	
"	Adam Smith	June 4, 1861	
Second Lieutenant	Jacob Rippstein	April 20, 1861	Resigned April 16, 1862.
"	Henry M. Pedan	April 16, 1862	
H			
Captain	Andrew Simpson	May 2, 1861	Resigned Oct. 4, 1862.
"	Oliver P. Squire	Oct. 4, 1862	
First Lieutenant	John W. Heartley	May 2, 1861	Resigned May 21, 1862.
"	Charles W. Powell	May 22, 1862	
Second Lieutenant	Oliver P. Squire	May 2, 1861	Promoted
"	Z. Pays'n Shumway	Oct. 4, 1862	
I			
Captain	Jonathan Morris	May 3, 1861	Promoted Major.
"	Jno. W. Meacham	May 24, 1861	Dismissed Nov. 11, 1862.
"	Erasmus D. Ward	Nov. 11, 1862	
First Lieutenant	Jno. W. Meacham	May 3, 1861	Promoted
"	Erasmus D. Ward	May 24, 1861	Promoted
"	Robert J. Henry	Nov. 11, 1862	
Second Lieutenant	Erasmus D. Ward	May 3, 1861	Promoted
"	Lawren W. Coe	May 24, 1861	
K			
Captain	William Cam	May 3, 1861	Promoted
"	Henry Case	Nov. 25, 1861	Transferred 7th Cavalry.
"	William W. Strong	March 2, 1862	
First Lieutenant	Henry Case	May 3, 1861	Promoted
"	William N. Shibley	Nov. 25, 1861	Resigned Nov. 4, 1862.
"	John Kirkham	Nov. 4, 1862	
Second Lieutenant	William H. Shibley	May 3, 1861	Promoted
"	William Mason	Nov. 25, 1861	

SCHEDULE G.—Continued.

Roster of Fifteenth Regiment, Illinois Volunteers.

Field and Staff.		Rank.	Remarks.
Colonel	Thomas J. Turner.	May 14, '61	Resigned Nov. 2, 1862
"	George C. Rogers.	Nov. 2, '62	
Lieut. Colonel	Edward F. Ellis	May 14, '61	Killed in battle, Shiloh
"	George C. Rogers.	April 7, '62	Promoted
"	James Rany	Nov. 2, '62	
Major	Wm. R. Goddard.	June 26, '61	Killed in battle, Shiloh
"	James Rany	April 7, '62	Promoted
"	Adam Nase	Nov. 2, '62	
Adjutant	Cyrenus C. Clark.	Sept. 4, '61	Transferred to staff
"	Charles F. Barber.	Oct. 26, '61	
Quartermaster	Samuel Hice, Jr.	Sept. 4, '61	Resigned Nov. 21, 1861
"	Ahiman V. Bohn.	Nov. 1, '61	
Surgeon	Wm. J. McKim.	May 14, '62	
1st Asst. Surgeon.	Harman A. Buck.	May 14, '61	Resigned March 13, '62
"	J. W. Van Valzah.	April 11, '62	
2d Asst. Surgeon.	Leonard L. Lake.	Nov. 8, '62	
Chaplain	David E. Halteman	May 24, '61	Resigned April 17, 1862
"	B. F. Rogers	Dec. 17, '62	

COMPANY A.

Captain	Louis D. Kelly	May 6, '61	Resigned Oct. 21, '62
"	Fred. W. Smith.	Oct. 21, '62	
First Lieutenant	Daniel C. Joslyn.	May 6, '61	Resigned Oct. 16, '61
"	Lawrence H. Jones	Oct. 26, '61	Dismissed Feb. 15, '62
"	Fred. W. Smith.	Feb. 15, '62	Promoted
"	Wm. H. Sherman.	Oct. 21, '62	
Second Lieutenant	Mark Hathaway.	May 6, '61	Resigned Oct. 16, '61
"	Fred. W. Smith.	Oct. 26, '61	Promoted
"	Wm. H. Sherman.	Feb. 15, '62	Promoted

B.

Captain	William Haywood.	May 24, '61	Resigned April 12, '62
"	David L. Baker.	April 12, '62	
First Lieutenant	David L. Baker.	May 24, '61	Promoted
"	Addison N. Longcer	April 12, '62	
Second Lieutenant	Addison N. Longcer	May 24, '61	Promoted
"	Wesley W. Jones.	April 12, '62	

C.

Captain	Holder Brownell.	May 14, '61	Killed at Shiloh
"	Geo. W. Bradley.	April 7, '62	
First Lieutenant	Cyrenus C. Clark.	May 14, '61	Adjutant
"	Geo. W. Bradley.	Sept. 4, '61	Promoted
"	Gideon V. Carr.	April 7, '62	
Second Lieutenant	Geo. W. Bradley.	May 14, '61	Promoted
"	Orville T. Andrews	Sept. 4, '61	Resigned Aug 21, 1862
"	Hampden S. Cottel	Aug. 21, '62	

D.

Captain	Harley Wayne	April 27, '61	Killed at Shiloh
"	Fred. A. Smith.	April 7, '62	
First Lieutenant	Frank S. Curtis.	April 27, '61	Resigned Sept. 12, '61
"	Fred. A. Smith.	April 16, '61	Promoted
"	Calvin H. Shapley.	April 7, '62	Resigned Sept. 3, '62
"	John Waldock	Sept. 3, '62	

SCHEDULE G.—Continued

		Rank.	Remarks.
Second Lieutenant	Fred. A. Smith	April 27, '61	Promoted
"	Peter J. Labaugh	Sept. 16, '61	Resigned April 18, '62
"	John Waldock	April 7, '62	Promoted
"	Mic'l Schommaker	Sept. 3, '62	

E.

Captain	James Rany	April 24, '61	Promoted Major
"	Daniel J. Benner	April 7, '62	
First Lieutenant	Daniel J. Benner	April 24, '61	Promoted
"	John W. Luke	April 7, '62	
Second Lieutenant	John W. Luke	April 24, '61	Promoted
"	Allen P. Barnes	April 7, '62	

F.

Captain	John H. Paddock	June 14, '61	
"	William Henry	Sept. 4, '61	Discharged Feb. 15, '62
"	Cyrenus C. Clark	Feb. 18, '62	
First Lieutenant	William Henry	June 14, '61	Promoted
"	Nelson A. Thomas	Sept. 4, '61	Declined
"	John J. Sears	Feb. 18, '62	
Second Lieutenant	John J. Sears	June 14, '61	Promoted
"	Frank D. Patterson	June 7, '62	

G.

Captain	Jas. O. P. Burnside	May 15,' 61	Mustered out April 2, 1862
"	R. C. McEathorn	April 2, '62	
First Lieutenant	R. C. McEathorn	April 24, '61	Promoted
"	Albert Bliss, Jr	April 2, '62	
Second Lieutenant	Albert Bliss, Jr	April 24, '61	Promoted
"	Hubbard P. Sweet	April 2, '62	

H.

Captain	Morton D. Swift	April 22, '61	
First Lieutenant	Thomas J. Hewitt	April 22, '61	Resigned Sept. 23, '62
"	William H. Gibbs	Sept. 23, '62	
Second Lieutenant	William H. Gibbs	April 22, '61	Promoted
"	John P. Newlands	Sept. 23, '62	

I.

Captain	Joseph B. Jones	April 25, '61	Resigned Sept. 4, '61
"	George C. Rogers	Sept. 4, '61	Promoted Lieut. Colonel
"	John S. Pratt	April 7, '62	
First Lieutenant	George C. Rogers	April 25, '61	Promoted
"	John S. Pratt	Sept. 4, '61	Promoted
"	William M. Reid	April 7, '62	
Second Lieutenant	John S. Pratt	April 25, '61	Promoted
"	William M. Reid	Sept. 4, '61	Promoted
"	Thomas Hewitt	April 7, '62	

K.

Captain	Adam Nase	April 25, '61	Promoted Major
"	Phineas D. Kenyon	Nov. 2, '62	
First Lieutenant	James O'Brien	April 25, '61,	Resigned April 16, '62
"	Phineas D. Kenyon	April 16, '62	Promoted
Second Lieutenant	J. W. Puterbaugh	June 6, '61	Killed at Shiloh
"	Wm. W. Wheelock	April 7, '62	

SCHEDULE G.—Continued.

Roster of Sixteenth Regiment Illinois Volunteers.

Field and Staff.		Rank.	Remarks.
Colonel.........	Robert F. Smith..	May 13, '61......	....
Lieut. Colonel....	Samuel Wilson...	May 13, '61......	Resigned Sept. 3, 1862.....
"	..James B. Cahill..	Sept. 3, '62......	....
Major...........	Samuel M. Hays..	May 13, '61......	Died August 6, '1862........
"	Charles Petrie...	Aug. 6, '62......	....
Adjutant........	Charles D. Kerr..	Sept. 21, '61.....	....
Quartermaster ...	Thomas J. Coulter	July 24, '61......	Transf'd to Brig. Quartermas'r
"	Lucius L. King...	May 3, '62.......	....
Surgeon.........	Louis Watson....	June 21, '61.....	....
1st Asst. Surgeon.	A. L. Ritchey.....	May 18, '62......	....
2d Asst. Surgeon.	....	....	....
Chaplain........	Richard Haney...	May 24, '61......	Resigned June 18, 1862....

COMPANY A.

Captain........	Virgil Y. Ralston.	April 26, '61.....	Resigned March 13, '62.....
"	..Benj. F. Pinckley.	March 13, '62....	Resigned July 11, '62......
"	..Eben White.....	July 11, '62......	....
First Lieutenant..	Benj. F. Pinckley.	April 26, '61.....	Promoted ....
"	..H. M. Bartholomew	March 13, '62 ...	....
Second Lieutenant	H. M. Bartholomew	May 3, '61........	Promoted ....
"	..Henry Gash.....	March 13, '62....	....

B.

Captain........	David P. Wells..	April 20, 1861...	Died April 7, 1862.........
"	Wm. L. Broadus..	April 7, 1862....	Resigned July 3, 1862......
"	James A. Chapman	July 3, 1862.....	....
First Lieutenant..	Wm. L. Broadus..	April 20, 1861 ...	Promoted ....
"	E. K. Westfall...	April 7, 1862.....	Resigned June 20, 1862.....
"	Jas. A. Chapman..	June 20, 1862....	Promoted ....
"	..Geo. W. McAllister	July 3, 1862.....	....
Second Lieutenant	Abram Rowe.....	April 20, 1861 ...	Promoted to Company C....
"	E. K. Westfall....	October 1, 1861..	Promoted ....
"	Jas. A. Chapman..	April 7, 1862.....	Promoted ....
"	..G. W. McAllister.	June 20, 1862....	Promoted ....
"	Benjamin Lowe..	July 3, 1862.....	....

C.

Captain........	George W. Patrick	May 14, 1861....	Mustered out Sept. 25, 1861
"	Abram Rowe....	Sept. 25, 1861....	....
First Lieutenant..	James P. Taylor..	May 14, 1861....	Resigned July 25, 1861.....
"	Edwin Moore....	July 26, 1861....	Major 21st Mo. Regiment...
"	James Donaldson.	June 27, 1862....	....
Second Lieutenant	Edwin Moore....	May 14, 1861....	Promoted ....
"	Thomas J. Coulter	July 26, 1861	Promoted Quartermaster ...
"	L. J. Crewdson...	Nov, 20, 1862....	....

D.

Captain........	James B. Cahill..	May 14, 1861....	Promoted ....
"	Isaac Davis......	Sept. 3, 1862....	....
First Lieutenant..	James B. Cahill..	May 4, 1861.....	Promoted ....
"	Francis Sample ..	May 14, 1861	....
"	..Wesley Clowse...	May 14, 1861....	Resigned Dec. 7, 1861......
"	..Isaac Davis......	Dec. 7, 1861.....	Promoted ....
"	..Wm. Summerville	Sept. 3, 1862	....
Second Lieutenant	Wesley Clowse...	May 14, 1861	Promoted ....

SCHEDULE G—Continued.

		Rank.	Remarks.
Second Lieutenant	Benj. F. Marsh, jr.	May 24, 1861	Resigned August 8, 1861
"	James Davis	Oct. 13, 1861	Promoted
"	Wm. Sommerville	Dec. 7, 1861	Promoted
"	William Congers	Sept. 3, 1862	

E.

Captain	Samuel E. Taylor	May 3, 1861	Resigned June 20, 1862
"	Calvin H. Wilson	June 20, 1862	
First Lieutenant	Calvin H. Wilson	May 3, 1861	Promoted
"	Jefferson Burton	June 20, 1862	Resigned December 4, 1862
Second Lieutenant	Jefferson Burton	May 3, 1861	Promoted
"	David Hederick	June 20, 1862	

F.

Captain	James Fritz	May 1, 1861	M. O. May 26, 1862
"	John W. Herbert	May 26, 1862	
First Lieutenant	John W. Herbert	May 1, 1861	Promoted
"	James G. Stewart	May 26, 1862	
Second Lieutenant	James G. Stewart	May 1, 1861	Promoted
"	Henry Watson	May 26, 1862	

G.

Captain	Wm. H. McAllister	May 10, 1861	Resigned June 21, 1862
"	Wm. G. Ritchey	June 21, 1862	
First Lieutenant	Wm. G. Ritchey	May 10, 1861	Promoted
"	M. D. L. Manlove	June 21, 1862	
Second Lieutenant	M. D. L. Manlove	May 10, 1861	Promoted
"	Geo. W. Parrott	June 21, 1862	

H.

Captain	Charles Petrie	May 9, 1861	Promoted
"	Clemens A. Ridder	August 6, 1862	
First Lieutenant	Theodore Weber	May 9, 1861	Dis'd by C. mars'l Aug. 20, '62
"	Clemens A. Ridder	Sept. 27, 1861	Promoted
"	Herman Lund	August 6, 1862	
Second Lieutenant	Charles Delabar	May 9, 1861	Resigned July 1, 1861
"	Casten Frinken	July 2, 1861	Resigned June 28, 1862
"	Herman Lund	June 28, 1862	Promoted
"	Thomas H. Smith	August 6, 1862	

I.

Captain	Smith Johnson	May 9, 1861	
First Lieutenant	Stedman Hatch	May 9, 1861	
Second Lieutenant	Robert Patterson	May 9, 1861	

K.

Captain	George D. Stewart	May 14, 1861	
First Lieutenant	James Hedger	May 14, 1861	Resigned
"	French B. Woodall	May 24, 1861	
Second Lieutenant	Rich'rd B. Higgins	May 14, 1861	Resigned July 3, 1862
"	Joseph E. Haines	July 3, 1862	

SCHEDULE G—Continued.

Roster of Seventeenth Regiment Illinois Volunteers.

Field and Staff.		Rank.	Remarks.
Colonel	Leonard Fulton Ross	May 20, '61	Promoted Brigadier Gen'l [April 25, '62.
"	Addison S. Norton	April 25, '62	
Lieut. Colonel	Enos P. Wood	May 20, '61	Resigned April 19, '62
"	Francis M. Smith	April 19, '62	
Major	Francis M. Smith	May 20, '61	Promoted
"	Frank F. Peats	April 25, '62	
Adjutant	Abraham H. Ryan	May 25, '61	Promoted Captain Co. A
"	William S. Reynolds	April 25, '62	
Quartermaster	Henry L. Smith	April 1, '62	
Surgeon	L. D. Kellogg	June 1, '61	
1st Ass't Surgeon	Charles B. Tompkins	May 20, '61	
2d Ass't Surgeon	Henry H. Penneman	Dec. 26, '62	
Chaplain	Sanford A. Kingsbury	Dec. 23, '61	

COMPANY A.

Captain	Addison S. Norton	April 19, '61	Promoted Colonel
"	Abraham H. Ryan	April 25, '62	
First Lieutenant	Abraham H. Ryan	April 19, '61	Rromoted
"	George W. Robson	May 20, '61	Promoted Co. B
"	Edmund E. Ryan	April 25, '62	
Second Lieutenant	George W. Robson	April 19, '61	Promoted
"	William S. Reynolds	May 20, '61	Adjutant
"	Gaun Wilkins	April 25, '62	

B.

Captain	Benjamin T. Baldwin	May 15, '61	Resigned
"	Frank F. Peats	July 3, '61	Promoted
"	George W. Robson	April 25, '62	
First Lieutenant	Joseph L. Dodds	May 15, '61	Resigned
"	John W. Miles	August 10, '61	Dismisssed Sept. 7, '62
"	John Hough	August 26, '61	Resigned April 16, '62
"	Albert W. Jones	April 16, '62	Resigned Sept. 13, '62
"	John A. Collier	Sept. 13, '62	
Second Lieutenant	Albert W. Jones	May 15, '61	Promoted
"	John A. Collier	April 16, '62	Promoted
"	Thomas McFarland	Sept. 13, '62	

C.

Captain	Allen D. Rose	May 13, '61	Resigned December 24, '61
"	George W. Wright	Dec. 24, '61	Resigned April 18, '62
"	Milton S. Kimball	April 18, '62	
First Lieutenant	William Walsh	May 13, '61	Resigned December 31, '61
"	William T. Dodds	Dec. 31, '61	Resigned April 18, '62
"	Chauncey Black	April 18, '62	
Second Lieutenant	David A. Parks	May 13, '61	Resigned December 27, '61
"	Chauncey Black	Dec. 27, '61	Promoted
"	James M. Moore	April 18, '62	

D.

Captain	Henry H. Bush	April 19, '61	
First Lieutenant	James McCartney	April 20, '61	Resigned March 28, '62
"	John J. Biggs	March 28, '62	Resigned as 2d Lieutenant
"	A. Curtis Mathews	April 18, '62	
Second Lieutenant	John J. Biggs	April 20, '61	Promoted
"	A. Curtis Mathews	March 28, '62	Promoted
"	Edmund C. D. Robbins	April 18, '62	

SCHEDULE G—Continued.

		Rank.	Remarks.

E.

Captain	Francis M. Smith	April 19, '61.	Promoted to Major
"	Roderick R. Harding	May 20, '61.	Resigned May 15, '62
"	George C. Smith	May 15, '62.	
First Lieutenant	Roderick R. Harding	April 19, '61.	Promoted
"	James C. Beswick	May 20, '61.	Mustered out April 2, '62.
"	William J. Merrill	April 2, '62.	
Second Lieutenant	James C. Beswick	April 19, '61.	Promoted
"	George C. Smith	May 20, '61.	Promoted
"	David Clough	May 15, '62.	

F.

Captain	Josiah Moore	April 20, '61.	
First Lieutenant	John R. Charter	April 20, '61.	Resigned September 3, '62.
"	Charles C. Williams	Sept. 3, '62.	
Second Lieutenant	Charles C. Williams	April 20, '61.	Promoted
"	William S. McClanahan	Sept. 3, '62.	

G.

Captain	Otis A. Burgess	May 13, '61.	Resigned April 24, '62.
"	Jonathan H. Rowell	April 24, '62.	
First Lieutenant	Jonathan H. Rowell	May 13, '61.	Promoted
"	Frederick W. Callsen	April 24, '62.	
Second Lieutenant	Frederick D. Callsen	May 13, '61.	Promoted
"	Henry D. Clark	April 24, '62.	

H.

Captain	Leonard F. Ross	May 13, '61.	Promoted
"	Thomas A. Boyd	May 20, '61.	Resigned April 24, '62.
"	William W. Hull	April 25, '62.	
First Lieutenant	Thomas A. Boyd	May 13, '61.	Promoted
"	Asias Willison	May 20, '61.	Resigned April 18, '62.
"	Milton S. Kimball	April 18, '62.	Promoted to Co. C
"	William C. Stockdale	April 25, '62.	
Second Lieutenant	Asias Willison	May 13, '61.	Promoted
"	Milton S. Kimball	May 20, '61.	Promoted
"	William E. Yarnell	April 25, '62.	

I.

Captain	Enos P. Wood	April 23, '61.	Promoted
"	Edward S. Bruington	May 20, '61.	Resigned July 8, '62.
"	George W. Sanders	July 8, '62.	
First Lieutenant	George W. Saunders	April 23, '61.	Promoted
"	William Avery	July 8, '62.	
Second Lieutenant	Edward S. Bruington	April 23, '61.	
"	William Avery	May 20, '61.	
"	William A. Lorimer	July 8, '62.	

K.

Captain	James P. Walker	April 23, '61.	Resigned April 27, '62.
"	Jacob Wheeler	April 27, '62.	
First Lieutenant	John Q. A. Jones	April 23, '61.	Died
"	Jacob Wheeler	Oct. 26, '61.	Promoted
"	Henry F. Hole	April 27, '62.	Resigned October 22, '62.
"	James H. Mitchell	Oct. 22, '62.	
Second Lieutenant	Andrew J. Bruner	April 23, '61.	Died
"	Alexander T. Davis	Dec. 11, '61.	Died
"	James H. Mitchell	July 2, '62.	Promoted
"	George R. Buck	Oct. 22, '62.	

SCHEDULE G—Continued.

Roster of the Eighteenth Regiment Illinois Volunteers.

Field and Staff.		Rank.	Remarks.
Colonel	Michael Lawler	May 20, 1861	
Lieut. Colonel	Thos. H. Burgess	May 20, 1861	Resigned Sept. 3, 1862
"	Daniel H. Brush	Sept. 3, 1862	
Major	Samuel Eaton	May 20, 1861	Resigned April 1, 1862
" e	Nathan Crews	April 1, 1862	Resigned July 8, 1862
"	Daniel H. Brush	July 8, 1862	Promoted
"	Samuel B. Marks	Sept. 3, 1862	
Adjutant	Wm. B. Fondey	August 6, 1861	Resigned October 13, 1861
"	Albert W. Adams	October 15, 1861	Died at Cairo, Feb. 12, 1862
"	Wm. H. Heath	February 12, 1862	Resigned Oct. 21, 1862, and
"	Samuel T. Brush	Sept. 5, 1862	[Lt. Colonel 33d Missouri.
Quartermaster	John Olney	May 30, 1861	Promoted Lt.Col.6th Cavalry
Surgeon	Jules C. Webber	August 18, 1861	
1st Ass't. Surgeon	Henry W. Davis	July 24, 1861	
2d Ass't. Surgeon	Orange B. Ormsby	August 26, 1861	
"	Wm. W. Hipolite	December 18, 1862	
Chaplain	Lewis Lambert	July 1, 1861	Resigned April 17, 1862
"	Mordecai B. Kelly	Sept. 6, 1862	
COMPANY A.			
Captain	James Baird	May 2, 1861	Resigned November 27, 1861
"	James S. Craig	Dec. 4, 1861	Killed in battle
"	Paul T. Jones	February 19, 1862	
First Lieutenant	James S. Craig	May 2, 1861	Promoted
"	Paul T. Jones	Dec. 4, 1862	Promoted
"	Alex. M. Brown	March 16, 1862	
Second Lieutenant	Henry S. Wilso	May 30, 1861	Promoted to Company B
"	Martin G. Kelson	August 18, 1861	Resigned Aug. 31, 1862
"	Cuthbert A. Jones	November 7, 1862	
B.			
Captain	Elias W. Jones	May 11, 1861	Resigned August 18, 1861
"	Henry S. Wilson	August 18, 1861	
First Lieutenant	Cornel's C. Weaver	May 11, 1861	
Second Lieutenant	William Scanland	May 11, 1861	Resigned Feb. 13, 1862
"	Emri C. Watson	February 13, 1862	Resigned Nov. 4, 1862
"	Chas. M. Edwards	November 4, 1862	
C.			
Captain	Wm. S. Crawford	May 9, 1861	Resigned Oct. 20, 1861
"	Wm. J. Dillon	Oct. 21, 1861	Killed at Shiloh
First Lieutenant	Wm. J. Dillon	May 9, 1861	Promoted
"	Andrew J. Ice	Oct. 21, 1861	Resigned Feb. 1, 1862
Second Lieutenant	Andrew J. Ice	May 9, 1861	Promoted
"	John D. Denning	Oct. 21, 1861	Mustered out April 1, 1862

[This company consolidated into others and new company enlisted and assigned C.]

Captain	Hezekiah C. Hodge	September 9, 1862	
First Lieutenant	Mich'l A. Killion	September 9, 1862	
Second Lieutenant	Benjamin Redfield	September 9, 1862	
D.			
Captain	Jos. T. Cormick	June 13, 1861	Resigned Nov. 16, 1861
"	Patrick Lawler	Nov. 16, 1861	
First Lieutenant	Wimer Bedford	June 13, 1861	Resigned Nov. 17, 1861
"	John G. Mansker	Nov. 18, 1861	Killed in battle
"	Chalon A. Towle	Feb. 16, 1862	
Second Lieutenant	George W. Green	June 13, 1861	Resigned January 10, 1862
"	Chalon A. Towle	Aug. 18, 1861	Promoted
"	Wm. L. Cross	Feb. 15, 1862	

Schedule G—Continued.

		Rank.	Remarks.
E.			
Captain	William Hunter..	May 6, 1861.....	Resigned Nov. 26, 1861....
"	Charles H. Reed..	October 14, 1861..	
First Lieutenant..	Edgar Potter....	May 6, 1861.....	Resigned Dec. 23, 1861....
"	Richard Kelly....	December 23, 1861	
Second Lieutenant	Charles Reed....	May 6, 1861.....	Promoted...............
"	Daniel W. Fick..	October 14, 1861.	Resigned Oct. 25, 1862.....
"	Peter McGowan..	October 25, 1862..	
F.			
Captain	Jabez J. Anderson	May 30, 1861....	
First Lieutenant..	John Olney......	May 30, 1861....	Revoked...............
"	Mordecai B. Kelly	May 30, 1861....	Promoted...............
"	George Miller....	Sept. 6, 1862....	
Second Lieutenant	Wm. M. Thompson	August 18, 1861..	Mustered out April 8, 1862..
"	George Miller....	April 8, 1862....	Promoted...............
"	Samuel P. Conner	October 6, 1862..	
G.			
Captain	Wilson M. Cooper	May 11, 1861....	Died...................
"	Nathan Crews....	Sept. 12, 1861....	Promoted...............
"	Ezekiel George...	April 1, 1862....	Died June 8, 1862..........
"	Daniel Haynes...	June 8, 1862.....	
First Lieutenant..	Nathan Crews....	May 11, 1861....	Promoted
"	Ezekiel George...	Sept. 12, 1861....	Promoted
"	Joseph B. Thorp..	April 1, 1862....	
Second Lieutenant	Wm. H. Robinson	May 11, 1861....	Resigned Oct. 20, 1861.....
"	Jos. M. Campbell.	Oct. 21, 1861....	Resigned April 27, 1862....
"	Benj. F. Staley...	April 27, 1862....	
H.			
Captain	Rich'd R. Hopkins	June 18, 1861....	Resigned March 28, 1862...
"	John Davis......	March 28, 1862...	
First Lieutenant..	John H. Moberly..	June 18, 1861....	Resigned Oct. 10, 1861.....
"	Wm. D. Harland..	October 18, 1861.	Died...................
"	Ezra N. Edwards.	Sept. 9, 1862....	
Second Lieutenant	Thos. G. Barnes..	June 18, 1861....	Resigned Oct. 17, 1861.....
"	John Davis......	October 18, 1861.	Promoted...............
"	Jonat'n K. Mosier	Sept. 9, 1862....	
I.			
Captain	Samuel B. Marks.	May 11, 1861....	Promoted...............
"	John Blackburn..	October 1, 1862..	
First Lieutenant..	John H. Barton..	May 11, 1861....	Resigned Nov. 17, 1861....
"	Wm. H. Heath...	November 17,1861	Promoted...............
"	John Blackburn..	Sept. 9, 1862.....	Promoted...............
"	Peter Dolan.....	October 1, 1862..	
Second Lieutenant	Joseph Williams.	May 11, 1861....	Resigned Dec. 28, 1861....
"	John Blackburn..	January 1, 1862..	Promoted...............
"	Charles Smith....	Sept. 9, 1862....	
K.			
Captain	Daniel H. Brush..	May 6, 1861.....	Promoted Major...........
"	Argill Conner....	July 8, 1862....	
First Lieutenant..	John W. Lawrence	May 6, 1861.....	Transferred to Ram Fleet as Ass't Surgeon, July 15, '62
"	Rowland R. Brush	June 25, 1862....	Resigned Dec. 10, 1862.....
"	John L. Tuthill...	Decemb'r 10, 1862	
Second Lieutenant	Argill Conner....	May 6, 1861.....	Promoted...............
"	John L. Tuthill...	July 8, 1862....	

SCHEDULE G—Continued.

Roster of Nineteenth Regiment of Illinois Volunteers.

Field and Staff.		Rank.	Remarks.
Colonel	John B. Turchin	June 22, '61	Resigned Aug. 6, '62; app.
"	Joseph R. Scott	Aug. 7, '62	..[Brig. Gen. July 17, '62.
Lieut. Colonel	Joseph R. Scott	June 22, '61	Resigned July 22, '62; pro-
"	Alex. W. Raffen	July 22, '62	......[moted Col. Aug. 7.
Major	Frederick Harding	June 22, '61	Resigned Sept. 6, '62
"	James B. Guthrie	Sept. 6, '62	
Adjutant	Chauncey Miller	Aug. 10, '61	Resigned July 12, '62
"	Lester G. Bangs	July 12, '62	
Quartermaster	Robert W. Wetherell	Aug. 10, '61	
Surgeon	Samuel C. Blake	June 25, '61	Transferred
"	Roswell G. Bogue	Aug. 5, '61	
1st Ass't Surgeon	Preston H. Bailhache	July 16, '61	
2d Ass't Surgeon			
Chaplain	Augustus H. Conant	July 31, '62	

COMPANY A.

Captain	James R. Hayden	May 6, '61	
First Lieutenant	Clifton T. Wharton	May 4, '61	
Second Lieutenant	John C. Long	May 4, '61	Transferred to U. S. army.
"	William B. Curtis	Aug. 6, '61	Resigned Aug. 17, '62
"	Thomas M. Beatty	Aug. 17, '62	

B.

Captain	Charles Stewart	July 30, '61	Resigned July 15, '62
"	Alexander Murchison	July 15, '62	
First Lieutenant	Stephen M. Hill	July 30, '61	Resigned Nov. 29, '61
"	Alexander Murchison, jr.	Oct. 30, '61	Promoted
"	William Jackson	July 15, '62	
Second Lieutenant	Alexander Murchison, jr.	July 30, '61	Promoted
"	William Jackson	Oct. 30, '61	Promoted
"	John H. Hunter	July 15, '62	

C.

Captain	James V. Guthrie	July 30, '61	Promoted
"	William Inness	Sept. 6, '62	
First Lieutenant	William Inness	July 30, '61	Promoted
"	Washington L. Wood	Sept. 6, '62	
Second Lieutenant	Leavens J. Keeler	July 30, '61	Ass't Surgeon 6th Ky. cav.
"	Edward A Filkins	Nov. 21, '62	

D.

Captain	Charles A. Colby	July 30, '61	
First Lieutenant	James R. Faulkner	July 30, '61	Resigned Oct. 31, '61
"	Samuel S. Boone	Oct. 31, '61	
Second Lieutenant	David A. Cunningham	July 30, '61	Resigned Nov. 25, '61
"	William A. Calhoun	Oct. 20, '61	

E.

Captain	Alexander W. Raffen	July 30, '61	Promoted
"	David F. Bremer	July 22, '62	
First Lieutenant	David F. Bremer	July 30, '61	Promoted
"	John Young	July 22, '62	
Second Lieutenant	John Young	July 30, '61	Promoted
"	James W. Raffen	July 22, '62	

SCHEDULE G—Continued.

		Rank.	Remarks.
F.			
Captain	Luther S. Allard	July 30, '61	Resigned Dec. 1, '61
"	Knowlton H. Chandler	Dec. 1, '61	
First Lieutenant	Knowlton H. Chandler	July 30, '61	Promoted
"	James G. Campbell	Dec. 1, '61	
Second Lieutenant	James G. Campbell	July 30, '61	Promoted
"	Samuel L. Hamilton	Dec. 1, '61	
G.			
Captain	Charles D. C. Williams	July 30, '61	Transferred to Marine Ar- [tillery.
"	Lyman Bridges	Jan. 1, '62	
First Lieutenant	Lyman Bridges	July 30, '61	Promoted
"	William Bishop	Jan. 1, '62	
Second Lieutenant	Charles H. Rowland	July 30, '61	
"	William Bishop	Sept. 13, '61	Promoted
"	Morris D. Temple	Jan. 1, '62	
H.			
Captain	Peachy A. Garriott	July 30, '61	
First Lieutenant	DeWitt C. Marshall	July 30, '61	Resigned Dec. 1, '61
"	Alvah Mansur	Dec. 1, '61	
Second Lieutenant	Alvah Mansur	July 30, '61	Promoted
"	Wellington Wood	Dec. 1, '61	
I.			
Captain	Bushrod B. Howard	July 30, '61	Killed
"	Charles H. Shepley	Oct. 18, '61	Died March 23, '62
"	John R. Madison	March 24, '62	Resigned Dec. 19, '62
First Lieutenant	Thaddeus G. Drum	July 30 '61	Resigned Oct. 31, '61
"	John R. Madison	Oct. 20, '61	Promoted
"	James Longhorn	March 24, '62	
Second Lieutenant	John R. Madison	July 30, '61	Promoted
"	William Quinton	Oct. 20, '61	
K.			
Captain	Presley N. Guthrie	July 30, '61	
First Lieutenant	Charles H. Shepley	July 30, '61	Promoted to Co. I
"	Cornelius F. Lamberson	Oct. 20, '61	
Second Lieutenant	Cornelius V. Lamberson	July 30, '61	Promoted
"	V. Bradford Bell	Oct. 20, '61	

SCHEDULE G—Continued.

Roster of Twentieth Regiment Illinois Volunteers.

Field and Staff.		Rank.	Remarks.
Colonel	C. Carroll Marsh	May 14, '61	
Lieut. Colonel	William Erwin	May 14, '61	Killed in battle at Fort
"	Evan Richards	Feb. 15, '62	[Donelson.
Major	John W. Goodwin	May 14, '61	Resigned Dec. 17, '61
"	Evan Richards	Dec. 17, '61	Promoted
"	Fred. A. Bartleson	Feb. 15, '62	
Adjutant	John E. Thompson	Nov. 10, '61	Killed at Shiloh, Ap'l 6, '62
"	John R. Conklin	April 7, '62	
Quartermaster	John Spicer	May 14, '61	
"	Joel H. Dix	Feb. 26, '62	Declined
"	Lysander Tiffany	Sept. 1, '62	
Surgeon	Christopher Goodbrake	May 19, '61	
1st Ass't Surgeon	Fred. K. Bailey	May 14, '61	Resigned Aug. 31, '62
2d Ass't Surgeon	Rolla T. Richards	Sept. 1, '62	
Chaplain	Charles Button	May 14, '61	
COMPANY A.			
Captain	John S. Wolfe	April 22, '61	Resigned Oct. 27, '61
"	Daniel Bradley	Nov. 1, '61	
First Lieutenant	Daniel Bradley	April 22, '61	Promoted
"	George W. Kennard	Aug. 31, '61	Promoted
"	William Archdeacon	Jan. 1, '62	Resigned May 30, '62
"	John H. Austin	June 1, '62	
Second Lieutenant	George W. Kennard	April 22, '61	Promoted
"	Eugene Fauntleroy	Aug. 31, '61	Dismissed Nov. 22, '62
B.			
Captain	Fred. A. Bartleson	April 22, '61	Promoted
"	John F. Cleghorn	Feb. 15, '62	
First Lieutenant	John W. Goodwin	April 22, '61	Promoted
"	John F. Cleghorn	May 14, '61	Promoted
"	Henry King	Feb. 15, '62	
Second Lieutenant	John F. Cleghorn	April 22, '61	Promoted
"	Henry King	May 14, '61	Promoted
"	Gideon Bernier	Feb. 15, '62	
C.			
Captain	John O. Pullen	April 22, '61	
First Lieutenant	John W. Champion	April 22, '61	Resigned Nov. 10, '61
"	Charles W. Spalding	Oct. 4, '61	
Second Lieutenant	Andrew J. Taylor	April 22, '61	Resigned Dec. 3, '61
"	William S. Sears	Dec. 3, '61	
D.			
Captain	John A. Hoskins	April 22, '61	Resigned Dec. 2, '61
"	Charles L. Page	Jan. 17, '62	
First Lieutenant	Joshua Whitmore	April 22, '61	Resigned March 28, '62
Second Lieutenant	John A. Fellows	April 22, '61	Resigned
"	George W. Newman	June 5, '61	Resigned Dec. 3, '61
"	Henry B. Reed	Jan. 17, '62	Resigned June 20, '62
"	Orlando H. Ross	Oct. 1, '62	
E.			
Captain	Evan Richards	May 10, '61	Promoted
"	James M. North	Jan. 1, '62	
First Lieutenant	Henry C. Pharres	May 10, '61	Resigned Jan. 30, '62
"	John A. Edmonston	Jan. 30, '62	
Second Lieutenant	James M. North	May 10, '61	Promoted
"	Vespasian Warner	Jan. 1, '62	

Schedule G — Continued.

		Rank.	Remarks.
F.			
Captain	William Erwin	April 24, '61	Promoted
"	Thomas Q. Hildebrand	May 14, '61	
First Lieutenant	James E. Shields	May 14, '61	Acting Quartermaster
"	David D. Wadsworth	Sept. 1, '61	
Second Lieutenant	James E. Shields	April 24, '61	Promoted
"	Jeremiah B. Bailey	May 14, '61	
G.			
Captain	James W. Burgess	April 24, '61	Resigned Aug. 20, '61
"	John Tunnison	Sept. 6, '61	Dismissed for neglect of duty, Nov. 16, '62
First Lieutenant	John Tunnison	April 24, '61	Promoted
"	James Hubbard	Sept. 6, '61	Resigned Oct. 4, '61
"	Edward P. Boas	Oct. 4, '61	
Second Lieutenant	Cephas Williams	Nov. 9, '61	Resigned May 2, '62
H.			
Captain	Orton Frisbie	May 8, '61	Dismissed for neglect of duty, Nov. 16, '62
First Lieutenant	Frank Whiting	June 16, '61	Resigned Oct. 31, '61
"	Victor H. Stevens	Nov. 1, '61	
Second Lieutenant	John M. Powell	June 16, '61	Promoted to Co. F., 2d Art.
"	William Ware	Oct. 8, '61	
I.			
Captain	George H. Walser	April 22, '61	Resigned Nov. 3, '61
"	George W. Kennard	Jan. 1, '62	
First Lientenant	George E. King	April 22, '61	Resigned Feb. 5, '62
"	Rowland N. Evans	March 1, '62	
Second Lieutenant	John C. Tobias	April 22, '61	Resigned Jan. 30, '62
"	Charles Taylor	March 1, '62	
K.			
Captain	Reuben F. Dyer	April 24, '61	Resigned March 13, '62
"	John W. Boyer	March 13, '62	
First Lieutenant	Benjamin Olin	May 24, '61	Resigned Oct. 29, '61
Second Lieutenant	John R. McKean	April 24, '61	Died Jan. 23, '62
"	John W. Boyer	Jan. 22, '62	Promoted

SCHEDULE G—Continued.

Roster of the Twenty-First Regiment Illinois Volunteers.

Field and Staff.		Rank.	Remarks.
Colonel	Ulysus S. Grant........	June 15, '61 .	Promoted to Brig. Gener'l
"	J. W. S. Alexander.....	August 23, '61	....
Lieutenant Colonel	George W. Peck........	Sept. 2, '61..	Discharged on account ill
"	Warren E. McMaken....	Sept. 19, '62.	[health, Sept. 19, 1862.
Major...........	Warren E. McMaken....	Sept. 25, '61..	Promoted ....
"	James E. Calloway......	Sept. 19, '62.	....
Adjutant	C. B. Steele	Sept. 6, '61..	....
Quartermaster ...	John E. Jones	May 15, '61..	....
Surgeon.........	Eden M. Seeley	August 21, '62	....
1st Ass't Surgeon.	Carl Munz.............	Oct. 6, '61...	Died....................
"	Samuel B. Ten Brook...	Feb. 16, '62..	....
2d Ass't Surgeon .	John E. Link..........	Nov. 5, '62 .	....
Chaplain	Elias D. Wilkins........	Oct. 12, '61..	....

COMAPNY A.

Captain	Simon S. Goode........	May 7, '61...	State service...........
"	George S. Dunning	May 17, '61..	Resigned October 24, 1862
"	George F. Eaton	Oct. 24, '62..	....
First Lieutenant..	George F. Eaton	May 7, '61...	Promoted ....
"	Edward D. Coxe........	Oct. 24, '62 .	....
Second Lieutenant	Jacob L. Bowman......	May 7, '61...	Resigned April 14, 1862..
"	Edward D. Coxe........	April 14, '62.	Promoted ....
"	Joseph C. Alvord.....	Oct. 24, '62..	....

B.

Captain	Jesse P. H. Stevenson...	May 7, '61...	....
First Lieutenant..	Philip Wolshimer	May 7, '61...	....
Second Lieutenant	Charles L. Smeidell.....	May 7, '61...	....

C.

Captain	Josiah W. Clark	May 3, '61...	Resigned March 14, 1862..
"	William H. Jamison	March 14, '62	....
First Lieutenant..	William H. Jamison	May 3, '61...	Promoted ....
"	Walter B. Hoag........	March 14, '62	....
Second Lieutenant	Walter B. Hoag........	May 3, '61...	Promoted ....
"	Emanuel Weigle	March 14, '62	....

D.

Captain	James E. Calaway......	May 7, '61...	Major...................
"	Benjamin F. Reed	Sept. 19, '62 .	....
First Lieutenant..	Benjamin F. Reed	May 7, '61...	Promoted ....
"	Joel T. Kirkman........	Sept. 19, '62.	....
Second Lieutenant	Joel F. Kirkman........	May 7, '61...	Promoted ....
"	Isaiah S. Taylor........	Sept. 19, '62.	....

E.

Captain	John Love	May 9, '61...	....
First Lieutenant..	Alfred Thayer.........	May 9, '61...	....
"	John A. Freeland......	Oct. 26, '61..	....
Second Lieutenant	John A. Freeland, jr....	May 9, '61 ...	Promoted ....
"	Benjamin F. Davis......	Oct. 28, '61..	....

SCHEDULE G — Continued.

		Rank.	Remarks.

F.

Captain	John W. S. Alexander	May 8, '61	Colonel
"	Enoch N. Moody	May 17, '61	Resigned Nov. 1, '61
"	David S. Blackburn	Nov. 16, '61	
First Lieutenant	Joseph W. Vance	May 8, '61	
Second Lieutenant	David S. Blackburn	May 8, '61	Promoted
"	William J. Hunter	Nov. 16, '61	

G.

Captain	Joseph Maher	May 10, '61	Resigned Dec. 13, 1861
"	Andrew George	Dec. 13, '61	
First Lieutenant	Robert D. E. Easley	May 10, '61	Resigned Oct. 20, 1862
"	Abraham W. Songer	Oct. 20, '61	
Second Lieutenant	Abraham W. Songer	May 10, '61	
"	Robert L. Smith	Oct. 20, '62	

H.

Captain	Edwin Harlan	May 2, '61	
First Lieutenant	Nineoch S. McKeen	May 2, '61	
Second Lieutenant	Alanson G. Austin	May 2, '61	

I.

Captain	George W. Peck	May 7, '61	Promoted
"	Chester K. Knight	Sept. 6, '61	
First Lieutenant	Clark B. Lagou	May 7, '61	Resigned June 8, 1862
"	Charles Howe	June 8, '62	
Second Lieutenant	Chester K. Knight	May 7, '61	Promoted
"	John L. Cox	Dec. 21, 61	

K.

Captain	Abner M. Pattison	May 12, '61	Resigned Nov. 21, 1862
First Lieutenant	George A. Armstrong	May 12, '61	Resigned Nov. 20, 1861
"	John L. Wilson	Nov. 25, '61	
Second Lieutenant	John L. Wilson	May 12, '61	Promoted
"	Joseph B. Berry	Nov. 26, '61	

SCHEDULE G—Continued.

Roster of Twenty-Second Regiment Illinois Volunteers.

Field and Staff.		Rank.	Remarks.
Colonel	Henry Dougherty	May 20, 1861	
Lieutenant Colonel	Harrison E. Hart	May 20, 1861	Died.
"	Francis Swanwick	Aug. 4, 1862	
Major	Enadies Probst	May 20, 1861	Resigned Jan'y 16, 1862..
"	Francis Swanwick	Jan. 17, 1862	Promoted
"	George Abbott	Aug. 4, 1862	
Adjutant	Robert H. Cliff	Feb. 11, 1862	
Quartermaster	Charles M. Hamilton	June 17, 1862	
Surgeon	George Coatsworth	July 16, 1861	Resigned May 28, 1862...
"	Benjamin Woodward	Sept. 17, 1862	
1st Ass't Surgeon	John Fitzer	July 16, 1861	Resigned Nov. 2, 1861....
"	Benjamin Woodward	Jan. 1, 1862	Promoted.
"	Russell J. Collins	Aug. 6, 1862	
2d Ass't Surgeon	Isaac W. Brown	Dec. 21, 1862	
Chaplain	Thomas F. Houts	Sept. 20, 1861	Resigned, May 28, 1862...

COMPANY A.

Captain	Samuel Johnson	May 11, 1861	
First Lieutenant	Theodore Wiseman	June 17, 1861	Resigned for promotion...
"	Samuel T. Mahlhorn	Dec. 14, 1861	
Second Lieutenant	William S. Ford	June 17, 1861	

B.

Captain	John Seaton	May 24, 1861	Resigned June 13, '62....
"	James N. Morgan	June 13, 1862	
First Lieutenant	Robert H. Clift	May 24, 1861	Promoted
"	James N. Morgan	Feb. 11, 1862	Promoted
"	Frank H. Allen	June 13, 1862	Resigned as 2d Lieut. June
Second Lieutenant	James N. Morgan	May 24, 1861	Promoted........[28, '62
"	Frank H. Allen	Feb. 11, 1862	Promoted
"	Robert McKenzie	June 13, 1862	

C.

Captain	Guide W. Stierlin	June 24, 1861	Resigned June 21, '62....
"	Wm. A. Gregory	June 21, 1862	
First Lieutenant	Wm. A. Gregory	Aug. 7, 1861	Promoted
"	Andrew J. Walsh	June 22, 1862	
Second Lieutenant	George C. Stevens	Aug. 7, 1861	Resigned Jan. 24, '62....
"	Edward M. McCarty	Jan. 24, 1862	Resigned June 13, '62....
"	James T. Stansifer	June 13, 1862	

D.

Captain	James A. Hubbard	May 11, 1861	
First Lieutenant	Elias J. C. Alexander	May 11, 1861	Resigned Jan. 5, '62......
"	Lemuel Adams	Jan. 5, 1862	Resigned Nov. 7, '62.....
"	John H. Phillips	Nov. 7, 1862	
Second Lieutenant	Lemuel Adams	May 11, 1861	Promoted
"	Edward Stearns	Jan. 5, 1862	Resigned June 8, '62.....
"	John H. Phillips	June 8, 1862	Promoted
"	Cyrus M. Galloway	Nov. 7, 1862	

E.

Captain	Samuel G. McAdams	June 17, 1861	
First Lieutenant	Charles M. Hamilton	June 17, 1861	Quartermaster
"	George Gibson	Dec. 13, 1861	
Second Lieutenant	George Gibson	June 17, 1861	Promoted
"	James M. McAdams	Dec. 13, 1861	

Schedule G—Continued.

		Rank.	Remarks.
F.			
Captain	George Abbott.........	May 11, '61..	Promoted Major.........
"	Hermann Bornemann....	Aug. 4, '62..	
First Lieutenant..	Hermann Bornemann....	May 11, '61..	Promoted ....
" ..	John Frohlich	Aug. 4, '62..	
Second Lieutenant	John Frohlich	May 11, '61..	Promoted ....
"	George Schenermann....	Aug. 4, '62..	
G.			
Captain.........	James S. Jackson	May 21, '61..	
First Lieutenant..	Solomon Smith.........	May 21, '61..	
Second Lieutenant	Edward J. Jackson	May 21, '61..	Resigned Nov. 27, '61....
"	Joseph C. Murphy......	Nov. 27, '61..	Resigned July 15, '62.....
"	John R. Smith.........	July 15, '62..	
H.			
Captain.........	Francis Swanwick	May 11, '61..	Promoted Lieut. Colonel .
"	Harvey Nevill..........	Jan. 17, '62..	
First Lieutenant..	Harvey Nevill..........	May 11, '61..	Promoted ....
" ..	Cave Montague.........	Jan. 17, '62..	
Second Lieutenant	Cave Montague	Aug. 11, '62..	Promoted ....
"	Wesley R. Graves.......	Jan. 17, '62..	
I.			
Captain	John A. Detrich.........	May 11, '61..	Resigned May 11, '62.....
"	Milton A. French.......	May 11, '62..	
First Lieutenant..	Milton A. French.......	May 11, '61..	Promoted ....
" ..	Hugh C. McCormack....	May 11, '62..	Resigned June 28, '62....
" ..	Samuel B. Hood.........	June 28, '62..	
Second Lieutenant	Robert H. Livingston....	May 11, '61..	Resigned Dec. 14, '61....
"	Hugh C. McCormack....	Dec. 14, '61..	Promoted ....
"	Samuel B. Hood.........	May 11, '62..	Promoted ....
"	William L. Wilson......	June 28, '62..	
K.			
Captain	Thomas Challener	May 11, '61..	Resigned Aug. 31, '62....
"	James L. Buchanan.....	Aug. 31, '62..	
First Lieutenant:..	Hugh Watson	May 11, '61'..	Resigned Dec. 14, '61.....
"	Frank H. Allen.........	Dec. 14, '61..	Declined ....
"	James L. Buchanan.....	Dec. 14, '61..	Promoted ....
"	Anthony Young.........	Aug. 31, '62..	
Second Lieutenant	William M. Lewis.......	May 11, '61..	Resigned Dec. 24, '61....
"	Anthony Young	Dec. 24, '61..	Promoted ....
"	William Leishman......	Aug. 31, '62..	

Schedule G—Continued.

Roster of Twenty-Third Regiment Illinois Volunteers.

Field and Staff.		Rank.	Remarks.
Colonel	James A. Mulligan	June 15, '61.	
Lieutenant Colonel	James Quirk	June 15, '61.	
Major	Charles E. Moore	June 15, '61.	
Adjutant	James F. Cosgrove	June 15, '61.	
Quartermaster	Quin Morton	Sept. 10, '61.	Resigned Feb. 6, '62.
Surgeon	Wm. D. Winer	June 15, '61.	Resigned Dec. 4, '62
"	Patrick Gregg	Dec. 15, '62.	
1st Ass't Surgeon	John S. Taylor	Feb. 14, '62.	
2d Ass't Surgeon	Charles W. Stinson	Nov. 24, '62.	
Chaplain	Thaddeus J. Buler	June 15, '61.	
Company A.			
Captain	John McDermott	June 15, '61.	
First Lieutenant	Patrick J. McDermott	June 15, '61.	
Second Lieutenant	John Dailey	June 15, '61.	
B.			
Captain	Michael Gleeson	June 15, '61.	
First Lieutenant	Daniel W. Quirk	June 15, '61.	
Second Lieutenant	Edward Murray	June 15, '61.	
C.			
Captain	Francis McMurray	June 15, '61.	Died.
"	Robert Adams	Aug. 5, '61.	
First Lieutenant	Patrick Higgins	June 15, '61.	Dishonorably dismissed May 7, '62.
"	John Gilman	May 9, '62.	Resigned May 31, '62.
Second Lieutenant	Robert Adams	June 15, '61.	Promoted
"	John Gilman	Aug. 5, '61.	Promoted
"	James Nugent	May 9, '62.	
D.			
Captain	Samuel Simison	June 15, '61.	
First Lieutenant	Thomas McClure	June 15, '61.	
Second Lieutenant	James Hudson	June 15, '61.	
E.			
Captain	Franklin K. Hulburd	June 15, '61.	Died at Chicago
"	Henry Pease	May 10, '62.	
First Lieutenant	George D. Kellogg	June 15, '61.	Transferred to reg. army.
"	Daniel Matteson	May 24, '62.	Resigned Oct. 15, '62
"	John J. Healy	Oct. 15, '62.	
Second Lieutenant	Henry Pease	June 15, '61.	Promoted
"	Thomas Brennan	May 24, '62.	
F.			
Captain	David P. Moriarty	June 15, '61.	
First Lieutenant	Lawrence Collins	June 15, '61.	M. O. for pro. Feb. 6, '62.
Second Lieutenant	Patrick O'Cane	June 15, '61.	
G.			
Captain	John C. Phillips	June 15, '61.	Resigned April 10, '62.
"	Martin Wallace	April 8, '62.	
First Lieutenant	John A. Hines	June 15, '61.	
Second Lieutenant	Martin Wallace	June 15, '61.	Promoted
"	James Kume	April 8, '62.	

SCHEDULE G — Continued.

		Rank.	Remarks.
H.			
Captain	Charles Coffee	June 15, '61.	
First Lieutenant	Thomas Hickey	June 15, '61.	
Second Lieutenant	Thomas J. Rae	June 15, '61.	
I.			
Captain	James Fitzgerald	June 15, '61.	
First Lieutenant	Timothy L. Shanly	June 15, '61.	Transferred to 69th N. Y.; killed in battle Antietam.
"	Patrick J. Ryan	March 1, '62.	
Second Lieutenant	Patrick J. Ryan	June 15, '61.	Promoted
"	John G. Healy	March 1, '62.	Promoted Co. E
"	John Lanigan	Oct. 15, '62.	
K.			
Captain	Daniel Quirk	June 15, '61.	
First Lieutenant	James H. Lane	June 15, '61.	
Second Lieutenant	Owen Cunningham	June 15, '61.	Resigned Nov. 15, '61
"	Bartholomew Quirk	Dec. 1, '61.	

Schedule G—Continued.

Roster of Twenty-Fourth Regiment Illinois Volunteers.

Field and Staff.		Rank.	Remarks.
Colonel	Frederick Hecker	June 17, '61.	Resigned Dec. 23, '61
"	Geza Mihalotzy	Dec. 23, '61.	
Lieutenant Colonel	Geza Mihalotzy	June 17, '61.	Promoted
"	John Van Horn	Dec. 23, '61.	
Major	Julian Kune	June 17, '61.	Resigned October 31, '61
"	Julius Standan	Dec. 23, '61.	Resigned July 3, '62
"	George A. Guenther	July 3, '62.	
Adjutant	Henry Ramming	June 17, '61.	In Missouri regiment
"	Julian Pann	Nov. 1, '61.	
Quartermaster	Henry Wendt	June 17, '61.	
Surgeon	William Wagner	June 16, '61.	
1st Ass't Surgeon.	Carl Stock	June 17, '61.	Resigned March 3, '62
"	Jerome B. Thomas	March 3, '62.	
2d Ass't Surgeon.	Theodore Wild	Nov. 16, '62.	
Chaplain			

Company A.

Captain	Thomas Lang	April 15, '61.	Resigned October 31, '61
"	George A. Guenther	Dec. 1, '61.	Promoted Major
"	Alexander Je Kalfalury	July 3, '62.	
First Lieutenant.	August Gerhardi	April 15, '61.	Resigned October 31, '61
"	E. F. C. Klokke	Jan. 1, '62.	
Second Lieutenant	Jacob Poull	April 15, '61.	Promoted Co. D
"	Jacob Leiser	Sept. 3, '62.	

B.

Captain	George Heinrichs	Dec. 1, '61.	
First Lieutenant.	Julius Fritsch	Dec. 1, '61.	Resigned March 3, '62
"	Andreas Jacobi	March 3, '62.	
Second Lieutenant	Otto W. Block	Jan. 1, '62	Promoted Co. C
"	Eugene W. Lippert	July 10, '62.	

C.

Captain	Anthony Sten	June 17, '61.	Resigned July 10, '62
"	H. F. W. Blanke	July 10, '62.	
First Lieutenant.	Emil Frey	Jan. 1, '62.	Resigned June 17, '62
"	Otto W. Block	July 10, '62.	
Second Lieutenant	H. F. W. Blanke	June 17, '61.	Promoted to Co. H
"	Albert Mauns	Jan. 1, '62.	Resigned August 12, '62
"	Edward Lohmann	Aug. 12, '62.	

D.

Captain	Leopold Becker	April 30, '61.	Resigned and reinstated
First Lieutenant.	Aloyo Mayer	Jan. 1, '62.	Resigned September 3, '62
"	Jacob Poull	Sept. 3, '62.	
Second Lieutenant	Rupert Russ	Jan. 1, '62.	Resigned August 13, '62
"	William Vocke	Aug. 18, '62.	

E.

Captain	August Mauff	June 5, '61.	
First Lieutenant.	Gustav A. Busse	June 5, '61.	Resigned October 31, '61
"	George Gunther	Jan. 1, '62.	Resigned June 17, '62
"	Frank Schweinfurth	June 17, '62.	
Second Lieutenant	Ernst F. C. Klokke	June 5, '61.	Resigned October 31, '61
"	Ami Smith	Jan. 1, '62.	Died Oct. 15, '62, in hospi-
"	Charles Friedrich	Oct. 15, '62.	[tal, Bowling Green, Ky.

Schedule G — Continued.

		Rank.	Remarks.
F.			
Captain	Augustus Kovats	June 22, '61.	Resigned October 31, '61..
First Lieutenant	Alexander Je Kalfalury	June 29, '61.	Promoted Capt. Co. A....
"	Hugo Gerhardt	July 3, '62.	
Second Lieutenant	Andreas Jacobi	June 22, '61.	Promoted to Co. B
"	Hugo Gerhardt	March 3, '62.	Promoted
"	Ernst Wilhelmi	July 3, '62.	
G.			
Captain	Julius Standan	July 8, '61.	Promoted
"	Augustus Gerhardy	Jan. 1, '62.	Resigned November 16, '62
First Lieutenant	George A. Guenther	July 8, '61.	Promoted to Co. A
"	Peter Hand	Dec. 1, '61.	Promoted to Co. K
"	Edward Bornemann	June 29, '62.	
Second Lieutenant	Peter Hand	July 8, '61.	Promoted
"	Edward Bornemann	Jan. 1, '62.	Promoted
"	August Bitter	June 29, '62.	
H.			
Captain	John Van Horn	June 15, '61.	Promoted
"	Frederick Hartman	Dec. 5, '61.	Died November 10, '62...
"	Herman H. Hinz	Nov. 10, '62.	
First Lieutenant	H. F. W. Blanke	Dec. 1, '61.	Promoted
"	Arthur Erbe	July 10, '62.	
Second Lieutenant	Arthur Erbe	Jan. 1, '62.	Promoted
"	Moritz Kaufman	July 10, '62.	
I.			
Captain	Henry J. Reed	June 16, '61.	Resigned October 31, '62..
"	George W. Fuchs	Dec. 1, '61.	Resigned March 1, '62....
"	August Steffens	March 1, '62.	
First Lieutenant	George W. Fuchs	June 16, '61.	Promoted
"	Hermann H. Hinz	Dec. 1, '61.	Promoted Captain Co. H..
"	S. Peter Hammerich	Nov. 10, '62.	
Second Lieutenant	Hermann H. Hinz	June 16, '61.	Promoted to Co. K
"	Francis Langelfeld	Jan. 1, '62.	Promoted
"	S. Peter Hammerich	March 1, '62.	Promoted
"	Julius Reichardt	Nov. 10, '62.	
K.			
Captain	Ferd'nd H. Rohlshausen	July 8, '61.	Resigned June 29, '62....
"	Peter Hand	June 29, '62.	
First Lieutenant	August Steffers	Dec. 1, '61.	Promoted
"	Francis Langelfeld	March 1, '62.	
Second Lieutenant	Frank Schweinfurth	Jan. 1, '62.	Promoted to Co. E
"	Charles Fritze	June 17, '62.	

Schedule G—Continued.

Roster of Twenty-Fifth Regiment Illinois Volunteers.

Field and Staff.		Rank.	Remarks.
Colonel	William N. Coler	Aug. 7, '61	Resigned Aug. 31, '62
"	Thomas D. Williams	Aug. 31, '62	
Lieutenant Colonel	James S. McClelland	Aug. 7, '61	
Major	Richard H. Nodine	Aug. 7, '61	
Adjutant	James D. Ellington	Aug. 7, '61	Resigned Dec. 23, '61
"	George W. Flynn	Dec. 23, '61	
Quartermaster	Caswell P. Ford	Aug. 7, '61	
Surgeon	Henry C. Winans	Sept. 1, '61	Resigned Dec. 20, '61
"	Joseph Blount	Jan. 15, '62	
1st Ass't Surgeon	Robert H. Brown	Nov. 1, '61	
2d Ass't Surgeon	Myron S. Brown	Aug. 13, '62	
Chaplain	Philip N. Minear	Aug. 7, '61	Resigned July 11, '62
"	Hiram H. Ashmore	July 11, '62	
Company A.			
Captain	Charles A. Clark	July 22, '61	Died Nov. 28, '62
"	Samuel Mitchell	Nov. 28, '62	
First Lieutenant	Theodore A. West	July 22, '62	
Second Lieutenant	Samuel Mitchell	July 22, '61	Promoted
"	Achilles Martin	Nov. 28, '62	
B.			
Captain	Samuel D. Wall	June 8, '61	
First Lieutenant	Thomas J. McKibbin	June 8, '61	
Second Lieutenant	E. Mosely Wright	June 8, '61	Resigned Feb. 17, '62
"	Joseph C. Grundy	Feb. 17, '62	
C.			
Captain	Charles A. Summers	Aug. 1, '61	Resigned April 3, '62
"	Zebulon Hall	April 3, '62	
First Lieutenant	Zebulon Hall	Aug. 1, '61	Promoted
"	Edward Hall	April 3, '62	
Second Lieutenant	Edward Hall	Aug. 1, '61	Promoted
"	Martin B. Thompson	April 3, '62	
D.			
Captain	William Osborn	Aug. 7, '61	Resigned Dec. 27, '62
First Lieutenant	Allen Varner	June 1, '61	
Second Lieutenant	Lyons Parker	June 1, '61	
E.			
Captain	Westford Taggert	June 1, '61	
First Lieutenant	William J. Sallie	June 1, '61	
Second Lieutenant	Thomas W. Brazelton	June 1, '61	
F.			
Captain	Ray W. Andrews	May 29, '61	Resigned Nov. 21, '62
"	John Smart	Nov. 21, '62	
First Lieutenant	Bellis H. Skeels	May 29, '61	Resigned Sept. 3, '62
"	John Smart	Sept. 3, '62	Promoted
"	James P. Martin	Nov. 21, '62	
Second Lieutenant	James P. Martin	May 29, '61	Promoted
"	Alexander H. South	Nov. 21, '62	

SCHEDULE G—Continued.

		Rank.	Remarks.

G.

Captain	Thomas D. Williams	Aug. 7, '61	Promoted Colonel
First Lieutenant	John F. Isom	Aug. 7, '62	
Second Lieutenant	John J. Hickman	Aug. 7, '61	Resigned Jan. 10, '62
"	Andrew J. Lake	Jan. 10, '61	Resigned Aug. 4, '62
"	Samuel Dickson	Aug. 4, '62	

H.

Captain	William Brian	July 20, '61	Resigned Dec. 30, '61
"	Benjamin F. Ford	Nov. 7, '61	
First Lieutenant	Allen Buckner	July 20, '61	Resigned June 13, '62
"	Henry C. Paddock	July 8, '62	Resigned Nov. 14, '62
"	Joshua H. Hastings	Nov. 14, '62	
Second Lieutenant	Archibald VanDeren	July 20, '61	Resigned July 15, '62
"	Joshua H. Hastings	July 15, '62	Promoted
"	John Scott	Nov. 14, '62	

I.

Captain	Samuel Houston	July 31, '61	
First Lieutenant	William W. Brown	July 31, '61	Resigned Dec. 27, '62
Second Lieutenant	Julius H. Brown	July 31, '61	Resigned Dec. 12, '61
"	Everett J. Knapp	Dec. 12, '61	

K.

Captain	Ezekiel Boyden	June 1, '61	Resigned Dec. 17, '62
First Lieutenant	Benjamin Burt	June 1, '61	Resigned July 15, '62
"	Guy D. Penfield	July 15, '62	
Second Lieutenant	George W. Flynn	June 1, '61	Promoted Adjutant
"	George N. Richards	Dec. 23, '61	Resigned June 20, '62
"	Edward L. Sherman	June 20, '62	

Schedule G—Continued.

Roster of Twenty-Sixth Regiment Illinois Volunteers.

Field and Staff.		Rank.	Remarks.
Colonel	John M. Loomis	Aug. 9, '61	
Lieutenant Colonel	Charles J. Tinkham	Aug. 29, '61	Resigned Oct. 7, '62
"	Robert A. Gilmore	Oct. 7, '62	
Major	Robert A. Gilmore	Aug. 29, '61	Promoted
"	John B. Harris	Oct. 7, '62	
Adjutant	Samuel A. Buckmaster, jr	Aug. 29, '61	Resigned April 15, '62
"	Edward A. Tucker	April 15, '62	
Quartermaster	Charles A. Nazra	Aug. 29, '61	Resigned June 18, '62
"	Charles E. Spring	June 18, '62	
Surgeon	Morse K. Taylor	Aug. 29, '61	Promoted Hospital Surgeon Aug. 8, '62
"	James C. Whitehill	Oct. 10, '62	
1st Ass't Surgeon.	Ezra A. Steele	Aug. 29, '61	Resigned Oct. 22, '62
2d Ass't Surgeon.	Charles Woodward	Oct. 11, '62	
Chaplain	Andrew B. Morrison	Feb. 16, '62	
COMPANY A.			
Captain	John J. Funkhouser	Aug. 10, '61	Resigned Nov. 24, '61
"	Benjamin F. Helm	Nov. 24, '61	
First Lieutenant	Sidney A. Newcomb	Aug. 10, '61	Resigned June 3, '62
"	Samuel N. King	June 3, '62	
Second Lieutenant	David P. Murphy	Aug. 10, '61	Resigned Jan. 12, '62
"	Samuel N. King	Jan. 12, '62	Promoted
"	Charles E. Linsley	June 3, '62	
B.			
Captain	James P. Davis	Aug. 28, '61	
First Lieutenant	George H. Reed	Aug. 28, '61	
Second Lieutenant	William Polk	Aug. 28, '61	
C.			
Captain	George U. Keener	Aug. 23, '61	Resigned April 1, '62
"	James A. Dugger	April 1, '62	
First Lieutenant	Thomas L. Vest	Aug. 23, '61	Resigned Feb. 20, '62
"	James A. Dugger	Feb. 20, '62	Promoted
"	Owen W. Walls	April 1, '62	
Second Lieutenant	James A. Dugger	Aug. 23, '61	Promoted
"	Edwin B. Wise	Feb. 20, '62	Resigned Nov. 18, '62
D.			
Captain	John B. Harris	Oct. 22, '61	Promoted
First Lieutenant	William W. Foutch	Aug. 27, '61	Died
"	George W. Kerlin	Sept. 26, '61	
Second Lieutenant	George W. Kerlin	Aug. 27, '61	Promoted
"	Calvin A. Peace	Sept. 26, 61	
E.			
Captain	Amos F. Jaquis	Aug. 15, '61	
First Lieutenant	Azro C. Putnam	Aug. 15, '61	Resigned Sept. 8, '62
"	John S. Lathrop	Sept. 8, '62	
Second Lieutenant	John S. Lathrop	Aug. 15, '61	Promoted
"	Ralph W. Buchanan	Sept. 8, '62	

SCHEDULE G—Continued.

		Rank.	Remarks.

F.

Captain	Charles J. Tinkham	Aug. 10, '61	Promoted Lieut. Colonel
"	John H. Folks	Aug. 24, '61	
First Lieutenant	George H. Knapp	Aug. 24, '61	Discharged July 14, '62
"	Samuel M. Custer	July 14, '62	
Second Lieutenant	Samuel M. Custer	Aug. 24, '61	Promoted
"	Ezekiel S. Cusick	July 14, '62	

G.

Captain	Thaddeus S. Updegraff	Aug. 23, '61	Resigned Aug. 31, '62
"	Bernard Flynn	Aug. 31, '62	
First Lieutenant	Bernard Flynn	Aug. 23, '61	Promoted
"	John Irwin	Aug. 31, '62	
Second Lieutenant	Joseph C. Baldwin	Aug. 23, '61	Resigned Feb. 4, '62
"	Orlando B. Howe	Feb. 4, '62	Mustered out July 9, '62
"	Joshua Ritter	July 9, '62	

H.

Captain	Andrew B. Morrison	Jan. 1, '62	Chaplain
"	Washington W. Woollard	Feb. 16, '62	Resigned Nov. 1, '62
"	James E. Merriman	Nov. 1, '62	
First Lieutenant	Washington W. Woollard	Dec. 17, '61	Promoted
"	Charles F. Wertz	Feb. 16, '62	
Second Lieutenant	Charles F. Wertz	Jan. 1, '62	Promoted
"	James E. Merriman	Feb. 16, '62	Promoted

I.

Captain	Washington C. Cassell	Jan. 29, '62	
First Lieutenant	John Archer	Jan. 29, '62	
Second Lieutenant	John W. Kelly	Jan. 29, '62	

K.

Captain	Ira J. Bloomfield	Jan. 28, '62	
First Lieutenant	Allen H. Dillon	Jan. 28, '62	Resigned Sept. 3, '62
Second Lieutenant	John B. Bruner	Jan. 28, '62	

Schedule G—Continued.

Roster of Twenty-Seventh Regiment Illinois Volunteers.

Field and Staff.		Rank.	Remarks.
Colonel.........	Napoleon B. Buford....	Aug. 10, '61.	Promoted Brig. Gen. April
"	Fazillo A. Harrington...	April 16, '62.	................[15, '62
Lieutenant Colonel	Fazillo A. Harrington...	Aug. 10, '61.	Promoted ....
"	Jonathan R. Miles	April 16, '62.	
Major......	Hall Wilson	Aug. 10, '61.	Promoted Col. 5th Cavalry
"	Jonathan R. Miles......	Dec. 18, '61..	Promoted ....
"	William A. Schmitt.....	April 15, '62.	
Adjutant........	Henry A. Rust.........	April 12, '61.	Promoted Captain Co. "F"
"	Simeon Sheldon.	Nov. 1, '62.	
Quartermaster ...	David B. Sears.........	Aug. 10, '61.	
Surgeon.........	Edward H. Bowman....	Sept. 11, '61.	
1st Ass't Surgeon.	Henry C. Barrell	Aug. 26, '61..	
2d Ass't Surgeon.			
Chaplain	S. Young McMasters....	Sept. 4, '61..	
Company A.			
Captain	William A. Schmitt....	Aug. 21, '61.	Promoted ....
"	Mathew Jansen.........	Aug. 16, '62.	
First Lieutenant..	William Shipley........	Aug. 21, '61.	Died.................
" ..	Joseph Voellinger......	Nov. 8, '61.	
Second Lieutenant	Joseph Voellinger......	Aug. 21, '61.	Promoted ....
"	Mathew Jansen.........	Nov. 8, '61..	Promoted ....
"	John A. Schmitt	April 16, '62.	
B.			
Captain	Henry W. Hitt	Aug. 12, '61.	Resigned June 11, '62....
"	Robert P. Lytle	June 11, '62.	
First Lieutenant..	George A. Dunlap......	Aug. 12, '61.	Resigned Nov. 16, '61...
"	Robert P. Lytle	Nov. 16, '61..	Promoted ....
" ..	Henry H. White........	Oct. 21, '62..	
Second Lieutenant	James M. Buchanan....	Aug. 12, '61.	Resigned Oct. 21, '61....
"	Duncan McCormick.....	Nov. 8, '61..	Resigned June 20, '61....
"	Richard A. Carwith.....	June 20, '62..	
C.			
Captain	Lemuel Parke..........	April 8, '61..	Resigned April 27, '62....
"	Lyman G. Allen........	April 27, '62.	Resigned Nov. 30, 62....
"	Laommi F. Williams....	Nov. 30, '62..	
First Lieutenant..	Lyman G. Allen........	Aug. 8, '61...	Promoted ....
" ..	Laommi F. Williams....	April 27, '62.	Promoted ....
" ..	Andrew J. Sides........	Nov. 30, '62..	
Second Lieutenant	Laommi F. Williams....	Aug. 8, '61...	Promoted ....
"	Andrew J. Sides........	April 27, '62.	Promoted ....
"	William B. Browning...	Nov. 30, '62..	
D.			
Captain	William N. Hart........	Aug. 23, '61..	Resigned Nov. 28, '61....
"	Horace Chapin.........	Nov. 28, '61..	
First Lieutenant..	Robert R. Murphy......	Aug. 23, '61..	
Second Lieutenant	John W. Brock.........	Aug. 23, '61..	
E.			
Captain	Robert S. Moore	Aug. 13, '61..	Promoted Colonel 85th...
"	William W. Stout......	Aug. 27, '62..	
First Lieutenant..	William W. Stout......	Aug. 13, '61..	Promoted ....
" ..	Royal W. Porter	Aug. 27, '62..	
Second Lieutenant	Royal W. Porter........	Aug. 13, '61..	Promoted ....
"	Isaac W. Chatfield......	Aug. 27, '62..	

SCHEDULE G — Continued.

		Rank.	Remarks.
F.			
Captain	Jonathan R. Miles	Aug. 10, '61.	Promoted Major
"	Thomas C. Meatyard	Jan. 1, '62	Resigned June 18, '62
"	Henry A. Rust	June 18, '62.	
First Lieutenant	Thomas C. Meatyard	Aug. 10, '61.	Promoted
"	Orson Hewitt	Jan. 1, '62	
Second Lieutenant	Orson Hewitt	Aug. 10, '61.	Promoted
"	Edward B. Meatyard	Jan. 1, '62	Resigned July 3, '62
"	John F. Glenn	July 3, '62	
G.			
Captain	Henry B. Southward	Aug. 23, '61.	
First Lieutenant	Simeon Sheldon	Aug. 23, '61.	Promoted Adjutant
"	Hugh M. Love	Nov. 1, '62.	
Second Lieutenant	Robert P. Lytle	Aug. 23, '61.	Promoted Co. B
"	George R. Beardsley	Jan. 1, '62	Resigned Oct. 26, '62
"	Hugh M. Love	Oct. 27, '62.	Promoted
"	Samuel Gideon	Nov. 1, '62	
H.			
Captain	McHenry Brooks	Aug. 28, '61.	
First Lieutenant	Frederick C. Bierer	Aug. 28, '61.	
Second Lieutenant	Daniel Worthen	Aug. 28, '61.	
I.			
Captain	Joseph W. Merrill	Aug. 28, '61.	
First Lieutenant	Thomas Sumner	Aug. 28, '61.	Resigned March 1, '62
"	John A. Russell	March 1, '62.	Resigned April 5, '62
"	Charles Grow	April 3, '62.	
Second Lieutenant	John A. Russell	Sept. 28, '61.	Promoted
"	Charles Grow	March 1, 62.	Promoted
"	William S. Bryan	April 3, '62.	
K.			
Captain	Abraham T. Bozarth	Aug. 22, '61.	
First Lieutenant	Horace Chapin	Aug. 22, '61.	Promoted Captain of D
"	Erastus S. Jones	Nov. 28, '61.	
Second Lieutenant	Erastus S. Jones	Aug. 22, '61.	Promoted
"	Lewis Hanback	Nov. 28, '61.	

Schedule G—Continued.

Roster of Twenty-Eighth Regiment Illinois Volunteers.

Field and Staff.		Rank.	Remarks.
Colonel..........	Amory K. Johnson.....	Sept. 21, '61..	....
Lieutenant Colonel	Louis H. Waters........	Aug. 22, '61..	Resigned Jan. 10, '62.....
" "	Thomas M. Killpatrick...	Jan. 10, '62..	Killed in battle at Shiloh..
" "	Richard Ritter.........	April 21, '62..	....
Major...........	Charles J. Sellon.......	Aug. 22, '61..	Resigned Jan. 8, '62.....
" "	Barclay C. Gillam......	Jan. 8, '62...	Resigned Nov. 21, '62....
" "	Hinman Rhodes.........	Nov. 21, '62...	....
Adjutant........	John B. T. Mead........	Aug. 27, '61..	Died Ap'l 21, '62, of wounds
" "	Thomas A. Ralston......	April 21, '62.	received at Shiloh.....
Quartermaster....	Hugh Ervin.............	Aug. 27, '61..	Resigned Jan. 31, '62....
" "	Arthur G. Burr.........	Feb. 1, '62...	....
Surgeon.........	James Bringhurst.......	Sept. 20, '61.	Resigned May 15, '62.....
" "	William F. West........	May 15, '62...	....
1st Ass't Surgeon.	William F. West........	Sept. 21, '61.	Promoted ....
" " "	John Kemper............	May 15, '62...	....
2d Ass't Surgeon.	....	....	....
Chaplain........	Bradley Hungerford.....	Sept. 4, '61..	....

Company A.

Captain..........	Richard Ritter..........	Aug. 2, '61...	Promoted Lieut. Colonel..
" "	James R. Walker........	April 21, '62.	....
First Lieutenant..	James R. Walker........	Aug. 2, '61...	Promoted ....
" "	William W. Noonan....	April 21, '62.	....
Second Lieutenant	Carl Reichman..........	Aug. 2, '61...	Resigned Nov. 14, '62....

B.

Captain..........	Thomas H. Butler.......	Aug. 20, '61.	Died....................
" "	George W. Stobie.......	Nov. 22, '61..	....
First Lieutenant..	Thomas Thompson......	Aug. 20, '61.	....
Second Lieutenant	George Stobie..........	Aug. 20, '61.	Promoted ....
" "	David C. Troutner......	Nov. 22, '61..	Died....................
" "	Cyrus K. Miller........	Aug. 20, 62..	....

C.

Captain..........	John H. Browne........	Aug. 10, '61.	....
First Lieutenant..	George W. P. Ebey.....	Aug. 10, '61.	Discharged for promotion.
" "	Ira Merchant	July 28, '62..	....
Second Lieutenant	Francis M. Springer.....	Aug. 10, '61.	Resigned Nov. 20, '61....
" "	Ira Merchant...........	Nov. 20, '61.	Promoted ....
" "	Charles C. Belford......	July 28, '62..	Killed at Hatchie........
" "	William J. Garland.....	Oct. 19, '62..	....

D

Captain..........	Louis H. Waters........	Aug. 10, '61.	Promoted Lieut. Colonel..
" "	Gladden L. Farwell.....	Aug. 27, '61	....
First Lieutenant..	Arthur G. Burr.........	Aug. 10, '61.	Promoted Quartermaster..
" "	John B. Pearson........	Feb. 1, '62...	....
Second Lieutenant	John B. Pearson........	Aug. 10, '61.	Promoted ....
" "	Charles Conover........	Feb. 1, '62...	....

E.

Captain..........	Thomas M. Killpatrick...	Aug. 23, '61.	Promoted Lieut. Colonel..
" "	John M. Griffin.........	Jan. 10, '62..	....
First Lieutenant..	John M. Griffin.........	Aug. 23, '61.	Promoted ....
" "	Fred. C. Bechdoldt.....	Jan. 10, '62..	....
Second Lieutenant	Burrell McPherson......	Aug. 23, '61.	....

Schedule G — Continued.

		Rank.	Remarks.

F.

Captain	William J. Estill	Aug. 15, '61	
First Lieutenant	Isaac B. Estill	Aug. 15, '61	
Second Lieutenant	Thomas Swaringuin	Aug. 15, '61	

G.

Captain	Barclay C. Gillum	Aug. 15, '61	Promoted Major
"	Oregon Richmond	Jan. 8, '62	Resigned March 14, '62
"	Reuben B. Presson	March 14, '62	
First Lieutenant	Oregon Richmond	Aug. 15, '61	Promoted
"	Reuben B. Presson	Jan. 8, '62	Promoted
"	Elias G. W. Bridgewater	March 14, '62	
Second Lieutenant	Reuben B. Presson	Aug. 15, '61	Promoted
"	Michael Gapin	Jan. 8, '62	

H.

Captain	Hinman Rhodes	Aug. 17, '61	Promoted Major
First Lieutenant	Isaiah Denness	Aug. 17, '61	
Second Lieutenant	Thomas A. Ralston	Aug. 17, '61	Promoted Adjutant
"	Edwin P. Durell	April 21, '62	

I.

Captain	Elisha Hurt	Aug. 25, '61	
First Lieutenant	Philip S. Likes	Aug. 25, '61	Resigned Oct. 29, '62
"	David Dixon	Oct. 29, '62	
Second Lieutenant	David Dixon	Aug. 25, '61	Promoted
"	Henry L. Hadsell	Oct. 29, '62	

K.

Captain	William R. Roberts	Aug. 12, '61	Resigned Dec. 31, '61
First Lieutenant	John Brewsaugh	Aug. 12, '61	Resigned Nov. 9, '61
"	Frederick Garternicht	Nov. 19, '61	Resigned Jan. 25, '62
"	John B. Newton	Jan. 25, '62	
Second Lieutenant	John B. Newton	Aug. 12, '61	Promoted
"	Albert G. Moses	Jan. 25, '62	

Schedule G—Continued.

Roster of Twenty-Ninth Regiment Illinois Volunteers.

Field and Staff.		Rank.	Remarks.
Colonel	James S. Rearden	Aug. 11, '61.	Resigned April 15, '62....
"	Mason Brayman	April 15, '62.	Promoted Brig. Gen. Sept.
"	Charles M. Ferrill	Sept. 24, '62.	[24, '62.
Lieutenant Colonel	James E. Dunlap	Aug. 27, '61.	Resigned March 14, '62...
"	Charles M. Ferrill	March 14, '62	Promoted
"	Loren Kent	Sept. 25, '62.	
Major	Mason Brayman	Aug. 29, '61.	Promoted Colonel
"	John A. Callicott	April 15, '62.	
Adjutant	Aaron R. Stout	Sept. 21, '61.	Resigned Nov. 20, '61....
"	Loren Kent	Dec. 1, '61.	Promoted Lieut. Colonel..
"	Richard M. Bozman	Sept. 25, '62.	
Quartermaster	Ebenezer Z. Ryan	Sept. 4, '61.	Resigned March 4, '62....
"	James A. Whiteside	March 4, '62.	
Surgeon	Charles C. Guard	Sept. 25, '61.	Died April 4, '62
"	Jared W. Tuttle	April 25, '62.	Resigned Oct. 31, '62.....
1st Ass't Surgeon.	Samuel L. Cheaney	March 16, '62	
2d Ass't Surgeon.			
Chaplain	Zenas S. Clifford	Aug. 30, '61.	

Company A.

Captain	Charles M. Ferrell	Aug. 19, '61.	Promoted Lieut. Col.....
"	Philip J. Howard	March 14, '62	
First Lieutenant	David R. Jones	Aug. 19, '61.	Resigned May 20, '62....
"	Lorenzo D. Martin	May 20, '62.	Resigned Sept. 17, '62....
Second Lieutenant	Lorenzo D. Martin	Aug. 19, '61.	Promoted
"	Daniel H. Smith	July 1, '62...	

B.

Captain	George W. McKenzie	Aug. 12, '61.	Resigned May 16, '62....
"	Charles H. Call	May 16, '62.	
First Lieutenant	John D. Jamison	Aug. 12, '61	Resigned March 14, '62 ..
"	Charles H. Call	March 14, '62	Promoted
"	George C. Gentry	May 15, '62.	
Second Lieutenant	George C. Jamison	Aug. 12, '61.	Resigned March 14, '62 ..
"	George C. Gentry	March 14, '62	Promoted
"	Richard A. Kent	Dec. 6, '62 ..	

C.

Captain	John A. Callicott	Aug. 15, '61.	Promoted Major
"	Eli W. Green	July 14, '62..	
First Lieutenant	John M. Eddy	Aug. 15, '61.	Resigned April 18, '62....
"	Thomas Rieling	July 14, '62..	
Second Lieutenant	Alfred DeWitt	Aug. 15, '61.	Died
"	William Boswell	March 1, '62.	Died April 6, '62
"	Sanford B. Kanady	Dec. 6, '62...	

D.

Captain	John S. Whiting	Aug. 20, '61.	Resigned March 4, '62....
"	James B. Hart	March 4, '62.	Resigned Oct. 25, '62....
"	Eberlee P. H. Stone	Oct. 25, '62.	
First Lieutenant	James B. Hart	Aug. 20, '61.	Promoted
"	Benjamin F. Berry	March 4, '62.	Dismissed
"	Samuel Bagsley	Nov. 1, '62.	
Second Lieutenant	Eberlee P. H. Stone	Aug. 20, '61.	Promoted
"	Pinkney B. Harris	Nov. 1, '62...	

Schedule G—Continued.

		Rank.	Remarks.
E.			
Captain	William H. Parish	Sept. 14, '61.	Resigned Oct. 26, '61....
"	William W. Burnett	Nov. 15, '61.	Died April 6, '62........
"	John Page Mitchell	April 9, '62..	....
First Lieutenant..	William Choisser	Aug. 20, '61.	....
Second Lieutenant	William W. Burnett	Sept. 14, '61.	Promoted ....
"	Richard M. Burnett	Nov. 15, '61.	....
F.			
Captain	James Roper	Sept. 9, '61..	Resigned May 16, '62.....
"	Edward Pendergast	May 16, '62,.	....
First Lieutenant..	Peter Belford	Sept. 9, '61..	....
Second Lieutenant	Richard M. Bozman	Aug. 17, '61.	Promoted Adjutant......
G.			
Captain	Solomon S. Brill	Aug. 28, '61.	....
First Lieutenant..	Henry Wakefield	Aug. 28, '61.	Resigned June 4, '62.....
"	Robert F. Stewart	Aug. 1, '62..	....
Second Lieutenant	Theodore Millspaugh	Aug. 28, '61.	Resigned July 13, '62.....
"	William J. Gossett	Aug. 1, '62..	....
H.			
Captain	Jason B. Sprague	Aug. 24, '61.	Killed in battle April 6, '62
"	Robert H. Collins	April 6, '62..	....
First Lieutenant..	Abner Hostetter	Aug. 24, '61.	Died March 29, '62......
"	Spencer Maynard	May 5, '62...	....
Second Lieutenant	William H. Stewart	Aug. 24, '61.	Resigned March 4, '62....
I.			
Captain	Augustus O. Millington	Sept. 14, '61.	Mustered out Nov. 13, '62.
"	Samuel H. Russell	Oct. 14, '62.	....
First Lieutenant..	Marshall M. McIntire	Sept. 14, '61.	Killed at Ft. Donelson....
"	Samuel H. Russell	Feb. 15, '62..	Promoted ....
"	Truman S. Post	Oct. 14, '62.	....
Second Lieutenant	Samuel H. Russell	Sept. 14, '61.	Promoted ....
"	Truman S. Post	Feb. 15, '62..	Promoted ....
K.			
Captain	John A. Carmichael	Aug. 17, '61.	Resigned May 27, '62 ....
"	Elijah P. Curtis	May 27, '62..	....
First Lieutenant..	Elijah P. Curtis	Aug. 17, '61.	Promoted ....
"	William T. Day	May 27, '62..	....
Second Lieutenant	William T. Day	Aug. 17, '61.	Promoted ....
"	Tenderson P. Smith	May 27, '62..	....

Schedule G — Continued.

Roster of Thirtieth Regiment Illinois Volunteers.

Field and Staff.		Rank.	Remarks.
Colonel	Philip B. Fouke	Aug. 28, '61	Resigned April 22, '62
"	Elias S. Dennis	April 21, '62	
Lieutenant Colonel	Elias S. Dennis	Aug. 28, '61	Promoted
"	George A. Bacon	April 22, '62	Resigned Oct. 8, '62
"	Warren Shedd	Oct. 8, '62	
Major	Thomas McClurken	Aug. 28, '61	Killed in battle of Belmont
"	George A. Bacon	Nov. 25, '61	Promoted
"	Warren Shedd	April 22, '62	Promoted
"	William C. Rhoads	Oct. 8, '62	
Adjutant	George A. Bacon	Aug. 28, 61	Promoted
"	Hiram H. Peyton	Feb. 16, '62	
Quartermaster	William Busbyshell	Aug. 28, '61	
Surgeon	William A. Gordon	Aug. 28, '61	Mustered out July 25, '62.
"	David N. Moore	July 25, '62	
1st Ass't Surgeon	John J. Turner	Sept. 27, '61	Died
"	William Feland	Oct. 1, '61	
2d Ass't Surgeon			
Chaplain	Williamson F. Boyakin	Aug. 28, '61	Resigned Aug. 21, '62
"	Williamson F. Boyakin	Aug. 31, '62	

Company A.

Captain	Warren Shedd	Aug. 28, '61	Promoted Major
"	Francis G. Burnett	April 22, '62	Resigned Sept. 3, '62
First Lieutenant	Nathaniel R. Kirkpatrick	Aug. 28, '61	Killed battle Ft. Donelson
"	Francis G. Burnett	Feb. 15, '62	Promoted
"	Elijah B. David	April 22, '62	
Second Lieutenant	Francis G. Burnett	Aug. 28, '61	Promoted
"	Elijah B. David	Feb. 15, '62	Promoted

B.

Captain	John P. Davis	Aug. 28, '61	
First Lieutenant	William R. Goodell	Aug. 28, '61	
Second Lieutenant	William Huffmaster	Aug. 28, '61	Resigned May 5, '62
"	Addison L. Page	May 5, '62	

C.

Captain	James R. Wilson	Aug. 28, '61	
First Lieutenant	Alexander M. Wilson	Aug. 28, '61	
Second Lieutenant	Alfred Parks	Aug. 28, '61	Resigned Jan. 28, '62
"	William M. Adair	Jan. 28, '62	

D.

Captain	Thomas G. Marckley	Aug. 28, '61	Killed at Belmont
"	Michael Langton	Nov. 27, '61	Resigned Oct. 22, '62
First Lieutenant	Michael Langton	April 28, '61	Promoted
"	Paterson Sharp	Jan. 28, '62	
Second Lieutenant	George L. Gordon	Aug. 28, '61	Resigned Jan. 28, '62
"	George E. Meily	Jan. 28, '62	

E.

Captain	John C. Johnson	Feb. 6, '62	
First Lieutenant	Benjamin H. Kline	Aug. 28, '61	Resigned Feb. 3, '62
"	J. K. Pearson	Feb. 20, '62	
Second Lieutenant	John C. Johnson	Aug. 28, '61	Promoted
"	Henry Beck	Feb. 6, '62	

SCHEDULE G—Continued.

		Rank.	Remarks.
F.			
Captain	Cyrus A. Bradshaw	Sept. 7, '61	Mustered out March 24,'62
"	John W. Martin	March 24, '62	
First Lieutenant	Alexander Bielaski	Aug. 10, '61	Killed at Belmont
"	Hiram H. Peyton	Aug. 28, '61	Promoted Adjutant
"	John W. Martin	Feb. 16, '62	Promoted
"	Ogden Greenough	March 24, '62	
Second Lieutenant	John W. Martin	Aug. 28, '61	Promoted
"	Ogden Greenough	Feb. 16, '62	Promoted
"	John Mars	March 24, '62	
G.			
Captain	James Burnett	Sept. 30, '61	
First Lieutenant	Henry G. Calhoun	Sept. 30, '61	Resigned Sept. 13, '62
Second Lieutenant	Orla C. Richardson	Sept. 30, '61	
H.			
Captain	William C. Rhoads	Aug. 28, '61	Promoted Major
"	Henry W. Strang	Oct. 8, '62	
First Lieutenant	Sidney Hall	Aug. 28, '61	Resigned May 23, '62
"	Henry W. Strang	May 23, '62	Promoted
"	Isaac R. Kidd	Oct. 8, '62	
Second Lieutenant	William M. Gibson	Aug. 28, '61	Resigned Dec. 31, '61
"	Henry W. Strang	Jan. 8, '62	Promoted
"	Isaac R. Kidd	May 23, '62	Promoted
"	Joel Harroll	Oct. 8, '62	
I.			
Captain	Robert Allen	Aug. 28, '61	
First Lieutenant	William C. Kesner	Feb. 28, '62	
Second Lieutenant	William H. Taylor	Aug. 28, '62	Resigned May 5, '62
"	Noah W. Reddick	May 5, '62	
K.			
Captain	Alexander H. Johnson	Aug. 28, '61	Resigned April 1, '62
"	John L. Nichols	April 1, '62	
First Lieutenant	John L. Nichols	Aug. 28, '61	Promoted
"	George C. Lockwood	April 1, '62	
Second Lieutenant	James L. Dougherty	Aug. 28, '62	Killed at Belmont
"	George C. Lockwood	Nov. 9, '61	Promoted
"	Abraham Smith	April 1, '62	

Schedule G — Continued.

Roster of Thirty-First Regiment Illinois Volunteers.

Field and Staff.		Rank.	Remarks.
Colonel.........	John A. Logan.........	Aug. 10, '61.	Promoted Brigadier General March 21, '62..
"	Lindorf Osborn........	April 1, '62.	
Lieutenant Colonel	John H. White........	Sep. 8, '61.	Killed at Fort Donelson, February 15, '62....
"	Edwin S. McCook.....	Feb. 16, '62.	
Major	Andrew J. Kuykendall..	Sept. 8, '61.	Resigned May 1, '62.....
"	John D. Reese.........		
Adjutant........	Charles H. Capehart....	Sept. 17, '61.	Resigned May 16, '62.....
"	Robert N. Pearson......	May 16, '62.	
Quartermaster...	Lindorf Osburn........	Sept. 8, '61.	Promoted Colonel.......
"	Michael F. Swortzcope..	April 2, '62.	
Surgeon.........			
1st Ass't Surgeon.	David T. Whitnell......	Sept. 8, '62.	
2d Ass't Surgeon.			
Chaplain........			

Company A.

Captain.........	John D. Rees..........	Sept. 8, '61.	Promoted Major..........
"	William B. Short.......	May 1, '62.	
First Lieutenant..	John Campbell........	Sept. 8, '61.	Died April 18, '62.......
" ..	Davidson C. Moore.....	April 18, '62.	
Second Lieutenant	Davidson C. Moore.....	Sept. 8, '61.	Promoted ... .
"	Isham E. Willis........	May 1, '62.	

B.

Captain.........	Thomas J. Cain........	Sept. 8, '61.	Resigned September 3, '62
First Lieutenant..	Cressa K. Davis........	Sept. 8, '61.	Promoted to Co. F. Sixth [Cavalry.
" ..	Sterne W. Foggy.......	Sept. 23, '61.	
Second Lieutenant	Sterne W. Foggy.......	Sept. 8, '61.	Promoted ....
"	George W. Youngblood..	Sept. 23, '61.	Died..................
"	Robert Lewis..........	Feb. 26, '62.	

C.

Captain.........	William A. Looney.....	Sept. 8, '61.	Resigned June 3, 1862....
"	George W. Goddard....	June 26, '62.	
First Lieutenant..	Daniel R. Pulley.......	Sept. 8, '61.	Resigned April 18, 1862..
" ..	Philander Jones........	April 18, '62.	
Second Lieutenant	John H. White.........	Sept. 8, '61.	Promoted...............
"	James M. Askew........	Sept. 9, '61.	

D.

Captain.........	James H. Williamson...	Sept. 8, '61.	Killed in battle at Fort [Donelson.
"	Levi B. Casey..........	Feb. 15, '62.	
First Lieutenant..	Robert C. Nelson.......	Sept. 8, '61.	Resigned...............
" ..	James P. Anderson.....	March 1, '62.	
Second Lieutenant	Levi B. Casey..........	Sept. 8, '61.	Promoted...............
"	James J. Bridges.......	Feb. 15, '62.	Resigned May 15, 1862...
"	Jasper Johnson........	May 15, '62.	

E.

Captain.........	Irvin G. Batson........	Sept. 8, '61.	Resigned May 20, 1862··.
"	Martin V. B. Murphy....	May 20, '62.	
First Lieutenant..	Josephus C. Gilliland....	Sept. 8, '61.	Resigned February 3, 1862
" ..	William Miller.........	Feb. 3, '62.	Resigned May 20, 1862...
" ..	William V. Sanders.....	May 20, '62.	Resigned Sept. 2, 1862...
" ..	Thomas M. Logan......	Sept. 2, '62.	.
Second Lieutenant	Robert E. Elmore......	Sept. 8, '61.	Resigned February 3, 1862
"	Martin V. B. Murphy....	Feb. 3, '62.	Promoted...............
"	Robert Moore..........	May 20, '62.	

SCHEDULE G—Continued.

		Rank.	Remarks.
F.			
Captain	John W. Rigby	Sept. 8, '61.	
First Lieutenant	George W. Goddard	Sept. 8, '61.	Resigned April 19, 1862.
"	Patrick H. Ayers	April 19, '62.	
Second Lieutenant	James M. Hale	Sept. 8, '61.	Died February 15, 1862.
"	Phillip Sipple	Feb. 15, '62.	
G.			
Captain	Willis A. Stricklin	Sept. 8, '61.	
First Lieutenant	Larkin M. Riley	Sept. 8, '61.	Died February 25, 1862.
"	Simpson S. Stricklin	Feb. 25, '62.	
Second Lieutenant	Simpson S. Stricklin	Sept. 8, '92.	Promoted
"	Benjamin Sisk	Feb. 25, '62.	
H.			
Captain	Orsamus Greenlee	Sept. 25, '61.	Resigned May 10, 1862.
"	Horace L. Bonyer	May 10, '62.	
First Lieutenant	Horace L. Bowyer	Sept. 25, '61.	Promoted
"	Jesse Robberds	May 10, '62.	
Second Lieutenant	Jesse Robberds	Sept. 25, '61.	Promoted
"	William N. Miller	May 10, '62.	
I.			
Captain	Edwin S. McCook	Aug. 10, '61.	Promoted Lieutenant Col.
"	Harry Almon	Feb. 17, '62.	
First Lieutenant	John Mooneyham	Aug. 10, '61.	Resigned March 13, 1862.
"	Robert R. Townes	Mar. 13, '62.	Transferred to General Lo-[gan's Staff.
"	John J. Curry	May 2, '62.	
Second Lieutenant	Robert A. Bowman	Aug. 10, '61.	Resigned April 29, 1862.
"	Carroll Moore	Mar. 29, '62.	
K.			
Captain	Alexander S. Somerville	Sept. 8, '61.	Dismissed
"	Thomas Hunter	Feb. 15, '62.	
First Lieutenant	Charles H. Capehart	Sept. 8, '61.	Promoted Adjutant
"	Henry F. Snyder	Oct. 11, '61.	Resigned April 24, 1862.
"	John S. Hoover	April 29, '62.	
Second Lieutenant	Levi E. Morris	Sept. 8, '61.	Resigned April 16, 1862.
"	Pinkney K. Watts	April 16, '62.	

Schedule G — Continued.

Roster of Thirty-Second Regiment Illinois Volunteers.

Field and Staff.		Rank.	Remarks.
Colonel	John Logan	Aug. 16, '61	
Lieutenant Colonel	John W. Ross	Aug. 16, '61	Killed in battle at Shiloh
"	William Hunter	April 12, '62	
Major	John S. Bishop	Nov. 12, '61	Resigned Dec. 6, '61
"	William Hunter	Dec. 31, '61	Promoted
"	George H. English	April 12, '62	
Adjutant	James F. Drish	Aug. 16, '61	Resigned April 22, '62
"	Alexander VanWinkle	April 22, '62	
Quartermaster	Charles A. Morton	Aug. 16, '61	Pro. Gen. Sherman's Staff
"	John S. Phelps	Sept. 10, '62	
Surgeon	William S. Edgar	Sept. 26, '61	
1st Ass't Surgeon	George B. Christy	Sept. 23, '61	
2d Ass't Surgeon	John J. Gilmer	Sept. 16, '62	
Chaplain	Asaph C. Vandewater	Sept. 16, '61	Resigned May 19, '62
"	Edward McMillian	May 19, '62	
Company A.			
Captain	Henry Davidson	Aug. 29, '61	
First Lieutenant	Joseph S. Rice	Aug. 29, '61	Killed at battle of Shiloh
"	John Berry	April 7, '62	
Second Lieutenant	John Berry	Aug. 29, '61	Promoted
"	William A. Burnett	April 7, '62	
B.			
Captain	William J. Pierce	Sept. 4, '61	Resigned Aug. 31, '62
First Lieutenant	James J. Searight	Aug. 22, '61	Dismissed Sept. 1, '62
Second Lieutenant	John H. Allen	Sept. 4, '61	Killed at Hatchie
"	George Ripley	Oct. 5, '62	
C.			
Captain	Thaddeus Phillips	Oct. 22, '61	Resigned Nov. 1, '62
"	Abram D. Keller	Nov. 1, '62	
First Lieutenant	Abram D. Keller	Oct. 22, '61	Promoted
"	William C. C. Logan	Nov. 1, '62	
Second Lieutenant	Josiah Borough	Oct. 22, '61	Resigned March 14, '62
"	William C. C. Logan	March 14, '62	Promoted
D.			
Captain	George H. English	Sept. 6, '61	Promoted Major
"	Daniel McLennan	April 16, '62	
First Lieutenant	Daniel McLennan	Sept. 6, '61	Promoted
"	Thomas A. Smith	April 8, '62	
Second Lieutenant	James W. Mitchel	Sept. 6, '61	
E.			
Captain	Alfred C. Campbell	Dec. 31, '61	
First Lieutenant	Richard W. Babbett	Dec. 31, '61	Promoted Captain Co. G
"	John A. Campbell	Sept. 29, '62	
Second Lieutenant	William H. Edgar	Dec. 31, '61	Resigned April 22, '62
"	John A. Campbell	April 22, '62	Promoted
"	John W. Lee	Sept. 29, '62	
F.			
Captain	George W. Jenks	Dec. 31, '61	Resigned Sept. 28, '62
"	Smith Townsend	Sept. 28, '62	
First Lieutenant	Smith Townsend	Dec. 31, '61	Promoted
"	David Glenn	Sept. 28, '62	
Second Lieutenant	John Laboytaux	Dec. 31, '61	Killed at Shiloh
"	Troy Moore	April 7, '62	

SCHEDULE G—Continued.

		Rank.	Remarks.
G.			
Captain	Jonathan Moore	Nov. 28, '61	Resigned June 30, '62
"	Richard W. Babbitt	Sept. 29, '62	
First Lieutenant	Robert H. Stevenson	Nov. 28, '61	Resigned April 8, '62
"	James S. Risley	April 8, '62	
Second Lieutenant	Charles A. Eames	Nov. 28, '61	Killed in battle at Shiloh
"	William W. Hitchcock	April 7, '62	
H.			
Captain	John B. Duncan	Dec. 31, '61	
First Lieutenant	Henry C. Wright	Dec. 31, '61	Resigned Sept. 3, '62
"	William H. York	Sept. 3, '62	
Second Lieutenant	John York	Dec. 31, '61	Killed at Shiloh
"	Alexander M. Wright	April 7, '62	
I.			
Captain	Samuel Cummings	Dec. 31, '61	Resigned Sept. 14, '62
"	Josiah Y. Ellas	Sept. 1, '62	
First Lieutenant	Josiah Y. Ellas	Nov. 27, '61	Promoted
"	Robert P. Drake	Sept. 1, '62	
Second Lieutenant	William Ulm	Dec. 31, '61	Resigned Sept. 3, '62
"	Richard Rucker	Sept. 3, '62	
K.			
Captain	Samuel B. Crowley	Dec. 31, '61	Resigned June 10, '62
"	John J. Rider	June 10, '62	
First Lieutenant	John J. Rider	Dec. 31, '61	Promoted
"	William B. Crowley	June 10, '62	
Second Lieutenant	Theodore Schifferstein	Dec. 31, '61	Resigned May 2, '62
"	Xavier Picquet	May 2, '62	

Schedule G—Continued.

Roster of Thirty-Third Regiment Illinois Volunteers.

Field and Staff.		Rank.	Remarks.
Colonel	Charles E. Hovey	Aug. 15, '61	Promoted Brig. Gen. Sept.
"	Charles E. Lippincott	Sept. 5, '62	['5, 62.
Lieutenant Colonel	William R. Lockwood	Oct. 4, '61	Resigned March 1, '62
"	Charles E. Lippincott	March 1, '62	Promoted
"	Edward R. Roe	Sept. 5, '62	
Major	Edward R. Roe	Aug. 15, '61	Promoted
"	Leander H. Potter	Sept. 5, '62	
Adjutant	Frederick M. Crandall	Aug. 15, '61	Promoted
"	E. Aaron Gove	Sept. 6, '62	
Quartermaster	Simeon Wright	Aug. 15, '61	
Surgeon	George P. Rex	Aug. 15, '61	
1st Ass't Surgeon	Nathan W. Abbott	Feb. 3, '62	M. O. for promotion
"	Edwin May	Aug. 25, '62	
2d Ass't Surgeon	Henry T. Antes	Nov. 21, '62	
Chaplain	Herman A. Eddy	Aug. 15, '61	

Company A.

Captain	Leander H. Potter	Sept. 18, '61	Promoted Major
"	J. Howard Burnham	Sept. 5, '62	
First Lieutenant	J. Howard Burnham	Sept. 18, '61	Promoted
"	G. Hyde Norton	Sept. 5, '62	
Second Lieutenant	G. Hyde Norton	Sept. 18, '61	Promoted
"	Harvey J. Dutton	Sept. 5, '62	

B.

Captain	Moses J. Morgan	Sept. 18, '61	
First Lieutenant	C. Judson Gill	Sept. 18, '61	
Second Lieutenant	E. Aaron Gove	Sept. 18, '61	Adjutant
"	Nelson G. Gill	Sept. 6, '62	

C.

Captain	Daniel B. Robinson	Sept. 18, '61	Resigned, Jan. 24, '62
"	Henry M. Kellogg	Jan. 24, '62	
First Lieutenant	Henry M. Kellogg	Sept. 18, '61	Promoted
"	Edward J. Lewis	Jan. 24, '62	
Second Lieutenant	George H. Fifer	Sept. 18, '61	

D.

Captain	Henry H. Pope	Sept. 18, '61	
First Lieutenant	William W. Mason	Sept. 18, '61	
Second Lieutenant	Franklin J. Duncklee	Sept. 18, '61	Resigned
"	Hiram V. Algur	Feb. 18, '62	

E.

Captain	Isaac H. Elliott	Sept. 18, '61	
First Lieutenant	Clarendon A. Stone	Sept. 18, '61	Resigned June 18, '62
"	Julian E. Bryant	June 18, '62	
Second Lieutenant	Julian E. Bryant	Sept. 18, 61	Promoted
"	Lyman M. Pratt	June 18, '62	

F.

Captain	Dermont C. Roberts	Sept. 18, '61	
First Lieutenant	Henry D. Winship	Sept. 18, 61	
Second Lieutenant	David A. Chumley	Sept. 18, '61	Resigned Aug. 5, '62
"	Elijah H. Gray	Aug. 5, '62	

SCHEDULE G—Continued.

		Rank.	Remarks.
G.			
Captain	Ira Moore	Sept. 18, '61.	
First Lieutenant	George P. Ela	Sept. 18, '61.	Resigned Sept. 7, '62
"	John S. Russell	Sept. 21, '62.	
Second Lieutenant	William Elbert	Sept. 18, '61.	
H.			
Captain	James A. McKenzie	Sept. 18, '61.	
First Lieutenant	George E. Smith	Sept. 18, '61.	
Second Lieutenant	Robert P. Williams	Sept. 18, '61.	
I.			
Captain	William W. H. Lawton	Sept. 18, '61.	
First Lieutenant	William T. Lyon	Sept. 18, '61.	
Second Lieutenant	Edward A. F. Allen	Sept. 18, '61.	Discharged
"	Charles Kinney	March 18, 62	
K.			
Captain	Charles E. Lippincott	Sept. 18, '61.	Promoted Lieut. Col.
"	William A. Nixon	March 1, '62.	Resigned July 1, '62
"	Edward H. Twining	July 1, '62.	
First Lieutenant	William A. Nixon	Sept. 18, '61.	Promoted
"	Franklin Adams	March 1, '62.	
Second Lieutenant	William H. Weaver	Sept. 18, 61.	Resigned March 22, '62
"	Edwin L. L. Higgins	March 22, 62.	

Schedule G — Continued.

Roster of Thirty-Fourth Regiment Illinois Volunteers.

Field and Staff.		Rank.	Remarks.
Colonel	Edward N. Kirk	Aug. 15, '61	
Lieutenant Colonel	Amos Bosworth	Aug. 15, '61	Resigned April 18, '62
"	Hiram W. Bristol	April 18, '62	
Major	Charles N. Levanway	Aug. 15, '61	Killed at Shiloh
"	Hiram W. Bristol	April 7, '62	Promoted
"	Alexander P. Dysart	April 18, '62	
Adjutant	David Leavitt	Aug. 15, '61	
Quartermaster	Abram Beeler	Aug. 15, '61	
Surgeon	Francis A. McNeil	Oct. 12, '61	Resigned Nov. 8, '61
"	Orson Q. Herrick	Jan. 13, '62	
1st Ass't Surgeon	George W. Hewitt	Oct. 2, '61	
2d Ass't Surgeon	John L. Hostetter	Dec. 10, '62	
Chaplain	Michael Decker	Oct. 1, '61	

Company A.

Captain	E. Brooks Ward	Aug. 15, '61	Resigned Dec. 5, '62
"	Peter Ege	Dec. 5, '62	
First Lieutenant	Peter Ege	Aug. 15, '61	Promoted
"	Jonathan A. Morgan	Dec. 5, '62	
Second Lieutenant	Jonathan A. Morgan	Aug. 15, '61	Promoted
"	Lorenzo D. Wescott	Dec. 5, '62	

B.

Captain	Hiram W. Bristol	Aug. 15, '61	Promoted Major
"	John A. Parrott	April 7, '62	
First Lieutenant	Cornelius Quackenbush	Aug. 15, '61	Resigned March 10, '62
"	John A. Parrott	March 10, '62	Promoted
"	Leland L. Johnson	April 7, '62	
Second Lieutenant	John A. Parrott	Aug. 15, '61	Promoted
"	Leland L. Johnson	March 10, '62	Promoted
"	David Cleveland	April 7, '62	

C.

Captain	Alexander P. Dysart	Aug. 15, '61	Promoted Major
"	Benson Wood	May 1, '62	
First Lieutenant	Benson Wood	Aug. 15, '61	Promoted
"	Daniel Riley	May 1, '62	
Second Lieutenant	Daniel Riley	Aug. 15, '61	Promoted
"	Peter F. Walker	May 1, '62	

D.

Captain	Truman L. Pratt	Aug. 15, '61	Resigned Aug. 18, '62
"	William S. Wood	Aug. 28, '62	
First Lieutenant	William S. Wood	Aug. 15, '61	Promoted
"	Simon B. Dexter	Aug. 28, '62	
Second Lieutenant	Simon B. Dexter	Aug. 15, '61	Promoted
"	Francis Forsyth	Aug. 28, '62	

E.

Captain	Henry Weld	Aug. 15, '61	Resigned March 26, '62
"	Samuel L. Patrick	March 28, '62	
First Lieutenant	Samuel L. Patrick	Aug. 15, '61	Promoted
"	Edward H. Weld	June 12, '62	
Second Lieutenant	Thomas Bell	Aug. 15, '61	Resigned Feb. 6, '62
"	Edward H. Weld	Aug. 15, '61	Promoted
"	Hollis S. Hall	June 12, '62	

Schedule G —Continued.

		Rank.	Remarks.
F.			
Captain	Oscar Van Tassel	Aug. 15, '61	
First Lieutenant	Uriah G. Galion	Aug. 15, '61	
Second Lieutenant	John Slaughter	Aug. 15, '61	
G.			
Captain	Mabry G. Greenwood	Sept. 4, '61	
First Lieutenant	John Hindman	Sept. 4, '61	Resigned Feb. 16, '62
"	Isaac Rawlings	Feb. 13, '62	
Second Lieutenant	Samuel R. Cavender	Sept. 4, '61	Resigned March 16, '62
"	Spencer C. Rawlings	March 16, '62	Resigned Nov. 16, '62
"	James H. Hindman	Nov. 16, '62	
H.			
Captain	John M. Miller	Aug. 15, '61	
First Lieutenant	David C. Wagner	Aug. 15, '61	Promoted Captain Co. K
"	Benjamin R. Wagner	Jan. 13, '62	Resigned Dec. 27, 62
Second Lieutenant	Benjamin R. Wagner	Aug. 15, '61	Promoted
"	Henry Hiller	Jan. 13, '62	Died
"	John M. Smith	May 1, '62	
I.			
Captain	Lewis Heffelfinger	Aug. 15, '61	Resigned April 18, '62
"	Amos W. Hostetter	April 18, '62	
First Lieutenant	Amos W. Hostetter	Aug. 15, '61	Promoted
"	Jackson Beaver	April 18, '62	
Second Lieutenant	James Watson	Aug. 15, '61	Resigned April 28, '62
"	Mason C. Fuller	May 4, '62	
K.			
Captain	Orson Q. Herrick	Oct. 2, '61	Promoted Surgeon
"	David C. Wagner	Jan. 13, '62	
First Lieutenant	Stephen Martin	Oct. 2, '61	
Second Lieutenant	David A. Zimmerman	Oct. 2, '61	Resigned Dec. 23, '61
"	Joseph Hollis	Dec. 23, '61	

Schedule G — Continued.

Roster of Thirty-Fifth Regiment Illinois Volunteers.

Field and Staff.		Rank.	Remarks.
Colonel	Gustavus A. Smith	July 3, '61	Promoted Brig. General.
Lieutenant Colonel	William P. Chandler	July 3, '61	[Sept. 19, '62
Major	John McIlwain	July 3, '61	
Adjutant	William J. Usrey	Sept. 1, '61	Resigned April 15, '62
"	Uriah J. Fox	April 15, '62	
Qurtermaster	John M. Miles	July 3, '61	
Surgeon	William J. Chenoweth	Sept. 25, '61	Resigned Dec. 14, '62
"	Sidney B. Hawley	Dec. 9, '62	
1st Ass't Surgeon	David C. Tidball	Sept. 25, '61	
2d Ass't Surgeon	Jonathan D. Wiley	Dec. 8, '6 ?	
Chaplain	Philip D. Hammond	July 3, '61	Resigned May 12, '62
"	Rice E. Harris	May 12, 62	

Company A.

Captain	Benjamin M. Tabler	July 3, '61	Resigned Dec. 20, '61
"	Pierre W. Thomas	Dec. 5, '61	
First Lieutenant	Pierre W. Thomas	July 3, '61	Promoted
"	George F. Dietz	Dec. 25, '61	
Second Lieutenant	James Shoaff	July 3, '61	Resigned Feb. 3, '62
"	George B. Peake	Feb. 3, '62	

B.

Captain	Charles W. Horr	July 3, '61	Resigned Oct. 20, '62
"	Theodore F. Tunison	Oct. 20, '62	
First Lieutenant	Theodore F. Tunison	July 3, '61	Promoted
"	Henry H. Reed	Oct. 20, '62	
Second Lieutenant	Henry H. Reed	July 3, '61	Promoted
"	William L. Warning	Oct. 20, '62	

C.

Captain	James F. Williams	July 3, '61	
First Lieutenant	Lewis H. Williams	July 3, '61	
Second Lieutenant	Truman C. Lapham	July 3, '61	

D.

Captain	William R. Timmons	July 3, '61	
First Lieutenant	Uriah J. Fox	July 3, '61	Promoted Adjutant
"	John W. Ball	April 18, '62	
Second Lieutenant	Josiah Timmons	July 3, '61	

E.

Captain	William L. Oliver	Sept. 1, '61	
First Lieutenant	Lewis J. Eyman	Sept. 1, '61	Canceled
"	Hiram Yoho	Nov. 11, '61	
Second Lieutenant	George C. Maxon	Sept. 1, '61	Resigned July 11, '62

F.

Captain	Allen C. Keys	July 3, '61	
First Lieutenant	John Q. A. Luddington	July 3, '61	Resigned Dec. 5, '61
"	Moses Snooks	Dec. 5, '61	
Second Lieutenant	James M. Sinks	July 3, '61	Resigned March 18, '62
"	Jacob Keiser	March 28, '62	

SCHEDULE G—Continued.

		Rank.	Remarks.
G.			
Captain	Beverly McHenry	July 3, '61	Resigned July 16, '62
"	William P. Smyth	July 16, '62	
First Lieutenant	William P. Smyth	Sept. 1, '61	Promoted
"	Hannibal C. St. Clair	July 16, '62	
Second Lieutenant	John Adams	Sept. 1, '61	Canceled
"	Hannibal C. St. Clair	March 1, '62	Promoted
H.			
Captain	James F. Han	July 3, '61	Mustered out April 15, '62
"	Collins P. Jones	July 16, '62	
First Lieutenant	Dudley H. Mabry	July 3, '61	Resigned July 16, '62
"	Collins P. Jones	July 16, '62	Promoted
"	Humphrey M. McConnell	July 16, '62	
Second Lieutenant	Andrew E. K. Surber	July 3, '61	Resigned Nov. 26, '61
"	Collins P. Jones	Dec. 16, '61	Promoted
"	Humphrey M. McConnell	July 16, '62	Promoted
I.			
Captain	Abraham B. B. Lewis	July 3, '61	Resigned Oct. 14, '62
"	Joseph Truax	Oct. 14, '62	
First Lieutenant	Joseph Truax	July 3, '61	Promoted
"	Milton Lee	Oct. 14, '62	
Second Lieutenant	Joseph F. Clise	July 3, '61	Died
"	Milton Lee	Oct. 14, '61	Promoted
"	Charles V. B. Smith	Oct. 14, '62	
K.			
Captain	Thomas H. Dobbs	July 3, '61	Resigned Oct. 14, '62
"	Jesse D. Jennings	Oct. 14, '62	
First Lieutenant	Joseph Moore	July 3, '61	Died
"	Jesse D. Jennings	April 9, '62	Promoted
"	Nelson Staats	Oct. 14, '62	
Second Lieutenant	Jesse D. Jennings	July 3, '61	Promoted
"	Nelson Staats	April 9, '62	Promoted
"	Daniel H. Kagay	Oct. 14, '62	

Schedule G — Continued.

Roster of Thirty-Sixth Regiment Illinois Volunteers.

Field and Staff.		Rank.	Remarks.
Colonel	Nicholas Greusel	Sept. 23, '61	
Lieutenant Colonel	Edward S. Joslyn	Aug. 20, '61	Discharged Sept. 18, '62
" "	Albert Jenks	Sept. 18, '62	
Major	Alonzo H. Barry	Aug. 20, '61	Discharged Sept. 18, '62
"	Silas Miller	Sept. 18, '62	
Adjutant	George A. Willis	Aug. 20, '61	Promoted Captain Cavalry.
Quartermaster	Isaac N. Buck	Aug. 20, '61	Resigned March 3, '62
"	John Van Pelt	March 3, '62	
Surgeon	Delos W. Young	Aug. 20, '61	
1st Ass't Surgeon	Sidney B. Hawley	Aug. 20, '61	Resigned Sept. 3, '62
" "	William P. Pierce	Sept. 3, '62	
2d Ass't Surgeon			
Chaplain	George G. Lyon	Sept. 23, '61	Mustered out April 1, '62.
"	William M. Haigh	Aug. 18, '62	

Company A.

Captain	Melvin B. Baldwin	Aug. 20, '61	Resigned June 8, '62
"	George D. Sherman	June 8, '62	
First Lieutenant	Edward S. Chappell	Aug. 20, '61	Died Oct. 16, '61
"	George Sherman	Oct. 19, '61	Promoted
"	Sanford H. Wakeman	June 8, '62	
Second Lieutenant	Isaac N. Buck	Aug. 20, '61	Promoted Quartermaster.
"	William S. Smith	Aug. 20, '61	Resigned July 9, '62
"	William Mitchell	Aug. 31, '62	

B.

Captain	Silas Miller	Aug. 20, '61	Promoted Major
"	Benjamin F. Campbell	Sept. 18, '62	
First Lieutenant	Joseph M. Walker	Aug. 20, '61	
Second Lieutenant	Benjamin F. Campbell	Aug. 20, '61	Promoted
"	George P. Douglas	Sept. 18, '62	

C.

Captain	Elias B. Baldwin	Aug. 20, '61	
First Lieutenant	James B. McNeal	Aug. 20, '61	
Second Lieutenant	Joseph M. Turnbull	Aug. 20, '61	

D.

Captain	William P. Pierce	Aug. 20, '61	Promoted Ass't Surgeon
"	George D. Parker	Sept. 3, '62	
First Lieutenant	John Van Pelt	Aug. 20, '61	Promoted Quartermaster
"	George D. Parker	March 3, '62	Promoted
"	Edward P. Cass	Sept. 3, '62	
Second Lieutenant	George D. Parker	Aug. 20, '61	Promoted
"	Edward P. Cass	March 3, '62	Promoted
"	Joseph C. Thompson	Sept. 3, '62	

E.

Captain	Charles D. Fish	Aug. 20, '61	Resigned July 16, '62
"	Albert M. Hobbs	July 16, '62	
First Lieutenant	Albert M. Hobbs	Aug. 20, '61	Promoted
"	William H. Clark	July 16, '62	
Second Lieutenant	William H. Clark	Aug. 20, '61	Promoted
"	George S. Bartlett	July 16, '62	

SCHEDULE G—Continued.

		Rank.	Remarks.
F.			
Captain	Porter C. Olson	Aug. 20, '61.	
First Lieutenant	George F. Stonax	Aug. 20, '61.	Resigned July 14, '62
"	George G. Biddolph	July 14, '62	
Second Lieutenant	Martin C. Wilson	Aug. 20, '61.	Resigned March 25, '62
"	George G. Biddolph	March 25, '62	Promoted
"	Loren L. Olsen	July 14, '62.	
G.			
Captain	Irving W. Parkhurst	Aug. 20, '61.	Resigned Nov. 8, '62
"	Abel Longworth	Nov. 8, '62	
First Lieutenant	Abel Longworth	Aug. 20, '61.	Promoted
"	Robert M. Denning	Nov. 8, '62	
Second Lieutenant	Robert M. Denning	Aug. 20, '61.	Promoted
"	Linus J. Austin	Nov. 8, 62	
H.			
Captain	Merrit L. Joslyn	Aug. 20, '61.	Resigned Sept. 3, '62
"	Theodore L. Griffin	Sept. 7, '62.	
First Lieutenant	Alfred H. Sellers	Aug. 20, '61.	Resigned July 14, '62
"	Charles F. Dyke	July 14, '62.	Resigned Aug. 31, '62
"	Morris Briggs	Sept. 7, '62.	
Second Lieutenant	Charles F. Dyke	Oct. 19, '61	Promoted
"	Theodore L. Griffin	July 14, '62.	Promoted
"	Myron A. Smith	Sept. 7, '62.	
I.			
Captain	Samuel C. Camp	Aug. 20, '61.	Resigned March 19, '62
"	Orville B. Merrill	March 19, 62	
First Lieutenant	William Walker	Aug. 20, '61.	Resigned
"	Orville B. Merrill	Sept. 11, '61.	Promoted
"	William F. Sutherland	March 19, '62	
Second Lieutenant	William F. Sutherland	Aug. 20, '61.	Promoted
"	Gustavus Voss	March 19, '62	Resigned Sept. 7, '62
"	David E. Shaw	Sept. 7, '62.	
K.			
Captain	John Q. Adams	Aug. 20, '61.	Resigned Sept. 7, '62
"	Aaron C. Holden	Sept. 7, '62.	
First Lieutenant	James Foley	Aug. 20, '61.	Resigned Feb. 15, '62
"	Aaron C. Holden	Feb. 15, '62.	Promoted
"	John F. Elliott	Sept. 7, '62.	
Second Lieutenant	Aaron C. Holdon	Sept. 20, '61.	Promoted
"	Matthew J. Hammond	Feb. 15, '62.	Resigned Sept. 7, '62
"	Charles E. Hazlehurst	Sept. 7, '62.	

SCHEDULE G.—Continued.

Roster of Thirty-Seventh Regiment Illinois Volunteers.

Field and Staff.		Rank.	Remarks.
Colonel	Julius White...........	July 26, '61..	Pro. Brig Gen., June 9, '62.
"	Myron S. Barnes	June 9, '62...	Dismissed Nov. 20, '62....
"	John C. Black	Nov. 20, '62...	....
Lieut. Colonel....	Myron S. Barnes	Aug. 1, '61 ..	Promoted ....
"	John Charles Black.....	June 9, '62...	Promoted ....
"	Henry N. Frisbie	Nov. 20, '62 .	....
Major..........	John Charles Black.....	Aug. 15, '61 .	Promoted ....
"	Henry N. Frisbie	June 9, '62 ..	Promoted ....
"	Eugene B. Payne	Nov. 20, '62 .	....
Adjutant	Anton Nieman	Aug. 15, '61 .	Resigned March 24, '62...
"	William M. Bandy	March 24, '62.	....
Quartermaster ...	John H. Peck...........	Aug. 5, '61 ..	....
Surgeon.........	Luther F. Humeston ...	Aug. 15, '61..	....
1st Asst. Surgeon.	Elijah A. Clark.........	Sept. 18, '61 .	....
2d Asst. Surgeon..	John Murphy	Aug. 6, '62...	....
Chaplain	Edward Anderson	Sept. 18, '61 .	Resigned April 25, '62....

COMPANY A.

Captain	John A. Jordan.........	Aug. 14, '61 .	Resigned Dec. 31, '61 .
"	Henry Curtis, jr	Dec. 31, '61 . .	Resigned July 20, '62 ....
"	Charles W. Hawes	July 20, '62...	....
First Lieutenant..	Henry Curtis, jr........	Aug. 14, '61..	Promoted ....
"	Charles W. Hawes	Dec. 31, '61..	Promoted ....
"	Lorenzo B. Morey.......	July 20, '62...	....
Second Lieutenant	Charles W. Hawes......	Aug. 14, '61..	Promoted..
"	Lorenzo B. Morey.......	Dec. 31, '61..	Promoted..
"	William H. Bigelow.....	July 20, '62...	....

B.

Captain	Charles V. Dickinson....	Aug. 19, '61 .	....
First Lieutenant..	Cassimir P. Jackson	Aug. 19, '61 .	Resigned July 9, '62......
"	Francis A. Jones........	July 9, '62...	....
Second Lieutenant	Francis A. Jones	Aug. 19, '61 .	Promoted ....
"	David L. Ash	July 9, '62...	....

C.

Captain	Eugene B. Payne	Aug. 1, '61 ..	Promoted Major..........
First Lieutenant..	Judson J. Huntley......	Aug. 1, '61 ..	....
Second Lieutenant	Chauncy C. Morse	Aug. 1, '61 ..	....

D.

Captain	John W. Laimbeer	Aug. 1, '61 ..	....
First Lieutenant..	Wells H. Blodgett	Aug. 1, '61 ..	....
Second Lieutenant	William Mazell.........	Aug. 1, '61 ..	Resigned Dec. 9, '61 .....
"	William Johnson	Dec. 9, '61...	....

E.

Captain	Phineas B. Rust	Aug. 20, '61 .	....
First Lieutenant..	Orville R. Powers.......	Aug. 20, '61 .	Killed in battle at Sugar Creek, March 7, '62 .
"	Charles W. Day	March 9, '62 .	Resigned Nov. 18, '62 ....
"	Henry L. Smith	Nov. 18, '62...	....
Second Lieutenant	Charles W. Day	Aug. 20, '61 .	Promoted ....
"	Henry L. Smith	March 9, '62.	Promoted ....
"	James P. Day...........	Nov. 18, '62 .	....

SCHEDULE G—Continued.

		Rank.	Remarks.

F.

Captain	Erwin B. Messer	Aug. 19, '61	
First Lieutenant	Andreas Greve	Aug. 19, '61	Resigned July 20, '62
"	Gallio H. Fairman	July 20, '62	
Second Lieutenant	Gallio H. Fairman	Aug. 19, '61	Promoted
"	Warren W. Doty	July 20, '62	

G.

Captain	Henry N. Frisbie	Aug. 1, '61	Promoted Major
"	George R Bell	June 9, '62	
First Lieutenant	George R. Bell	Aug. 8, '61	Promoted
"	Manning F. Atkinson	June 9, '62	
Second Lieutenant	Manning F. Atkinson	Aug. 15, '61	Promoted
"	Charles H. Newton	June 9, '62	

H.

Captain	John B. Frick	Aug. 12, '61	Resigned Feb. 8, '62
"	Herman Wolford	Feb. 8, '62	
First Lieutenant	Herman Wolford	Aug. 12, '61	Promoted
"	Joseph Eaton	Feb. 8, '62	
Second Lieutenant	Joseph Eaton	Aug. 12, '61	Promoted
"	William C. Willson	June 30, '62	

I.

Captain	Ransom Kennicott	Aug. 1, '61	
First Lieutenant	Frederick Abbey	Aug. 1, '61	
Second Lieutenant	Isaac C. Dodge	Aug. 1, '61	

K.

Captain	William P. Black	Aug. 15, '61	
First Lieutenant	William K. Fithian	Aug. 15, '61	Resigned April 12, '62
"	William M. Bandy	April 12, '62	Promoted Adjutant
"	Napoleon B. Hicks	March 24, '62	
Second Lieutenant	William M. Bandy	Aug. 15, '61	Promoted
"	Napoleon B. Hicks	April 12, '62	Promoted
"	Martin H. Leonard	March 24, '62	

SCHEDULE G—Continued.

Roster of Thirty-Eighth Regiment Illinois Volunteers.

Field and Staff.		Rank.	Remarks.
Colonel	William P. Carlin	Aug. 15, '61.	
Lieutenant Colonel	Mortimer O'Kean	Sept. 9, '61.	Resigned September 5, '62
"	Daniel H. Gilmer	Oct. 25, '62.	
Major	Daniel H. Gilmer	Sept. 9, '61.	Promoted
Adjutant	Arthur Lee Bailhache	Aug. 15, '61.	Died
"	James R. Willette	Jan. 29, '62.	
Quartermaster			
Surgeon	John L. Teed	Sept. 10, '61.	
1st Ass't Surgeon	Dudley W. Stewart	Sept. 10, '61.	
2d Ass't Surgeon	Edward J. Tichener	Aug. 11, '62.	
Chaplain	Jacob E. Reed	June 1, '62.	

COMPANY A.

Captain	Henry N. Alden	Aug. 15, '61.	
First Lieutenant	George H. Alcoke	Aug. 15, '61.	Resigned April 18, '62
"	Walter E. Carlin	April 18, '62.	
Second Lieutenant	Walter E. Carlin	Aug. 15, '61.	Promoted
"	Charles H. Wells	April 18, '62.	

B.

Captain	David Young	Aug. 15, '61.	Resigned December 6, '61.
"	Harrison Tyner	Dec. 6, '61.	
First Lieutenant	Robert M. Rankin	Aug. 15, '61.	Resigned March 31, '62
"	William F. White	April 1, '62.	
Second Lieutenant	Harrison Tyner	Aug. 15, '61.	Promoted
"	John F. Sisson	Dec. 6, '61.	

C.

Captain	Theodore C. Roding	Aug. 15, '61.	Resigned November 3, '61
"	Thomas Cole	Nov. 3, '61.	
First Lieutenant	Thomas Cole	Aug. 15, '61.	Promoted
"	James Mullen	Nov. 3, '61.	
Second Lieutenant	James Mullen	Aug. 15, '61.	Promoted
"	Amos D. Hartsock	Nov. 3, '61.	

D.

Captain	Alexander G. Sutherland	Aug. 15, '61.	
First Lieutenant	James A. Moore	Aug. 15, '61.	
Second Lieutenant	Robert Plunkett	Aug. 15, '61.	

E.

Captain	James M. True	Aug. 15, '61.	Resigned December 26, '61
"	John McKinstry	Dec. 26, '61.	Resigned June 2, '62
"	Samuel P. Voris	June 8, '62.	
First Lieutenant	John McKinstry	Aug. 15, '61.	Promoted
"	John L. Dillon	Dec. 26, '61.	
Second Lieutenant	John L. Dillon	Aug. 15, '61.	Promoted
"	William W. Gwinn	Dec. 26, '61.	

F.

Captain	James P. Mead	Aug. 15, '61.	
First Lieutenant	William P. Hunt	Aug. 15, '61.	Resigned July 15, '62
"	Willis G. Whitehurst	July 15, '62.	
Second Lieutenant	Willis G. Whitehurst	Aug. 15, '61.	Promoted
"	Lemuel K. Wescott	July 15, '62.	

SCHEDULE G — Continued.

		Rank.	Remarks.
G.			
Captain	Andrew M. Pollard	Aug. 15, '61.	
First Lieutenant	William F. Chapman	Aug. 15, '61.	
Second Lieutenant	Andrew J. Rankin	Aug. 15, '61.	Resigned February 8, '62.
"	Abraham Golden	Feb. 8, '62.	
H.			
Captain	Charles Yelton	Aug. 15, '61.	
First Lieutenant	Abraham E. Goble	Aug. 15, '61.	
Second Lieutenant	Charles H. Miller	Nov. 1, '61.	Canceled.
"	Luther M. DeMotte	Nov. 1, '61.	
I.			
Captain	Charles Churchill	Aug. 15, '61.	
First Lieutenant	William Ferriman	Aug. 15, '61.	
Second Lieutenant	Edward Colyer	Aug. 15, '61.	
K.			
Captain	William C. Harris	Aug. 15, '61.	
First Lieutenant	Bushwood W. Harris	Aug. 15, '61.	
Second Lieutenant	Isaiah Foote	Aug. 15, '61.	Resigned January 10, '62.
"	Peter N. Scott	Feb. 10, '62.	

Schedule G—Continued.

Roster of Thirty-Ninth Regiment Illinois Volunteers.

Field and Staff.		Rank.	Remarks.
Colonel	Austin Light	Aug. 5, '61.	Dismissed
"	Thomas O. Osborn	Dec. 1, '61.	
Lieutenant Colonel	Thomas O. Osborn	July 22, '61.	Promoted
"	Orrin L. Mann	Dec. 1, '61.	
Major	Orrin L. Mann	Aug. 12, '61.	Promoted
"	Sylvester W. Munn	Dec. 1, '61.	
Adjutant	Frank B. Marshall	Aug. 5, '61.	Resigned July 15, '62
"	Joseph D. Walker	July 15, '62.	
Quartermaster	Joseph A. Cutler	July 22, '61.	Resigned June 12, '62
"	Jonathan F. Linton	June 12, '62.	
Surgeon	Samuel C. Blake	Aug. 5, '61.	Resigned June 3, '62
"	Charles M. Clark	June 3, '62.	
1st Ass't Surgeon	Charles M. Clark	Aug. 5, '61.	Promoted
"	James Crozier	Dec. 6, '62.	
2d Ass't Surgeon	William Woodward	Dec. 9, '62.	
Chaplain	Charles S. Macreading	Oct. 9, '61.	

Company A.

Captain	Sylvester W. Munn	Aug. 5, '61.	Promoted Major
"	Leroy A. Baker	Dec. 1, '61.	
First Lieutenant	Joseph W. Richerson	Aug. 5, '61.	Died
"	Leroy A. Baker	Nov. 17, '61.	Promoted
"	Allen B. Johnson	Dec. 1, '61.	
Second Lieutenant	Leroy A. Baker	Aug. 5, '61.	Promoted
"	Allen B. Johnson	Nov. 17, '61.	Promoted
"	James Burrill	Dec. 1, '61.	

B.

Captain	Isaiah W. Wilmerth	Aug. 12, '61.	Resigned May 26, '62
"	David F. Sellards	May 26, '62.	Discharged on account of ill health Nov. 28, '62.
First Lieutenant	David F. Sellards	Aug. 12, '61.	Promoted
"	George T. Heritage	May 26, '62.	
Second Lieutenant	James Haldeman	Aug. 12, '61.	Resigned May 26, '62
"	James Gibson	May 26, '62.	

C.

Captain	John Gray	Aug. 12, '61.	Resigned May 26, '62
"	James Wightman	May 26, '62.	
First Lieutenant	Wallace Lord	Aug. 12, '61.	Resigned January 24, '62.
"	James Wightman	Jan. 24, '62.	Promoted
"	Simon S. Brucker	May 26, '62.	
Second Lieutenant	Simon S. Brucker	Aug. 12, '61.	Promoted
"	James Henderson	May 26, '62.	

D.

Captain	Samuel S. Linton	Aug. 9, '61.	
First Lieutenant	Jonathan F. Linton	Aug. 9, '61.	Promoted Quartermaster
"	George O. Snowden	June 12, '62.	
Second Lieutenant	Austin Towner	Aug. 9, '61.	Resigned September 4, '62
"	Cyrus F. Knapp	Sept. 4, '62.	

E.

Captain	James H. Hooker	Sept. 20, '61.	Resigned May 26, '62
"	Lewis Whipple	May 26, '62.	
First Lieutenant	Lewis Whipple	Sept. 20, '61.	Promoted
"	Norman C. Warner	May 26, '62.	
Second Lieutenant	Norman C. Warner	Sept. 20, '61.	Promoted
"	John Conelly	May 20, '62.	

SCHEDULE G—Continued.

		Rank.	Remarks.
F.			
Captain	Amasa Kennicott	Aug. 27, '61.	Resigned August 7, '62
"	John W. McIntosh	Aug. 7, '62.	
First Lieutenant	John W. McIntosh	Aug. 27, '61.	Promoted
"	Patrick Seary	Aug. 7, '62.	
Second Lieutenant	Patrick Seary	Nov. 15, '61.	Promoted
"	Adolphus B. Hoffman	Aug. 7, '62.	
G.			
Captain	William B. Slaughter	Aug. 5, '61.	Resigned July 20, '62
"	Oscar F. Rudd	July 20, '62.	
First Lieutenant	Oscar F. Rudd	Aug. 5, '61.	Promoted
"	Amos Savage	July 20, '62.	
Second Lieutenant	Amos Savage	Aug. 5, '61.	Promoted
"	James M. Harrington	July 20, '62.	
H.			
Captain	Casper S. F. Dericks	Aug. 5, '61.	Resigned
"	Edmund O. Freeman	Aug. 3, '61.	Resigned
"	Chauncey Williams	July 11, '62.	
First Lieutenant	Charles J. Wilder	Mar. 24, '62.	
Second Lieutenant	Charles Flickinger	Aug. 3, '61.	Resigned March 11, '62
"	George Searing	July 11, '62.	
I.			
Captain	Hiram M. Phillips	Sept. 6, '61.	
First Lieutenant	Emory L. Waller	Sept. 6, '61.	Resigned June 14, '62
"	James D. Lemon	June 14, '62.	
Second Lieutenant	Albert W. Fellows	Sept. 6, '61.	
K.			
Captain	Joseph Woodruff	Aug. 20, '61.	
First Lieutenant	Oscar S. Belcher	Aug. 20, '61.	Resigned March 11, '62
"	Donald A. Nicholson	Mar. 15, '62.	Resigned June 14, '62
"	Andrew W. Wheeler	June 14, '62.	
Second Lieutenant	Donald A. Nicholson	Aug. 20, '61.	Promoted
"	Andrew W. Wheeler	Mar. 15, '62.	Promoted
"	Marion L. Butterfield	June 14, '62.	

Schedule G—Continued.

Roster of Fortieth Regiment Illinois Volunteers.

Field and Staff.		Rank.	Remarks.
Colonel........	Stephen G. Hicks......	July 25, '61..	Honorably discharged Nov.
Lieut. Colonel....	James W. Boothe......	July 25, '61,..	[1, '62..............
Major..........	John B. Smith........	July 25, '61..	Resigned May 26, '62...:.
" "	Rigden S. Barnhill....	May 26, '61..	....
Adjutant........	Rigden S. Barnhill......	July 25, '61..	Promoted Major.........
" "	James Roy............	July 23, '62..	....
Quartermaster...	Albion F. Taylor.......	July 25, '61..	....
Surgeon........	Samuel W. Thompson...	July 25, '61 .	Resigned June 3, '62.....
" "	William M. Elliott.....	June 3, '62..	....
1st Ass't Surgeon.	William Graham.......	Aug. 15, '61..	....
2d Ass't Surgeon.	Joseph W. Edwards....	Oct. 21, '62..	....
Chaplain'........	Richard Massey........	July 25, '61..	....

Company A.

Captain........	Hiram W. Hall.........	July 25, '61..	....
First Lieutenant..	Flavius J. Carpenter....	July 25, '61..	Resigned Nov. 15, '61....
" " ..	Benjamin W. Herrelson.	Nov. 15, '61..	....
Second Lieutenant	Benjamin W. Herrelson.	July 25, '61..	Promoted ....
" "	John McLean..........	Nov. 15, '61..	Resigned Sept. 23, '62....
" "	William B. Heard......	Sept. 23, '62 .	....

B.

Captain........	William T. Sprouse.....	July 25, '61..	....
First Lieutenant .	Joshua Goodwin........	July 25, '61..	....
Second Lieutenant	Elijah D. Martin........	July 25, '61..	Resigned Oct. 21, '62.....
" "	Robert G. Nance.......	Oct. 21, '62..	....

C.

Captain........	Elias Stuart...........	July 25, '61..	Resigned May 15, '62 ....
" "	William Merritt.......	May 15, '62..	....
First Lieutenant..	Samuel S. Emery.......	July 25, '61..	Resigned Oct. 21, '62.....
" "	John Phipps...........	Oct. 21, '62..	....
Second Lieutenant	William Merritt........	July 25, '61..	Promoted ....
" "	John Phipps...........	May 15, '62..	Promoted ....
" "	James Fields...........	Oct. 21, '62..	....

D.

Captain.........	Samuel Hooper.........	July 25, '61..	Killed at Shiloh ....
" "	William Stuart........	April 7, '62..	....
First Lieutenant..	William Stuart.........	July 25, '61..	Promoted ....
" " ..	Joseph P. Rider........	April 7, '62..	Resigned June 3, '62.....
" " ..	William C. Murphy.....	June 3, '62 ..	....
Second Lieutenant	Joseph P. Rider........	July 25, '61..	Promoted ....
" "	Gilbert J. George.......	April 7, '62..	....

E.

Captain........	Daniel N. Ulm.........	July 25, '61..	....
First Lieutenant..	Andrew F. Nesbit.......	July 25, '61..	Resigned Sept. 27, 61....
" " ..	William H. Summers ...	Sept. 27, '61 .	....
Second Lieutenant	William H. Summers....	July 25, '61..	Promoted ....
" "	Benjamin F. Best.......	Sept. 27, '61 .	Resigned Sept 6, '62 .....
" "	William W. Dunlap.....	Sept. 6, '62..	....

SCHEDULE G — Continued.

		Rank.	Remarks.
F.			
Captain	Tillman Shirley	July 25, '61.	Resigned Oct. 29, 1862
"	William T. Ingram	Oct. 29, '62.	
First Lieutenant	William T. Ingram	July 25, '61.	Promoted
"	Chistopher Ing	Oct. 29, '62.	
Second Lieutenant	Joseph Ing	July 25, '61.	Resigned March 11, 1862.
"	Isaac A. Ingram	Mar. 11, '62.	Died of wounds
"	Christopher Ing	July 23, '62.	Promoted
"	John W. Baugh	Oct. 29, '62.	
G.			
Captain	William F. Scott	July 25, '61.	Resigned April 1, 1862
"	Carlisle C. Hopkins	April 1, '62.	
First Lieutenant	Carlisle C. Hopkins	July 25, '61.	Promoted
"	Jonah Morlan	April 1, '62.	
Second Lieutenant	Jonah Morlan	July 25, '61.	Promoted
"	Samuel H. Watson	April 1, '62.	
H.			
Captain	Samuel D. Stuart	July 25, '61.	Honorably discharged November 1, 1862
First Lieutenant	John G. Lane	July 25, '61.	Resigned Nov. 26, 1861
"	Thomas F. Galvin	Nov. 26, '61.	
Second Lieutenant	Thomas F. Galvin	July 25, '61.	Promoted
"	Thomas G. Kelly	Nov. 26, '61.	
I.			
Captain	Gamaliel Hoskinson	July 25, '61.	Resigned June 3, 1862
"	Abraham L. Hammaker	June 3, '62.	
First Lieutenant	George D. Humphries	July 25, '61.	Died of wounds May 2, '62
"	Samuel B. Lingenfelter	May 2, '62.	Died.
Second Lieutenant	Henry Crackel	July 25, '61.	Promoted
"	Abraham L. Hammaker	Oct. 11, '61.	
"	Isaac Ingersoll	June 3, '62.	
K.			
Captain	Jacob L. Moore	July 25, '61.	
First Lieutenant	Woodruff Blacklidge	July 25, '61.	
Second Lieutenant	Joseph B. Figg	July 25, '61.	Resigned Oct. 14, 1861
"	Howlett H. Cook	Oct. 14, '61.	Died of wounds
"	Robert F. Davidson	April 11, '62.	

SCHEDULE G—Continued.

Roster of Forty-First Regiment Illinois Volunteers.

Field and Staff.		Rank.	Remarks.
Colonel..........	Isaac C. Pugh..........	July 27, '61..	....
Lieutenant Colonel	Ansel Tupper..........	July 27, '61..	Killed in battle Shiloh, Ap'l 6, '62..............
"	John Warner..........	April 8, '62..	Discharged Sept. 1, '62...
"	John H. Nale..........	Sept. 1, '62..	....
Major..........	John Warner..........	July 27, '61..	Promoted ....
"	John H. Nale..........	April 8, '62..	Promoted ....
"	Francis M. Long	Sept. 1, '62..	....
Adjutant........	Bartley G. Pugh........	Dec. 12, '61..	Resigned March 17, '62...
"	William C. B. Gillespie..	March 17, '62	....
Quartermaster ...	Henry C. Bradsby.......	July 27, '61..	Resigned June 19, '62....
"	Isaac R. Pugh..........	Sept. 30, '62..	....
Surgeon........	William M. Gray.......	Aug. 4, '61..	Mustered out March 29, '62
"	Charles Carle	March 29, '62	....
1st Ass't Surgeon.	George W. Short.......	July 27, '61..	Resigned ....
"	George M. Warmoth....	April 12, '62..	....
2d Ass't Surgeon.	John W. Coleman......	Sept. 30, '62..	....
Chaplain	Henry C. McCook	Oct. 1, '61...	Resigned Jan. 8, '62......
"	Benjamin C. Swartz.....	Feb. 10, 62..	Resigned May 23, '62.....

COMPANY A

Captain	John H. Nale..........	July 27, '61..	Promoted Major..........
"	Michael F. Kanan......	April 8, '62 ..	....
First Lieutenant..	Michael F. Kanan......	July 27, '61..	Promoted ....
"	George R. Steele.......	April 8, '62..	....
Second Lieutenant	George R. Steele	July 27, '61..	Promoted ....
"	Rolando Bell	April 8, '62..	....

B

Captain	Alsey B. Lee..........	July 27, '61..	....
First Lieutenant..	John H. Davis	July 27, '61..	....
Second Lieutenant	Jackson H. Aldrich.....	July 27, '61..	Died at Mound City, March
"	William H. Palmer	April 7, '62..	.... [1, '62.

C

Captain	John Conklin	July 27, '61..	Resigned March 17, '62...
"	Michael Danison.......	March 17, '62	....
First Lieutenant..	William C. Campbell....	July 27, '61..	Resigned Nov. 12, '61.....
"	Michael Danison	Nov. 15, '61..	Promoted ....
"	William W. Hickman...	March 17, '62	Resigned Oct. 15, '62 ....
"	John W. Bullock.......	Oct. 15, '62..	....
Second Lieutenant	Michael Danison	July 27, '61..	Promoted ....
"	John W. Bullock.......	Nov. 15, '61..	Promoted ....
"	Philip F. McGowan.....	Oct. 15, '62..	....

D

Captain	Edmund W. True.......	July 27, '61..	Killed at Shiloh..........
"	Robert H. McFadden....	Feb. 15, '62..	....
First Lieutenant..	Robert H. McFadden....	July 27, '61..	Promoted ....
"	Francis A. Norvell......	Feb. 15, '62..	....
Second Lieutenant	Francis A. Norvell......	July 27, '61..	Promoted ....
"	Theodore E. True.......	Feb. 15, '62..	....

E.

Captain	John L. Armstrong.....	July 27, '61..	Died Dec. 11, '61 ....
"	Willis S. Oglesby.......	Dec. 12, '61..	Killed at Shiloh ....
"	Oscar Strait	Sept. 1, '62 ..	....

SCHEDULE G — Continued.

		Rank.	Remarks.
First Lieutenant..	Willis S. Oglesby.......	July 27, '61..	Promoted...............
" ..	Robert Warwick.......	Dec. 12, '61..	Dismissed by court martial.
" ..	James A. Wilson.......	April 8, '62..	
Second Lieutenant	Robert Warwick.......	July 27, '61..	Promoted...............
"	James M. Taylor........	Dec. 12, '61..	Resigned April 26, 62....
"	Simeon R. Appleton....	Sept. 30, '62.	Resigned Nov. 18, '62....
"	Joseph Catherwood.....	Nov. 18, '62..	

F.

Captain.........	David P. Brown........	July 27, '61..	Resigned, March 28, '62...
"	John C. Lewis.........	March 28, '62	Resigned, Oct. 16, '62....
"	Jesse F Harrold........	Oct. 16, '62..	
First Lieutenant..	Henry C. McCook......	July 27, '61..	Promoted Chaplain.......
" ..	Henry Bevis............	Oct. 1, '61..	Resigned, Feb. 10, '62....
" ..	John C. Lewis.........	Feb. 10, '62..	Promoted...............
" ..	Jesse F. Harrold........	March 28, 62.	Promoted...............
" ..	William H. Taylor......	Oct. 16, '62..	
Second Lieutenant	John C. Lewis.........	July 27, '61..	Promoted...............
"	Jesse F. Harrold........	Feb. 10, 62..	Promoted...............
"	William H. Taylor......	March 28, '62	Promoted...............
"	Edward C. Sackett......	Oct. 16, '62..	

G.

Captain.........	Francis M. Long	July 27, '61..	Promoted Major..........
"	Daniel K. Hall.........	Sept. 1, '62..	
First Lieutenant..	Daniel K. Hall	July 27, '61..	Promoted...............
" ..	John B. Butler..........	Sept. 1, '62..	Killed at Shiloh..........
Second Lieutenant	John C. Cox............	July 27, '61..	Promoted...............
"	John B. Butler.........	April 10, '62.	
"	Thomas J. Anderson	Sept. 1, '62..	

H.

Captain.........	Hiram Blackstone......	July 27, '61..	Resigned Jan. 14, '62....
"	John H. Huffner........	Jan. 28, '62..	Killed at Shiloh..........
"	Luther H. Wilber	April 7, '62..	Died April 28, '62........
"	William F. Turney......	April 29, '62.	
First Lieutenant..	James S. Steen.........	July 27, '61..	Resigned Dec. 21, '61....
" ..	John H. Huffner........	Dec. 25, 61.	Promoted...............
" ..	Luther H. Wilber.......	Jan. 28. '62..	Promoted...............
" ..	Daniel M. Turney......	April 29, '62.	
Second Lieutenant	William F. Turney......	July 27, '61..	Resigned Dec. 17, '61....
"	Henry H. Hardy........	Dec. 25, '61..	Resigned May 21, '62.....
"	Christopher Corneley ...	May 22, '62..	

I.

Captain.........	Benjamin B. Bacon.....	July 27, '61..	Resigned March 4, '62....
"	Francis M. Green.......	March 5, '62.	
First Lieutenant..	Benjamin R. Parish.....	July 27, '61..	Resigned Sept. 28, '62 ...
" ..	Leander Green.........	Sept. 28, '62.	
Second Lieutenant	Francis M. Green.......	July 27, '61..	Promoted...............
"	Leander Green.........	March 5, '62.	Promoted...............
"	Philip J. Frederick.....	Sept. 28, '62.	

K.

Captain.........	Alexander Kelly........	July 27, '61..	Resigned Dec. 17, '61.....
"	Samuel Winegardner....	Jan. 15, '62..	
First Lieutenant..	Samuel Woodward......	July 27, '61..	
Second Lieutenant	Thomas Davis...........	July 27, '61..	Resigned Jan. 8, '62.....
"	James M. Warren	Jan. 8, '62...	

Schedule G—Continued.

Roster of Forty-Second Regiment Illinois Volunteers.

Field and Staff.		Rank.	Remarks.
Colonel	William A. Webb	July 22, '61	Died Dec. 24, '61
"	George W. Roberts	Dec. 24, '61	
Lieutenant Colon'l	David Stuart	July 22, '61	Promoted to Colonel 55th
"	Charles Northrop	Dec. 24, '61	Resigned Sept. 26, '62
"	Nathan H. Walworth	Sept. 26, '62	
Major	George W. Roberts	July 22, '61	Promoted Colonel
"	Nathan H. Walworth	Dec. 24, '61	Promoted Lieut. Colonel
"	John A. Hottenstein	Sept. 26, '62	
Adjutant	Edward H. Brown	July 22, '61	
Quartermaster	Edward D. Swartout	July 22, '61	Resigned Oct. 18, '61
"	J. Condit Smith	Oct. 7, '61	
Surgeon	Edwin Powell	July 28, '61	Resigned Jan. 11, '62
"	Thomas D. Fitch	Jan. 11, '62	
1st Ass't Surgeon	E. O. F. Roler	July 28, '61	Promoted Surgeon 55th In-
"	Zenas P. Hanson	Jan. 11, '62	[fantry.
2d Ass't Surgeon	Octave P. F. Ravenot	Dec. 18, '62	
Chaplain	G. L. S. Stuff	July 22, '61	
COMPANY A.			
Captain	Charles Northrop	July 22, '61	Promoted Lieut. Colonel
"	Hamilton M. Way	Dec. 24, '61	Resigned May 28, '62
"	Elijah S. Church	May 28, '62	
First Lieutenant	Hamilton M. Way	July 22, '61	Promoted
"	Elijah S. Church	Dec. 24, '61	Promoted
"	Frederick A. Atwater	May 28, '62	
Second Lieutenant	Elijah S. Church	July 22, '61	Promoted
"	Frederick A. Atwater	Dec. 24, '61	Promoted
"	John G. McFadden	May 28, '62	
B.			
Captain	George Vardan	July 22, '61	Died Sept. 18, '62
First Lieutenant	Alexander F. Stevenson	July 22, '61	
Second Lieutenant	Julius Lettman	July 22, '61	
C.			
Captain	Nathan H. Walworth	July 22, '61	Promoted Major
"	James Lighton	Dec. 24, '61	
First Lieutenant	James Lighton	July 22, '61	Promoted
"	Nicholas P. Ferguson	Dec. 24, '61	Resigned June 13, '62
Second Lieutenant	Nicholas P. Ferguson	July 22, '61	Promoted
"	Levi Preston	Dec. 24, '61	
D.			
Captain	Bela P. Clark	July 22, '61	Resigned July 14, '62
First Lieutenant	Robert Ranny	July 22, '61	Promoted Captain Co. K
"	Jared W. Richards	April 8, '62	
Second Lieutenant	Jared W. Richards	July 22, '61	Promoted
"	Mendez C. Bryant	April 8, '62	
E.			
Captain	David W. Norton	July 22, '61	
First Lieutenant	William R. Townsend	July 22, '61	
Second Lieutenant	Nathaniel H. DuFoe	July 22, '61	Resigned May 11, '62

SCHEDULE G—Continued.

		Rank.	Remarks.
F.			
Captain	Charles C. Phillips	July 22, '61	Resigned Aug. 31, '62
First Lieutenant	William D. Williams	July 22, '61	Resigned Oct. 27, '62
Second Lieutenant	Andrew H. Granger	July 22, '61	
G.			
Captain	William H. Boomer	July 22, '61	
First Lieutenant	Joseph N. Gettman	July 22, '61	Resigned April 8, '62
"	John W. Scott	April 8, '62	
Second Lieutenant	John W. Scott	July 22, '61	Promoted
"	Alfred O. Johnson	April 8, '62	
H.			
Captain	John H. Henstein	July 22, '61	Promoted Major
First Lieutenant	George D. Curtis	July 22, '61	Promoted
"	Alexander J. H. Brewer	Nov. 25, '61	Resigned Nov. 25, '61
Second Lieutenant	Alexander J. H. Brewer	July 22, '61	Resigned June 8, '62
"	Ezra A. Montgomery	Nov. 25, '61	
I.			
Captain	Edgar D. Swain	July 22, '61	
First Lieutenant	Wesley P. Andrews	July 22, '61	Resigned June 13, '62
Second Lieutenant	Ogden Lovell	July 22, '61	
K.			
Captain	Jesse D. Butts	July 22, '61	Resigned April 8, '62
"	Robert Raney	April 8, '62	
First Lieutenant	Joseph W. Foster	July 22, '61	
Second Lieutenant	Gilbert L. Barnes	July 22, '61	Died Oct. 24, '61
"	Abram O. Garlock	Oct. 24, '61	Resigned June 16 '62

SCHEDULE G—Continued.

Roster of Forty-Third Regiment Illinois Volunteers.

Field and Staff.		Rank.	Remarks.
Colonel	Julius Raith	Sept. 1, '61	Died, April 11, 1862, of
"	Adolphus Engelmann	April 12, '62	[wounds at Shiloh.
Lieutenant Colonel	Adolphus Engelmann	Sept. 1, '61	Promoted
"	Adolph Dengler	April 12, '62	
Major	Adolph Dengler	Sept. 1, '61	Promoted
"	Hugo M. Starkloff	April 7, '62	Commission returned
"	Charles Stephani	July 1, '62	
Adjutant	John Peetz	Oct. 1, '61	Promoted to Capt. Co. A.
"	Ernst W. Decker	Sept. 1, '62	
Quartermaster	Albert Potthoff	Sept. 18, '61	
Surgeon	Hugo M. Starkloff	May 8, '62	
1st Ass't Surgeon.			
2d Ass't Surgeon.			
Chaplain	John L. Walther	Oct. 1, '61	Killed in battle at Shiloh.

COMPANY A.

Captain	William Ehrhard	Sept. 1, '61	Resigned Aug. 31, '62
"	John Peetz	Sept. 1, '62	
First Lieutenant	Peter Druckenbrodt	Sept. 1, '61	Promoted to Company F.
"	Henry Millitzer	Dec. 30, '61	
Second Lieutenant	August Fritz	Sept. 1, '61	

B.

Captain	Samuel Schimminger	Sept. 1, '61	
First Lieutenant	George H. Hoering	Sept. 1, '61	Promoted to Co. K
"	Henry Strassinger	Sept. 1, '62	
Second Lieutenant	Henry Strassinger	Sept. 1, '61	Promoted
"	John Wolz	Sept. 1, '62	

C.

Captain	Hugo M. Starkloff	Sept. 1, '61	Promoted Major
"	Olof S. Edvall	October 1, '61	Died May 7, '62
"	Carl Arosenius	October 9, '62	
First Lieutenant	Olof S. Edvall	Sept. 1, '61	Promoted
"	John P. Andberg	Feb. 13, '62	
Second Lieutenant	Nels P. McCool	Sept. 1, '61	Dead
"	Nels Knutson	Feb. 13, '62	

D.

Captain	Louis Mauss	Sept. 1, '61	Died April 7, '62
"	Ernst W. Decker	May 1, '62	Resigned
"	Reimer C. Fieldcamp	May 31, '62	
First Lieutenant	Henry Johns	Sept. 1, '61	Resigned April 30, '62
"	Reimer C. Fieldcamp	May 1, '62	Promoted
Second Lieutenant	Reimer C. Fieldcamp	Sept. 1, '61	Promoted
"	Samuel Keymer	May 1, '62	

E.

Captain	John Tobien	Sept. 1, '61	
First Lieutenant	Henry Kroeger	Sept. 1, '61	Promoted Captain Co. I.
"	Charles Engel	Sept. 1, '62	
Second Lieutenant	John Peetz	Sept. 1, '61	Promoted Adjutant
"	John Oppendick	Oct. 1, '61	Killed April 6, '62
"	Charles Engel	April 8, '62	Promoted
"	Gustav Wagenfucher	Sept. 1, '62	

Schedule G.—Continued.

		Rank.	Remarks.
F.			
Captain	George Frick	Sept. 1, '61	Resigned
"	Ernst W. Decker	Nov. 1, '61	Resigned
"	Peter Druckenbrodt	Dec. 30, '61	Resigned Nov. 12, '62
First Lieutenant	Henry Struisbig	Sept. 1, '62	Resigned Dec. 31, '61
"	Ernst Wuerple	Dec. 31, '61	
Second Lieutenant	Henry Rose	Sept. 1, '61	Resigned April 19, '62
G.			
Captain	Franz Grimm	Sept. 1, '61	Died April 6, '62
"	Charles Hoenny	April 8, '62	
First Lieutenant	Charles Hoenny	Sept. 1, '61	Promoted
"	Charles Storck	April 8, '62	
Second Lieutenant	John Lindroth	Sept. 1, '61	Died April 6, '62
"	Frederick Exter	April 8, '62	
H.			
Captain	Hugo Westermann	Sept. 1, '61	
First Lieutenant	Louis Westermann	Sept. 1, '61	Resigned February 5, 62
"	John Harnni	Feb. 8, '62	
Second Lieutenant	John W. Florence	Oct. 15, '61	Resigned February 4, '62
"	Joseph Fuess	April 8, '62	
I.			
Captain	Charles Stephani	Oct. 1, '61	Promoted Major
"	Henry Kroeger	Sept. 1, '62	
First Lieutenant	Henry Sacker	Oct. 1, '61	Died April 6, '62
"	John J. Meyer	April 8, '62	
Second Lieutenant	Julius Phillips	Sept. 11, '61	Resigned July 17, '62
K.			
Captain	George H. Hoering	Sept. 1, '62	
First Lieutenant	Peter Schmitt	April 17, '62	
Second Lieutenant	Daniel C. Anderson	April 17, '62	

Schedule G—Continued.

Roster of Forty-Fourth Regiment Illinois Volunteers.

Field and Staff.		Rank.	Remarks.
Colonel	Charles Knobelsdorf	Aug. 14, '61	
Lieut. Colonel	William J. Stephenson	Aug. 14, '61	Resigned Aug. 2, 1862
"	William J. Stephenson	Dec. 16, '62	
Major	Thomas J. Hobart	Aug. 14, '61	
Adjutant	Charles T. Dake	Aug. 14, '61	Promoted Capt. Co. H
"	James S. Ransom	June 7, '62	
Quartermaster	William H. Gale	Aug. 14, '61	
Surgeon	Ferdinand Weitzc	July 1, '61	
1st Ass't Surgeon			
2d Ass't Surgeon	William D. Carter	Oct. 1, '62	
Chaplain	George Erwin	Aug. 14, '61	Resigned June 13, '62

Company A.

Captain	George Zelle	Aug. 14, '61	Resigned March 31, '62
First Lieutenant	Nicholas Davis	Aug. 14, '61	Mustered out June 27, '62
"	Henry Schmitdz	Aug. 20, '62	Resigned Nov. 18, '62
Second Lieutenant	Charles J. Hulbig	Aug. 14, '61	Mustered out May 23, '62
"	Henry Schmitdz	May 23, '62	Promoted
"	Peter Weyhrich	Aug. 20, '62	

B.

Captain	Wallace W. Barrett	Aug. 14, '61	
First Lieutenant	Lemon G. Hine	Aug. 14, '61	Resigned April 7, '62
"	Samuel N. Andrews	April 7, '62	
Second Lieutenant	Samuel N. Andrews	Aug. 14, '61	Promoted
"	Silas L. Parker	April 7, '62	

C.

Captain	John Russell	Aug. 14, '61	
First Lieutenant	John B. Stoner	Aug. 14, '61	
Second Lieutenant	Eli R. Manley	Aug. 14, '61	

D.

Captain	Edwin L. Hays	Aug. 14, '61	Resigned Sept. 3, '62
First Lieutenant	David O. Livermore	Aug. 14, '61	Resigned Aug. 31, '62
Second Lieutenant	Jacob C. Hoffmire	Aug. 14, '61	

E.

Captain	Lothar Lippert	Aug. 14, '61	Resigned for promotion
"	Ernst Moldenhawer	Feb. 9, '62	
First Lieutenant	John A. Commerell	Aug. 14, '61	Resigned Dec. 27, '61
"	Ernst Moldenhawer	Dec. 27, '61	Promoted
"	Charles R. Harnisch	Feb. 9, '62	
Second Lieutenant	William H. Gale	Aug. 14, '61	Quartermaster
"	Ernst Moldenhawer	Aug. 14, '61	Promoted
"	Charles R. Harnisch	Dec. 27, '61	Promoted
"	Frederick Abrahams	Feb. 9, '62	

F.

Captain	Andrew J. Hosmer	Aug. 14, '61	
First Lieutenant	William Hicks	Aug. 14, '61	Resigned April 5, '62
"	James M. Stephenson	April 5, '62	
Second Lieutenant	James M. Stephenson	Aug. 14, '61	Promoted
"	Oliver A. Dickerman	April 5, '62	

Schedule G — Continued.

		Rank.	Remarks.

G.

Captain	Luther M. Sabine	Aug. 14, '61	
First Lieutenant	Randolph D. Hobart	Aug. 14, '61	Resigned April 19, '62
"	Reuben C. Norton	April 19, '62	
Second Lieutenant	Robert Penman	Aug. 14, '61	Resigned Feb. 28, '62
"	Gustavus Freysleben	Feb. 28, '62	

H.

Captain	James H. Barrett	Aug. 14, '61	Resigned Feb. 1, '62
"	Charles T. Dake	June 7, '62	
First Lieutenant	Charles T. Dake	Aug. 14, '61	Promoted Adjutant
"	James S. Ransom	Oct. 31, '61	Promoted Adjutant
"	William H. Friccius	June 7, '62	Dismissed Dec. 18, '62
Second Lieutenant	James S. Ransom	Aug. 14, '61	Promoted
"	William H. Friccius	Oct. 31, '61	Promoted
"	George B. Cooley	June 7, '62	

I.

Captain	Jasper Partridge	Aug. 14, '61	
First Lieutenant	Thomas B. Lacey	Aug. 14, '61	Canceled
"	Russell Brown	Sept. 13, '61	
Second Lieutenant	Jesse C. Bliss	Aug. 14, '61	

K.

Captain	Hermann Stach	Aug. 14, '61	Resigned Nov. 22, '62
First Lieutenant	Martin Reininger	Aug. 14, '61	
Second Lieutenant	William Gebhardt	Aug. 14, '61	Resigned Jan. 16, '62
"	William Schnoeckel	Jan. 16, '62	

SCHEDULE G.—Continued.

Roster of Forty-Fifth Regiment Illinois Volunteers.

Field and Staff.		Rank.	Remarks.
Colonel	John Eugene Smith	July 23, '61	
Lieut. Colonel	Jasper A. Maltby	Sept. 17, '61	
Major	Melancthon Smith	Oct. 31, '61	
Adjutant	William T. Frohock	Oct. 31, '61	
Quartermaster	John Pyatt	Sept. 10, '61	Resigned
"	Evans Blake	Nov. 25, '61	
Surgeon	Edward D. Kittoe	Aug. 30, '61	
1st Asst. Surgeon	Francis Weaver	Nov. 18, '61	Died
"	Frank W. Reilley	March 21, '62	
2d Asst. Surgeon	William Lyman	Sept. 5, '62	
Chaplain	George W. Woodward	Jan. 1, '62	

COMPANY A.

Captain	Abraham Polsgrove	Aug. 30, '61	
First Lieutenant	William T. Frohock	Aug. 30, '61	Promoted Adjutant
"	George Moore	Nov. 1, '61	Died
"	Joseph Myers	April 9, '62	
Second Lieutenant	George Moore	Aug. 30, '61	Promoted
"	Joseph Myers	Dec. 1, '61	Promoted
"	David Williams	May 1, '62	

B.

Captain	Luther H. Cowen	Aug. 30, '61	
First Lieutenant	Nesbit Banger	Aug. 30, '61	Died May 16, '62
"	Joshua Vandewort	June 1, '62	
Second Lieutenant	Samuel H. Townsend	Aug. 30, '61	Resigned June 4, 1862
"	Daniel W. Cowen	June 4, '62	

C.

Captain	Thomas Burns	Sept. 2, '61	Resigned May 5, '62
"	James Rouse	May 5, '62	
First Lieutenant	James Rouse	Sept. 2, '61	Promoted
"	Joseph Vincent	May 9, '62	
Second Lieutenant	John Byrne	Sept. 2, '61	Resigned May 16, '62
"	James Clifford	June 1, '62	

D.

Captain	Thomas D. Connor	Sept. 3, '61	Killed at Shiloh
"	John O. Duer	April 6, '62	
First Lieutenant	William R. Rowley	Nov. 13, '61	Pro. to Gen. Grant's Staff
"	John O. Duer	March 1, '62	Promoted
"	Joseph W. Miller	April 6, '62	
Second Lieutenant	John O. Duer	Sept. 3, '61	Promoted
"	Joseph W. Miller	March 1, '62	Promoted
"	Otto C. Hager	May 1, '62	

E.

Captain	Leander B. Fisk	Sept. 14, '61	
First Lieutenant	Charles D. Overstreet	Sept. 14, '61	Resigned Nov. 4, '62
Second Lieutenant	John M. Adair	Dec. 1, '61	

SCHEDULE G—Continued.

		Rank.	Remarks.
F.			
Captain	Melancthon Smith	Sept. 17, '61	Promoted Major
"	Alfred Johnson	Dec. 29, '61	Killed at Shiloh April 7, '62
"	James J. Palmer	April 8, '62	
First Lieutenant	Robert P. Seely	Sept. 17, '61	Promoted Co. G
" "	James J. Palmer	Dec. 29, '61	Promoted
" "	Edwin L. Lawrence	April 8, '62	Resigned Sept. 2, '62
Second Lieutenant	Dennis W. Griffin	Sept. 17, '61	Resigned
"	Edwin L. Lawrence	Dec. 29, '61	Promoted
"	John A. Rollins	June 1, '62	
G.			
Captain	Robert P. Seely	Nov. 1, '61	
First Lieutenant	Dennis W. Griffin	Nov. 1, '61	Resigned June 1, '62
" "	Syrice M. Budlong	June 1, '62	
Second Lieutenant	Syrice M. Budlong	Dec. 1, '61	Promoted
" "	Giles H. Bush	June 1, '62	
H.			
Captain	John B. Hawley	Dec. 24, '61	Resigned May 26, '62
"	William B. Seymour	May 26, '62	
First Lieutenant	William B. Seymour	Dec. 24, '61	Promoted
" "	Thomas C. Morris	May 26, '62	
Second Lieutenant	Thomas C. Morris	Dec. 24, '61	Promoted
"	David O. Reid	June 1, '62	
I.			
Captain	Oliver A. Bridgford	Dec. 24, '61	Resigned Sept. 3, '62
First Lieutenant	James Balfour	Dec. 24, '61	Died
" "	Henry H. Boyce	May 19, '62	Resigned Aug. 31, '62
Second Lieutenant	Henry H. Boyce	Dec. 24, '61	Promoted
" "	William L. Green	June 1, '62	
K.			
Captain	Benjamin F. Holcomb	Dec. 24, '61	
First Lieutenant	John Gray	Dec. 24, '61	
Second Lieutenant	Luther B. Hunt	Dec. 24, '61	Resigned June 1, '62
" "	Henry O. Harkness	June 1, '62	

SCHEDULE G—Continued.

Roster of Forty-Sixth Regiment Illinois Volunteers.

Field and Staff.		Rank.	Remarks.
Colonel	John A. Davis	Sept. 12, '61.	Died at Boliver Oct. 10, '62
"	Benjamin Dornblaser	Oct. 11, '62.	[of wounds receiv'd Hatchie
Lieut. Colonel	William O. Jones	Sept. 12, '61.	Resigned Dec. 31, 1861...
"	John J. Jones	Jan. 1, '62.	
Major	Frederick A. Starring	Sept. 12, '61.	Promoted Major 2d Ill. Art.
"	Benjamin Dornblaser	Feb. 8, '62.	Promoted Colonel
"	John M. McCracken	Oct. 11, '62.	
Adjutant	Benjamin Dornblaser	Oct. 11, '61.	Promoted Major
"	Edward R. Lord	July 17, '62.	Resigned Nov. 19, 1862
Quartermaster	Frank Fuller	Sept. 12, '61.	Resigned to Governer
"	James L. Willson	Sept. 18, '61.	Resigned January 15, 1862
"	David S. Pride	Jan. 15, '62.	Promoted Chaplain Co. I.
"	Edwin R. Gillitt	Sept. 1, '62.	
Surgeon	Elias C. DePuy	Sept. 23, '61.	Resigned Sept. 3, '62
"	Elias C. DePuy	Dec. 9, '62.	
1st Ass't. Surgeon	Charles Carle	Feb. 16, '62.	Promoted Surgeon 41st Reg
"	Benjamin H. Bradshaw	Sept. 12, '61.	
2d Ass't. Surgeon			
Chaplain	David Teed	Oct. 11, '61.	Resigned Sept. 1, 1862
"	Hezekiah R. Lewis	Oct. 21, '62.	

COMPANY A.

Captain	John Musser	Sept. 10, '61.	Died April 24, 1862
"	Joseph Clingman	April 24, '62.	
First Lieutenant	William O. Saxton	Sept. 10, '61.	Resigned April 1, '62
"	Isaac A. Arnold	April 1, '62.	
Second Lieutenant	Isaac A. Arnold	Sept. 10, '61.	Promoted
"	George S. Dickey	April 1, '62.	

B.

Captain	Rollin V. Ankeny	Sept. 14, '61.	
First Lieutenant	Henry Roush	Sept. 14, '61.	Resigned April 18, 1862
"	William J. Reitzell	July 10, '62.	
Second Lieutenant	Thomas J. Hathaway	Sept. 14, '61.	Resigned June 10, 1862
"	William J. Reitzell	June 10, '62	Promoted
"	Emanuel Faust	July 10, '62	

C.

Captain	Frederick Khrumne	Sept. 10, '61.	Resigned April 23, '62
"	Philip Arno	April 23, '62.	
First Lieutenant	Philip Arno	Sept. 10, '61.	Promoted
"	Harbert Harberts	April 23, '62.	
Second Lieutenant	Addo Borchers	Sept. 18, '61.	Resigned Sept. 29, '62
"	Edward Wike	Sept. 29, '62.	

D.

Captain	William F. Wilder	Dec. 1, '61	Resigned Nov. 24, '62
First Lieutenant	Joel L. Coe	Dec. 1, '61	Resigned Nov. 12, '62
Second Lieutenant	Henry H. Woodbury	Dec. 1, '61	

E.

Captain	John M. Marble	Dec. 1, '61	
First Lieutenant	William Lane	Dec. 1, '61	Discharged Sept. 11,'62
"	Frederick H. Marsh	Sept. 11, '62	
Second Lieutenant	William Plantz	Dec. 1, 61	Resigned May 23, '62
"	Albert Siezick	May 23, '62.	

SCHEDULE G—Continued.

		Rank.	Remarks.
F.			
Captain	Thomas Wakefield	Dec. 30, '61	
First Lieutenant	John W. Barr	Oct. 15, '61	
Second Lieutenant	Winfield S. Ingraham	Dec. 30, '61	Killed at Shiloh
"	John Shaw	April 7, '62	
G.			
Captain	William Young	Oct. 15, '61	
First Lieutenant	Thomas M. Hood	Oct. 15, '61	Killed at Shiloh
"	Moses R. Thompson	April 7, '62	Killed at Hatchie
"	Robert Smith	Oct. 6, '62	
Second Lieutenant	Moses R. Thompson	Oct. 15, '61	Promoted
"	Robert Smith	April 7, '62	Promoted
"	Thomas Allen	Oct. 6, '62	
H.			
Captain	John Stevens	Dec. 1, '61	Killed at Shiloh
"	John A. Hughes	April 7, '62	
First Lieutenant	John A. Hughes	Dec. 1, '61	Promoted
"	Frederick W. Pike	April 7, '62	
Second Lieutenant	Frederick W. Pike	Dec. 1, '61	Promoted
"	Edward A. Snyder	April 7, '62	
I.			
Captain	Charles P. Stimson	Dec. 1, '61	Resigned Feb. 26, '62
"	Rosiel D. Campbell	Feb. 26, '62	Resigned August 31, 1862
"	David S. Pride	Sept. 1, '62	
First Lieutenant	James Ballard	Dec. 1, '61	Resigned Nov. 19, 1862
Second Lieutenant	William H. Howell	Dec. 1, '61	Killed at Shiloh
"	Hezekiah Bullock	April 7, '62	
K.			
Captain	John M. McCracken	Dec. 30, '61	Promoted Major
"	William Stewart	Oct. 11, '62	
First Lieutenant	William Stewart	Oct. 15, '61	Promoted
"	Joseph M. McKibbon	Oct. 11, '62	
Second Lieutenant	Beverly W. Whitney	Dec. 30, '61	Resigned July 16, 1862
"	Joseph M. McKibbon	July 16, '62	Promoted
"	Oley F. Johnson	Oct. 11, '62	

SCHEDULE G — Continued.

Roster of Forty-Seventh Regiment Illinois Volunteers.

Field and Staff.		Rank.	Remarks.
Colonel	John Bryner	July 27, '61	Resigned Sept. 2, 1862
"	William A. Thrush	Sept. 2, '62	Killed in battle Oct. 3, '62.
"	John N. Cromwell	Oct. 3, '62	
Lieutenant Colonel	Daniel L. Miles	Aug. 25, '61	Killed in battle May 9, '62
"	William A. Thrush	May 9, '62	Promoted
"	Samuel R. Baker	Sept. 2, '62	
Major	William A. Thrush	Aug. 25, '61	Promoted
"	John N. Cromwell	May 9, '62	Promoted
"	Rush W. Chambers	Oct. 3, '62	Resigned Oct. 31, '62
Adjutant	Rush W Chambers	Aug. 25, '61	Promoted
"	Joseph R. Vail	Oct. 31, '62	
Quartermaster	William Stewart	Aug. 25, '61	
Surgeon	George L. Lucas	Aug. 14, '61	
1st. Ass't Surgeon	Timothy Babb	Aug. 14, '61	
2d Ass't Surgeon	Luther M. Andrews	Dec. 5. '62	
Chaplain	Jeremiah Hazen	Sept. 20, '61	Resigned Nov. 1, '62

COMPANY A.

Captain	John N. Cromwell	Aug. 25. '61	Promoted Major
"	Converse Southard	May 9, '62	Resigned Oct. 29, '62
"	John T. Bowen	Oct. 29, '62	
First Lieutenant	Converse Southard	Aug. 25, '61	Promoted
"	John W. Dodds	May 9, '62	Resigned June 17, '62
"	John T. Bowen	June 17, '62	Promoted
"	William W. Poole	Oct. 29, '62	
Second Lieutenant	John W. Dodds	Aug. 25, '61	Promoted
"	John T. Bowen	May 9, '62	Promoted
"	Charles S. Blood	June 17, '62	

B.

Captain	Joseph B. Miles	Aug. 25, '61	
First Lieutenant	Benjamin F. Biser	Aug. 25, '61	
Second Lieutenant	George Kinnear	Aug. 25, '61	

C.

Captain	John D. McLure	Aug. 25, '61	
First Lieutenant	Silas Chapple	Aug. 25, '61	Resigned June 17, '62
"	George Broad	June 17, '62	
Second Lieutenant	George Broad	Aug. 25, '61	Promoted
"	Samuel A. L. Law	June 17, '62	

D.

Captain	John C. Townsend	Aug. 25, '61	
First Lieutenant	Orlando Fountain	Aug. 25, '61	Resigned March 26, '62
"	George F. Townsend	March 26, '62	
Second Lieutenant	James P. Warrell	Sept. 20, '61	Resigned April 12, '62
"	Theophilus F. Clapp	April 12, '62	

E.

Captain	Samuel R. Baker	Aug. 25, '61	Promoted Lieut. Colonel.
"	George Puterbaugh	Sept. 2, '62	
First Lieutenant	George Puterbaugh	Aug. 25, '61	Promoted
"	William W. Pierce	Sept. 2, '62	
Second Lieutenant	William W. Pierce	Aug. 25, '61	Promoted
"	Edgar Isbell	Sept. 2, '62	

SCHEDULE G — Continued.

		Rank.	Remarks.
F.			
Captain	Lyman W. Clark	Aug. 25, '61	Resigned Dec. 27, '61
"	Theodore M. Lowe	Dec. 28, '61	
First Lieutenant	Theodore M. Lowe	Aug. 25, '61	Promoted
"	Joseph H. Moulton	Dec. 28, '61	Resigned Oct. 22, '62
Second Lieutenant	Joseph Moulton	Aug. 25, '61	Promoted
"	William E. Kuhn	Dec. 28, '61	
G.			
Captain	Harmon Andrews	Aug. 25, '61	
First Lieutenant	William Armmtrout	Aug. 25, '61	Resigned Dec. 30, '61
"	Thomas R. Henderson	Dec. 30, '61	Resigned Nov. 27, '62
"	Edward E. Tobey	Nov. 27, '62	
Second Lieutenant	Abel Bradley	Oct. 1, '61	Resigned Dec. 30, '61
"	Edward E. Tobey	Dec. 31, '61	Promoted
"	Edward Bonham	Nov. 27, '62	
H.			
Captain	Thompson Gordon	Aug. 25, '61	
First Lieutenant	George A. Wilkins	Aug. 25' '61	
Second Lieutenant	James Brassfield	Aug. 25, '61	Resigned June 16, '62
"	Thomas Gray	June 16, '62	
I.			
Captain	Samuel S. Jackman	Aug. 25, '61	Resigned March 26, '62
"	Chester Andrews	March 26, '62	
First Lieutenant	James Tisdale	Aug. 25, '61	Resigned April 12, '62
"	Charles H. Robinson	April 12, '62	
Second Lieutenant	Chester Andrews	Aug. 25, '61	Promoted
"	Joseph H. Wylie	March 27, '62	
K.			
Captain	Jacob Jemison	Aug 25, '61	Resigned March 26, '62
"	David DeWolf	March 26, '62	Killed in battle Corinth
"	John M. Brown	Oct. 3, '62	[Oct 3, '62.
First Lieutenant	David DeWolf	Aug. 25, '61	Promoted
"	James A. Henderson	March 26, '62	Resigned June 16, '62
"	John M. Brown	June 16, '62	Promoted
"	William H. Denchfield	Oct. 3, '62	
Second Lieutenant	Amos Tucker	Aug. 25, '61	Resigned March 26, '62
"	William H. Denchfield	March 26, '62	Promoted
"	John Hawks	Oct. 3, '62	

Schedule G.—Continued.

Roster of Forty-Eighth Regiment Illinois Volunteers.

Field and Staff.		Rank.	Remarks.
Colonel	Isham N. Haynie	Aug. 18, '61	Resigned Nov. 21, '62
Lieutenant Colonel	Thomas H. Smith	Aug. 18, '61	Killed at Fort Donelson
"	William W. Sanford	Feb. 16, '62	[Feb. 15, '62.
Major	William W. Sanford	Aug. 18, '61	Promoted
"	Manning Mayfield	Feb. 16, '62	Honorably discharged Oct.
"	Lucian Greathouse	Oct. 9, '62	[9, '62
Adjutant	William Prescott	Sept. 24, '61	Resigned April 27, '62
"	Wimer Bedford	May 17, '62	
Quartermaster	Jonathan C. Willis	Sept. 24, '61	Resigned June 3, '62
"	George W. Haynie	June 3, '62	
Surgeon	William Hill	Sept. 24, '61	Resigned April 27, '62
"	Asher Goslin	May 1, '62	
1st Ass't Surgeon	Henry H. Deshon	Sept. 27, '61	Died November 20, '61
"	Stephen J. Young	Feb. 2, '62	
2d Ass't Surgeon	Thomas Williams	Aug. 26, '62	
Chaplain	Robert H. Manier	Sept. 24, '61	Resigned June 16, '62
"	Isaac Bundy	Oct. 7, '62	

Company A.

Captain	Manning Mayfield	Sept. 2, '61	Promoted Major
"	John F. Johnston	Feb. 16, '62	Dismissed Nov. 11, '62
"	Stephen F. Grimes	Nov. 11, '62	
First Lieutenant	Malcolm J. Walker	Sept. 2, '61	Deceased
"	John W. Stokes	Feb. 16, '62	Resigned October 11, '62
Second Lieutenant	John F. Johnston	Sept. 2, '61	Promoted
"	William L. Crosby	Feb. 16, '62	

B.

Captain	William J. Stephenson	Sept. 10, '61	
First Lieutenant	Ferdinand D. Stephenson	Sept. 10, '61	
Second Lieutenant	William Sneed	Sept. 10, '61	Died
"	Elbert S. Apperson	April 14, '62	

C.

Captain	Lucian Greathouse	Sept. 10, '61	Promoted Major
"	Jacob G. Stewart	Oct. 9, '62	
First Lieutenant	Robert P. Randolph	Sept. 10, '61	Died
"	Jacob G. Stewart	July 1, '62	Promoted
"	Frank Farrell	Oct. 9, '62	
Second Lieutenant	Jacob G. Stewart	Sept. 10, '61	Promoted
"	William J. Holt	Nov. 1, '62	

D.

Captain	William H. Reddin	Sept. 10, '61	
First Lieutenant	Hartwell P. Farrar	Sept. 10, '61	
Second Lieutenant	Thomas W. Anderson	Sept. 10, '61	

E.

Captain	Jackson G. Young	Sept. 10, '61	Resigned August 31, '62
"	Abner B. Smith	Aug. 31, '62	
First Lieutenant	Hiram B. Chadwick	Sept. 10, '61	Died December 6, '61
"	Abner B. Smith	Dec. 11, '61	Promoted
Second Lieutenant	Abner B. Smith	Sept. 10, '61	Promoted
"	William H. Hoyt	Feb. 16, '62	

Schedule G — Continued.

		Rank.	Remarks.
F.			
Captain	Milton H. Lydick	Nov. 10, '61	
First Lieutenant	Alexander L. Wellman	Nov. 10, '61	
Second Lieutenant	John R. Daily	Nov. 10, '61	
G.			
Captain	William B. Beall	Sept. 25, '61	Resigned March 24, '62
"	Edward Adams	Mar. 24, '62	
First Lieutenant	Edward Adams	Sept. 25, '61	Promoted
Second Lieutenant	George Rank	Sept. 25, '61	Mustered out Feb. 15, '62
"	Hepburn Comrie	Mar. 24, '62	
H.			
Captain	Asher Goslin	Sept. 25, '61	Promoted Surgeon
"	Frank Lindsay	Aug. 14, '62	
First Lieutenant	Sullerd F. Sellers	Sept. 25, '61	Resigned September 3, '62
"	George B. Parker	Sept. 3, '62	
Second Lieutenant	George B. Parker	Sept. 25, '61	Promoted
"	Vincent Anderson	Sept. 3, '62	
I.			
Captain	Ashley T. Galraith	Sept. 25, '61	
First Lieutenant	Elias M. Holmes	Sept. 25, '61	Killed at Shiloh
"	Stephen F. Grimes	April 7, '62	Promoted
"	Thomas L. B. Weens	Nov. 11, '62	
Second Lieutenant	Stephen F. Grimes	Sept. 25, '61	Promoted
"	Thomas L. B. Weens	April 7, '62	Promoted
"	William M. Galbraith	Nov. 11, '62	
K.			
Captain	Benjamin F. Reynolds	Nov. 10, '61	Resigned April 19, '62
First Lieutenant	Jefferson Farris	Nov. 10, '61	Resigned April 19, '62
Second Lieutenant	William N. Berkely	Mar. 22, '62	

Schedule G — Continued.

Roster of Forty-Ninth Regiment Illinois Volunteers.

Field and Staff.		Rank.	Remarks.
Colonel	William R. Morrison	Aug. 30, '61	Resigned Dec. 13, '62
Lieutenant Colonel	Thomas G. Allen	Sept. 9, '61	Resigned Nov. 26, '61
" "	Phineas Pease	Dec. 31, '61	
Major	John B. Hay	Sept. 9, '61	Resigned Dec. 18, '61
"	William W. Bishop	Dec. 31, '61	
Adjutant	James Morrison	Sept. 14, '61	Resigned Sept. 3, 62
"	William Martin	Sept. 3, '62	
Quartermaster	James W. Davis	Oct. 15, '61	
Surgeon	William H. Medcalfe	Dec. 1, '61	
1st Ass't Surgeon	Andrew B. Beatty	Oct. 15, '61	Resigned April 22, '62
2d Ass't Surgeon			
Chaplain	James B. Corrington	July 1, '62	Declined
"	John H. Lockwood	Oct. 8, '62	

Company A.

Captain	Thomas W. Morgan	Sept. 12, '61	
First Lieutenant	Nicholas C. Chester	Sept. 12, '61	Died of wounds received at Ft. Donelson, May 3, '62.
" "	William Cogan	May 3, '62	
Second Lieutenant	William H. Rogers	Sept. 12, '61	Killed at Shiloh
"	William Cogan	April 8, '62	Promoted
"	Andy K. Demint	May 3, '62	

B.

Captain	William P. Moore	Dec. 31, '61	
First Lieutenant	James P. Burns	Oct. 15, '61	Died April 1, '62
"	John L. Stanley	April 1, '62	
Second Lieutenant	William Wesley	Jan. 1, '62	Resigned Jan. 2, '62
"	John L. Stanley	Jan. 2, '62	Promoted
"	Andrew J. McGregor	April 1, '62	

C.

Captain	Louis Kinghoff	Dec. 30, '61	
First Lieutenant	Philip Doll	Oct. 15, '61	Killed at Shiloh
"	Simeon Spira	April 8, '62	
Second Lieutenant	Simeon Spira	Dec. 30, '61	Promoted
"	Christian Dohrman	April 8, '62	

D.

Captain	John W. Brokaw	Dec. 30, '61	Killed at Ft. Donelson
"	James W. Cheney	Feb. 13, '62	
First Lieutenant	James W. Cheney	Oct. 15, '61	Promoted
"	Emory B. Harlan	Feb. 13, '62	
Second Lieutenant	Emory B. Harlan	Dec. 30, '61	Promoted
"	Albert S. Rowley	Feb. 13, '62	

E.

Captain	John G. Berrey	Dec. 31, '61	
First Lieutenant	James M. Maguire	Oct. 23, '61	Died of wounds May 8, '62
"	Henry W. Kerr	May 8, '62	
Second Lieutenant	Henry W. Kerr	Dec. 31, '61	Promoted
"	James Mitchell	May 8, '62	

Schedule G — Continued.

		Rank.	Remarks.
F.			
Captain	Benjamin W. Jones	Dec. 31, '61	Resigned June 7, '62
"	John A. Logan	June 7, '62	
First Lieutenant	Ransom C. Hagerman	Nov. 17, '61	Died May 11, '62
"	John A. Logan	May 11, '62	Promoted
"	James A. Reed	June 7, '62	
Second Lieutenant	William T. Freeland	Dec. 31, '61	Died of wounds Ap'l 22, '62
"	James A. Reed	April 22, '62	Promoted
"	Lewis Dobblemann	June 7, '62	
G.			
Captain	Lewis W. Moore	Dec. 31, '61	
First Lieutenant	William W. Bliss	Oct. 25, '61	
Second Lieutenant	William M. Whaling	Dec. 31, '61	
H.			
Captain	Jacob E. Gauen	Oct. 23, '61	
First Lieutenant	Service Sonday	Sept. 16, '61	
Second Lieutenant	Jacob Fischer	Oct. 23, '61	
I.			
Captain	Archibald W. Thompson	Dec. 31, '61	Resigned March 28, '62
"	Thomas Alexander	March 28, '62	
First Lieutenant	James L. McClurken	Oct. 15, '61	Resigned May 7, '62
"	John B. Houston	May 7, '62	
Second Lieutenant	George L. Watts	Dec. 31, '61	Resigned May 5, '62
"	George Y. McClure	May 5, '62	
K.			
Captain	Benjamin T. Wood	Dec. 30, '61	Resigned June 10, '62
"	Joseph Laur	June 10, '62	
First Lieutenant	Joseph Laur	Oct. 19, '61	Promoted
"	James Lemmon	June 10, '62	
Second Lieutenant	James G. Gilbert	Dec. 30, '61	Resigned March 5, '62
"	James Lemmon	March 5, '62	Promoted
"	Edward Barbee	June 10, '62	

Schedule G—Continued.

Roster of Fiftieth Regiment Illinois Volunteers.

Field and Staff.		Rank.	Remarks.
Colonel	Moses M. Bane	Aug. 21, '61	
Lieutenant Colonel	William Swarthout	Sept. 12, '61	
Major	George W. Randall	Sept. 12, '61	Resigned April 28, '62
"	Samuel R. Glenn	April 28, '62	Discharged Oct. 9, '62
"	Thomas W. Gaines	Oct. 9, '62	
Adjutant	Thomas J. Brown	Sept. 12, '61	Resigned April 28, '62
"	Theodore W. Letton	April 28, '62	
Quartermaster	William Keal	Sept. 12, '61	
Surgeon	Henry W. Kendall	Sept. 12, '61	
1st Ass't Surgeon	Garner H. Bane	Sept. 12, '61	Resigned Nov. 22, '62
2d Ass't Surgeon			
Chaplain			

Company A.

Captain	Edgar Pickett	Sept. 12, '61	Resigned Feb. 5, '62
"	Henry P. W. Cramer	Feb. 5, '62	
First Lieutenant	Henry P. W. Cramer	Sept. 12, '61	Promoted
"	Sergeant Moody	Feb. 5, '62	
Second Lieutenant	Sergeant Moody	Sept. 12, '61	Promoted
"	Henry C. Bissell	Feb. 5, '62	

B.

Captain	John W. Smith	Sept. 12, '61	Resigned June 1, '62
"	Henry E. Horn	June 1, '62	
First Lieutenant	Henry E. Horn	Sept. 1, '61	Promoted
"	William H. Harbison	June 1, '62	
Second Lieutenant	William H. Harbison	Sept. 12, '61	Promoted
"	James W. Anderson	June 1, '62	

C.

Captain	William M. Gooding	Sept. 12, '61	Resigned July 10, '62
"	Horace L. Burnham	July 10, '62	
First Lieutenant	Theodore W. Letton	Sept. 12, '61	Promoted Adjutant
"	George R. Naylor	July 10, '62	
Second Lieutenant	Horace L. Burnham	Sept. 12, '61	Promoted
"	Samuel W. Sterrett	July 10, '62	

D.

Captain	Thomas W. Gaines	Sept. 12, '61	Promoted Major
"	William K. Hazlewood	Oct. 9, '62	Resigned Nov. 14, '62
First Lieutenant	Henry Cusick	Sept. 12, '61	Resigned April 1, '62
"	William K. Hazlewood	April 1, '62	Promoted
"	John W. Rickart	Oct. 9, '62	
Second Lieutenant	William K. Hazlewood	Sept. 12, '61	Promoted
"	Jesse C. Rodgers	April 1, '62	Resigned Oct. 22, '62
"	Charles H. Floyd	Oct. 22, '62	

E.

Captain	William Hanna	Sept. 12, '61	
First Lieutenant	Albert Pickett	Sept. 12, '61	Resigned March 15, '62
"	William W. Birchard	March 15, '62	Resigned Oct. 12, '62
"	John M. Cyrus	Oct. 12, '62	
Second Lieutenant	William W. Birchard	Sept. 12, '61	Promoted
"	John M. Cyrus	March 15, '62	Promoted
"	William C. Ross	Oct. 12, '62	

SCHEDULE G—Continued.

		Rank.	Remarks.
F.			
Captain	William B. Snyder	Sept. 12, '61	
First Lieutenant	Charles J. May	Sept. 12, '61	Resigned April 27, '62
"	Charles M. Harris	April 27, '62	Resigned June 20, '62
"	Charles J. Early	June 20, '62	Resigned Nov. 15, '62
"	Charles D. Fee	Nov. 15, '62	
Second Lieutenant	Charles M. Harris	Sept. 12, '61	Promoted
"	Charles J. Early	April 27, '62	Promoted
"	Charles D. Fee	June 20, '62	Promoted
"	William L. Weakley	Nov. 15, '62	
G.			
Captain	George W. Brown	Sept. 12, '61	Resigned Dec. 12, '61
"	Selah W. King	Dec. 12, '61	
First Lieutenant	Selah W. King	Sept. 12, '61	Promoted
"	Edward P. Barrett	Dec. 12, '61	Resigned July 13, '62
"	Lewis Zolman	July 13, '62	Canceled
"	Mervin Converse	July 13, '62	
Second Lieutenant	Edward P. Barrett	Sept. 12, '61	Promoted
"	Lewis Zolman	Dec. 12, '61	Resigned Aug. 31, '62
"	Henry Comstock	July 13, '62	Canceled
H.			
Captain	Samuel R. Glenn	Oct. 1, '61	Resigned June 30, '62
"	Miles D. Murphy	June 27, '62	Resigned Sept. 2, '62
"	Walter S. Wait	Sept. 2, '62	
First Lieutenant	William S. Ishmel	Oct. 1, '61	Resigned March 3, '62
"	Miles D. Murphy	March 3, '62	Promoted
"	John Cooper	June 27, '62	
Second Lieutenant	John Cooper	Oct. 1, '61	Promoted
"	Fielding T. Glenn	June 27, '62	
I.			
Captain	Joseph D. Wolf	Sept. 15, '61	Mustered out May 19, '62
"	Horace L. Dunlap	May 19, '62	Resigned Nov. 22, '62
First Lieutenant	Horace L. Dunlap	Sept. 15, '61	Promoted
"	George W. Elliott	May 19, '62	Resigned Nov. 15, '62
Second Lieutenant	George W. Elliott	Sept. 15, '61	Promoted
"	Jonas D. Corwin	May 19, '62	Killed at Corinth
"	Cornelius F. Kitchen	Oct. 4, '62	
K.			
Captain	Timothy D. McGillicuddy	Oct. 5, '61	
First Lieutenant	Jefferson White	Nov. 1, '61	
Second Lieutenant	William A. Shane	Jan. 1, '62	Resigned June 20, '62
"	Edward Jonas	Nov. 6, '62	

SCHEDULE G—Continued.

Roster of Fifty-First Regiment Illinois Volunteers.

Field and Staff.		Rank.	Remarks.
Colonel	Gilbert W. Cumming	Sept. 20, '61	Resigned Sept. 30, 1862
"	Luther P. Bradley	Sept. 30, '62	
Lieutenant Colonel	Luther P. Bradley	Sept. 20, '61	Promoted
"	Samuel B. Raymond	Sept. 30, '62	
Major	Samuel B. Raymond	Sept. 20, '61	Promoted
"	Charles W. Davis	Sept. 30, '62	
Adjutant	Charles W. Davis	Oct. 15, '61	Promoted
"	Henry W. Hall	Sept. 30, '62	
Quartermaster	Henry Howland	Sept. 20, ,61	Promoted Brigade Quar-
"	Albert C. Coe	June 9, '62	[termaster.
Surgeon	William C. Hunt	Oct. 21, '61	Resigned April 14, '62
"	Jerome F. Weeks	May 15, '62	
1st Ass't Surgeon	John S. Pashley	Oct. 28, '61	Mustered out July 26, '62
"	Francis W. Lytle	Sept. 25, '62	
2d Ass't Surgeon	Thomas L. Magee	Nov. 25, '62	
Chaplain			
COMPANY A.			
Captain	Henry F. Wescott	Dec. 14, '61	
First Lieutenant	James E. Montandon	Dec. 24, '61	
Second Lieutenant	Antonio DeAnguera	Dec. 24, '61	Resigned June 13, 1862
"	John S. Keith	June 13, '62	
B.			
Captain	Isaac K. Gardner	Dec. 24, '61	Resigned June 28, 1862
"	Henry W. Hall	June 28, '62	Adjutant
First Lieutenant	Henry W. Hall	Dec. 24, '61	Promoted
"	George J. Waterman	June 28, '62	
Second Lieutenant	George J. Waterman	Jan. 17, '62	Promoted
"	Ansel Bates	June 28, '62	
C.			
Captain	Nathaniel B. Petts	Dec. 24, '61	Resigned Nov. 17, 1862
"	Albert M. Tilton	Nov. 17, '62	
First Lieutenant	Albert M. Tilton	Dec. 24, '61	Promoted
"	Albert Eads	Nov. 17, '62	
Second Lieutenant	Albert Eads	Dec. 24, '61	Promoted
"	Adam S. Hatfield	Nov. 17, '62	
D.			
Captain	Ezra L. Brainard	Mar. 1, '62	Mustered out July 8, 1862
"	Theodore F. Brown	July 8, '62	
First Lieutenant	Theodore F. Brown	Mar. 1, '62	Promoted
"	James S. Boyd	July 8, '62	
Second Lieutenant	James S. Boyd	Dec. 24, '61	Promoted
"	Thomas W. Cummings	July 8, '62	
E.			
Captain	John G. McWilliams	Dec. 24, '61	
First Lieutenant	Thomas T. Lester	Dec. 24, '61	
Second Lieutenant	Augustus B. Sweeney	Dec. 24, '61	Resigned Oct. 28, 1862
F.			
Captain	George L. Bellows	July 18, '62	
First Lieutenant	Robert Houston	July 18, '62	
Second Lieutenant	Andrew H. Frasier	July 18, '62	

SCHEDULE G.—Continued

		Rank.	Remarks.
G			
Captain	George H. Wentz	Dec. 24, '61	Resigned October 28, '62.
"	Charles C. Merrick	Sept. 11, '62	
First Lieutenant	Merritt B. Atwater	Dec. 24, '61	
Second Lieutenant	Orin S. Johnson	Dec. 24, '61	Resigned June 28, '62
"	Charles C. Merrick	June 28, '62	Promoted
"	Albert C. Simons	Sept. 11, '62	
H			
Captain	John T. Whitson	Mar. 1, '62	Died July 15, '62
"	Charles B. Whitson	July 15, '62	
First Lieutenant	William H. Greenwood	Jan. 17, '62	
Second Lieutenant	Charles B. Whitson	Mar. 1, '62	Promoted
"	Osman L. Cole	July 15, '62	
K			
Captain	Rufus Rose	Dec. 24, '61	
First Lieutenant	Otis Moody	Dec. 24, '61	
Second Lieutenant	Albert L. Coe	Dec. 24, '61	Promoted Quartermaster.
"	Edward G. Blathemick	June 9, '61	

SCHEDULE G — Continued.

Roster of the Fifty-Second Regiment Illinois Volunteers.

Field and Staff.		Rank.	Remarks.
Colonel	Isaac G. Wilson	Sept. 6, '61	Resigned Dec. 6, '61
"	Thomas W. Sweeney	Jan. 21, '62	
Lieutenant Colonel	John S. Wilcox	Oct. 14, '61	
Major	Henry Stark	Oct. 14, '61	Resigned May 10, '62
"	Edwin A. Bowen	May 10, '62	
Adjutant	Ethan J. Allen	Sept. 14, '61	Resigned Sept. 12, '62
"	Edward Brainard	Sept. 13, '62	Killed in battle at Hatchie
"	Edward S. Wilcox	Oct. 18, '62	
Quartermaster	Charles B. Wells	Sept. 13, '61	
Surgeon	Leland H. Angel	Oct. 2, '61	Resigned March 7, '62
"	Edgar Winchester	March 15, '62	
1st. Ass't Surgeon	Phineas K. Guild	Oct. 14, '61	Resigned March 18, '62
"	Wesley Humphrey	April 10, '62	
2d Ass't Surgeon	George W. Rhor	July 15, '62	
Chaplain	Benjamin Thomas	Oct. 14, '61	
COMPANY A.			
Captain	Smith G. Ward	Aug. 2, '61	Honorably discharged, Oct. [7, '62.
"	George E. Young	Oct. 7, '62	
First Lieutenant	George E. Young	Oct. 1, '61	Promoted
"	Charles R. White	Oct. 7, '62	
Second Lieutenant	Charles R. White	Oct. 1, '61	Promoted
"	Thomas W. Mack	Oct. 7, '62	
B.			
Captain	Edwin A. Bowen	Oct. 8, '61	Promoted Major
"	David D. Bailey	May 10, '62	
First Lieutenant	Solomon L. Roth	Oct. 8, '61	
Second Lieutenant	George W. Graves	Oct. 8, '61	Resigned May 29, '62
"	Charles H. Fish	May 29, '62	
C.			
Captain	John S. Brown	Oct. 1, '61	Resigned Feb. 18, '62
"	Edward M. Knapp	Feb. 18, '62	Killed in battle at Corinth.
"	James Compton	April 7, '62	
First Lieutenant	Edward M. Knapp	Oct. 1,'61	Promoted
"	James Compton	March 4, '62	Promoted
"	Erskin M. Hoyt	April 7, '62	Resigned July 15, '62
"	Oscar W. Phelps	July 15, '62	
Second Lieutenant	Erskin M. Hoyt	Oct. 1, '61	Promoted
"	Oscar W. Phelps	April 7, '62	Promoted
"	Albert C. Perry	July 15, '62	
D.			
Captain	Jacob Grimes	Sept. 23, '61	Resigned Dec. 14, '61
"	D. Carlos Newton	Dec. 14, '61	
First Lieutenant	D. Carlos Newton	Sept. 23, '61	Promoted
"	Lewis H. Everts	Dec. 14, '61	
Second Lieutenant	Lewis H. Everts	Sept. 23, '61	Promoted
"	Joseph J. Kelser	Dec. 14, '61	
E.			
Captain	Wesley Boyd	Nov, 23, '61	
First Lieutenant	Edward Brainard	Nov. 23,'61	Promoted Adjutant
"	DeWitt C. Hurd	Sept. 13, '62	
Second Lieutenant	Henry C. Barker	Nov. 23, '61	Resigned June 7, '62
"	DeWitt C. Hurd	June 7, '62	Promoted
"	Edward B. Spalding	Sept. 13, '62	

SCHEDULE G—Continued.

		Rank.	Remarks.

F.

Captain	Nathan P. Herrington	Oct. 10, '61	Resigned April 8, '62
"	Slocum S. Dunn	April 18, '62	
First Lieutenant	Slocum S. Dunn	Oct. 10, '61	Promoted
"	Lucien S. Kinney	April 18, '62	
Second Lieutenant	John Dyer	Oct. 10, '61	Resigned March 6, '62
"	Arthur P. Vaughn	March 7, '62	

G.

Captain	Francis H. Bowman	Oct. 15, '31	Resigned April 19, '62
"	William H. Wilcox	April 19, '62	
First Lieutenant	William H. Wilcox	Oct. 15, '61	Promoted
"	James Davidson	April 19, '62	
Second Lieutenant	William H. Earl	Oct. 15, '61	Resigned May 15, '62
"	George R. Robinson	May 15, '62	

H.

Captain	Alvah P. Maffatt	Oct. 1, '61	Resigned April 8, '62
"	Luther C. Lee	April 8, '62	Resigned Nov. 7, '62
"	Morris J. McGrath	Nov. 7, '62	
First Lieutenant	Luther C. Lee	Oct. 1, '61	Promoted
"	Morris J. McGrath	April 8, '62	Promoted
"	Cornelius Snyder	Nov. 7, '62	
Second Lieutenant	Morris J. McGrath	Oct. 1, '61	Promoted
"	Cornelius Snyder	April 8, '62	Promoted
"	Alfred Billing	Nov. 7, '62	

I.

Captain	Joseph T. Brown	Sept. 13, '61	
First Lieutenant	Charles B. Wells	Sept. 13, '61	Promoted Quartermaster
"	Joseph E. Ewell	Sept. 13, '61	Resigned April 18, '62
"	Henry G. Wilmarth	April 18, '62	Resigned Sept. 3, '62
"	Thomas H. Thompson	Sept. 2, '62	
Second Lieutenant	Henry G. Wilmarth	Sept. 13, '61	Promoted
"	Thomas H. Thompson	April 18, '62	Promoted
"	Jerome D. Davis	Sept. 3, '62	

K.

Captain	John S. Wilcox	Sept. 14, '61	Promoted Lieut. Colonel
"	Alphonso Barto	Oct. 16, '61	
First Lieutenant	Ethan J. Allen	Sept. 14, '61	Promoted Adjutant
"	Edward S. Wilcox	Nov. 1, '61	Promoted Adjutant
Second Lieutenant	Alphonso Barto	Sept. 14, '61	Promoted
"	E. Sanford Wilcox	Oct. 16, '61	Promoted
"	Henry S. Doty	Nov. 1, '61	

Schedule G—Continued.

Roster of the Fifty-Third Regiment Illinois Volunteers.

Field and Staff.		Rank.	Remarks.
Colonel	Wm. H. W. Cushman	Sept. 23, '61	Resigned Sept. 3, '62
"	Daniel F. Hitt	Sept. 3, '62	
Lieutenant Colonel	Daniel F. Hitt	Sept. 23, '61	Promoted
"	Seth C. Earl	Sept. 3, '62	
Major	Theodore C. Gibson	Jan. 1, '62	Resigned May 23, '62
"	Seth C. Earl	May 23, '62	Promoted
"	John W. McClanahan	Sept. 3, '62	
Adjutant	Seth W. Hardin	Jan. 1, '62	Resigned Sept. 2, '62
"	Charles H. Brush	Nov. 26, '62	
Quartermaster	Philo Lindley	Sept. 23, '61	
Surgeon	William W. Welsh	Jan. 1, '62	
1st Ass't Surgeon	James O. Harris	Nov. 1, '61	Resigned Nov. 18, '62
"	George O. Smith	Dec. 13, '62	
2d Ass't Surgeon			
Chaplain	Festus P. Cleveland	Nov. 11, '61	

Company A.

Captain	Josiah B. Wright	Dec. 1, '61	
First Lieutenant	William Armstrong	Dec. 1, '61	
Second Lieutenant	Daniel Slattery	Dec. 1, '61	Dismissed October 1, '62

B.

Captain	Rolland H. Allison	Jan. 1, '62	
First Lieutenant	Seldon B. Griswold	Jan. 1, '62	Resigned Sept. 29, '62
"	Jarvis B. Smith	Sept. 29, '62	
Second Lieutenant	Jarvis B. Smith	Jan. 1, '62	Promoted

C.

Captain	Joseph E. Skinner	Jan. 1, '62	Dismissed October 1, '62
First Lieutenant	William F. Dewey	Jan. 1, '62	
Second Lieutenant	Carser R. May	Feb. 1, '62	

D.

Captain	James E. Hudson	Dec. 1, '61	
First Lieutenant	Warren H. Norton	Dec. 28, '61	
Second Lieutenant	Albert S. Kinsloe	Jan. 1, '62	

E.

Captain	Charles M. Vaughn	Jan. 1, '62	Wounded at Hatchie, died [October 30, '62.
First Lieutenant	Alonzo W. Buell	Jan. 1, '62	Transferred to Co. I
"	Mark C. Wheeler	March 1, '62	Resigned August 31, '62
"	Frank J. Crawford	Aug. 31, '62	
Second Lieutenant	Mark C. Wheeler	Jan. 1, '62	Promoted
"	Frank J. Crawford	March 1, '62	Promoted
"	Mark M. Bassett	Aug. 31, '62	

F.

Captain	Seth C. Earl	Sept. 23, '61	Promoted Major
"	Daniel L. Houston	May 23, '62	
First Lieutenant	Daniel L. Houston	Jan. 1, '62	Promoted
"	William G. Earl	May 23, '62	Resigned Nov. 18, '62
"	John Potter	Nov. 18, '62	
Second Lieutenant	William G. Earl	Jan. 1, '62	Promoted
"	John Potter	May 23, '62	Promoted
"	Cornelius G. W. Hyde	Nov. 18, '62	

SCHEDULE G — Continued.

		Rank.	Remarks.
G.			
Captain	Morgan L. Payne	March 1, '62.	Dismissed October 1, '62..
First Lieutenant	George R. Lodge	Feb. 1, '62.	
Second Lieutenant	John H. Elwood	March 1, '62.	
H.			
Captain	John W. McClanahan	Nov. 2, '62.	Promoted Major
"	Timothy W. Atwood	Sept. 3, '62.	
First Lieutenant	Timothy W. Atwood	March 1, '62.	Promoted
"	Simeon Rathbun	Sept. 3, '62.	Dismissed October 1, '62..
"	John D. Hatfield	Oct. 1, '62.	
Second Lieutenant	Simeon Rathbun	March 1, '62.	Promoted
"	John D. Hatfield	Sept. 3, '62.	Promoted
"	Christopher Starr	Oct. 1, '62.	
I.			
Captain			
First Lieutenant	Alonzo W. Bull	March 1, '62.	
Second Lieutenant			
K.			
Captain	Michael Leahey	Jan. 1, '62.	
First Lieutenant	Patrick Buckley	Jan. 1, '62.	
Second Lieutenant	George R. Lodge	Jan. 1, '62.	Promoted to Company G..
"	Robert V. Simpson	Feb. 1, '62.	Resigned April 22, '62....
"	Roger Warner	Sept. 1, '62.	

SCHEDULE G—Continued.

Roster of the Fifty-Fourth Regiment Illinois Volunteers.

Field and Staff.		Rank.	Remarks.
Colonel	Thomas W. Harris	Oct. 10, '61	
Lieutenant Colonel	Greenville M. Mitchell	Oct. 10, '61	
Major	Augustus H. Chapman	Oct. 10, '61	
Adjutant	John W. True	Oct. 10, '61	
Quartermaster	George Monroe	Oct. 10, '61	
Surgeon	Shubal York	Oct. 10, '61	
1st Ass't Surgeon	Thomas Wilkins	Oct. 10, '61	Resigned May 24, '62
" "	Ethan A. Lee	Dec. 16, '62	
2d Ass't Surgeon			
Chaplain	Sidney L. Harkey	Oct. 10, '61	Resigned June 30, '62
"	William M. Jones	July 1, '62	

COMPANY A.

Captain	Charles P. Woodruff	Feb. 12, '62	
First Lieutenant	Russell W. Williams	Feb. 12, '62	
Second Lieutenant	William W. Purinton	Feb. 12, '62	

B.

Captain	Samuel B. Logan	Feb. 12, '62	
First Lieutenant	Johnson White	Feb. 12, '62	Died April 21, '62
"	Alexander M. Houstin	April 22, '62	
Second Lieutenant	Alexander M. Houstin	Feb. 12, '62	Promoted
"	Alfred B. Balch	April 22, '62	

C.

Captain	Bird Monroe	Feb. 12, '62	Resigned Nov. 27, '62
"	Moses W. Robbins	Nov. 27, '62	
First Lieutenant	Moses W. Robbins	Feb. 12, '62	Promoted
"	Joseph Ledbetter	Nov. 27, '62	
Second Lieutenant	Joseph Ledbetter	Feb. 12, '62	Promoted
"	William A. Brasleton	Nov. 27, '62	

D.

Captain	Presley B. O'dear	Feb. 12, '62	
First Lieutenant	Merit B. Redding	Feb. 12, '62	
Second Lieutenant	John F. Barkley	Feb. 12, '62	

E.

Captain	Neil Fisher	Feb. 12, '62	
First Lieutenant	Thomas R. Miller	Feb. 12, '62	
Second Lieutenant	Chapman Sutton	Feb. 12, '62	

F

Captain	John B. Hanah	Feb. 12, '62	
First Lieutenant	James Chapman	Feb. 12, '62	
Second Lieutenant	Stephen L. Latimer	Feb. 12, '62	

G.

Captain	Richard W. Belknap	Feb. 12, '62	Resigned Sept. 16, 1862
"	Newton J. Blankenbaker	Sept. 16, '62	
First Lieutenant	Newton J. Blankenbaker	Feb. 12, '62	Promoted
"	Jacob M. Ryan	Sept. 16, '62	
Second Lieutenant	Jacob M. Ryan	Feb. 12, '62	Promoted
"	William A. Kline	Sept. 16, '62	

SCHEDULE G—Continued.

		Rank.	Remarks.
H			
Captain	Edward Roessler	Feb. 12, '62	Dismissed Nov. 22, 1862
"	Hiram M. Scarborough	Nov. 22, '62	
First Lieutenant	John W. Johnson	Feb. 12, '62	Resigned October 15, '62
"	Hiram M. Scarborough	Oct. 15, '62	Promoted
"	John A. P. Fleming	Nov. 22, '62	
Second Lieutenant	Hiram M. Scarborough	Feb. 12, '62	Promoted
"	John A. P. Fleming	Oct. 15, '62	Promoted
"	John M. Heart	Nov. 22, '62	
I			
Captain	Jeremiah W. Boatman	Feb. 12, '62	
First Lieutenant	Joseph T. Barkley	Feb. 12, '62	
Second Lieutenant	Reson W. Ashbrook	Feb. 12, '62	Resigned October 1, 1862
"	David McKinney	Oct. 1, '62	
K			
Captain	Theodore C. Rodrig	Feb. 12, '62	Dismissed
"	John H. Bailey	July 9, '62	
First Lieutenant	John H. Bailey	Feb. 12, '62	Promoted
"	Charles T. Kimble	July 9, '62	Resigned Nov. 15, 1862
"	William M. Kelly	Nov. 15, '62	
Second Lieutenant	Charles T. Kimble	Feb. 12, '62	Promoted
"	William M. Kelly	July 9, '62	Promoted
"	Thomas P. James	Nov. 15, '62	

SCHEDULE G—Continued.

Roster of Fifty-Fifth Regiment Illinois Volunteers.

Field and Staff.		Rank.	Remarks.
Colonel	David Stuart	Oct. 31, '61	Promoted Brig. Gen.
"	Oscar Malmborg	Dec. 19, '62	
Lieutenant Colonel	Oscar Malmborg	Oct. 31, '61	Promoted Colonel
"	William D. Sanger	Dec. 19, '62	
Major	William D. Sanger	Oct. 31, '61	Honorably discharg'd Nov.
"	Theodore C. Chandler	Dec. 19 62	....[1, '62. Promoted.
Adjutant	George L. Thurston	Oct. 31, 61	Resigned Sept. 3, '62
"	Henry S. Nourse	April 30, '62	
Quartermaster	Henry W. Jones	Oct. 31, '61	
Surgeon	E. O. F. Roler	Oct. 31, '61	
1st Ass't Surgeon	Charles Winne	Nov. 25, '61	Promoted Surgeon 77th
2d Ass't Surgeon			[infantry.
Chaplain	Milton L. Haney	Oct. 31, '61	

COMPANY A.

Captain	William N. Presson	Oct. 31, '61	Resigned March 13, '62
"	Jacob M. Augustine	March 15, '62	
First Lieutenant	Jacob M. Augustine	Oct. 31, '61	Promoted
"	Casper Shleich	March 15, '62	Promoted Co. F
Second Lieutenant	Casper Shleich	Oct. 31, '61	Promoted
"	Henry Augustine	Aug. 1, '62	

B.

Captain	Thomas B. Mackey	Oct. 31, '61	Resigned Dec. 28, '61
First Lieutenant	Albert F. Merrill	Oct. 31, '61	
Second Lieutenant	Ashabel C. Smith	Oct. 31, '61	Resigned March 5, '62
"	Elijah C. Lawrence	March 5, '62	

C.

Captain	Rhenodyne A. Bird	Oct. 31, '61	Resigned June 6, '62
"	Francis H. Shaw	July 1, '62	
First Lieutenant	Daniel McIntosh	Oct. 31, '61	
Second Lieutenant	Squire A. Wright	Oct. 31, '61	Died May 12, '62
"	John T. McAuley	July 1, '62	

D.

Captain	Theodore C. Chandler	Oct. 31, '61	Promoted Major
First Lieutenant	Francis H. Shaw	Oct. 31, '61	Promoted to Co. C
"	Joseph R. Roberts	July 1, '62	
Second Lieutenant	William S. Johnson	Oct. 31, '61	Resigned March 5, '62

E.

Captain	Charles Tazewell	Oct. 31, '61	Resigned Aug. 31, '62
First Lieutenant	William H. Dixon	Oct. 31, '61	Resigned March 13, '62
"	Josiah E. Keyes	March 13, '62	
Second Lieutenant	William R. Halligan	Oct. 31, '61	Resigned March 5, '62

F.

Captain	Milton L. Haney	Oct. 31, '61	Resigned March 14, '62
"	Casper Shleich	July 1, '62	
First Lieutenant	Harrison Presson	Oct. 31, '61	Resigned March 5, '62
"	Joseph W. Parks	March 8, '62	
Second Lieutenant	Joseph W. Parks	Oct. 31, '62	Promoted
"	John B. Johnson	March 8, '62	

SCHEDULE G—Continued.

		Rank.	Remarks.
G.			
Captain	Joseph Clay	Oct. 31, '61	Dismissed Sept. 16, '62
First Lieutenant	Cyrus M. Brown	Oct. 31, '61	
Second Lieutenant	Albert A. Whipple	Oct. 31, '61	
H.			
Captain	James J. Heffernan	Oct. 31, '61	
First Lieutenant	James Weldon	Oct. 31, '61	
Second Lieutenant	Nicholas Angason	March 1, '62	
I.			
Captain	Timothy Slattery	Feb. 18, '62	
First Lieutenant	Phillip Seelbach	Oct. 31, '61	Resigned March 5, '62
"	Lucien B. Crooker	March 5, '62	
Second Lieutenant	Timothy Slattery	Oct. 31, '61	Promoted
"	Charles A. Andress	March 5, '62	
K.			
Captain	Joseph Black	Oct. 31, '61	
First Lieutenant	Benjamin C. Swarts	Oct. 31, '61	Resigned March 13, '62
"	John H. Fillmore	March 13, '62	
Second Lieutenant	Andrew J. Gillett	Oct. 31, '61	Resigned April 7, '62
"	H. H. Kendrick	April 7, '62	

Schedule G—Continued.

Roster Fifty-Sixth Regiment of Illinois Volunteers.

Field and Staff.		Rank.	Remarks.
Colonel	Robert Kirkham	Sept. 28, '61	Resigned June 26, '62
"	William R. Brown	June 26, '62	Resigned Aug. 31, '62
"	Green B. Raum	Aug. 31, '62	
Lieutenant Colonel	William R. Brown	Sept. 28, '61	Promoted
"	Green B. Raum	June 26, '62	Promoted
"	James F. Cooper	Aug. 31, '62	
Major	Green B. Raum	Sept. 28, '61	Promoted
"	James F. Cooper	June 26, '62	Promoted
"	John P. Hall	Aug. 31, '62	
Adjutant	John M. Baker	Feb. 27, '62	Resigned Oct. 17, '62
"	Marmaduke Nicholson	Oct. 17, '62	
Quartermaster	John N. Williams	Feb. 27, '62	Resigned April 14, '62
"	Walter C. Hulbut	April 14, '62	
Surgeon	Francis B. Thompson	Feb. 27, '62	Resigned Nov. 27, '62
"	James S. Whitmire	May 26, '62	
1st Ass't Surgeon	Randall Poindexter	Feb. 27, '62	Resigned Oct. 23, '62
2d Ass't Surgeon			
Chaplain	David P. Bunn	Feb. 27, '62	Resigned May 28, '62
"	William B. Brunner	July 19, '62	

Company A.

Captain	James F. Cooper	Feb. 27, '62	Promoted Major
"	Samuel Atwell	Sept. 29, '62	
First Lieutenant	William Armstrong	Feb. 27, '62	Resigned April 22, '62
"	Benjamin Rankin	April 22, '62	Resigned Sept. 29, '62
"	Andrew E. Walbright	Sept. 29, '62	
Second Lieutenant	Benjamin Rankin	Feb. 27, '62	Promoted
"	Andrew E. Walbright	April 22, '62	Promoted
"	George W. Rankin	Sept. 29, '62	

B.

Captain	Sanford Cochran	Feb. 27, '62	
First Lieutenant	William McKinzie	Feb. 27, '62	Resigned Sept. 3, '62
"	James C. Tanguary	Sept. 3, '62	
Second Lieutenant	William L. Rankin	Feb. 27, '62	Deserted
"	James C. Tanguary	Aug. 19, '62	Promoted
"	Joshua M. Field	Sept. 3, '62	

C.

Captain	Pinckney J. Welsh	Feb. 27, '62	
First Lieutenant	James W. Flannigan	Feb. 27, '62	Resigned Sept. 3, '62
"	John E. Barker	Sept. 3, '62	
Second Lieutenant	George O. Griggs	Feb. 27, '62	

D.

Captain	David Slenger	Feb. 27, '62	Resigned Oct. 12, '62
First Lieutenant	William F. Williams	Feb. 27, '62	Died
"	Sylvester R. Cone	May 21, '62	
Second Lieutenant	Sylvester R. Cone	Feb. 27, '62	Promoted
"	Michael J. Dempsey	May 21, '62	

Schedule G — Continued.

		Rank.	Remarks.

E.

Captain	Henry T. Massey	Feb. 27, '62..	Resigned Sept. 28, '62....
"	William E. Webber	Sept. 28, '62.	
First Lieutenant..	Doddrige B. Gratton	Feb. 27, '62..	Resigned June 26, '62....
"	William E. Webber	June 26, '62.	Promoted
"	Josiah Joiner	Sept. 28, '62.	
Second Lieutenant	William E. Webber	Feb. 27, '62..	Promoted
"	Josiah Joiner	June 26, '62.	Promoted

F.

Captain	John P. Hall	Feb. 27, '62..	Promoted Major
"	John W. O'Neal	Aug. 31, '62.	
First Lieutenant..	John W. O'Neal	Feb. 27, '62..	Promoted
Second Lieutenant	Marmaduke Nicholson	Feb. 27, '62..	Promoted Adjutant

G.

Captain	William Reavis	Feb. 27, '62..	Resigned Oct. 29, '62
"	Edward Keffer	Oct. 29, '62..	
First Lieutenant..	Thomas H. Edwards	Feb. 27, '62..	Resigned Sept. 29, '62....
"	Edward Keffer	Sept. 29, '62.	Promoted
"	Thomas S. Campbell	Oct. 29, '62..	
Second Lieutenant	Edward Keffer	Feb. 27, '62..	Promoted
"	Thomas S. Campbell	Sept. 29, '62.	Promoted
"	Osmand C. Griswold	Oct. 29, '62..	

H.

Captain	James P Files	Feb. 27, '62..	
First Lieutenant..	Aaron E. Scott	Feb. 27, '62..	
Second Lieutenant	John J. Scott	Feb. 27, '62..	

I.

Captain	William B. Dillon	Feb. 27, '62..	Resigned Aug. 31, '62....
First Lieutenant..	James M. Akens	Feb. 27, '62..	Resigned Oct. 29, '62
Second Lieutenant	Erastus M. Gates	Feb. 27, '62..	Deserter
"	Elisha Dillon	Aug. 18, '62..	

K.

Captain	William R. Floyd	Feb. 27, '62..	Resigned Oct. 29, '62....
"	Samuel Roper	Oct. 29, '62..	
First Lieutenant..	Samuel Roper	Feb. 27, '62..	Promoted
Second Lieutenant	Philip B. Cheney	Feb. 27, '62..	Resigned Sept. 3, '62
"	John L. Hase	Oct. 3, '62..	

SCHEDULE G—Continued.

Roster of Fifty-Seventh Regiment Illinois Volunteers.

Field and Staff.		Rank.	Remarks.
Colonel............	Silas D. Baldwin........	Dec. 26, '61..	
Lieutenant Colonel	Frederick J. Hurlburt...	Dec. 26, '61..	
Major	Norman B. Page........	Dec. 26, '61..	Killed at Shiloh..........
"	Eric Forsee...........	April 15, '62..	
Adjutant........	Norman E. Hahn.......	Oct. 1, '61..	Resigned Sept. 29, '62....
"	Nelson Flansbury.......	Sept. 29, '61..	
Quartermaster ...	Edward Hamilton	Oct. 1, '61..	Resigned Sept. 26, '62....
" ...	Nathan Linton........	Sept. 26, '62..	
Surgeon........	James Zearing.........	Dec. 26, '61..	
1st Ass't Surgeon.	Henry S. Blood	Dec. 26, '61..	Died..............
"	George W. Crossley	March 7, '62..	
2d Ass't Surgeon.	....	....	
Chaplain........	....	....	

COMPANY A.

Captain	John Phillips..........	Dec. 26, '61..	
First Lieutenant..	John N. Schilling.......	Dec. 26, '61..	Deserted June 7, 1862....
" ..	William F. Conkey......	June 7, '62..	
Second Lieutenant	William F. Conkey......	Dec. 26, '61..	Promoted ....
"	Eli Barnum...........	June 7, '62..	

B.

Captain........	Alfred H. Manzer.......	Dec. 26, '61..	Resigned July 14, 1862...
"	Linas Vansteinburg.....	July 16, '62..	
First Lieutenant..	Nathan Linton.........	Dec. 26, '61..	Promoted Quartermaster..
" ..	George N. Barr.........	Sept. 26, '62..	
Second Lieutenant	John R. Larkin.........	Dec. 26, '61..	

C.

Captain........	William S. Swan.......	Dec. 30, '61..	
First Lieutenant..	Robert B. Morse........	Dec. 30, '61..	Resigned June 7, 1862....
" ..	Moses S. Lord..........	June 7, '62..	Resigned Sept. 26, 1862..
" ..	Jacob S. Sills..........	Sept. 26, '62..	
Second Lieutenant	Moses S. Lord..........	Dec. 30, '61..	Promoted ....
"	Archibald B. McLane...	June 7, '62..	Dismissed Nov. 8, 1862...
"	Frederick Laycock	Nov. 8, '62..	

D.

Captain........	Eric Forsee............	Dec. 26, '61..	Promoted Major..........
"	Eric Johnson	April 15, '62.	Resigned Sept. 3, 1862...
"	Peter M. Wickstrum....	Sept. 3, '62..	
First Lieutenant..	Eric Johnson	Dec. 26, '61..	Promoted ....
" ..	Eric Berglend.........	April 15, '62	
Second Lieutenant	Eric Berglend.........	Dec. 26, '62..	Promoted ....
"	Peter M. Wickstrum....	April 15, '62.	Promoted ....
"	George E. Rodeen......	Sept. 3, '62..	

E.

Captain	Robert D. Adams.......	Dec. 26, '61..	Killed at Shiloh..........
"	Bradley D. Salter.......	April 7, '62..	
First Lieutenant..	Bradley D. Salter.......	Dec. 26, '61..	Promoted ....
" ..	David Kenyan..........	April 7, '62.	
Second Lieutenant	Albert L. Otis..........	Dec. 26, '61..	Resigned April 1, 1862...
"	Edward Martin........	April 7, '62..	

SCHEDULE G—Continued.

		Rank.	Remarks.

F.

Captain	Frederick A. Battey	Dec. 26, '61	
First Lieutenant	Joseph W. Harris	Dec. 26, '61	
Second Lieutenant	Joseph T. Cook	Dec. 26, '61	Resigned June 17, 1862
"	Andrew Anderson	June 17, '62	

G.

Captain	Gustav A. Busse	Dec. 26, '61	
First Lieutenant	Fritz Busse	Dec. 26, '61	
Second Lieutenant	Charles W. Rosenthal	Dec. 26, '61	

H.

Captain	Josiah Robbins, jr	Dec. 26, '61	
First Lieutenant	Nelson Flansbury	Dec. 26, '61	Promoted Adjutant
Second Lieutenant	George Welch	Dec. 26, '61	Resigned Aug. 31, 1862
"	John H. Weirick	Aug. 31, '62	

I.

Captain	Benjamin H. Chadburn	Dec. 26, '61	Resigned Sept. 2, 1862
"	Charles Ratteray	Sept. 2, '62	
First Lieutenant	Theodore M. Dogett	Dec. 26, '61	Killed at Shiloh
"	Frank W. Cutler	April 10, '62	
Second Lieutenant	William S. Hendricks	Dec. 26, '61	

K.

Captain	Augustus C. Barry	Dec. 26, '61	Resigned June 20, 1862
"	Harlan Page	June 20, '62	
First Lieutenant	Harlan Page	Dec. 26, '61	Promoted
"	William Starling	June 20, '62	
Second Lieutenant	William Brewer	Dec. 26, '61	Resigned October 29, 1862
"	Jacob S. Carper	Oct. 29, '62	

SCHEDULE G—Continued.

Roster of Fifty-Eighth Regiment Illinois Volunteers.

Field and Staff.		Rank.	Remarks.
Colonel	William F. Lynch	Jan. 25, '62	
Lieutenant Colonel	Isaac Rutishowser	Jan. 25, '62	
Major	Thomas Newlan	Jan. 25, '62	
Adjutant	Lewis H. Martin	Jan. 25, '62	Resigned March 26, '62
"	Joseph G. Burt	March 26, '62	Died Nov. 9, '62
"	Charles L. Healy	Nov. 25, '62	
Quartermaster	George Sawin	Nov. 1, '61	
Surgeon	Henry M. Crawford	Jan. 25, 62	
1st Ass't Surgeon	Emory A. Merrifield	Jan. 25, 62	
2d Ass't Surgeon			
Chaplain			

COMPANY A.

Captain	Robert W. Healy	Dec. 24, '61	
First Lieutenant	Eugene Lynch	Dec. 24, '61	Resigned Oct. 12 '62
"	John Murphy	Oct. 12, '62	
Second Lieutenant	Hiram M. VanArman	Dec. 24, '61	Resigned June 20, '62
"	John Murphy	July 1, '62	Promoted
"	Francis X. Cotten	Oct. 12, '62	

B.

Captain	Thomas D. Griffin	Dec. 24, '61	Resigned March 26, 1862
"	John W. Babbitt	March 26, '62	Resigned July 3, '62
"	David J. Lynch	July 3, '62	
First Lieutenant	Abraham Vandenburgh	Dec. 24, '61	Dropped from rolls April
"	Job Moxom	April 18, '62	[29, '62.
Second Lieutenant	John W. Babbitt	Dec. 24, '61	Promoted
"	James E. Moss	March 26 '62	

C.

Captain	George W. Kittell	Dec. 25, '61	
First Lieutenant	Sanford W. Smith	Dec. 25, '61	Resigned May 10, '62
"	Henry Smith	May 10, '62	
Second Lieutenant	Joseph G. Burt	Dec. 25, '61	Promoted Adjutant
"	Henry Smith	March 26, '62	Promoted
"	George C. Willson	May 10, '62	

D.

Captain	Nicklaus Nicklaus	Jan. 28, '62	Resigned April 18, '62
"	George Glassner	April 18, '62	
First Lieutenant	George Glassner	Jan. 28, '62	Promoted
"	Gustav C. Kothe	April 18, '62	
Second Lieutenant	Gustav C. Kothe	Jan. 28, '62	Promoted
"	Charles Maager	April 18, '62	

E.

Captain	Karl A. Rutishauser	Dec. 25, '61	Died of wounds at St. Louis
"	Charles Christianson	July 1, '62	[May 18, '62.
First Lieutenant	Charles Kittel	Dec. 25, '61	
Second Lieutenant	Joseph Stauffer	Dec. 25, '61	Resigned Dec. 2, '61
"	Emery P. Dustin	June 6, '62	

F.

Captain	Frederick Kurth	Dec. 31, '61	
First Lieutenant	Julius Kurth	Dec. 31, '61	Died Sept. 8, '62
Second Lieutenant	Louis W. Pfeif	Dec. 31, '61	Killed in battle at Shiloh
"	Frederick Wilhelmi	April 7, '62	

SCHEDULE G—Continued.

		Rank.	Remarks.
G.			
Captain	James A. Bewley	Dec. 31, '61	Killed at Shiloh
"	Loring P. Fuller	April 8, '62	
First Lieutenant	Loring P. Fuller	Dec. 31, '61	Promoted
"	Robert H. Winslow	April 8, '62	
Second Lieutenant	Robert H. Winslow	Dec. 31, '61	Promoted
"	John C. Parker	Sept. 1, '62	
H.			
Captain	Lawrence Collins	Feb. 7, '62	
First Lieutenant	John C. Lonergan	Feb. 7, '62	Died of wounds May 25,'62
"	James Carey	May 28, '62	
Second Lieutenant	Danforth L. Scott	Feb. 7, '62	Dismissed
"	Nicholas Murphy	April 18, '62	
I.			
Captain	Philip R. Heelan	Dec. 24, '61	
First Lieutenant	David J. Lynch	Dec. 24, '61	Promoted to Co. B
"	John O. Kane	July 3, '62	
Second Lieutenant	Job Moxom	Dec. 24, '61	Promoted Co. B
"	John O. Kane	April 18, '62	Promoted
"	James M. Howard	Nov. 28, '62	
K.			
Captain	Patrick Gregg	Dec. 31, '61	Promoted Surgeon 23d [Regiment.
"	John Tobin	Dec. 15, '62	
First Lieutenant	John Tobin	Dec. 31, '61	Promoted
"	John W. Gregg	Dec. 15, '62	
Second Lieutenant	John W. Gregg	Dec. 31, '61	Promoted
"	John Clark	Dec. 15, '62	

Schedule G—Continued.

Roster of Fifty-Ninth Regiment Illinois Volunteers.

Field and Staff		Rank	Remarks
Colonel	P. Sidney Post	March 1, '62	
Lieutenant Colonel	Charles H. Frederick	June 17, '62	
Major	Joshua C. Winters	March 1, '62	
Adjutant	Samuel West	March 1, '62	
Quartermaster	Frederick Brasher	Sept. 18, '62	
Surgeon			
1st Ass't Surgeon	Charles Bunce	Oct. 25, '62	
2d Ass't Surgeon			
Chaplain			

Company A.

Captain			
First Lieutenant			
Second Lieutenant			

B.

Captain	Hendrick E. Paine	July 17, '61	
First Lieutenant	John H. Johnson	July 27, '61	Resigned Dec. 22, 1862
Second Lieutenant	Andrew R. Johnson	Aug. 6, '61	Killed at Perryville
"	James Johnson	Oct. 8, '62	

C.

Captain	Barzillai M. Veatch	Aug. 5, '61	
First Lieutenant	Daniel W. Henderson	April 14, '62	
Second Lieutenant	Heslip Phillips	April 14, '62	

D

Captain	Orlando W. Frazier	Nov. 2, '62	
First Lieutenant	Emanuel Mennet	Nov. 21, '62	
Second Lieutenant	Cherley A. Mossmans	Nov. 3, '62	

E.

Captain	James M. Stookey	Aug. 17, '61	
First Lieutenant	James H. Knight	March 15, '62	
Second Lieutenant	Robert Gooding	March 15, '62	

F.

Captain	George E. Currie	April 14, '62	
First Lieutenant	Reuben Maddox	Sept. 15, '62	
Second Lieutenant	Henry C. Bonham	Oct. 1, 62	

G.

Captain	Joseph S. Hackney	April 1, '62	
First Lieutenant	Horace W. Starkey	April 1, '62	
Second Lieutenant	Thomas B. Johnson	April 1, '62	

H.

Captain	Albert Anthony	June 17, '62	
First Lieutenant	Hamilton W. Hall	June 17, '62	
Second Lieutenant	Henry W. Wiley	June 17, '62	

SCHEDULE G — Continued.

		Rank.	Remarks.

I.

Captain	Charles F. Adams	May 12, '62	Died of wounds Oct. 16, '62,
"	James A. Beach	Oct. 16, '62	
First Lieutenant	James A. Beach	Sept. 29, '62	
"	Charles C. Doolittle	Oct. 16, '62	
Second Lieutenant	Charles C. Doolittle	Sept. 29, '62	Promoted

K.

Captain	Henry N. Snyder	Sept. 6, '61	
First Lieutenant	John M. Van Osdel	Aug. 11, '62	
Second Lieutenant			

Schedule G—Continued.

Roster of Sixtieth Regiment Illinois Volunteers.

Field and Staff.		Rank.	Remarks.
Colonel	Silas C. Toler	Oct. 15, '61	
Lieutenant Colonel	William B. Anderson	Feb. 12, '62	
Major	Samuel Hess	Feb. 12, '62	
Adjutant	Thomas G. Barnes	Oct. 15, '61	
Quartermaster	Cloyd Crouch	Feb. 9, '62	
Surgeon	Joseph T. Miller	Feb. 12, '62	Resigned Sept. 3, '62
"	William M. Gray	Oct. 28, '62	
1st Ass't Surgeon	Ford S. Dodds	Jan. 13, '62	
2d Ass't Surgeon	John A. Sheriff	Dec. 6, '62	
Chaplain	Levi S. Walker	Feb. 12, '62	

Company A.

Captain	Francis M. Davidson	Feb. 17, '62	Resigned July 3, '62
"	William E. Short	July 3, '62	Died July 20, '62
"	Thomas J. Rhodes	July 20, '62	
First Lieutenant	William E. Short	Feb. 17, '62	Promoted
"	Aurelius Hight	July 3, '62	
Second Lieutenant	Jerome M. Ingram	Feb. 17, '62	Resigned July 13, '62
"	Walter P. Moore	July 13, '62	

B.

Captain	James H. McDonald	Feb. 12, '62	
First Lieutenant	Isaac S. Boswell	Feb. 12, '62	
Second Lieutenant	DeWitt Anderson	Feb. 12, '62	Resigned July 9, '62
"	Thomas J. Thrash	July 9, '62	

C.

Captain	John R. Moss	Feb. 21, '62	Resigned Dec. 19, '62
First Lieutenant	Thomas J. Rhodes	Feb. 21, '62	Promoted Co. A
"	Marks Hailes	July 20, '62	
Second Lieutenant	Marks Hailes	Feb. 21, '62	Promoted
"	Simeon Walker	July 20, '62	

D.

Captain	Alfred Davis	Feb. 17, '62	Resigned March 31, '62
"	Luke S. Wilbanks	March 31, '62	
First Lieutenant	Edmund D. Choisser	Feb. 17, '62	Resigned Aug. 31, '62
"	John B. Coleman	Nov. 12, '62	
Second Lieutenant	James Stull	Feb. 17, '62	Resigned Nov. 18, '62
"	Anozi Kniffin	Nov. 18, '62	

E.

Captain	George W. Evans	Feb. 17, '62	
First Lieutenant	Hamilton Wiggs	Feb. 17, '62	Died June 20, '62
"	Stephen Fogarty	July 20, '62	
Second Lieutenant	William Baker	Feb. 17, '62	Resigned, March 31, '62
"	Franklin M. Bing	April 26, '62	Resigned June 23, '62
"	William N. Mitchell	June 23, '62	Resigned Nov. 18, '62
"	John Q. Adams	Nov. 18, '62	

Schedule G.—Continued.

		Rank.	Remarks.
F.			
Captain	William May	Feb. 17, '62	Resigned Nov. 21, '62
"	Robert B. Stinson	Nov. 21, '62	
First Lieutenant	Gallatin A. Wood	Feb. 17, '62	Resigned Aug. 31, '62
"	Robert B. Stinson	Sept. 1, '62	Promoted
"	Thomas G. Stokes	Nov. 21, '62	
Second Lieutenant	Robert B. Stinson	Feb. 17, '62	Promoted
"	Thomas G. Stokes	Sept. 1, '62	Promoted
G.			
Captain	Andrew J. Alden	Feb. 17, '62	Resigned Sept. 3, '62
"	Jehu J. Maxey	Sept. 3, 62	
First Lieutenant	Jehu J. Maxey	Feb. 17, '62	Promoted
"	Cornelius N. Breeze	Nov. 12, '62	
Second Lieutenant	William H. Campbell	Feb. 17, '62	
H.			
Captain	David Ragains	Feb. 17, '62	
First Lieutenant	Joseph F. McKee	Feb. 17, '62	
Second Lieutenant	John S. Cochennour	Feb. 17, '62	
I.			
Captain	John Frizell	Feb. 17, '62	Resigned Sept. 3, '62
"	John Gibson	Sept. 3, '62	
First Lieutenant	John Gibson	Feb. 17, '62	Promoted
Second Lieutenant	E. W. Hulbert	Feb. 17, '62	Resigned July 16, '62
"	Asa Hawkins	July 16, '62	
K.			
Captain	William C. Goddard	Feb. 17, '62	
First Lieutenant	James M. Benson	Feb. 17, '62	Resigned Aug. 31, '62
"	John S. Bridges	Aug. 31, '62	
Second Lieutenant	William E. Goddard	Feb. 17, '62	Resigned March 31, '62
"	John S. Bridges	March 31, '62	Promoted
"	Lyman A. Miller	Nov. 12, '62	

Schedule G — Continued.

Roster of Sixty-First Regiment Illinois Volunteers.

Field and Staff.		Rank.	Remarks.
Colonel	Jacob Fry	Nov. 1, 61	
Lieutenant Colonel			
Major	Simon P. Ohr	March 7, 62	
Adjutant	Francis M. Posey	Feb. 5, '62	Promoted Captain Co. A
"	Henry S. Goodspeed	Oct. 9, '62	
Quartermaster	Francis P. Vedder	Feb. 5, '62	Dismissed May 21, 1862.
Surgeon	Leonidas Clemens	Feb. 5, '62	Resigned August 31, 1862
1st Ass't Surgeon	George H. Knapp	Nov. 20, 61	
2d Ass't Surgeon			
Chaplain	Edward Rutledge	May 16, '62	Resigned September 3, '62
"	Benjamin B. Hamilton	Oct. 30, '62	

Company A.

Captain	Simon P. Ohr	Feb. 5, '62	Promoted Major
"	Francis M. Posey	March 7, 62	
First Lieutenant	David G. Culver	Feb. 5, '62	Killed at Shiloh
"	William M. Potts	April 15, '62	
Second Lieutenant	William H. Armstrong	Feb. 5, '62	

B.

Captain	Martin J. Mann	Feb. 5, '62	
First Lieutenant	George Chism	Feb. 5, '62	Resigned October 16, 1862
"	Samuel T. Carrico	Oct. 16, '62	
Second Lieutenant	Samuel T. Carrico	Feb. 5, '62	Promoted
"	Charles W. Mann	Oct. 15, '62	

C.

Captain	Warren Ihrie	Feb. 5, '62	Died Sept. 9, 1862
"	John T. Hesser	Sept. 9, '62	
First Lieutenant	John T. Hesser	March 7, '62	Promoted
"	Marshall S. Parker	Sept. 9, '62	
Second Lieutenant	John T. Hesser	Feb. 5, '62	Promoted
"	Marshall S. Parker	March 7, '62	Promoted
"	John W. Judd	Sept. 9, '62	

D.

Captain	John H. Reddish	March 7, '62	
First Lieutenant	John H. Reddish	Feb. 5, '62	Promoted
"	Daniel S. Kelly	March 7, '62	
Second Lieutenant	John R. McWylder	March 7, '62	Resigned Sept. 3, '62

E.

Captain	Henry W. Manning	March 7, '62	
First Lieutenant	Henry W. Manning	Feb. 5, 62	Promoted
"	Jedediah Beals	March 7, '62	Dead
"	Charles E. McDougall	July 1, '62	
Second Lieutenant	James D. Ballou	March 7, '62	Dead
"	Charles E. McDougall	May 1, '62	Promoted
"	John C. Judy	July 1, '62	

F

Captain	Robert E. Haggard	March 24, '62	
First Lieutenant	Robert E. Haggard	Feb. 5, '62	Promoted
"	William L. Stuart	March 24, '62	
Second Lieutenant	Charles B. Smith	March 24, '62	

Schedule G — Continued.

		Rank.	Remarks.

G.

Captain	Jerome B. Nulton	Feb. 5, '62	
First Lieutenant	William B. Taylor	March 7, '62	Resigned Sept. 3, 1862
Second Lieutenant	Jacob L. Marshall	March 7, '62	

H.

Captain			
First Lieutenant	Daniel Grass	March 7, '62	
Second Lieutenant			

I.

Captain	James Lawrence	March 28, '62	
First Lieutenant	Frederick Mattern	March 28, '62	Resigned July 8, 1862
"	Charles J. Dawes	July 8, '62	
Second Lieutenant	James Lawrence	March 7, '62	Promoted
"	Joseph H. Buffington	March 28, '62	Resigned June 5, 1862
"	Henry S. Goodspeed	June 5, '62	Promoted Adjutant

K.

Captain			
First Lieutenant			
Second Lieutenant			

SCHEDULE G—Continued.

Roster of the Sixty-Second Regiment Illinois Volunteers.

Field and Staff.		Rank.	Remarks.
Colonel	James M. True	Dec. 1, '61	
Lieutenant Colonel	Daniel B. Robinson	Feb. 18, '62	
Major	Stephen M. Meeker	Jan. 1, '62	
Adjutant	Louis C. True	March 10, '62	Promoted Captain of Co. D
"	Edmund R. Wiley, jr.	Jan. 17, 62	
Quartermaster	John Nabb	Feb. 1, '62	
Surgeon	John W. McKinney	March 6, '62	Resigned Aug. 31, 1862.
"	Charles L. Wundt	March 26, '62	
1st Ass't Surgeon.	John W. Cameron	Jan. 24, '62	
2d Ass't Surgeon.	Vernon R. Bridges	Oct. 13, '62	
Chaplain	Hiram M. Trimble	March 25, '62	

COMPANY A.

Captain	Henry C. McCleave	Jan. 15, '62	Resigned Sept. 11, 1862.
"	Thomas J. Warner	Sept. 11, '62	
First Lieutenant	Thomas J. Warner	Jan. 15, '62	Promoted
"	Jacob J. Applegate	Sept. 11, '62	
Second Lieutenant	Benjamin F. Stinger	Jan. 15, '62	Resigned Sept. 3, 1862.
"	George M. Evans	Sept. 3, '62	

B.

Captain	Henry P. Ingram	Jan. 15, '62	
First Lieutenant	Edwin M. Jordon	Jan. 15, '62	
Second Lieutenant	John H. Askins	Jan. 15, '62	

C.

Captain	Silas Overmire	April 10, '62	
First Lieutenant	William G. McConnell	April 10, '62	
Second Lieutenant	William D. Wilson	April 10, '62	Resigned Nov. 7, 1862.
"	John Fisher	Nov. 7, '62	

D.

Captain	Mairston M. Doyle	April 10, '62	Resigned June 17, 1862.
"	Lewis C. True	June 17, '62	
First Lieutenant	Robert J. Ford	April 10, '62	
Second Lieutenant	John N. Hackett	April 10, '62	Resigned Sept. 11, 1862.
"	Elijah C. Compton	Sept. 11, '62	

E.

Captain	William E. Robinson	Jan. 15, '62	
First Lieutenant	Hamilton Nabb	Jan. 15, '62	
Second Lieutenant	Pleasington Nabb	Jan. 15, '62	

F.

Captain	Jesse Crooks	Jan. 15, '62	
First Lieutenant	James J. McGrew	Jan. 15, '62	Resigned Sept. 11, 1862.
"	Guy S. Alexander	Sept. 11, '62	
Second Lieutenant	Guy S. Alexander	Jan. 15, '62	Promoted
"	Thomas H. Magee	Sept. 11, '62	

G.

Captain	James L. Garretson	April 10, '62	
First Lieutenant	Joseph W. Filler	April 10, '62	
Second Lieutenant	William S. Barrickman	April 10, '62	Resigned Oct. 13, 1862.
"	James F. True	Oct. 14, '62	

SCHEDULE G—Continued.

		Rank.	Remarks.
H.			
Captain	Samuel Sherman	April 10, '62.	Resigned Sept. 23, 1862..
"	John Foley	Sept. 23, '62.	
First Lieutenant	John Foley	April 10, '62.	Promoted
"	Robert B. Wilson	Sept. 23, '62	
Second Lieutenant	Robert B. Wilson	April 10, '62	Promoted
"	Read Anderson	Sept. 23, '62.	
I.			
Captain	Joseph McLain	April 10, '62.	
First Lieutenant	John J. Wyatt	April 10, '62.	
Second Lieutenant	John C. Parcel	April 10, '62.	
K.			
Captain	Charles A. Mertz	Jan. 15, '62..	
First Lieutenant	David Trimble	Jan. 15, '62..	
Second Lieutenant	John W. Hannah	Jan. 15, '62..	

Schedule G—Continued.

Roster of Sixty-Third Regiment Illinois Volunteers.

Field and Staff.		Rank.	Remarks.
Colonel.........	Francis Mora..........	Dec. 1, '61...	Resigned Sept. 29, 1862..
"	Joseph B. McCown......	Sept. 29.....	
Lieutenant Colonel	Joseph B. McCown......	April 10, '62.	Promoted ....
"	Henry Glaze...........	Sept. 29, '62.	
Major...........	Henry Glaze...........	April 10, '62.	Promoted ....
Adjutant........	Charlie S. Chambers....	April 10, '62.	
Quartermaster ...	John M. Maris.........	Feb. 28, '62.	
Surgeon	William M. Gray.......	May 26, '62..	Resigned Sept. 12, 1862..
"	John W. McKinney.....	Sept. 15, '62.	
1st. Ass't. Surgeon	Lyman Hall............	April 10, '62.	
2d Asst. Surgeon.	Alexander A. Lodge....	Dec. 6, '62..	
Chaplain	Stephen Blair..........	April 10, '62.	

Company A.

Captain.........	Richard McClure.......	April 10, '62.	
First Lieutenant..	Charles E. Cartwright...	April 10, '62.	
Second Lieutenant	Victor E. Phillips	April 10, '62.	

B.

Captain	George J. Johns.........	April 10, '62.	Resigned Nov. 27, 1862..
First Lieutenant..	John C. Grayson.......	April 10, '62.	Resigned Oct. 13, 1862...
" ..	Arnot L. McCoy.......	Oct. 13, '62..	
Second Lieutenant	Arnot L. McCoy........	April 10, '62.	Promoted ....
"	William A. Harris......	Oct. 13, '62..	

C.

Captain.........	William M. Boughan....	April 10, '62.	
First Lieutenant..	Alfred Laws...........	April 10, '62.	
Second Lieutenant	Jacob Lewis...........	April 10, '62.	

D.

Captain	John W. Champion.....	April 10, '62.	
First Lieutenant..	James Isaminger.......	April 10, '62.	
Second Lieutenant	Benjamin M. Tabler.....	April 10, '62.	

E.

Captain	Henry Gilbert.......	April 10, '62.	Deserted ....
" ..	Hiram H. Walser.......	Aug. 4, '62...	
First Lieutenant..	Hiram H. Walser.......	April 10, '62	Promoted ....
" ..	William C. Keen........	Aug. 4, '62...	
Second Lieutenant	William C. Keen	April 10, '62.	Promoted ....

F.

Captain	Joseph Lemon	April 10, '62.	
First Lieutenant..	Alfred Davis....	April 10, '62.	
Second Lieutenant	James M. Hunter.......	April 10, '62.	

G.

Captain	Joseph R. Stanford.....	April 10, '62.	
First Lieutenant..	Westford B. Russell....	April 10, '62	
Second Lieutenant	William P. Richardson..	April 10, '62.	

SCHEDULE G — Continued.

		Rank.	Remarks.
H.			
Captain	Sylvester G. Parker	April 10, '62.	
First Lieutenant	John M. Davis	April 10, '62.	
Second Lieutenant	James Houselman	April 10, '62.	
I.			
Captain	John B. Craig	April 10, '62.	
First Lieutenant	George F. Glossbrenner	April 10, '62.	
Second Lieutenant	Joseph H. C. Dill	April 10, '62.	
K.			
Captain	James H. Briggs	April 10, '62.	Resigned Oct. 1, '62
"	Andrew A. Ricketts	Oct. 1, '62	
First Lieutenant	Andrew A. Ricketts	April 10, '62.	Promoted
"	William Leamon	Oct. 1, '62	
Second Lieutenant	William Leamon	April 10, '62.	Promoted
"	Ingham Starkey	Oct. 1, '62	

Schedule G—Continued.

Roster of Sixty-Fourth Regiment Illinois Volunteers.

Field and Staff.		Rank.	Remarks.
Colonel............	....		
Lieutenant Colonel	David E. Williams.......	Sept. 3, '61..	Discharg'd, ill health, Sept.
"	John Morrill............	Sept. 12, '62.	................[12, '62.
Major............	Frederick W. Matteson..	Sept. 25, '61.	Died Aug. 8, '62.........
"	George W. Stipp.......	Aug. 8, '62 ..	Resigned Nov. 19, '62....
Adjutant........	Oliver H. Payne........	Sept. 25, '61.	Promoted Captain Co. F.
"	Aaron E. May..........	Jan. 12, '62..	Resigned June 28, '62....
"	Thomas C. Fullerton....	June 28, '62..	....
Quartermaster ...	Alexander F. Cameron ..	Nov. 1, '61..	....
Surgeon.........	James T. Stewart.......	Dec. 31, '61..	....
1st Ass't Surgeon	Noble Holton..........	April 22, '62.	....
2d Ass't Surgeon.	....		
Chaplain........	Charles Cain...........	Dec. 10, '61..	....

Company A.

Captain.........	John Morrill...........	Sept. 26, '61.	Promoted Lieut. Colonel..
"	James C. Cameron......	Sept. 12, '62.	....
First Lieutenant..	James C. Cameron......	Sept. 26, '61.	Promoted ....
"	Charles J. Conger......	Sept. 12, '62.	....
Second Lieutenant	Charles J. Conger	Sept. 26, '61.	Promoted ....
"	Frank Smith...........	Sept. 12, '62.	....

B.

Captain.........	George W. Stipp.......	Sept. 27, '61.	Promoted Major.........
"	Samuel B. Thompson ...	Aug. 8, '62..	....
First Lieutenant..	Samuel B. Thompson ...	Sept. 27, '61.	Promoted ....
"	Robert R. Gibbons......	Aug. 8, '62..	....
Second Lieutenant	Robert R. Gibbons......	Sept. 27, '61.	Promoted ....
"	George Bell............	Aug. 8, '62..	....

C.

Captain.........	Christian B. Keasey.....	Dec. 16, '61..	Resigned June 29, '62....
First Lieutenant..	George E. Doran.......	Dec. 16, '61..	Resigned June 25, '62....
Second Lieutenant	George A. Caine........	Dec. 16, '61..	Resigned Sept. 3, '62.....
"	John Keasey...........	Sept. 3, '62..	....

D.

Captain.........	John W. Stewart.......	Dec. 16, '61..	....
First Lieutenant..	William N. Stewart.....	Dec. 16, '61..	Resigned June 20, '62.....
"	George W. Reid........	June 20, '62..	....
Second Lieutenant	George W. Reid........	Dec. 16, '61..	Promoted ....
"	Duncan Reid...........	June 20, '62..	....

E.

Captain.........	David G. Grover.......	Dec. 31, 61..	Killed in battle Oct. 11, '62
"	Michael W. Manning....	Oct. 4, '62...	....
First Lieutenant..	Michael W. Manning....	Dec. 31, '61..	Promoted ....
"	Edwin H. Moore........	Oct. 4, '62...	....
Second Lieutenant	Edwin H. Moore........	Dec. 31, '61..	Promoted ....

SCHEDULE G—Continued.

		Rank.	Remarks.
F.			
Captain	Oliver H. Payne	Dec. 31, '61	Pro. Lieut. Col. Ohio Reg.
"	Joshua W. Baker	Sept. 2, '62	
First Lieutenant	Joshua W. Baker	Dec. 31, '61	Promoted
"	Joseph H. Reynolds	Sept. 2, '62	
Second Lieutenant	Joseph H. Reynolds	Dec. 31, '61	Promoted
"	Ward Knickerbocker	Sept. 2, '62	
G.			
Captain			
First Lieutenant			
Second Lieutenant			
H.			
Captain			
First Lieutenant			
Second Lieutenant			
I.			
Captain			
First Lieutenant			
Second Lieutenant			
K.			
Captain			
First Lieutenant			
Second Lieutenant			

SCHEDULE G—Continued.

Roster of Sixty-Fifth Regiment Illinois Volunteers.

Field and Staff.		Rank.	Remarks.
Colonel	Daniel Cameron, jr	May 1, '61	
Lieutenant Colonel	Daniel Cameron, jr	March 24, '62	Promoted
"	William S. Stewart	May 1, '62	
Major	William S. Stewart	March 24, '62	Promoted
"	John Wood	May 1, '62	
Adjutant	David C. Bradley	March 1, '62	
Quartermaster	James C. Rankin	Feb. 1, '62	
Surgeon	George H. Park	March 1, '62	
1st Ass't Surgeon	Ira Brown	May 1, '62	
2d Ass't Surgeon	Henry T. Mesler	July 2, '62	
Chaplain	Charles H. Roe	May 1, '62	

COMPANY A.

Captain	John Wood	March 17, '62	Promoted Major
"	James Duguid	May 1, '62	
First Lieutenant	James Duguid	March 17, '62	Promoted
"	Clandine George	May 1, '62	
Second Lieutenant	Clandine George	March 17, '62	Promoted
"	James Miller	May 1, '62	Promoted to Co. H
"	James L. Kee	Aug. 1, '62	

B.

Captain	Robert S. Montgomery	March 12, '62	
First Lieutenant	James W. Ballard	Feb. 13, '62	
Second Lieutenant	Henry H. Jones	March 15, '62	

C.

Captain	John J. Boyd	March 15, '62	Resigned Dec. 12, 1862
"	Henry Fisher	Dec. 12, '62	
First Lieutenant	Henry Fisher	March 1, '62	Promoted
"	Andrew Young	Dec. 12, '62	
Second Lieutenant	Andrew Young	March 12, '62	Promoted
"	Cornelius Wilson	Dec. 12, '62	

D.

Captain	Van Ness Billings	March 15, '62	
First Lieutenant	Ai D. Ewer	March 1, '62	Resigned August 1, 1862
"	William A. Kipp	Aug. 1, '62	
Second Lieutenant	Benjamin Harding	March 15, '62	Resigned August 1, 1862
"	Charles R. Manning	Sept. 1, '62	

E.

Captain	George H. Kennedy	March 15, '62	
First Lieutenant	John R. Floyd	March 1, '62	
Second Lieutenant	Arthur M. Tanney	March 15, '62	Resigned August 17, 1862
"	Hugh Adams	Aug. 17, '62	

F.

Captain	James S. Putnam	April 26, '62	
First Lieutenant	Samuel D. Tobey	April 1, '62	Resigned August 17, 1862
Second Lieutenant	Harrison W. Mallory	April 26, '62	Resigned Sept. 5, 1862

G.

Captain	Iranoff Willentzki	May 1, '62	
First Lieutenant	Alexander W. Diller	May 1, '62	Hon. disch'g'd Oct. 21, '62
Second Lieutenant	Louis H. Higgins	May 1, '62	

SCHEDULE G—Continued.

		Rank.	Remarks.

H.

Captain	Alexander McDonald	May 15, '62	
First Lieutenant	Lysander Tiffany	May 15, '62	Resigned August 1, 1862
"	James Miller	Aug. 1, '62	
Second Lieutenant	John J. Littler	May 15, '62	

I.

Captain	William H. Mapes	May 15, '62	
First Lieutenant	William Knowles	May 15, '62	
Second Lieutenant	Benjamin B. Adams	May 15, '62	

K.

Captain	Henry M. Fuller	May 15, '62	
First Lieutenant	William Robertson	April 25, '62	Resigned Dec. 20, 1862
Second Lieutenant	John Blain	June 10, '62	

212

SCHEDULE G — Continued.

Roster of Sixty-Sixth Regiment Illinois Volunteers.

Field and Staff.		Rank.	Remarks.
Colonel.........	Patrick E. Burke......	June 18, '62.	
Lieutenant Colonel	Charles W. Smith......	April 13, '62.	
Major...........	George Pipe...........	April 13, '62.	
Adjutant........	William Wilson........	April 30, '62.	
Quartermaster...	Nicholas Brown........	Dec. 10, '62..	
Surgeon.........	Joseph Pogue.........	April 19, '62.	
1st Ass't Surgeon.	Edward Vogel.........	April 13, '62.	
2d Ass't Surgeon.	David O. McCord......	May 9, '62...	
Chaplain........	James M. Alexander....	Sept. 17, '61.	

COMPANY A.

Captain.........	William S. Boyd......	Dec. 5, '61...	
First Lieutenant..	Frederick Ullrich......	Nov. 8, '61...	
Second Lieutenant	Austin S. Davidson.....	Dec. 5, '61...	

B.

Captain.........	Henry Eads...........	Nov. 13, '61..	
First Lieutenant .	Frank M. Bingham......	April 30, '62.	
Second Lieutenant	Samuel B. Brightman...	April 30, '62.	

C.

Captain.........	Ensign Conklin........	Nov. 9, '61..	
First Lieutenant..	Robert J. Adams.......	April 30, '62.	
Second Lieutenant	Francis A. Hartzell.....	April 30, '62.	

D.

Captain.........	John Piper............	Nov. 7, '61..	
First Lieutenant..	....		
Second Lieutenant	George W. Lusk.......	June 30, '62..	

E.

Captain.........	Andrew K. Campbell...	Oct. 10, '61..	
First Lieutenant..	William H. H. Simpkins.	Sept. 10, '61.	
Second Lieutenant	John V. Bovell........	Sept. 1, '62..	

F.

Captain	Michael Piggott........	April 30, '62.	
First Lieutenant..	Cyrus A. Lemon.......	April 30, '62.	
Second Lieutenant	....		

G

Captain.........	Benjamin D. Longstreth	April 30, '62.	
First Lieutenant..	Perry P. Ellis..........	Aug. 31, '62.	
Second Lieutenant	Philip C. Diedrich......	Aug. 31, '62.	

H.

Captain.........	Thomas B. Mitchell.....	Aug. 31, '62.	
First Lieutenant..	Joseph Lidack.........	June 30, '62.	
Second Lieutenant	Nicholas R. Park.......	June 30, '62.	

Schedule G—Continued.

		Rank.	Remarks.

I.

Captain	Jerry N. Hill	April 30, '62	
First Lieutenant	John L. Hays	Sept. 9, '62	
Second Lieutenant	John L. Hays	April 30, '62	Promoted
"	Samuel J. Smith	Sept. 9, '62	

K.

Captain	George A. Taylor	April 7, '62	
First Lieutenant	Alvin H. Davis	April 7, '62	
Second Lieutenant	William C. Jones	Aug. 30, '62	

SCHEDULE G—Continued.

Roster of Sixty-Seventh Regiment Illinois Volunteers.

Field and Staff.		Rank.	Remarks.
Colonel	Rosell M. Hough	June 13, '62	
Lieutenant Colonel	Eugene H. Oakley	June 13, '62	
Major	William H. Haskell	June 13, '62	
Adjutant	Daniel T. Hale	June 13, '62	
Quartermaster	Isaac N. Buck	June 13, '62	
Surgeon	Brock McVickar	June 4, '62	
1st Ass't Surgeon	Roscoe L. Hall	June 13, '62	
2d Ass't Surgeon			
Chaplain	William H. Ryder	June 13, '62	

COMPANY A.

Captain	Charles B. Hull	June 13, '62	
First Lieutenant	King H. Milliken	June 13, '62	
Second Lieutenant	Judson Ellison	June 13, '62	

B.

Captain	John F. Scanlan	June 13, '62	
First Lieutenant	Peter Caldwell	June 13, '62	
Second Lieutenant	David F. Maloney	June 13, '62	

C.

Captain	Hiram R. Enoch	June 13, '62	
First Lieutenant	James B. Kerr	June 13, '62	
Second Lieutenant	Joseph S. Berry	June 13, '62	

D.

Captain	Judson W. Read	June 13, '62	
First Lieutenant	Frederick W. Cole	June 13, '62	
Second Lieutenant	William Sharp	June 13, '62	

E.

Captain	Charles A. Heilig	June 13, '62	
First Lieutenant	James A. Sexton	June 13, '62	
Second Lieutenant	Charles H. Vogel	June 13, '62	

F.

Captain	William H. Frites	June 13, '62	
First Lieutenant	Abram D. Van Veckten	June 13, '62	
Second Lieutenant	Horace E. Dyer	June 13, '62	

G.

Captain	Charles K. Purple	June 13, '62	
First Lieutenant	Jeremiah Dockstater	June 13, '62	
Second Lieutenant	Edward K. Valentine	June 13, '62	

H.

Captain	James W. Crane	June 13, '62	
First Lieutenant	Stephen Allen	June 13, '62	
Second Lieutenant	Alonzo Hilliard	June 13, '62	

SCHEDULE G—Continued.

		Rank.	Remarks.

I.

Captain	Ruel G. Rounds	June 13, '62	
First Lieutenant	Kelsey Bond	June 13, '62	
Second Lieutenant	John Murphy	June 13, '62	

K.

Captain	S. W. McKown	June 13, '62	
First Lieutenant	Edward Bailey	June 13, '62	
Second Lieutenant	James Wright	June 13, '62	

SCHEDULE G—Continued.

Roster of Sixty-Eighth Regiment Illinois Volunteers.

Field and Staff.		Rank.	Remarks.
Colonel	Elias Stuart	July 16, '62	
Lieutenant Colonel	Houston L. Taylor	June 20, '62	
Major	George W. Lackey	June 20, '62	
Adjutant	John S. Bishop	June 20, '62	
Quartermaster	Samuel F. True	June 20, '62	
Surgeon	Albert H. Lanphier	June 20, '62	
1st Ass't Surgeon			
2d Ass't Surgeon			
Chaplain			

COMPANY A.

Captain	John W. King	June 23, '62	Resigned Dec. 24, '62
First Lieutenant	William H. Harrison	June 23, '62	
Second Lieutenant	Martin V. B. Parker	June 23, '61	

B.

Captain	Daniel F. Coffey	June 23, '62	
First Lieutenant	Judson J. C. Gillespie	June 23, '62	
Second Lieutenant	William Reynolds	June 23, '62	

C.

Captain	John P. St. John	June 23, '62	
First Lieutenant	Elsey Blake	June 23, '62	
Second Lieutenant	Green B. Davis	June 23, '62	

D.

Captain	John C. Hull	June 23, '62	
First Lieutenant	Thomas K. Jenkins	June 23, '62	
Second Lieutenant	Hugh B. McKnight	June 23, '62	

E.

Captain	Henry Davey	June 23, '62	
First Lieutenant	George H. Whiteman	June 23, '62	
Second Lieutenant	Isaac N. Coltrin	June 23, '62	

F.

Captain	John W. Morris	June 23, '62	
First Lieutenant	John R. Larrimore	June 23, '62	
Second Lieutenant	Lewis Ijamis	June 23, '62	

G.

Captain	James P. Moore	June 23, '62	
First Lieutenant	Harvey C. DeMotte	June 23, '62	
Second Lieutenant	John H. Stout	June 23, '62	

H.

Captain	Leroy T. Brown	June 23, '62	
First Lieutenant	John W. Hamilton	June 23, '62	
Second Lieutenant	Adam H. Bogardus	June 23, '62	

Schedule G—Continued.

		Rank.	Remarks.

I.

Captain	John W. Bear	June 23, '62.	
First Lieutenant	Samuel B. Crisky	June 23, '62.	
Second Lieutenant	S. Wheaton West	June 23, '62.	

K.

Captain	Edward J. Jones	June 23, '62.	
First Lieutenant	Thomas L. Masters	June 23, '62.	
Second Lieutenant	Hiram L. Dunn	June 23, '62.	

SCHEDULE G — Continued.

Roster of Sixty-Ninth Regiment Illinois Volunteers.

Field and Staff.		Rank.	Remarks.
Colonel	Joseph H. Tucker	June 12, '62.	
Lieutenant Colonel	Thomas J. Pickett	June 14, '62.	
Major	George P. Smith	June 14, '62.	
Adjutant	Abram H. Van Buren	June 14, '62.	
Quartermaster	Charles W. Cringle	June 14, '62.	
Surgeon	Isaiah P. Lynn	June 19, '62.	
1st Ass't Surgeon	Azro E. Goodwin	June 14, '62.	
2d Ass't Surgeon			
Chaplain	William W. Everts	July 14, '62.	

COMPANY A.

Captain	Abram Lash, jr	June 14, '62.	
First Lieutenant	David Robinson, jr	June 14, '62.	
Second Lieutenant	Edward R. Virden	June 14, '62.	

B.

Captain	Jonathan Kimball	June 14, '62.	
First Lieutenant	Samuel H. Hunter	June 14, '62.	
Second Lieutenant	Thomas W. Tefft	June 14, '62.	

C.

Captain	Lansing B. Tucker	June 14, '62.	Died Aug. 18, 1862
"	James O. McClellan	Aug. 18, '62.	
First Lieutenant	James O. McClellan	June 14, '62.	Promoted
"	John S. Mabie	Aug. 18, '62.	
Second Lieutenant	John S. Mabie	June 14, '62.	Promoted
"	Charles Case	Aug. 18, '62.	

D.

Captain	Frank J. Bush	June 14, '62.	
First Lieutenant	Warfield B. Todd	June 14, '62.	
Second Lieutenant	Robert Irwin	June 14, '62.	

E.

Captain	Tidel Schlund	June 14, '62.	
First Lieutenant	Charles Varges	June 14, '62.	
Second Lieutenant	August W. Willige	June 14, '62.	

F.

Captain	Frazer Wilson	June 14, '62.	
First Lieutenant	Ezra M. Beardsley	June 14, '62.	
Second Lieutenant	George Schemerhorn	June 14, '62.	

G.

Captain	Joseph A. Vincent	June 14, '62.	
First Lieutenant	E. S. Scribner	June 14, '62.	
Second Lieutenant	John Herbert	June 14, '62.	

H.

Captain	James W. Rearden	June 14, '62.	
First Lieutenant	Eli B. Baker	June 14, '62.	
Second Lieutenant	Edwin F. Bennett	June 14, '62.	

SCHEDULE G—Continued.

		Rank.	Remarks.

I.

Captain	William C. Hale	June 14, '62.	
First Lieutenant	Charles L. Peny	June 14, '62.	
Second Lieutenant	Alvah R. Jordan	June 14, '62.	

K.

Captain	John Coakley	June 14, '62.	
First Lieutenant	William H. Tousley	June 14, '62.	
Second Lieutenant	Isaac H. Allen	June 14, '62.	

SCHEDULE G—Continued.

Roster of Seventieth Regiment Illinois Volunteers.

Field and Staff.		Rank.	Remarks.
Colonel	Owen T. Reeves	July 23, '62	
Lieutenant Colonel	John D. Sage	July 23, '62	
Major	Joseph H. Scibird	July 23, '62	
Adjutant	James B. Breese	July 23, '62	
Quartermaster	John B. Burrows	July 10, '62	
Surgeon			
1st Ass't Surgeon	Madison Reece	Aug. 5, '62	
2d Ass't Surgeon			
Chaplain	William C. Lacy	July 23, '62	

COMPANY A.

Captain	Gilbert Summe	July 4, '62	
First Lieutenant	Samuel E. Wishhard	July 4, '62	
Second Lieutenant	Benjamin Hove	July 4, '62	

B.

Captain	William Perce	July 23, '62	
First Lieutenant	Benjamin G. Bills	July 23, '62	
Second Lieutenant	John S. Clark	July 23, '62	

C.

Captain	John T. Maddux	July 4, '62	
First Lieutenant	Thomas G. Black	July 4, '62	
Second Lieutenant	James G. Seward	July 4, '62	

D.

Captain	George W. Fox	July 4, '62	
First Lieutenant	Isaac P. Wilson	July 4, '62	
Second Lieutenant	William M. Lewis	Aug. 21, '62	

E.

Captain	Daniel D. Snyder	July 4, '62	
First Lieutenant	William H. Hinman	July 4, '62	
Second Lieutenant	George Dempsey	July 4, '62	

F.

Captain	Alfred Comings	July 4, '62	
First Lieutenant	Charles P. Fleshbein	July 4, '62	
Second Lieutenant	William J. Allen	July 4, '62	

G.

Captain	Newton Harlan	July 4, '62	
First Lieutenant	Joseph Beyles	July 4, '62	
Second Lieutenant	Daniel O. Martin	July 4, '62	

H.

Captain	Owen T. Reeves	July 4, '62	Promoted Colonel
"	James O. Donald	July 23, '62	
First Lieutenant	James O. Donald	July 4, '62	Promoted
"	John A. Robinson	July 23, '62	
Second Lieutenant	Albert Braxton	July 4, '62	

SCHEDULE G—Continued.

		Rank.	Remarks.
I.			
Captain	James Hudson	July 4, '62	
First Lieutenant	George Wilderboor	July 4, '62	
Second Lieutenant	William T. Hudson	July 4, '62	
K.			
Captain	George R. Brumlay	July 4, '62	
First Lieutenant	Robert W. Musgrave	July 4, '62	
Second Lieutenant	Henry A. Club	July 4, '62	

SCHEDULE G — Continued.

Roster of Seventy-First Regiment Illinois Volunteers.

Field and Staff.		Rank.	Remarks.
Colonel	Othniel Gilbert	July 26, '62	
Lieutenant Colonel	James O. P. Burnside	July 26, '62	
Major	DeWitt C. Marshall	July 26, '62	
Adjutant	Henry G. Hicks	July 26, '62	
Quartermaster	James H. Moore	July 22, '62	
Surgeon			
1st Ass't Surgeon			
2d Ass't Surgeon			
Chaplain	William C. Mason	July 26, '62	

COMPANY A.

Captain	Jerome B. Fuller	July 26, '62	
First Lieutenant	Edward Lafferty	July 26, '61	
Second Lieutenant	Charles C. Jamison	July 26, '62	

B.

Captain	Luther W. Black	July 22, '62	
First Lieutenant	George W. Snyder	July 22, '62	
Second Lieutenant	Emanuel Stover	July 22, '62	

C.

Captain	Charles A. Summers	July 22, '62	
First Lieutenant	Charles E. Hartman	July 22, '62	
Second Lieutenant	Solomon N. Nebleck	July 22, '62	

D.

Captain	Horatio G. Coykendall	July 26, '62	
First Lieutenant	James L. Smedley	July 26, '62	
Second Lieutenant	Charles C. Huntley	July 26, '62	

E.

Captain	Charles Parker	July 22, '62	
First Lieutenant	Aaron S. Hadley	July 22, '62	
Second Lieutenant	William D. Lattimer	July 22, '62	

F.

Captain	Pliny L. Fox	July 22, '62	
First Lieutenant	Benjamin H. Towner	July 22, '62	
Second Lieutenant	James N. Phillips	July 22, '62	

G.

Captain	William H. Weaver	July 26, '62	
First Lieutenant	James C. Tice	July 26, '62	
Second Lieutenant	Thomas B. Collins	July 26, '62	

H.

Captain	Theodore M. Brown	July 26, '62	
First Lieutenant	James W. Heffington	July 26, '62	
Second Lieutenant	George W. Pittman	July 26, '62	

SCHEDULE G — Continued.

		Rank.	Remarks.
	I.		
Captain	Jesse P. M. Howard	July 26, '62	
First Lieutenant	David P. Murphy	July 26, '62	
Second Lieutenant	John M. Loy	July 26, '62	
	K.		
Captain	James Creed	July 26, '62	
First Lieutenant	Flavius J. Carpenter	July 26, '62	
Second Lieutenant	Absalom A. Lasater	July 26, '62	

SCHEDULE G—Continued.

Roster of Seventy-Second Regiment Illinois Volunteers.

Field and Staff.		Rank.	Remarks.
Colonel	Frederick A. Starring	Aug. 21, '62	
Lieutenant Colonel	Joseph C. Wright	Aug. 21, '62	
Major	Henry W. Chester	Aug. 21, '62	
Adjutant	Ebenezer Bacon	Aug. 21, '62	
Quartermaster	Benjamin W. Thomas	July 31, '62	
Surgeon	Edwin Powell	Aug. 22, '62	
1st Ass't Surgeon	Benjamin Durham, jr.	Aug. 22, '62	
2d Ass't Surgeon	Edwin A. Beers	Oct. 17, '62	
Chaplain	Henry Barnes	Aug. 22, '62	

COMPANY A.

Captain	Joseph Stockton	Aug. 21, '62	
First Lieutenant	George B. Randall	Aug. 21, '62	
Second Lieutenant	William B. Gallaher	Aug. 21, '62	

B.

Captain	Jacob S. Curtis	Aug. 21, '62	
First Lieutenant	David W. Perkins	Aug. 21, '62	
Second Lieutenant	Daniel W. Whittle	Aug. 21, '62	

C.

Captain	William James, jr.	Aug. 21, '62	
First Lieutenant	Glen C. Ledyard	Aug. 21, '62	
Second Lieutenant	Clifford Stickney	Aug. 21, '62	

D.

Captain	James A. Sexton	Aug. 21, '62	
First Lieutenant	Benjamin C. Underwood	Aug. 21, '62	
Second Lieutenant	Nathan C. Underwood	Aug. 21, '62	

E.

Captain	William B. Holbrook	Aug. 21, '62	
First Lieutenant	Henry C. Mowry	Aug. 21, '62	
Second Lieutenant	Porter A. Ransom	Aug. 21, '62	

F.

Captain	Isaiah H. Williams	Aug. 21, '62	
First Lieutenant	George W. Colby	Aug. 21, '62	
Second Lieutenant	Richard Pomeroy	Aug. 21, '62	

G.

Captain	Henry D. French	Aug. 21, '62	
First Lieutenant	James H. Smith	Aug. 21, '62	
Second Lieutenant	James A. Bingham	Aug. 21, '62	

H.

Captain	Edwin C. Prior	Aug. 21, '62	
First Lieutenant	John W. Murray	Aug. 21, '62	
Second Lieutenant	Hezekiah Stout	Aug. 21, '62	

Schedule G — Continued.

		Rank.	Remarks.
I.			
Captain	James W. Harvey	Aug. 21, '62.	Resigned Oct. 16, '62
"	Abner E. Barnes	Oct. 16, '62.	
First Lieutenant	Abner E. Barnes	Aug. 21, '62.	Promoted
"	Spencer B. Carter	Oct. 16, '62.	
Second Lieutenant	John W. Abbott	Aug. 21, '62.	
K.			
Captain	John Reid	Aug. 21, '62.	
First Lieutenant	Charles Gladding	Aug. 21, '62.	
Second Lieutenant	Edwin Small	Aug. 21, '62.	

Schedule G — Continued.

Roster of Seventy-Third Regiment Illinois Volunteers.

Field and Staff.		Rank.	Remarks.
Colonel	James F. Jaquess	Aug. 21, '62.	
Lieutenant Colonel	Benjamin F. Northcutt.	Aug. 21, '62.	
Major	William A. Presson	Aug. 21, '62.	
Adjutant	Richard R. Randall	Aug. 21, '62.	
Qurtermaster	James W. Slavens	Aug. 29, '62.	
Surgeon	George O. Pond	Aug. 21, '62.	
1st Ass't Surgeon.	Robert E. Stevenson	Aug. 21, '62.	
2d Ass't Surgeon.	Kendall E. Rich	Sept. 23, '62.	
Chaplain	John S. Barger	Aug. 21, '62.	

Company A.

Captain	William E. Smith	Aug. 21, '62.	
First Lieutenant.	Edward W. Bennett	Aug. 21, '62.	
Second Lieutenant	Thomas G. Underwood.	Aug. 21, '62.	Resigned Dec. 19, '62

B.

Captain	Wilder B. M. Colt	Aug. 21, '62.	Resigned Dec. 1, '62
First Lieutenant.	Harvey Pratt	Aug. 21, '62.	
Second Lieutenant	Samuel W. McCormack.	Aug. 21, '62.	

C.

Captain	Peterson McNabb	Aug. 21, '62.	
First Lieutenant.	Mark D. Haws	Aug. 21, '62.	Resigned Nov. 28, '62
Second Lieutenant	Richard N. Davis	Aug. 21, '62.	Resigned Nov. 20, '62

D.

Captain	Thomas Motherspaw	Aug. 21, '62.	
First Lieutenant.	Jonas Jones	Aug. 21, '62.	
Second Lieutenant	Reuben B. Winchester.	Aug. 21, '62.	Resigned Dec. 19, '62

E.

Captain	Wilson Burroughs	Aug. 21, '62.	
First Lieutenant.	Charles Tilton	Aug. 21, '62.	
Second Lieutenant	David Blosser	Aug. 21, '62.	Resigned Dec. 24, '62

F.

Captain	George Montgomery	Aug. 21, '62.	Resigned Dec. 19, '62
First Lieutenant.	William Barrick	Aug. 21, '62.	
Second Lieutenant	Edwin Allsop	Aug. 21, '62.	

G.

Captain	John Sutton	Aug. 21, '62.	
First Lieutenant.	James F. Bowen	Aug. 21, '62.	Resigned Dec. 24, '62
Second Lieutenant	Uriah Warrington	Aug. 21, '62.	

H.

Captain	James J. Davidson	Aug. 21, '62.	
First Lieutenant.	Samson Purcell	Aug. 21, 62.	
Second Lieutenant	Clement S. Shinn	Aug. 21, '62.	Resigned Dec. 19, '62

SCHEDULE G—Continued.

		Rank.	Remarks.

I.

Captain	Peter Wallace	Aug. 21, '62	
First Lieutenant	John L. Barger	Aug. 21, '62	Resigned Dec. 16, '62
Second Lieutenant	James M. Turpin	Aug. 21, '62	

K.

Captain	Reuben W. Laughlin	Aug. 21, '62	
First Lieutenant	James Lancaster	Aug. 21, '62	Resigned Dec. 24, '62
Second Lieutenant			

Schedule G — Continued.

Roster of Seventy-Fourth Regiment Illinois Volunteers.

Field and Staff.		Rank.	Remarks.
Colonel	Jason Marsh	Sept. 4, '62	
Lieutenant Colonel	James B. Kerr	Sept. 4, '62	
Major	Edward F. Dutcher	Sept. 4, '62	
Adjutant	Edward A. Blodgett	Aug. 14, '62	
Quartermaster	Lewis Williams	Sept. 4, '62	
Surgeon	Charles N. Ellinwood	Sept. 28, '62	
1st Ass't Surgeon	Henry Strong	Sept. 28, '62	
2d Ass't Surgeon	Chesseldon Fisher	Sept. 28, '62	
Chaplain			

Company A.

Captain	Thomas J. L. Remington	Sept. 4, '62	
First Lieutenant	Josiah W. Leffingwell	Sept. 4, '62	
Second Lieutenant	Alfred Barker	Sept. 4, '62	

B.

Captain	David O. Buttolph	Sept. 4, '62	
First Lieutenant	Augustus W. Thompson	Sept. 4, '62	
Second Lieutenant	Edwin Swift	Sept. 4, '62	

C.

Captain	Hampton P. Sloan	Sept. 4, '62	
First Lieutenant	Christopher M. Brazee	Sept. 4, '62	
Second Lieutenant	Richard P. Blaisdell	Sept. 4, '62	Resigned Sept. 4, 1862
"	John F. Squire	Sept. 4, '62	

D.

Captain	Jonathan H. Douglas	Sept. 4, '62	
First Lieutenant	Hobert H. Hatch	Sept. 4, '62	
Second Lieutenant	John H. Nye	Sept. 4, '62	

E.

Captain	Elias Cosper	Sept. 4, '62	
First Lieutenant	Elias Cosper	Sept. 4, '62	Promoted
"	William Powell	Sept. 4, '62	Resigned
Second Lieutenant	William Powell	Sept. 4, '62	Promoted
"	Alpheus M. Blakely	Sept. 4, '62	

F.

Captain	Henry C. Barker	Sept. 4, '62	
First Lieutenant	Jerome E. Andrews	Sept. 4, '62	
Second Lieutenant	Cyrenius N. Woods	Sept. 4, '61	

G.

Captain	Bowman W. Bacon	Sept. 4, '62	
First Lieutenant	William R. Hoadley	Sept. 4, '62	
Second Lieutenant	David McKaig	Sept. 4, '62	

H.

Captain	Timothy B. Taylor	Sept. 4, '62	
First Lieutenant	Samuel Whitmyer	Sept. 4, '62	
Second Lieutenant	Andrew J. Belts	Sept. 4, '62	Mustered out Oct. 10, '62

Schedule G—Continued.

		Rank.	Remarks.

I.

Captain	Willliam Irvin	Sept. 4, '62	
First Lieutenant	Frederick W. Stegner	Sept. 4, '62	
Second Lieutenant	Daniel Cronemiller	Sept. 4, '62	

K.

Captain	Butler Ward	Sept. 4, '62	
First Lieutenant	Henry N. Baker	Sept. 4, '62	
Second Lieutenant	Albert G. Lakin	Sept. 4, '62	

Schedule G — Continued.

Roster of Seventy-Fifth Regiment Illinois Volunteers.

Field and Staff.		Rank.	Remarks.
Colonel	George Ryan	Sept. 2, '62	Resigned Dec. 20, 1862
"	John E. Bennett	Dec. 20, '62	
Lieutenant Colonel	John E. Bennett	Sept. 2, '62	Promoted
"	William M. Kilgour	Dec. 20, '62	
Major	William M. Kilgour	Sept. 2, '62	Promoted Lieut. Colonel
"	James A. Watson	Dec. 20, '62	
Adjutant	Jerome W. Hollenbeck	Sept. 2, '62	Resigned Dec. 19, '62
Quartermaster	John E. Remington	Sept. 2, '62	
Surgeon	George W. Phillips	Sept. 18, '62	
1st Ass't Surgeon	John C. Corbus	Sept. 2, '62	
2d Ass't Surgeon	Henry Utley	Sept. 18, '62	Resigned Dec. 10, '61
Chaplain	William H. Smith	Sept. 12, '62	

Company A.

Captain	James A. Watson	Sept. 2, '62	Promoted Major
First Lieutenant	Ezekiel Giles	Sept. 2, '62	
Second Lieutenant	William Parker, jr	Sept. 2, '62	

B.

Captain	John Whallon	Sept. 2, '62	
First Lieutenant	Albert M. Gillett	Sept. 2, '62	
Second Lieutenant	James Blean	Sept. 2, '62	

C.

Captain	Ernst Altman	Sept. 2, '62	
First Lieutenant	George R. Shaw	Sept. 2, '62	
Second Lieutenant	Prentiss S. Bannister	Sept. 2, '62	

D.

Captain	Andrew McMoore	Sept. 2, '62	
First Lieutenant	Joseph E. Colby	Sept. 2, '62	
Second Lieutenant	Edward H. Barlow	Sept. 2, '62	

E.

Captain	William S. Erost	Sept. 2, '62	
First Lieutenant	Franklin H. Eels	Sept. 2, '62	Killed in action
"	James H. Blodgett	Oct. 8, '62	
Second Lieutenant	James H. Blodgett	Sept. 2, '62	Promoted
"	Henry Hill, jr	Oct. 8, '62	

F.

Captain	Addison S. Vorrey	Sept. 2, '62	
First Lieutenant	James Tourtillott	Sept. 2, '62	
Second Lieutenant	Dennis Hannifin	Sept. 2, '62	

G.

Captain	Joseph Williams	Sept. 2, '62	Resigned Dec. 19, '62
First Lieutenant	David Sanford	Sept. 2, '62	
Second Lieutenant	Robert L. Irvine	Sept. 2, '62	

SCHEDULE G—Continued.

		Rank.	Remarks.

H.

Captain	John G. Price	Sept. 2, '62	
First Lieutenant	Joseph W. R. Stanbaugh	Sept. 2, '62	
Second Lieutenant	Abner R. Hurless	Sept. 2, '62	

I.

Captain	Robert Hale	Sept. 2, '62	
First Lieutenant	Joel A. Fife	Sept. 2, '62	
Second Lieutenant	Ezekiel Kilgour	Sept. 2, '62	

K.

Captain	David M. Roberts	Sept. 2, '62	
First Lieutenant	William H. Thompson	Sept. 2, '62	
Second Lieutenant	Isaac L. Hunt	Sept. 2, '62	

Schedule G—Continued.

Roster of Seventh-Sixth Regiment Illinois Volunteers.

Field and Staff.		Rank.	Remarks.
Colonel	Alonzo W. Mack	Aug. 22, '62	
Lieutenant Colonel	Samuel T. Busey	Aug. 22, '62	
Major	William A. Dubois	Aug. 22, '62	
Adjutant	John F. Huntoon	July 31, '62	
Quartermaster	George J. Hodges	Aug. 1, '62	
Surgeon	Franklin Blades	Aug. 22, '62	
1st Ass't Surgeon	William A. Babcock	Aug. 22, '62	
2d Ass't Surgeon	Edmund Ridgeway	Sept. 26, '62	
Chaplain	John W. Flower	Aug. 22, '62	

Company A.

Captain	George C. Harrington	Aug. 22, '62	
First Lieutenant	Abraham Andrea	Aug. 22, '62	
Second Lieutenant	James R. Elliott	Aug. 22, '62	

B.

Captain	Homer W. Ayers	Aug. 22, '62	
First Lieutenant	Homer W. Ayers	Aug. 22, '62	Promoted
"	Ning A. Riley	Aug. 22, '62	
Second Lieutenant	James E. Smith	Aug. 22, '62	

C.

Captain	Charles C. Jones	Aug. 22, '62	
First Lieutenant	William Reardon, jr	Aug. 22, '62	
Second Lieutenant	Richard Hughes	Aug. 22, '62	

D.

Captain	Francis Seguin	Aug. 22, '62	
First Lieutenant	Charles O. Savoil	Aug. 22, '62	
Second Lieutenant	Noel Brosseau	Aug. 22, '62	

E.

Captain	Abram Irvin	Aug. 22, '62	
First Lieutenant	Peter J. Williams	Aug. 22, '62	
Second Lieutenant	Cornelius L. Hoyle	Aug. 22, '62	

F.

Captain	George Cooper	Aug. 22, '62	
First Lieutenant	William P. Mitchell	Aug. 22, '62	
Second Lieutenant	David Palmer	Aug. 22, '62	

G.

Captain	Joseph Park	Aug. 22, '62	
First Lieutenant	Joseph Ingersoll	Aug. 22, '62	
Second Lieutenant	James R. Dunlap	Aug. 22, '62	

H.

Captain	Daniel Plummer	Aug. 22, '62	
First Lieutenant	Peter Nichols	Aug. 22, '62	
Second Lieutenant	Jacob Ruger	Aug. 22, '62	

Schedule G—Continued.

		Rank.	Remarks.

I.

Captain	Walter W. Todd	Aug. 22, '62.	
First Lieutenant	J. B. Durham	Aug. 22, '62.	
Second Lieutenant	Warren R. Hickox	Aug. 22, '62.	

K.

Captain	Joseph Davis	Aug. 22, '62.	
First Lieutenant	Charles R. Ford	Aug. 22, '62.	
Second Lieutenant	John B. Dille	Aug. 22, '62.	

SCHEDULE G—Continued.

Roster of Seventy-Seventh Regiment Illinois Volunteers.

Field and Staff.		Rank.	Remarks.
Colonel	Charles Ballance	Aug. 18, '62	Resigned
"	David P. Grier	Sept. 12, 62	
Lieutenant Colonel	Lysander R. Webb	Sept. 3, '62	
Major	Memoir V. Hotchkiss	Sept. 3, '62	
Adjutant	John Hough	Sept. 6, '62	
Quartermaster	David McKinney	Sept. 12, '62	
Surgeon	Charles Winnie	Dec. 6, '62	
1st Ass't Surgeon	Jesse M. Cowen	Sept. 30, '62	
2d Ass't Surgeon	John Stoner	Sept. 30, '62	
Chaplain	William G. Pierce	Sept. 12, '62	

COMPANY A.

Captain	John A. Burdett	Sept. 2, '62	
First Lieutenant	Gardner G. Stearns	Sept. 2, '62	
Second Lieutenant	Merritt M. Clark	Sept. 2, '62	

B.

Captain	Robert Irwin	Sept. 2, '62	
First Lieutenant	Henry B. Kays	Sept. 2, '62	
Second Lieutenant	Addison E. McCaleb	Sept. 2, '62	

C.

Captain	Joseph M. McCullock	Sept. 2, '62	
First Lieutenant	William A. Woodruff	Sept. 2, '62	
Second Lieutenant	Phillip Jenkins	Sept. 2, '62	

D.

Captain	Robert H. Brock	Sept. 2, '62	
First Lieutenant	William J. Goodrich	Sept. 2, '62	
Second Lieutenant	John M. Shields	Sept. 2, '62	

E.

Captain	Edwin Stevens	Sept. 2, '62	
First Lieutenant	Samuel J. Smith	Sept. 2, '62	
Second Lieutenant	James H. Schnebly	Sept. 2, '62	

F

Captain	William W. Crandall	Sept. 2, '62	
First Lieutenant	William O. Hammers	Sept 2, '62	
Second Lieutenant	James A. Secord	Sept. 2, '62	

G.

Captain	John D. Rouse	Sept. 2, '62	
First Lieutenant	Charles Island	Sept. 2, '62	
Second Lieutenant	Frederick H. Osgood	Sept. 2, '62	

H.

Captain	Lewis G. Keedy	Sept. 2, '62	
First Lieutenant	Milgrove B. Parmeter	Sept. 2, '62	
Second Lieutenant	John Filger	Sept. 2, '62	

SCHEDULE G—Continued.

		Rank.	Remarks.

I.

Captain	Wayne O. Donald	Sept. 2, '62	
First Lieutenant	Silas J. Wagoner	Sept. 2, '62	
Second Lieutenant	John H. Em	Sept. 2, '62	

K.

Captain	Ephraim C. Rynearson	Sept. 2, '62	Resigned Oct. 21, '62
"	William H. White	Oct. 21, '62	
First Lieutenant	William H. White	Sept. 2, '62	Promoted
"	Sylvester S. Edwards	Oct. 21, '62	
Second Lieutenant	Sylvester S. Edwards	Sept. 2, '62	Promoted
"	Marcus O. Harkness	Oct. 21, '62	

SCHEDULE G—Continued.

Roster of Seventy-Eighth Regiment Illinois Volunteers.

Field and Staff.		Rank.	Remarks.
Colonel	William H. Bennison	Sept. 1, '62	
Lieutenant Colonel	Carter Van Vleck	Sept. 1, '62	
Major	William L. Broddus	Sept. 15, '62	
Adjutant	George Greene	Sept. 1, '62	
Quartermaster	Abner V. Humphrey	Aug. 6, '62	
Surgeon	Thomas M. Jordan	Sept. 1, '62	
1st Ass't Surgeon	Elisha S. McIntire	Sept. 1, '62	
2d Ass't Surgeon	Samuel C. Moss	Nov. 28, '62	
Chaplain	Robert F. Taylor	Sept. 1, '62	

COMPANY A.

Captain	Robert S. Blackburn	Sept. 1, '62	
First Lieutenant	Phillip Chipman	Sept. 1, '62	
Second Lieutenant	Archibald H. Graham	Sept. 1, '62	

B.

Captain	John C. Anderson	Sept. 1, '62	
First Lieutenant	William D. Ruddell	Sept. 1, '62	
Second Lieutenant	David M. Taylor	Sept. 1, '62	

C.

Captain	Charles R. Hume	Sept. 1, '62	
First Lieutenant	Oliver P. Cartwright	Sept. 1, '62	
Second Lieutenant	George W. Blandin	Sept. 1, '62	

D.

Captain	Robert M. Black	Sept. 1, '62	
First Lieutenant	John B. Warroll	Sept. 1, '62	
Second Lieutenant	Isaac N. Kincheloe	Sept. 1, '62	

E.

Captain	George Pollock	Sept. 1, '62	
First Lieutenant	Matthew Henry	Sept. 1, '62	
Second Lieutenant	John J. Mercer	Sept. 1, '62	

F.

Captain	Henry E. Hawkins	Sept. 1, '62	
First Lieutenant	Clinton B. Cannon	Sept. 1, '62	
Second Lieutenant	Seldon G. Earl	Sept. 1, '62	Resigned Dec. 21, 1862

G.

Captain	Jacob F. Joseph	Sept. 1, '62	
First Lieutenant	Thomas L. Howden	Sept. 1, '62	
Second Lieutenant	Pleasant M. Herndon	Sept. 1, '62	

H.

Captain	John K. Allen	Sept. 1, '62	
First Lieutenant	George T. Beers	Sept. 1, '62	
Second Lieutenant	Samuel Simmons	Sept. 1, '62	

SCHEDULE G—Continued.

		Rank.	Remarks.

I.

Captain	Granville H. Reynolds	Sept. 1, '62	
First Lieutenant	Hardin Hovey	Sept. 1, '62	
Second Lieutenant	James H. McCandless	Sept. 1, '62	

K.

Captain	Maris R. Vernon	Sept. 1, '62	
First Lieutenant	Jeremiah Parsons	Sept. 1, '62	
Second Lieutenant	William B. Akins	Sept. 1, '62	

238

SCHEDULE G—Continued.

Roster of Seventy-Ninth Regiment Illinois Volunteers.

Field and Staff.		Rank.	Remarks.
Colonel	Lyman Guinnip	Aug. 28, '62	Resigned October 17, 1862
"	Sheridan P. Read	Oct. 17, '62	
Lieutenant Colonel	Sheridan P. Read	Aug. 28, '62	Promoted
"	Henry E. Rives	Nov. 29, '62	
Major	Allen Buckner	Aug. 28, '62	
Adjutant	William H. Lamb	Aug. 28, '62	
Quartermaster	Charles E. Woodward	Aug. 5, '62	
Surgeon			
1st Ass't Surgeon	Henry C. McAllister	Aug. 28, '62	
2d Ass't Surgeon	Thomas J. Wheeler	Aug. 28, '62	
Chaplain	Cornelius G. Bradshaw	Aug. 28, '62	

COMPANY A.

Captain	Terrance Clark	Aug. 28, '62	
First Lieutenant	James S. Price	Aug. 28, '62	
Second Lieutenant	John Mitchell	Aug. 28, '62	

B.

Captain	Archibald Vanderin	Aug. 28, '62	
First Lieutenant	Seth L. Woodworth	Aug. 28, '62	
Second Lieutenant	Horace W. Rideout	Aug. 28, '62	

C.

Captain	David S. Curtis	Aug. 28, '62	
First Lieutenant	William S. Hendrix	Aug. 28, '62	Resigned Dec. 8, 1862
"	John H. Patton	Dec. 8, '62	
Second Lieutenant	John H. Patton	Aug. 28, '62	Promoted
"	Henry C. Beyls	Dec. 8, '62	

D.

Captain	Thomas A. Young	Aug. 28, '62	
First Lieutenant	David B. Elliott	Aug. 28, '62	
Second Lieutenant	John P. Vance	Aug. 28, '62	Resigned Nov. 28, 1862
"	Ike P. Hartsock	Nov. 28, '62	

E.

Captain	William A. Low	Aug. 28, '62	
First Lieutenant	Harvey J. Bassell	Aug. 28, '62	Resigned Nov. 20, 1862
"	Henry S. Albin	Nov. 20, '62	
Second Lieutenant	Henry S. Albin	Aug. 28, '62	Promoted
"	Harvey W. Peters	Nov. 20, '62	

F.

Captain	Thomas Handy	Aug. 28, '62	
First Lieutenant	David S. Williams	Aug. 28, '62	
Second Lieutenant	James R. Patten	Aug. 28, '62	

G.

Captain	Oliver O. Bagley	Aug. 28, '62	
First Lieutenant	Martin L. Lininger	Aug. 28, '62	Died Nov. 19, '62 by fall of [tree.
"	Thomas B. Jacobs	Nov. 19, '62	
Second Lieutenant	Thomas B. Jacobs	Aug. 28, '62	Promoted
"	Albert J. Jones	Nov. 19, '62	

Schedule G—Continued.

		Rank.	Remarks.

H.

Captain	Willis O. Pennell	Aug. 28, '62	
First Lieutenant	James T. Braddock	Aug. 28, '62	
Second Lieutenant	Andrew J. Bigelow	Aug. 28, '62	

I.

Captain	Robert Lacy	Aug. 28, '62	
First Lieutenant	Henry Week	Aug. 28, '62	
Second Lieutenant	Samuel Sharp	Aug. 28, '62	Resigned Sept. 26, 1862
"	William C. Willard	Sept. 26, '62	

K.

Captain	Hezekiah D. Martin	Aug. 28, '62	
First Lieutenant	William W. Davis	Aug. 28, '62	
Second Lieutenant	Moses Hunter	Aug. 28, '62	Resigned Oct. 19, 1862
"	Isaac P. C. Taylor	Oct. 19, '62	

SCHEDULE G — Continued.

Roster of Eightieth Regiment Illinois Volunteers.

Field and Staff.		Rank.	Remarks.
Colonel	Thomas G. Allen	Aug. 25, '62.	
Lieutenant Colonel	Andrew F. Rogers	Aug. 25, '62.	
Major	Erastus N. Baker	Aug. 25, '62.	
Adjutant	James C. Jones	Sept. 18, '62.	
Quartermaster	Robert J. Harmer	Aug. 25, '62.	
Surgeon	Nathan W. Abbott	Aug. 25, '62.	
1st Ass't Surgeon	Ebenezer Rodgers	Aug. 25, '62.	
2d Ass't Surgeon			
Chaplain	John W. Lane	Aug. 28, '62.	

COMPANY A.

Captain	James L. Mann	Aug. 25, '62.	
First Lieutenant	Samuel T. Jones	Aug. 25, '62.	
Second Lieutenant	Goodwin Scudmore	Aug. 25, '62.	

B.

Captain	George W. Carr	Aug. 25, '62.	
First Lieutenant	William R. Wright	Aug. 25, '62.	
Second Lieutenant	Henry C. Smith	Aug. 25, '62.	

C.

Captain	Henry Zeis	Aug. 25, '62.	
First Lieutenant	Herman Steinscke	Aug. 25, '62.	
Second Lieutenant	Benjamin Kohln	Aug. 25, '62.	

D.

Captain	Carter C. Williams	Aug. 25, '62.	
First Lieutenant	James Neville	Aug. 25, '62.	
Second Lieutenant	Alexander Van Kendle	Aug. 25, '62.	

E.

Captain	Stephen T. Stratton	Aug. 25, '62.	
First Lieutenant	Newton C. Pace	Aug. 25, '62.	
Second Lieutenant	Charles W. Pavey	Aug. 25, '62.	

F.

Captain	Edmund R. Jones	Aug. 25, '62.	
First Lieutenant	John Woods	Aug. 25, '62.	
Second Lieutenant	Albert Foster	Aug. 25, '62.	

G.

Captain	Andrew Wilson	Aug. 25, '62.	
First Lieutenant	John W. McCormack	Aug. 25, '62.	
Second Lieutenant	John W. McCormack	Aug. 25, '62.	Promoted
"	William H. McDill	Aug. 25, '62.	

H.

Captain	James Cunningham	Aug. 25, '62.	
First Lieutenant	James Cunningham	Aug. 25, '62.	Promoted
"	Samuel G. Andrews	Aug. 25, '62.	
Second Lieutenant	Samuel G. Andrews	Aug. 25, '62.	Promoted
"	John R. Cunningham	Aug. 25, '62.	

Schedule G—Continued.

		Rank.	Remarks.
I.			
Captain	Daniel Hay	Aug. 25, '62.	
First Lieutenant	James Adams	Aug. 25, '62.	
Second Lieutenant	Richard M. Davis	Aug. 25, '62.	
K.			
Captain	Alexander Hodge	Aug. 25, '62.	
First Lieutenant	Edmund D. Kiersey	Aug. 25, '62.	
Second Lieutenant	John A. Miller	Aug. 25, '62.	

SCHEDULE G—Continued.

Roster of Eighty-First Regiment Illinois Volunteers.

Field and Staff.		Rank.	Remarks.
Colonel	James J. Dollins	Aug. 26, '62	
Lieutenant Colonel	Franklin Campbell	Aug. 26, '62	
Major	Andrew W. Rogers	Aug. 26, '62	
Adjutant	Zebedee Hammock	Aug. 26, '62	
Quartermaster	Logan H. Roots	Aug. 26, '62	
Surgeon	Lewis Dyer	Aug. 26, '62	
1st Ass't Surgeon		Aug. 26, '62	
2d Ass't Surgeon		Aug. 26, '62	
Chaplain	William S. Post	Aug. 26, '62	

COMPANY A.

Captain	James P. Cowan	Aug. 26, '62	
First Lieutenant	Samuel Payne	Aug. 26, '62	
Second Lieutenant	William McNeill	Aug. 26, '62	

B.

Captain	Thomas Hightower	Aug. 26, '62	
First Lieutenant	John W. Grammar	Aug. 26, '62	
Second Lieutenant	Josiah Goodwin	Aug. 26, '62	

C.

Captain	John C. Armstrong	Aug. 26, '62	
First Lieutenant	Mortimer C. Edwards	Aug. 26, '62	
Second Lieutenant	Thomas B. McClure	Aug. 26, '62	Died Oct. 24, '62
"	Abraham L. Lippincott	Oct. 24, '62	

D.

Captain	Cornelius S. Ward	Aug. 26, '62	
First Lieutenant	Logan Wheeler	Aug. 26, '62	
Second Lieutenant	Isaac Rapp	Aug. 26, '62	

E.

Captain	Marmaduke F. Smith	Aug. 26, '62	
First Lieutenant	John P. Reese	Aug. 26, '62	
Second Lieutenant	David R. Sanders	Aug. 26, '62	

F.

Captain	Samuel L. Campbell	Aug. 26, '62	
First Lieutenant	Jacob W. Sanders	Aug. 26, '62	
Second Lieutenant	George W. Kelly	Aug. 26, '62	

G.

Captain	George W. Sisney	Aug. 26, '62	
First Lieutenant	William W. Russell	Aug. 36, '62	
Second Lieutenant	William L. Farmer	Aug. 26, '62	

H.

Captain	Albert F. Crane	Aug. 26, '62	
First Lieutenant	William A. Stewart	Aug. 26, '62	
Second Lieutenant	James V. Pierce	Aug. 26, '62	

Schedule G—Continued.

		Rank.	Remarks.
I.			
Captain	John W. Felt	Aug. 26, '62.	
First Lieutenant	James Bartleson	Aug. 26, '62.	
Second Lieutenant	Charles J. Minnick	Aug. 26, '62.	
K.			
Captain	Samuel Pyle	Aug. 26, '62.	
First Lieutenant	Lycurgus Rees	Aug. 26, '62.	
Second Lieutenant	William Needham	Aug. 26, '62.	

Schedule G — Continued.

Roster of Eighty-Second Regiment Illinois Volunteers.

Field and Staff.		Rank.	Remarks.
Colonel	Frederic Hecker	Oct. 23, '62	
Lieutenant Colonel	Edward S. Solomon	Sept. 26, '62	
Major	Ferdinand Rolshanson	Sept. 26, '62	
Adjutant	Eugene F. Weigel	Sept. 26, '62	
Quartermaster	Hermann Panse	Aug. 1, '62	
Surgeon	George Schloetzer	Sept. 26, '62	
1st Ass't Surgeon	Emil Brendel	Aug. 20, '62	
2d Ass't Surgeon	Oscar Julius Bergk	Oct. 11, '62	
Chaplain	Emanuel Julius Richhelm	Sept. 23, '62	

Company A.

Captain	Anton Bruhn	Sept. 26, '62	
First Lieutenant	Edward Kafka	Sept. 26, '62	
Second Lieutenant	Charles E. Stueven	Sept. 26, '62	

B.

Captain	Augustus Bruning	Aug. 15, '62	
First Lieutenant	George Heinzmann	Aug. 15, '62	
Second Lieutenant	Charles Lanzendorfer	Aug. 25, '62	

C.

Captain	Jacob Lasalle	Sept. 26, '62	
First Lieutenant	Mayer A. Frank	Sept. 26, '62	
Second Lieutenant	Frederick Bechstein	Sept. 26, '62	

D.

Captain	Matthew Marx	Aug. 28, '62	
First Lieutenant	William Warner	Aug. 28, '62	
Second Lieutenant	Frank Kirchner	Aug. 28, '62	

E.

Captain	Robert Lender	Sept. 26, '62	
First Lieutenant	Rudolph Mueller	Sept. 26, '62	
Second Lieutenant	John Brech Celler	Sept. 26, '62	

F.

Captain	Frederick L. Webber	Sept. 26, '62	
First Lieutenant	Erich Hoppe	Sept. 26, '62	
Second Lieutenant	Lorenz Spoenemann	Sept. 26, '62	

G.

Captain	William Neussel	Sept. 26, '62	
First Lieutenant	Joseph Gottlob	Sept. 26, '62	
Second Lieutenant	Conrad Schonder	Sept. 26, '62	

H.

Captain	Emil Frey	Sept. 26, '62	
First Lieutenant	Johann Sporre	Sept. 26, '62	
Second Lieutenant	Joseph Riegert	Sept. 26, '62	

SCHEDULE G—Continued.

		Rank.	Remarks.

I.

Captain	Ivar Alexander Weid	Aug. 30, '62.	
First Lieutenant	John Hillborg	Aug. 30, '62.	
Second Lieutenant	Peter Hanson	Aug. 30, '62.	Resigned Dec. 10, 1862

K.

Captain	Joseph B. Greenhut	Oct. 23, '62.	
First Lieutenant	George W. Fuchs	Oct. 23, '62.	
Second Lieutenant	Dominicus Klutsch	Oct. 23, '62.	

Schedule G—Continued.

Roster of Eighty-Third Regiment Illinois Volunteers.

Field and Staff.		Rank.	Remarks.
Colonel	Abner C. Harding	Aug. 21, '62	
Lieutenant Colonel	Arthur A. Smith	Aug. 21, '62	
Major	Elijah C. Brott	Sept. 30, '62	
Adjutant	Wesley B. Casey	Aug. 21, '62	
Quartermaster	John B. Cotton	Aug. 21, '62	
Surgeon	Esaias S. Cooper	Nov. 14, '62	
1st Ass't Surgeon	John P. McClanahan	Aug. 21, '62	
2d Ass't Surgeon	Richard Morris	Sept. 30, '62	Promoted Surgeon 103d
Chaplain	Adam C. Higgins	Aug. 21, '62	

Company A.

Captain	Philo C. Reed	Aug. 21, '62	
First Lieutenant	George H. Palmer	Aug. 21, '62	
Second Lieutenant	Davis M. Clark	Aug. 21, '62	

B.

Captain	John McClanahan	Aug. 21, '62	
First Lieutenant	James Moore	Aug. 21, '62	
Second Lieutenant	William W. Turnbull	Aug. 21, '62	

C.

Captain	Lyman B. Cutler	Aug. 21, '62	
First Lieutenant	John C. Gamball	Aug. 21, '62	
Second Lieutenant	Samuel L. Stephenson	Aug. 21, '62	

D.

Captain	Joshua M. Snyder	Aug. 21, '62	
First Lieutenant	Hugh M. Robb	Aug. 21, '62	
Second Lieutenant	Francis M. Sykes	Aug. 21, '62	

E.

Captain	Elijah C. Brott	Aug. 21, '62	Promoted Major
"	James M. Gilson	Oct. 22, '62	
First Lieutenant	James M. Gilson	Aug. 21, '62	Promoted Captain
"	Erastus H. Pierce	Oct. 22, '62	
Second Lieutenant	Erastus H. Pierce	Aug. 21, '62	Promoted
"	John L. Parsons	Oct. 22, '62	

F.

Captain	John T. Morgan	Aug. 21, '62	
First Lieutenant	Joseph A. Boyington	Aug. 21, '62	
Second Lieutenant	James W. Morgan	Aug. 21, '62	

G.

Captain	James G. Hammick	Aug. 21, '62	
First Lieutenant	Horace Jones	Aug. 21, '62	
Second Lieutenant	John Jones	Aug. 21, '62	

H.

Captain	William G. Bond	Aug. 21, '62	
First Lieutenant	Walter N. Bond	Aug. 21, '62	
Second Lieutenant	James C. Johnson	Aug. 21, '62	

Schedule G—Continued.

		Rank.	Remarks.

I.

Captain	Joseph B. Dowley	Aug. 21, '62	
First Lieutenant	Daniel D. Shoop	Aug. 21, '62	
Second Lieutenant	William S. Latimer	Aug. 21, '62	

K.

Captain	George W. Reynolds	Aug. 21, '62	
First Lieutenant	Richard D. Russell	Aug. 21, '62	
Second Lieutenant	John S. Garrett	Aug. 21, '62	

248

SCHEDULE G—Continued.

Roster of Eighty-Fourth Regiment Illinois Volunteers.

Field and Staff.		Rank.	Remarks.
Colonel	Louis H. Waters	Sept. 1, '62	
Lieutenant Colonel	Thomas Hamer	Sept. 1, '62	
Major	Charles H. Morton	Sept. 1, '62	
Adjutant	Charles E. Waters	Sept. 1, '62	
Quartermaster	Samuel L. Roe	Aug. 9, '62	Resigned Nov. 18, '62
"	James A. Russell	Nov. 19, '62	
Surgeon	James B. Kyle	Sept. 1, '62	
1st Ass't Surgeon	David McDill	Sept. 3, '62	
2d Ass't Surgeon	Elijah L. Marshall	Sept. 12, '62	
Chaplain	Ralph Harris	Sept 3, '62	

COMPANY A.

Captain	John P. Higgins	Sept. 1, '62	
First Lieutenant	Thomas G. Wisdom	Sept. 1, '62	
Second Lieutenant	William F. Stearns	Sept. 1, '62	

B.

Captain	Vincent M. Grewell	Sept. 1, '62	
First Lieutenant	Lemuel L. Scott	Sept. 1, '62	
Second Lieutenant	James A. Russell	Sept. 1, '62	Quartermaster

C.

Captain	William Ervin	Sept. 1, '62	
First Lieutenant	Epaphroditus C. Coulson	Sept. 1, '62	
Second Lieutenant	William P. Pearson	Sept. 1, '62	

D.

Captain	Moses W. Davis	Sept. 1, '62	
First Lieutenant	Thomas D. Adams	Sept. 1, '62	
Second Lieutenant	Walter Scaggan	Sept. 1, '62	

E.

Captain	Miron G. Tousley	Sept. 1, '62	
First Lieutenant	Hiram P. Roberts	Sept. 1, '62	
Second Lieutenant	Henry V. Lewis	Sept. 1, '62	

F.

Captain	Caleb B. Cox	Sept. 1 '62	
First Lieutenant	Joseph Nelson	Sept. 1, '62	
Second Lieutenant	Samuel Frost	Sept. 1, '62	

G.

Captain	Frederick Garternicht	Aug. 12, '62	
First Lieutenant	William H. Fuller	Sept. 1, '62	
Second Lieutenant	Russell W. Caswell	Sept. 1, '62	

H.

Captain	John C. Pepper	Sept. 1, '62	
First Lieutenant	Luther T. Ball	Sept. 1, '62	
Second Lieutenant	Henry E. Abercrombie	Sept. 1, '62	

Schedule G — Continued.

		Rank.	Remarks.

I.

Captain	Albert J. Griffith	Sept. 2, '62	
First Lieutenant	William Scott	Sept. 1, '62	
Second Lieutenant	Thomas F. Kendrick	Sept. 1, '62	

K.

Captain	John B. McGaw	Sept. 1, '62	
First Lieutenant	Alexander P. Nelson	Sept. 1, '62	
Second Lieutenant	Hiram H. Mills	Sept. 1, '62	

SCHEDULE G—Continued.

Roster of Eighty-Fifth Regiment Illinois Volunteers.

Field and Staff.		Rank.	Remarks.
Colonel	Robert S. Moore	Aug. 27, '62	
Lieutenant Colonel	Caleb J. Dilworth	Aug. 27, '62	
Major	Samuel P. Cummings	Aug. 27, '62	
Adjutant	John B. Wright	Aug. 27, '62	
Quartermaster	Samuel F. Wright	Aug. 9, '62	
Surgeon	James P. Walker	Aug. 22, '62	
1st Ass't Surgeon.	Philip L. Duffenbecker	Aug. 27, '62	
2d Ass't Surgeon.			
Chaplain			

COMPANY A.

Captain	Matthew Langston	Aug. 27, '62	
First Lieutenant	Thomas R. Roberts	Aug. 27, '62	
Second Lieutenant	John W. Neal	Aug. 27, '62	Resigned Nov. 12, '62
"	Daniel Westfall	Nov. 12, '62	

B.

Captain	James R. Griffith	Aug. 27, '62	
First Lieutenant	Charles W. Pierce	Aug. 27, '62	
Second Lieutenant	John A. Mallory	Aug. 27, '62	

C.

Captain	Samuel Black	Aug. 27, '62	
First Lieutenant	George A. Blanchard	Aug. 27, '62	
Second Lieutenant	William W. Walker	Aug. 27, '62	

D.

Captain	Charles W. Houghton	Aug. 27, '62	
First Lieutenant	Comfort H. Raymon	Aug. 27, '62	Resigned Dec. 21, '62
Second Lieutenant	Charles H. Chatfield	Aug. 27, '62	

E.

Captain	Pleasant S. Scott	Aug. 27, '62	
First Lieutenant	Joseph M. Plunckett	Aug. 27, '62	Resigned Dec. 21, '62
Second Lieutenant	Abraham Clarry	Aug. 27, '62	

F.

Captain	John Kennedy	Aug. 27, '62	
First Lieutenant	Robert A. Bowman	Aug. 27, '62	
Second Lieutenant	Richard W. Tenney	Aug. 27, '62	

G

Captain	William McClelland	Aug. 27, '62	Resigned Dec. 21, '62
First Lieutenant	Lafayette Curless	Aug. 27, '62	Resigned Nov. 12, '62
"	John M. Robinson	Nov. 12, '62	
Second Lieutenant	John M. Robinson	Aug. 27, '62	Promoted

H.

Captain	Nathaniel McClelland	Aug. 27, '62	Resigned Nov. 12, '62
"	David Maxwell	Nov. 12, '62	
First Lieutenant	Luke Elliott	Aug. 27, '62	Resigned Nov. 21, '62
"	James T. McNeill	Nov. 21, '62	
Second Lieutenant	William Cohren	Aug. 27, '62	Resigned Nov. 12, '62
"	Washington M. Sheilds	Nov. 12, '62	

Schedule G.—Continued

		Rank.	Remarks.
I.			
Captain	William H. Marble	Aug. 27, '62	
First Lieutenant	David M. Holstead	Aug. 27, '62	
Second Lieutenant	Hugh McHugh	Aug. 27, '62	
K.			
Captain	Robert G. Rider	Aug. 27, '62	
First Lieutenant	Samuel Yates	Aug. 27, '62	
Second Lieutenant	Isaac C. Short	Aug. 27, '62	

Schedule G—Continued.

Roster of Eighty-Sixth Regiment Illinois Volunteers.

Field and Staff.		Rank.	Remarks.
Colonel	David D. Irons	Aug. 27, '62.	
Lieutenant Colonel	David W. Magee	Aug. 27, '62.	
Major	James S. Bean	Aug. 27, '62.	Resigned Dec. 26, '62.
Adjutant	James E. Prescott	Aug. 27, '62	Resigned Dec. 26, '62
Quartermaster	Charles H. Dean	Aug. 11, '62.	
Surgeon	Massena M. Hooton	Aug. 27, '62.	
1st Ass't Surgeon.	John Gregory	Aug. 27, '62.	
2d Ass't Surgeon.	Israel J. Gruth	Aug. 27, '62.	
Chaplain	Geo. W. Brown	Aug. 27, '62.	

Company A.

Captain	William S. Magarity	Aug. 27, '62.	
First Lieutenant	Joseph Major	Aug. 27, '62.	
Second Lieutenant	Samuel T. Rogers	Aug. 27, '62.	

B.

Captain	Elias C. Breasley	Aug. 27, '62.	
First Lieutenant	Jonathan C. Kingsley	Aug. 27, '62.	
Second Lieutenant	Nelson McVicker	Aug. 27, '62.	

C.

Captain	Joseph F. Thomas	Aug. 27, '62	
First Lieutenant	John H. Bachelder	Aug. 27, '62	
Second Lieutenant	Reuben B. Beebe	Aug. 27, '62.	

D.

Captain	Frank Hitchcock	Aug. 27, '62.	
First Lieutenant	William D. Faulkner	Aug. 27, '62.	
Second Lieutenant	William H. Hall	Aug. 27, '62.	

E.

Captain	Orlando Fountain	Aug. 27, '62.	
First Lieutenant	Malchi Grave	Aug. 27, '62.	
Second Lieutenant	Solomon H. Williams	Aug. 27, '62	

F.

Captain	James L. Buckhalter	Aug. 27, '62.	
First Lieutenant	Nelson D. Combs	Aug. 27, '62	
Second Lieutenant	John Hall	Aug. 27, '62.	

G.

Captain	William B. Bogardus	Aug. 27, '62.	
First Lieutenant	Solomon L. Zinser	Aug. 27, '62.	
Second Lieutenant	Martin Kingman	Aug. 27, '62.	

H.

Captain	John H. Hall	Aug. 27, '62.	
First Lieutenant	Edwin E. Peters	Aug. 27, '62.	
Second Lieutenant	Davilla W. Merwin	Aug. 27, '62.	Dishonorably discharged,
"	Wilber F. Hodge	Nov. 21, '62.	[Nov. 21, '62

SCHEDULE G — Continued.

		Rank.	Remarks.
I.			
Captain	Allen L. Fahnestock	Aug. 27, '62.	
First Lieutenant	Abner A. Lee	Aug. 27, '62.	
Second Lieutenant	Jacob L. Fahnestock	Aug. 27, '62.	
K.			
Captain	John F. French	Aug. 27, '62.	
First Lieutenant	James B. Peet	Aug. 27, '62.	[Nov. 29, '62
Second Lieutenant	Henry F. Irvin	April 27, '62.	Dishonorably discharged

SCHEDULE G — Continued.

Roster of Eighty-Seventh Regiment Illinois Volunteers.

Field and Staff.		Rank.	Remarks.
Colonel	John E. Whiting	Oct. 3, '62	
Lieutenant Colonel	John M. Crebs	Oct. 3, '62	
Major	George W. Land	Oct. 3, '62	
Adjutant	John D. Martin	Oct. 3, '62	
Quartermaster	John H. Cooper	Oct. 1, '62	
Surgeon	Elan L. Stewart	Oct. 3, '62	
1st. Ass't Surgeon	John Poindexter	Oct. 3, '62	
2d Ass't Surgeon			
Chaplain	Albert Ransom	Oct. 1, '62	

Company A.

Captain	John S. Anderson	Sept. 22, '62	
First Lieutenant	Robert L. Meador	Sept. 22, '62	
Second Lieutenant	John W. Richardson	Sept. 22, '62	

B.

Captain	Thomas J. Enlow	Sept. 22, '62	
First Lieutenant	William T. Prunty	Sept. 22, '62	
Second Lieutenant	Archibald Spring	Sept. 22, '62	

C.

Captain	Edmund Emery	Sept. 22, '62	
First Lieutenant	James A. Miller	Sept. 22, '62	
Second Lieutenant	Robert Pomroy	Sept. 22, '62	

D.

Captain	Jacob B. Borah	Sept. 22, '62	
First Lieutenant	James T. Price	Sept. 22, '62	
Second Lieutenant	Lewis Mayo	Sept. 22, '62	

E.

Captain	Milton Carpenter	Sept. 22, '62	
First Lieutenant	James H. Wright	Sept. 22, '62	
Second Lieutenant	Theophilus L. Jones	Sept. 22, '62	

F.

Captain	James Fackney	Sept. 22, '62	
First Lieutenant	John H. Wasson	Sept. 22, '62	
Second Lieutenant	Nathaniel B. Hodsdun	Sept. 22, '62	

G.

Captain	Samuel J. Foster	Sept. 22, '62	
First Lieutenant	Edwin B. Emerson	Sept. 22, '62	
Second Lieutenant	John Graham	Sept. 22, 62	

H.

Captain	James R. Jacobs	Sept. 22, '62	
First Lieutenant	William H. Johns	Sept. 22, '62	
Second Lieutenant	James Chism	Sept. 22, '62	

SCHEDULE G—Continued.

		Rank.	Remarks.

I.

Captain	James P. Thomas	Sept. 22, '62.	
First Lieutenant	Benjamin F. Brockett	Sept. 22, '62.	
Second Lieutenant	Ross Graham	Sept. 22, '62.	

K.

Captain	Martin Vaught	Sept. 22, '62.	
First Lieutenant	Thomas Sheridan	Sept. 22, '62.	
Second Lieutenant	William H. McHenry	Sept. 22, '62.	

Schedule G—Continued.

Roster of Eighty-Eighth Regiment Illinois Volunteers.

Field and Staff.		Rank.	Remarks.
Colonel	Francis T. Sherman	Sept. 4, '62	
Lieutenant Colon'l	Alexander S. Chadburn	Sept. 4, '62	
Major	George W. Chandler	Sept. 4, '62	
Adjutant	Joshua S. Bullard	Sept. 4, '62	
Quartermaster	Nathaniel S. Bouton	Sept. 4, '62	
Surgeon	George Coatsworth	Sept. 4, '62	
1st Ass't Surgeon	Arthur C. Rankin	Sept. 4, '62	
2d Ass't Surgeon	Frank N. Burdick	Sept. 4, '62	Resigned Nov. 26, '62
Chaplain	Joseph C. Thomas	Sept. 17, '62	

Company A.

Captain	John A. Bross	Sept. 4, '62	
First Lieutenant	John P. D. Gibson	Sept. 4, '62	
Second Lieutenant	Lewis B. Cole	Sept. 4, '62	

B.

Captain	George W. Smith	Sept. 4, '62	
First Lieutenant	George Chandler	Sept. 4, '62	
Second Lieutenant	Gilbert F. Bigelow	Sept. 4, '62	

C.

Captain	Webster A. Whiting	Sept. 4, '62	
First Lieutenant	Henry H. Cushing	Sept. 4, '62	
Second Lieutenant	Charles H. Lane	Sept. 4, '62	

D.

Captain	George A. Sheridan	Sept. 4, '62	
First Lieutenant	Thomas F. W. Gullich	Sept. 4, '62	
Second Lieutenant	Alex. C. McMurtry	Sept. 4, '62	

E.

Captain	Levi P. Holden	Sept. 4, '62	
First Lieutenant	Sylvester Titsworth	Sept. 4, '62	
Second Lieutenant	Lorenzo Brown	Sept. 4, '62	

F.

Captain	John W. Chickering	Sept. 4, '62	
First Lieutenant	James A. S. Hanford	Sept. 4, '62	
Second Lieutenant	James Watts	Sept. 4, '62	

G.

Captain	Gurdon S. Hubbard, jr.	Sept. 4, '62	
First Lieutenant	Frederick C. Goodwin	Sept. 4, '62	
Second Lieutenant	Dean R. Chester	Sept. 4, '62	

H.

Captain	Alex. C. McClurg	Sept. 4, '62	
First Lieutenant	Charles T. Boal	Sept. 4, '62	
Second Lieutenant	Daniel B. Rice	Sept. 4, '62	

Schedule G — Continued.

		Rank.	Remarks.

I.

Captain	Joel J. Spalding	Sept. 4, '62	
First Lieutenant	Orson C. Miller	Sept. 4, '62	
Second Lieutenant	Jesse Ball	Sept. 4, '62	

K.

Captain	Daniel E. Barnard	Sept. 4, '62	
First Lieutenant	Homer C. McDonald	Sept. 4, '62	
Second Lieutenant	Edmund E. Tucker	Sept. 4, '62	

Schedule G — Continued.

Roster of Eighty-Ninth Regiment Illinois Volunteers.

Field and Staff.		Rank.	Remarks.
Colonel	John Christopher	Aug. 25, '62	
Lieutenant Colonel	Charles T. Hotchkiss	Aug. 25, '62	
Major	Duncan J. Hall	Sept. 4, '62	
Adjutant	Edward F. Bishop	Aug. 25, '62	
Quartermaster	Frederick L. Lake	Aug. 25, '62	
Surgeon	Samuel F. Hance	Aug. 25, '62	
1st Ass't Surgeon			
2d Ass't Surgeon	Herman B. Tuttle	Aug. 25, '62	
Chaplain	James H. Dill	Aug. 25, '62	

Company A.

Captain	Duncan J. Hall	Aug. 25, '62	Promoted Major
"	Edward A. Smith	Sept. 4, '62	Resigned
"	William H. Rice	Dec. 2, '62	
First Lieutenant	Edward A. Smith	Aug. 25, '62	Promoted
"	William H. Rice	Sept 4, '62	Promoted
Second Lieutenant	William H. Rice	Aug. 25, '62	Promoted
"	Jacob N. Hopper	Sept. 4, '62	

B.

Captain	Thomas O. Spencer	Aug. 25, '62	
First Lieutenant	Henry W. Smith	Aug. 25, '62	
Second Lieutenant	Horace W. Adams	Aug. 25, '62	

C.

Captain	Henry L. Rowell	Aug. 25, '62	
First Lieutenant	Samuel A. Ellis	Aug. 25, '62	
Second Lieutenant	John R. Dawsey	Aug. 25, '62	

D.

Captain	John W. Spink	Aug. 25, '62	
First Lieutenant	George F. Robinson	Aug. 25, '62	
Second Lieutenant	William D. Clark	Aug. 25, '62	Resigned Dec. 14, '62

E.

Captain	Bruce H. Kidder	Aug. 25, '62	
First Lieutenant	John B. Watkins	Aug. 25, '62	
Second Lieutenant	George W. White	Aug. 25, '62	

F.

Captain	William D. Williams	Aug. 23, '62	
First Lieutenant	Ebenezer T. Wells	Aug. 23, '62	
Second Lieutenant	Laertes F. Dimick	Aug. 23, '62	

G.

Captain	Thomas Whiting	Aug. 25, '62	
First Lieutenant	Isaac Copley	Aug. 25, '62	
Second Lieutenant	William H. Howell	Aug. 25, '62	

SCHEDULE G—Continued.

		Rank.	Remarks.

H.

Captain	Henry S. Willett	Aug. 25, '62.	
First Lieutenant	Franklin M. Hobbs	Aug. 25, '62.	
Second Lieutenant	William Harkness	Aug. 25, '62.	

I.

Captain	Samuel C. Comstock	Aug. 25, '62.	
First Lieutenant	William H. Phelps	Aug. 25, '62.	
Second Lieutenant	Jesse Hale	Aug. 25, '62.	

K.

Captain	Herbert M. Blake	Aug. 25, '62.	
First Lieutenant	William A. Sampson	Aug. 25, '62.	
Second Lieutenant	James A. Jackson	Aug. 25, '62.	

Schedule G—Continued.

Roster of Ninetieth Regiment Illinois Volunteers.

Field and Staff.		Rank.	Remarks.
Colonel	Timothy O'Meara	Nov. 22, '62	
Lieutenant Colonel	Timothy O'Meara	Sept. 23, '62	Promoted
" "	Smith McCleavy	Nov. 23, '62	
Major	Owen Stuart	Sept. 23, '62	
Adjutant	Edwin S. Davis	Sept. 23, '62	
Quartermaster	Redmond Sheridan	Sept. 23, '62	
Surgeon			
1st Ass't Surgeon	John B. Davidson	Nov. 1, '62	
2d Ass't Surgeon	Darwin Hinckley	Nov. 22, '62	
Chaplain	Thomas F. Kelley	Sept. 23, '62	

Company A.

Captain	Patrick Flynn	Aug. 1, '62	
First Lieutenant	James Conway	Aug. 1, '62	
Second Lieutenant	Daniel Corcoran	Aug. 1, '62	

B.

Captain	Michael W. Murphy	Sept. 6, '62	
First Lieutenant	Thomas Gray	Sept. 6, '62	
Second Lieutenant	Charles Billingale	Sept. 6, '62	

C.

Captain	Patrick O'Marah	Aug. 28, '62	
First Lieutenant	John C. Harrington	Aug. 28, '62	
Second Lieutenant	Thomas Murray	Aug. 28, '62	

D.

Captain	David O'Conner	Aug. 29, '62	
First Lieutenant	John W. Kelley	Aug. 29, '62	
Second Lieutenant	Peter O'Brine	Aug. 29, '62	

E.

Captain	Matthew Leonard	Sept. 5, '62	
First Lieutenant	John McAssey	Sept. 5, '62	
Second Lieutenant	Lawrence S. McCarthy	Sept. 5, '62	

F.

Captain	Richard C. Kelley	Sept. 6, '62	
First Lieutenant	Patrick Feeney	Sept. 6, '62	
Second Lieutenant	William White	Sept. 6, '62	

G.

Captain	John Murphy	Sept. 6, '62	
First Lieutenant	David Duffy	Sept. 6, '62	
Second Lieutenant	Patrick Campion	Sept. 6, '62	

H.

Captain	Peter Casey	Sept. 15, '62	
First Lieutenant	Andrew Liddle	Sept. 15, '62	
Second Lieutenant	George W. McDonald	Sept. 15, '62	

SCHEDULE G—Continued.

| | | Rank. | Remarks. |
|---|---|---|---|//

I.

Captain	William Cunningham	Oct. 31, '62	
First Lieutenant	Joseph Teahon	Oct. 31, '62	
Second Lieutenant	John J. O'Leary	Oct. 31, '62	

K.

Captain	Thomas K. Barrett	Nov. 22, '62	
First Lieutenant	Peter Real	Nov. 22, '62	
Second Lieutenant	John Larkin	Nov. 22, '62	

Schedule G — Continued.

Roster of Ninety-First Regiment Illinois Volunteers.

Field and Staff.		Rank.	Remarks.
Colonel	Henry M. Day	Sept. 8, '62	
Lieutenant Colonel	Harry S. Smith	Sept. 9, '62	
Major	Harry S. Smith	Sept. 8, '62	Promoted
"	George A. Day	Oct. 6, '62	
Adjutant	George A. Day	Aug. 18, '62	Promoted
"	William Grant	Oct. 6, '62	
Quartermaster	Eugene M. Wiswell	Aug. 15, '62	
Surgeon	David LeRoy	Sept. 6, '62	
1st. Ass't Surgeon	Edgar L. Phillips	Nov. 18, '62	
2nd Ass't Surgeon	William T. Day	Sept. 27, '62	
Chaplain	John C. Sargent	Oct. 4, '62	

Company A.

Captain	Isaac Skillman	Sept. 8, '62	
First Lieutenant	William R. Pack	Sept. 8, '62	
Second Lieutenant	James T. Renbart	Sept. 8, '62	

B.

Captain	Joseph A. James	Sept. 8, '62	
First Lieutenant	John M. Marrah	Sept. 8, '62	
Second Lieutenant	Matthew Shaw	Sept. 8, '62	

C.

Captain	John McKinney	Sept. 8, '62	
First Lieutenant	Caswell Hanna	Sept. 8, '62	
Second Lieutenant	Jonathan P. Long	Sept. 8, '62	

D.

Captain	Edwin I. Fosha	Sept. 8, '62	
First Lieutenant	Phillip Seelback	Sept. 8, '62	
Second Lieutenant	Daniel N. Van Antwerp	Sept. 8, '62	

E.

Captain	Thomes B. Hanna	Sept. 8, '62	
First Lieutenant	Edwin Brown	Sept. 8, '62	
Second Lieutenant	John Q. A. Rider	Sept. 8, '62	

F.

Captain	Elmers Ryan	Sept. 8, '62	
First Lieutenant	Alfred H. Grass	Sept. 8, '62	
Second Lieutenant	Nathan B. Hoff	Sept. 8, '62	

G.

Captain	James D. Roodhouse	Sept. 8, '62	Resigned Oct. 25, 1862
"	John H. Wilson	Oct. 25, '62	
First Lieutenant	John C. Sargeant	Sept. 8, '62	Promoted to Chaplain
"	John H. Wilson	Oct. 4, '62	Promoted
"	Isaac N. Oaks	Oct. 25, '62	
Second Lieutenant	John H. Wilson	Sept. 8, '62	Promoted
"	Isaac N. Oaks	Oct. 4, '62	Promoted
"	Ebenezer I. Pearce	Oct. 25, '62	

H.

Captain	Jordan Lakin	Sept. 8, '62	
First Lieutenant	James Coates	Sept. 8, '62	
Second Lieutenant	John Jones	Sept. 8, '62	

SCHEDULE G—Continued.

		Rank.	Remarks.
I.			
Captain	Slocum H. Culver	Sept. 8, '62	
First Lieutenant	Robert Dennis	Sept. 8, '62	
Second Lieutenant	Theodore P. Hackney	Sept. 8, '62	
K.			
Captain	Benjamin Newman	Sept. 8, '62	
First Lieutenant	John F. Collins	Sept. 8, '62	
Second Lieutenant	Alexander S. Denton	Sept. 8, '62	

SCHEDULE G — Continued.

Roster of Ninety-Second Regiment Illinois Volunteers.

Field and Staff.		Rank.	Remarks.
Colonel	Smith D. Atkins	Sept. 4, '62	
Lieutenant Colonel	Benjamin F. Sheets	Sept. 4, '62	
Major	John H. Bohn	Sept. 4, '62	
Adjutant	Isan C. Lawver	Sept. 4, '62	
Quartermaster	George W. Marshall	Sept. 4, '62	
Surgeon	Clinton Helm	Sept. 4, '62	
1st Ass't Surgeon	Thomas Winston	Sept. 4, '62	
2d Ass't Surgeon	Nathan Stephenson	Oct. 11, '62	
Chaplain			

COMPANY A.

Captain	William J. Bollinger	Sept. 4, '62	Resigned Dec. 15, '62
First Lieutenant	Harvey W. Timms	Sept. 4, '62	
Second Lieutenant	William Cox	Sept. 4, '62	

B.

Captain	Wilber W. Dennis	Sept. 4, '62	
First Lieutenant	William H. Crowell	Sept. 4, '62	
Second Lieutenant	Ephraim F. Blander	Sept. 4, '62	

C.

Captain	William Stouffer	Sept. 4, '62	
First Lieutenant	Robert M. A. Hawk	Sept. 4, '62	
Second Lieutenant	Norman Lewis	Sept. 4, '62	

D.

Captain	Lyman Preston	Sept. 4, '62	
First Lieutenant	George R. Skinner	Sept. 4, '62	
Second Lieutenant	Oscar F. Samis	Sept. 4, '62	

E.

Captain	Matthew Van Buskirk	Sept. 4, '62	
First Lieutenant	Joseph L. Spear	Sept. 4, '62	
Second Lieutenant	Jeremiah Vorhis	Sept. 4, '62	

F.

Captain	Christopher T. Dunham	Sept. 4, '62	
First Lieutenant	Alfred G. Dunham	Sept. 4, '62	
Second Lieutenant	William C. Dove	Sept. 4, '62	Resigned Dec. 24, '62
"	William B. Mayers	Dec. 24, '62	

G.

Captain	John M. Schermerhorn	Sept. 4, '62	
First Lieutenant	John Gishwiller	Sept. 4, '62	
Second Lieutenant	Justin N. Parker	Sept. 4, '62	

H.

Captain	James Brice	Sept. 4, '62	
First Lieutenant	James Dawson	Sept. 4, '62	
Second Lieutenant	Edward C. Mason	Sept. 4, '62	

SCHEDULE G—Continued.

		Rank.	Remarks.

I.

Captain	Egbert Q. E. Becker	Sept. 4, '62	
First Lieutenant	David B. Colhour	Sept. 4, '62	
Second Lieutenant	Alexander M. York	Sept. 4, '62	

K.

Captain	Albert Woodcock	Sept. 4, '62	
First Lieutenant	Horace J. Smith	Sept. 4, '62	
Second Lieutenant	Horace C. Scoville	Sept. 4, '62	

Schedule G—Continued.

Roster of Ninety-Third Regiment Illinois Volunteers.

Field and Staff.		Rank.	Remarks.
Colonel	Holden Putnam	Oct. 13, '62	
Lieutenant Colonel	Nicholas C. Buswell	Oct. 13, '62	
Major	James M. Fisher	Oct. 13, '62	
Adjutant	David W. Sparks	Oct. 13, '62	Resigned Nov. 15, '62
"	Henry G. Hicks	Nov. 15, 62	
Quartermaster	Edward S. Johnson	Oct. 13, '62	
Surgeon	Joseph Huyett	Oct. 13, '62	
1st Ass't Surgeon	Samuel A. Hopkins	Oct. 13, '62	
2d Ass't Surgeon	Charles A. Griswold	Oct. 13, '62	
Chaplain	Thomas H. Hagerty	Oct. 13, '62	

COMPANY A.

Captain	Lewis S. Ashbaugh	Aug. 23, '62	
First Lieutenant	William M. Morris	Oct. 13, '62	
Second Lieutenant	Samuel F. McDonald	Oct. 13, '62	

B.

Captain	John W. Hopkins	Oct. 13, '62	
First Lieutenant	David Deselms	Oct. 13, '62	
Second Lieutenant	James W. Lee	Oct. 13, '62	

C.

Captain	William J. Brown	Oct. 13, '62	
First Lieutenant	William Yonson	Oct. 13, '62	
Second Lieutenant	Thomas I. Lockwood	Oct. 13, '62	

D.

Captain	Charles F. Taggart	Oct. 13, '62	
First Lieutenant	Alpheus P. Goddard	Oct. 13, '62	
Second Lieutenant	George S. Kleckner	Oct. 13, '62	

E.

Captain	Alfred F. Knight	Oct. 13, '62	
First Lieutenant	John Dyer	Oct. 13, '62	
Second Lieutenant	William A. Payne	Oct. 13, '62	

F.

Captain	Orrin Wilkinson	Oct. 13, '62	
First Lieutenant	Lyman J. Wilkinson	Oct. 13, '62	
Second Lieutenant	William C. Kinney	Oct. 13, '62	

G.

Captain	Joseph P. Reed	Oct. 13, '62	
First Lieutenant	George W. Hartsough	Oct. 13, '62	
Second Lieutenant	Jeremiah J. Piersol	Oct. 13, '62	

H.

Captain	John A. Russell	Oct. 13, '62	
First Lieutenant	Samuel Dorr	Oct. 13, '62	
Second Lieutenant	Gad C. Lowrey	Oct. 13, '62	

SCHEDULE G—Continued.

		Rank.	Remarks.

I.

Captain	Ellis Fisher	Oct. 13, '62	
First Lieutenant	Elijah Sapp	Oct. 13, '62	
Second Lieutenant	Mills C. Clark	Oct. 13, '62	

K.

Captain	David Loyd	Oct. 13, '62	
First Lieutenant	Clark Gray	Oct. 13, '62	
Second Lieutenant	Harrison I. Davis	Oct. 13, '62	

Schedule G — Continued.

Roster of Ninety-Fourth Regiment Illinois Volunteers.

Field and Staff.		Rank.	Remarks.
Colonel	William W. Orme	Aug. 20, '62	
Lieutenant Colonel	John McNulta	Aug. 20, '62	
Major	Rankin K. Laughlin	Aug. 20, '62	
Adjutant	Hudson Burr	Aug. 18, '62	
Quartermaster	Martin L. Moore	Aug. 18, '62	
Surgeon	Joseph C. Ross	Nov. 19, '62	
1st Ass't Surgeon			
2d Ass't Surgeon			
Chaplain			

Company A.

Captain	Alexander T. Briscoe	Aug. 20, '62	
First Lieutenant	Guy A. Carlton	Aug. 20, '62	
Second Lieutenant	Algernon S. Lawrence	Aug. 20, '62	

B.

Captain	James C. McFarland	Aug. 20, '62	
First Lieutenant	Patrick Gorman	Aug. 20, '62	
Second Lieutenant	William W. Elder	Aug. 20, '62	

C.

Captain	John Franklin	Aug. 20, '62	
First Lieutenant	George B. Okeson	Aug. 20, '62	
Second Lieutenant	James A. Elder	Aug. 20, '62	

D.

Captain	George W. Brown	Aug. 20, '62	
First Lieutenant	Timothy Owen	Aug. 20, '62	
Second Lieutenant	William Vangundy	Aug. 20, '62	

E.

Captain	John L. Routt	Aug. 20, '62	
First Lieutenant	William H. Wright	Aug. 20, '62	
Second Lieutenant	Joseph B. Hopkins	Aug. 20, '62	

F.

Captain	Aaron W. Walden	Aug. 20, '62	
First Lieutenant	Joseph Dennison	Aug. 20, '62	
Second Lieutenant	John W. Batey	Aug. 20, '62	

G.

Captain	Aaron Buckles	Aug. 20, '62	
First Lieutenant	Peter Vansta	Aug. 20, '62	
Second Lieutenant	Marcus E. Ferguson	Aug. 20, '62	

H.

Captain	Joseph P. Orme	Aug. 20, '62	
First Lieutenant	Lyman S. Johnston	Aug. 20, '62	Dismissed Dec. 8, '62
"	Henry C. Steere	Dec. 8, '62	
Second Lieutenant	Henry C. Steere	Aug. 20, '62	Promoted
"	Charles E. Orme	Dec. 8, '62	

Schedule G — Continued.

		Rank.	Remarks.

I.

Captain	William H. Mann	Aug. 20, '62	
First Lieutenant	Osborn Barnard	Aug. 20, '62	
Second Lieutenant	Samuel P. Howell	Aug. 20, '62	

K.

Captain	James M. Burch	Aug. 20, '62	
First Lieutenant	George Hayes	Aug. 20, '62	
Second Lieutenant	William J. Bowlby	Aug. 20, '62	

SCHEDULE G—Continued.

Roster of Ninety-Fifth Regiment Illinois Volunteers.

Field and Staff.		Rank.	Remarks.
Colonel...........	Lawrence S. Church....	Sept. 4, '62..	....
Lieutenant Colonel	Thomas W. Humphrey ..	Sept. 4, '62..	....
Major............	Leander Blanden.......	Sept. 4, '62..	....
Adjutant.........	Wales W. Wood	Sept. 4, '62..	....
Quartermaster ...	Henry D. Bates	Sept. 4, '62..	....
Surgeon.........	George N. Woodward...	Oct. 10, '62..	....
1st Ass't Surgeon.	A. D. Merritt	Oct. 28, '62..	....
2d Ass't Surgeon.	Walter F. Suiter	Oct. 7, '62..	....
Chaplain	Thomas R. Satterfield...	Oct. 9, '62..	....

COMPANY A.

Captain..........	William Avery.........	Sept. 4, '62..	....
First Lieutenant..	Alexander S. Stewart...	Sept. 4, '62..	....
Second Lieutenant	James E. Sponable......	Sept. 4, '62..	....

B.

Captain..........	Charles B. Loop........	Sept. 4, '62..	....
First Lieutenant..	Milton E. Keeler........	Sept. 4, '62..	....
Second Lieutenant	Aaron F. Randall.......	July 28, '62..	....

C.

Captain..........	Jason B. Manzer	Sept. 4, '62..	....
First Lieutenant..	William W. Wedgewood.	Sept. 4, '62..	....
Second Lieutenant	Otis H. Smith..........	Sept. 4, '62..	....

D.

Captain..........	Edward J. Cook........	Sept. 4, '62..	....
First Lieutenant..	John E. Beckley........	Sept. 4, '62..	....
Second Lieutenant	William H. Heiffman....	Sept. 4, '62..	....

E.

Captain..........	John Eddy	Sept. 4, '62..	....
First Lieutenant..	Asa Farnam............	Sept. 4, '62..	....
Second Lieutenant	Oscar E. Dow..........	Sept. 4, '62..	....

F.

Captain..........	William H. Stewart.....	Sept. 4, '62..	....
First Lieutenant..	Sabine Van Curen......	Sept. 4, '62..	....
Second Lieutenant	Phineas H. Kerr........	Sept. 4, '62..	....

G.

Captain..........	Elliott N. Bush	Sept. 4, '62..	....
First Lieutenant..	Henry M. Bush.........	Sept. 4, '62..	....
Second Lieutenant	Joseph M. Collier	Sept. 4, '62..	....

H.

Captain..........	Charles H. Tryon.......	Sept. 4, '62..	....
First Lieutenant..	James H. Wetmore.....	Sept. 4, '62..	....
Second Lieutenant	William B. Walker.....	Sept. 4, '62..	....

SCHEDULE G—Continued.

		Rank.	Remarks.

I.

Captain	James Nish	Sept. 4, '62	
First Lieutenant	Gardnier S. Southworth	Sept. 4, '62	
Second Lieutenant	Converse Pierce	Sept. 4, '62	

K.

Captain	Gabriel E. Cornwell	Sept. 4, '62	
First Lieutenant	Almon Schellenger	Sept. 4, '62	
Second Lieutenant	Alonzo Brooks	Sept. 4, '62	

Schedule G—Continued.

Roster of Ninety-Sixth Regiment Illinois Volunteers.

Field and Staff.		Rank.	Remarks.
Colonel	Thomas E. Champion	Sept. 6, '62	
Lieutenant Colonel	Isaac L. Clark	Sept. 6, '62	
Major	John C. Smith	Sept. 6, '62	
Adjutant			
Quartermaster	Stephen Jeffers	Sept. 6, '62	
Surgeon	Charles Martin	Sept. 6, '62	
1st Ass't Surgeon	Moses Evans	Sept. 6, '62	
2d Ass't Surgeon	Daniel A. Sheffield	Oct. 31, '62	
Chaplain	Jonathan M. Clendenning	Sept. 8, '62	

Company A.

Captain	George Hicks	Sept. 6, '62	
First Lieutenant	William Vincent	Sept. 6, '62	
Second Lieutenant	Robert Pool	Sept. 6, '62	

B.

Captain	David Salisbury	Sept. 6, '62	
First Lieutenant	Rollin H. Trumbull	Sept. 6, '62	
Second Lieutenant	Allen B. Whitney	Sept. 6, '62	

C.

Captain	John R. Pollock	Sept. 6, '62	
First Lieutenant	Addison B. Partridge	Sept. 6, '62	
Second Lieutenant	William M. Laughlin	Sept. 6, '62	

D.

Captain	Asiel Z. Blodgett	Sept. 6, '62	
First Lieutenant	Caleb A. Montgomery	Sept. 6, '62	
Second Lieutenant	Walter Hastings	Sept. 6, '62	

E.

Captain	Joseph P. Black	Sept. 6, '61	
First Lieutenant	William F. Taylor	Sept. 6, '62	
Second Lieutenant	Halsey H. Richardson	Sept. 6, '62	

F.

Captain	Thomas A. Green	Sept. 6, '62	Resigned Nov. 24, 1862
"	Charles E. Rowan	Nov. 24, '62	
First Lieutenant	Charles E. Rowan	Sept. 6, '62	Promoted
"	Nelson R. Simms	Nov. 24, '62	
Second Lieutenant	Nelson R. Simms	Sept. 6, '62	Promoted
"	William Dawson	Nov. 24, '62	

G.

Captain	James H. Clark	Sept. 6, '62	
First Lieutenant	David James	Sept. 6, '62	
Second Lieutenant	Benjamin G. Blouney	Sept. 6, '62	

H.

Captain	Alexander Burnette	Sept. 6, '62	
First Lieutenant	Samuel H. Bayne	Sept. 6, '62	
Second Lieutenant	Reuben L. Root	Sept. 6, '62	

Schedule G—Continued.

		Rank.	Remarks.

I.

Captain	John Barker	Sept. 6, '62	
First Lieutenant	John P. Tarpley	Sept. 6, '62	
Second Lieutenant	George W. Moore	Sept. 6, '62	

K.

Captain	Timothy D. Rose	Sept. 6, '62	
First Lieutenant	Edward E. Townsend	Sept. 6, '62	
Second Lieutenant	George W. Pepoon	Sept. 6, '62	

Schedule G — Continued.

Roster of Ninety-Seventh Regiment Illinois Volunteers.

Field and Staff.		Rank.	Remarks.
Colonel	Friend S. Rutherford	Sept. 16, '62	
Lieutenant Colonel	Lewis D. Martin	Sept. 16, '62	
Major	Stephen W. Horten	Sept. 20, '62	
Adjutant	Victor Vifquain	Sept. 1, '62	
Quartermaster	George C. Cockerel	Sept. 15, '62	
Surgeon	Samuel Willard	Sept. 5, '62	
1st Ass't Surgeon	Charles Davis	Sept. 23, '62	
2d Ass't Surgeon	Constantine M. Smith	Oct. 2, '62	
Chaplain	William M. Baker	Sept. 24, '62	

Company A.

Captain	William H. Willard	Sept. 8, '62	
First Lieutenant	Richard H. Wood	Sept. 8, '62	
Second Lieutenant	Alexander C. Atchison	Sept. 8, '62	

B.

Captain	James G. Buchanan	Sept. 8, '62	
First Lieutenant	James A. Goodell	Sept. 8, '62	
Second Lieutenant	Alfred Miller	Sept. 8, '62	

C.

Captain	John Nairn	Sept. 8, '62	
First Lieutenant	J. George Ruckstahl	Sept. 8, '62	
Second Lieutenant	William H. Minessinger	Sept. 8, '62	

D.

Captain	James W. Wisner	Sept. 8, '62	
First Lieutenant	Henry Dalgar	Sept. 8, '62	
Second Lieutenant	Harvey S. Titus	Sept. 8, '62	

E.

Captain	Jonathan B. Denoman	Sept. 8, '62	
First Lieutenant	George C. Harding	Sept. 8, '62	
Second Lieutenant	Francis M. Denman	Sept. 8, '62	

F.

Captain	John H. Welch	Sept. 8, '62	
First Lieutenant	George W. Bolt	Sept. 8, '62	
Second Lieutenant	Andrew Ray	Sept. 8, '62	

G.

Captain	John Trible	Sept. 8, '62	
First Lieutenant	James W. Davis	Sept. 8, '62	
Second Lieutenant	Frederick F. Lewis	Sept. 8, '62	

H.

Captain	Mortimer B. Scott	Sept. 8, '62	
First Lieutenant	James M. Erwin	Sept. 8, '62	
Second Lieutenant	Jacob P. Lurton	Sept. 8, '62	

Schedule G—Continued.

		Rank.	Remarks.

I.

Captain	William Achenbach	Sept. 8, '62	
First Lieutenant	Samuel R. Howard	Sept. 8, '62	
Second Lieutenant	Wilson Campbell	Sept. 8, '62	

K.

Captain	Benjamin F. Slaton	Sept. 8, '62	
First Lieutenant	Thomas B. Spaulding	Sept. 8, '62	
Second Lieutenant	Mathias W. Archer	Sept. 8, '62	

Schedule G — Continued.

Roster of Ninety-Eighth Regiment Illinois Volunteers.

Field and Staff.		Rank.	Remarks.
Colonel	John J. Funkhouser	Sept. 3, '62	
Lieutenant Colonel	Edward Kitchell	Sept. 3, '62	
Major	William B. Cooper	Sept. 3, '62	
Adjutant	John H. J. Lacy	Sept. 3, '62	
Quartermaster	Finney D. Preston	Sept. 3, '62	
Surgeon	Robert M. Lackey	Dec. 15, '62	
1st Ass't Surgeon	Samuel W. Vortrees	Sept. 3, '62	
2d Ass't Surgeon	Allen T. Barnes	Sept. 3, '62	
Chaplain	William Cliffe	Oct. 7, '62	

Company A.

Captain	Enoch P. Turner	Sept. 3, '62	
First Lieutenant	George W. Foster	Sept. 3, '62	Resigned Nov. 18, '62
"	Silas Jones	Nov. 18, '62	
Second Lieutenant	Joseph C. Gadd	Sept. 3, '62	

B.

Captain	David D. Marquis	Sept. 3, '62	
First Lieutenant	William E. Hoffman	Sept. 3, '62	
Second Lieutenant	William C. Rickard	Sept. 3, '62	

C.

Captain	William McCracken	Sept. 3, '62	
First Lieutenant	Stephen I. Williams	Sept. 3, '62	Resigned December 19, '62
"	John P. Powell	Dec. 19, '62	
Second Lieutenant	John P. Powell	Sept. 3, '62	Promoted
"	Henry S. Watson	Dec. 19, '62	

D.

Captain	William Wood	Sept. 3, '62	
First Lieutenant	James H. Watts	Sept. 3, '62	
Second Lieutenant	William G. Young	Sept. 3, '62	

E.

Captain	John T. Cox	Sept. 3, '62	
First Lieutenant	Ira A. Flood	Sept. 3, '62	
Second Lieutenant	Charles Willard	Sept. 3, '62	

F.

Captain	Albert W. Lacrone	Sept. 3, '62	
First Lieutenant	Wiot Cook	Sept. 3, '62	
Second Lieutenant	George W. Hobbs	Sept. 3, '62	

G.

Captain	Frederick A. Johns	Sept. 3, '62	
First Lieutenant	Lindsy D. Laws	Sept. 3, '62	
Second Lieutenant	William Jobes	Sept. 3, '62	Resigned Nov. 17, '62
"	Edwin E. Sellers	Nov. 17, '62	

H.

Captain	Thomas Johnson	Sept. 3, '62	
First Lieutenant	Ephraim Martin	Sept. 3, '62	
Second Lieutenant	George Moutray	Sept. 3, '62	

SCHEDULE G—Continued.

		Rank.	Remarks.

I.

Captain	William H. Wade	Sept. 3, '62	
First Lieutenant	Simon S. Foster	Sept. 3, '62	
Second Lieutenant	Lawrence Banta	Sept. 3, '62	

K.

Captain	Orvilla L. Kelley	Sept. 3, '62	Killed Sept. 8, '62
"	Alexander S. Moffitt	Sept. 8, '62	
First Lieutenant	Alexander S. Moffitt	Sept. 3, '62	Promoted
"	William Torrent	Sept. 8, '62	
Second Lieutenant	William Torrent	Sept. 3, '62	Promoted
"	Andrew M. Kirkpatrick	Sept. 8, '62	

SCHEDULE G—Continued.

Roster of Ninety-Ninth Regiment Illinois Volunteers.

Field and Staff.		Rank.	Remarks.
Colonel	George W. K. Bailey	Sept. 22, '62	
Lieutenant Colonel	Lemuel Parke	Aug. 23, '62	
Major	Edwin A. Crandall	Aug. 23, '62	
Adjutant	Marcellus Ross	Aug. 23, '62	
Quartermaster	Isaac G. Hodgen	Aug. 18, '62	
Surgeon	Joseph H. Ledlie	Aug. 20, '62	
1st Ass't Surgeon	Archibald E. McNeal	Sept. 5, '62	
2d Ass't Surgeon	Abner T. Spencer	Sept. 5, '62	
Chaplain	Oliver A. Topliff	Sept. 23, '62	

COMPANY A.

Captain	George T. Edwards	Aug. 23, '62	
First Lieutenant	James K. Smith	Aug. 23, '62	
Second Lieutenant	James F. Stobie	Aug. 23, '62	Hon. Disch'd Nov. 25, '62.
"	Thomas A. Hubbard	Nov. 25, '62	

B.

Captain	Benjamin L. Matthews	Aug. 23, '62	Resigned Dec. 24, '62
First Lieutenant	James W. Fee	Aug. 23, '62	
Second Lieutenant	James A. Elledge	Aug. 23, '62	

C.

Captain	Asa C. Matthews	Aug. 23, '62	
First Lieutenant	Joshua K. Sitton	Aug. 23, '62	
Second Lieutenant	Lucien W. Shaw	Aug. 23, '62	

D.

Captain	John F. Richards	Aug. 23, '62	
First Lieutenant	Francis M. Dabney	Aug. 23, '62	
Second Lieutenant	William T. Mitchell	Aug. 23, '62	

E.

Captain	John C. Dinsmore	Aug. 23, '62	
First Lieutenant	Joseph G. Colvin	Aug. 23, '62	
Second Lieutenant	Allen D. Richards	Aug. 23, '62	

F.

Captain	Eli R. Smith	Aug. 23, '62	
First Lieutenant	Leonard Greaton	Aug. 23, '62	
Second Lieutenant	Daniel McDonald	Aug. 23, '62	

G.

Captain	Henry D. Hull	Aug. 23, '62	
First Lieutenant	James H. Crane	Aug. 23, '62	
Second Lieutenant	Lewis Dutton	Aug. 23, '62	

H.

Captain	Lewis Hull	Aug. 23, '62	
First Lieutenant	Melville D. Massie	Aug. 23, '62	
Second Lieutenant	Gottfried Wenzell	Aug. 23, '62	

SCHEDULE G—Continued.

		Rank.	Remarks.
I.			
Captain	Joseph G. Johnson	Aug. 23, '62	
First Lieutenant	John G. Sever	Aug. 23, '62	
Second Lieutenant	Robert E. Gilleland	Aug. 23, '62	
K.			
Captain	Isaiah Cooper	Aug. 23, '62	
First Lieutenant	William Gray	Aug. 23, '62	
Second Lieutenant	Thomas J. Kinman	Aug. 23, '62	

SCHEDULE G—Continued.

Roster of One Hundredth Regiment Illinois Volunteers.

Field and Staff.		Rank.	Remarks.
Colonel	Frederick A. Bartleson	Aug. 30, '62.	
Lieutenant Colonel	A. W. Waterman	Aug. 30, '62.	
Major	Charles M. Hammond	Aug. 30, '62.	
Adjutant	George W. Rouse	Aug. 30, '62.	
Quartermaster	Thomas S. Wilson	Aug. 30, '62.	
Surgeon	Adolphus W. Heise	Aug. 30, '62.	
1st Ass't Surgeon	Elves Harwood	Aug. 30, '62.	
2d Ass't Surgeon	Henry T. Woodruff	Aug. 30, '62.	
Chaplain	Hooper Crews	Aug. 30, '62.	

COMPANY A.

Captain	Rodney S. Bowen	Aug. 30, '62.	
First Lieutenant	Malcolm N. M. Stewart	Aug. 30, '62.	
Second Lieutenant	Charles F. Mitchell	Aug. 30, '62.	

B.

Captain	James G. Elwood	Aug. 30, '62.	
First Lieutenant	Augustus A. Osgood	Aug. 30, '62.	
Second Lieutenant	Ethan A. Howard	Aug. 30, '62.	

C.

Captain	Charles H. Bacon	Aug. 30, '62.	
First Lieutenant	George Bez	Aug. 30, '62.	
Second Lieutenant	Jonathan S. McDonald	Aug. 30, '62.	

D.

Captain	Albert Amsden	Aug. 30, '62.	
First Lieutenant	John A. Burrell	Aug. 30, '62.	
Second Lieutenant	Horatio N. Wicks	Aug. 30, '62.	

E.

Captain	William W. Bartlett	Aug. 30, '62.	
First Lieutenant	Anson Patterson	Aug. 30, '62.	
Second Lieutenant	James R. Letts	Aug. 30, '62.	

F.

Captain	Richard S. McClaughry	Aug. 30, '62.	
First Lieutenant	Nathan D. Ingraham	Aug. 30, '62.	
Second Lieutenant	John M. Powell	Aug. 30, '62.	

G.

Captain	William A. Mungers	Aug. 30, '62.	
First Lieutenant	Julius C. Williams	Aug. 30, '62.	
Second Lieutenant	Henry I. Ewen	Aug. 30, '62.	

H.

Captain	Harlow B. Goddard	Aug. 30, '62.	
First Lieutenant	Samuel G. Nelson	Aug. 30, '62.	
Second Lieutenant	Charles Meacham	Aug. 30, '62.	Resigned Oct. 27, '62

SCHEDULE G—Continued.

		Rank.	Remarks.

I.

Captain	Hezekiah Gardner	Aug. 30, '62	....
First Lieutenant	John H. McConnell	Aug. 30, '62	....
Second Lieutenant	George C. Schoonmaker	Aug. 30, '62	....

K.

Captain	David Kelley	Aug. 30, '62	....
First Lieutenant	John A. Kelley	Aug. 30, '62	....
Second Lieutenant	Morson Worthanham	Aug. 30, ,62	....

SCHEDULE G — Continued.

Roster of One Hundred and First Regiment Illinois Volunteers.

Field and Staff.		Rank.	Remarks.
Colonel	Charles H. Fox	Sept. 2, '62	
Lieutenant Colonel	William J. Wyatt	Sept. 2, '62	
Major	Jesse T. Newman	Sept. 2, 62	
Adjutant	Harrison O. Cassell	Sept. 12, '62	
Quartermaster	John M. Snyder	Sept. 2, '62	
Surgeon	Clarke Roberts	Oct. 8, '62	
1st Ass't Surgeon	James Miner	Sept. 22, '62	
2d Ass't Surgeon	Alonzo L. Kimber	Oct. 1, '62	
Chaplain	Wyngate J. Newman	Sept. 2, '62	

COMPANY A.

Captain	John B. Lesage	Sept. 2, '62	
First Lieutenant	Charles Heinz	Sept. 2, '62	
Second Lieutenant	Nimrod B. McPherson	Sept. 2, '62	

B.

Captain	Napoleon B. Brown	Sept. 2, '62	
First Lieutenant	Thomas J. Moss	Sept. 2, '62	
Second Lieutenant	Thomas B. Woff	Sept. 2, '62	

C.

Captain	Horace E. May	Sept. 2, '62	
First Lieutenant	C. Augustus Catlin	Sept. 2, '62	
Second Lieutenant	Joseph H. Belt	Sept. 2, '62	

D.

Captain	Henry C. Coffman	Sept. 2, '62	
First Lieutenant	J. Newton Gillham	Sept. 2, '62	
Second Lieutenant	Robert C. Bruce	Sept. 2, '62	

E.

Captain	Charles Sample	Sept. 2, '62	
First Lieutenant	Myron H. Lamb	Sept. 2, '62	
Second Lieutenant	Liberty Courtney	Sept. 2, '62	

F.

Captain	George W. Fanning	Sept. 2, '62	
First Lieutenant	James L. Wyatt	Sept. 2, '62	
Second Lieutenant	John W. Shelton	Sept. 2, '62	

G.

Captain	Robert McKee	Sept. 2, '62	
First Lieutenant	Willis Meacham	Sept. 2, '62	
Second Lieutenant	John Hardin	Sept. 2, '62	

H.

Captain	Joab M. Fanning	Sept. 2, '62	
First Lieutenant	William S. Wright	Sept. 2, '62	Deceased
"	William R. Seymour	Oct. 6, '62	
Second Lieutenant	William R. Seymour	Sept. 2, '62	Promoted
"	William T. Luttrell	Oct. 6, '62	

Schedule G — Continued.

		Rank.	Remarks.

I.

Captain	John A. Lightfoot	Sept. 2, '62	....
First Lieutenant	Frederick E. Shafer	Sept. 2, '62	....
Second Lieutenant	Thomas M. Guy	Sept. 2, '62	....

K.

Captain	Sylvester L. Moore	Sept. 2, '62	....
First Lieutenant	Thomas B. O'Rear	Sept. 2, '62	....
Second Lieutenant	David B. Henderson	Sept. 2, '62	....

Schedule G—Continued.

Roster of One Hundred and Second Regiment Illinois Volunteers.

Field and Staff.		Rank.	Remarks.
Colonel	William McMurtry	Sept. 8, '62	
Lieutenant Colonel	Frank C. Smith	Sept. 8, '62	
Major	James M. Mannon	Sept. 23, '62	
Adjutant	John W. Pitman	Sept. 8, '62	
Quartermaster	Francis H. Rugar	Aug. 16, '62	
Surgeon	David B. Rice	Sept. 30, '62	
1st Ass't Surgeon	William Hamilton	Aug. 25, '62	
2d Ass't Surgeon	Thomas S. Stanway	Dec. 23, '62	
Chaplain	Amos K. Tullis	Sept. 8, '62	Resigned December 21, '62

Company A.

Captain	Roderick R. Harding	Sept. 2, '62	
First Lieutenant	Levi F. Gentry	Sept. 2, '62	
Second Lieutenant	Charles M. Barnett	Sept. 2, '62	

B.

Captain	Elisha C. Atchison	Sept. 2, '62	
First Lieutenant	William Armstrong	Sept. 2, '62	
Second Lieutenant	James C. Beswick	Sept. 2, '62	

C.

Captain	Frank Shedd	Sept. 2, '62	
First Lieutenant	Almond Shaw	Sept. 2, '62	
Second Lieutenant	Watson C. Trego	Sept. 2, '62	Resigned Nov. 18, '62

D.

Captain	Horace H. Welsie	Sept. 2, '62	
First Lieutenant	Highland H. Clay	Sept. 2, '62	
Second Lieutenant	John B. Nixon	Sept. 2, '62	

E.

Captain	Thomas Likely	Sept. 2, '62	
First Lieutenant	Daniel W. Sedwick	Sept. 2, '62	
Second Lieutenant	Thomas G. Brown	Sept. 2, '62	

F.

Captain	Charles H. Jackson	Sept. 2, '62	
First Lieutenant	Orlando J. Sullivan	Sept. 2, '62	
Second Lieutenant	Ethan A. Cornwell	Sept. 2, '62	Resigned Nov. 24, '62

G.

Captain	Joseph P. Wycoff	Sept. 2, '62	Resigned Dec. 27, '62
First Lieutenant	Isaac McManus	Sept. 2, '62	
Second Lieutenant	William H. Bridgeford	Sept. 2, '62	

H.

Captain	Lemuel D. Shinn	Sept. 2, '62	
First Lieutenant	Hiram Elliott	Sept. 2, '62	
Second Lieutenant	John Thomas	Sept. 2, '62	

SCHEDULE G—Continued.

		Rank.	Remarks.
I.			
Captain	George H. King	Sept. 2, '62	
First Lieutenant	Edwin H. Congon	Sept. 2, '62	
Second Lieutenant	John L. Bonnell	Sept. 2, '62	
K.			
Captain	Sanderson H. Rodgers	Sept. 2, '62	
First Lieutenant	William A. Wilson	Sept. 2, '62	
Second Lieutenant	Van Willits	Sept. 2, '62	Resigned Nov. 17, '62
"	James Y. Merritt	Nov. 17, '62	

Schedule G—Continued.

Roster of One Hundred and Third Regiment Illinois Volunteers.

Field and Staff.		Rank.	Remarks.
Colonel.........	Amos C. Babcock......	Oct. 2, '62...	Resigned Oct. 18, '62.....
"	Willard A. Dickerman..	Oct. 18, '62...	....
Lieutenant Colonel	Parley C. Stearns.......	Oct. 2, '62...	Resigned Oct. 18, '62.....
"	George W. Wright......	Oct. 18, '62...	....
Major...........	George W. Wright......	Oct. 2, '62...	Promoted ....
"	Asias Willison	Oct. 18, '62...	....
Adjutant........	Samuel S. Tipton.......	Oct. 2, '62...	....
Quartermaster....	Willard A. Dickerman...	Aug. 25, '62.	Promoted Colonel ....
"	William Mellor.........	Oct. 18, '62.	....
Surgeon.........	Richard Morris.........	Nov. 15, '62 .	....
1st Ass't Surgeon.	Sidney S. Buck.........	Oct. 2, '62...	....
2d Ass't Surgeon..	James W. Van Brunt....	Oct. 3, '62...	....
Chaplain	William S. Peterson	Oct. 2, '62...	....

Company A.

Captain	Asias Willison	Oct. 2, '62...	Promoted Major..........
"	William W. Bishop	Oct. 18, '62...	....
First Lieutenant..	William W. Bishop.....	Oct. 2, '62...	Promoted ....
" ..	Isaiah C. Worley	Oct. 18, '62...	....
Second Lieutenant	Isaiah C. Worley	Oct. 2, '62...	Promoted ....
"	Howard Willison.......	Oct. 18, '62...	....

B.

Captain	Orramel D. Carpenter ...	Oct. 2, '62...	....
First Lieutenant..	John S. Gardner........	Oct. 2, '62...	....
Second Lieutenant	William Walsh.........	Oct. 2, '62...	....

C.

Captain	Sidney A. Stockdale ...	Oct. 2, '62...	....
First Lieutenant..	Henry L. Nicolet.......	Oct. 2, '62...	....
Second Lieutenant	John S. Smith	Oct. 2, '62...	....

D.

Captain	John S. Wyckoff.......	Oct. 2, '62...	....
First Lieutenant..	Benjamin F. Wyckoff....	Oct. 2, '62...	....
Second Lieutenant	Isaac McBean..........	Oct. 2, '62. .	....

E.

Captain	Franklin C. Post	Oct. 2, '62...	....
First Lieutenant..	William S. Johnson.....	Oct. 2, '62...	....
Second Lieutenant	Charles H. Suydam	Oct. 2, '62...	....

F.

Captain	William Vanderander...	Oct. 2, '62...	....
First Lieutenant..	Bernard Kelly..........	Oct. 2, '62...	....
Second Lieutenant	William Mellor.........	Oct. 2, '62...	Promoted Quartermaster..
"	James H. Bailey........	Oct. 18, '62..	....

G.

Captain	Charles Wills..........	Oct. 2, '62...	....
First Lieutenant..	Charles F. Matleson.....	Oct. 2, '62...	....
Second Lieutenant	John H. Dorrence	Oct. 2, '62...	....

SCHEDULE G—Continued.

		Rank.	Remarks.

H.

Captain	James J. Hale	Oct. 2, '62	
First Lieutenant	William Boyd	Oct. 2, '62	
Second Lieutenant	Samuel D. Woodson	Oct. 2, '62	

I.

Captain	Phillip Medley	Oct. 2, '62	
First Lieutenant	Nathaniel P. Montgomery	Oct. 2, '62	
Second Lieutenant	Samuel H. Brown	Oct. 2, '62	

K.

Captain	James C. King	Oct. 2, '62	
First Lieutenant	Augustus B. Smith	Oct. 2, '62	
Second Lieutenant	Aaron Amesley	Oct. 2, '62	

SCHEDULE G—Continued.

Roster of One Hundred and Fourth Regiment Illinois Volunteers.

Field and Staff.		Rank.	Remarks.
Colonel............	Absalom B. Moore......	Aug. 27, '62..	
Lieutenant Colonel	Douglas Hapeman......	Oct. 3, '62..	
Major	John H. Widmer	Sept. 25, '62..	
Adjutant........	Rufus C. Stevens	Aug. 27, '62..	
Quartermaster ...	Edward L. Herrick	Aug. 23, '62..	
Surgeon..........	Reuben F. Dyer........	Aug. 25, '62	
1st Ass't Surgeon.	Julius A. Freeman......	Aug. 25, '62..	
2d Ass't Surgeon.	Thomas B. Hamilton....	Aug. 27, '62..	
Chaplain.........			

COMPANY A.

Captain	James H. Leighton.....	Aug. 27, '62.	
First Lieutenant..	Moses Osman	Aug. 27, '62.	
Second Lieutenant	Alphonso Prescott......	Aug. 27, '62.	

B.

Captain	George W. Howe.......	Aug. 27, '62.	
First Lieutenant..	Moses M. Randolph.....	Aug. 27, '62.	
Second Lieutenant	Samuel A. Porter	Aug. 27, '62.	

C.

Captain	Samuel M. Heslet.......	Aug. 27, '62.	
First Lieutenant ..	Malcomb W. Tewksbury.	Aug. 27, '62.	
Second Lieutenant	David C. Rynearson.....	Aug. 27, '62.	

D.

Captain	William H. Collins.....	Aug. 27, '62.	
First Lieutenant..	William E. Brush.......	Aug. 27, '62.	
Second Lieutenant	James Snedaker........	Aug. 27, '62.	Resigned Dec. 31, '62 ....

E.

Captain	John S. H. Doty........	Aug. 27, '62.	
First Lieutenant..	Milton Straun..........	Aug. 27, '62.	
Second Lieutenant	Ransom P. Dewey......	Aug. 27, '62.	

F.

Captain	James I. McKernan	Aug. 27, '62.	
First Lieutenant..	William Strawn........	Aug. 27, '62.	
Second Lieutenant	John C. Lindsley.......	Aug. 27, '62.	

G.

Captain	Johnson Misner........	Aug. 27, '62.	
First Lieutenant..	Robert V. Simpson.....	Aug. 27, '62.	
Second Lieutenant	Samuel I. Haney........	Aug. 27, '62.	

H.

Captain	Lewis Ludington	Aug. 27, '62.	
First Lieutenant..	Orrin S. Davidson......	Aug. 27, '62.	
Second Lieutenant	John N. Wood.........	Aug. 27, '62.	

SCHEDULE G — Continued.

		Rank.	Remarks.

I.

Captain	John Wadleigh	Aug. 27, '62	
First Lieutenant	Willard Proctor	Aug. 27, '62	
Second Lieutenant	Charles E. Webber	Aug. 27, '62	

K.

Captain	Justus W. Palmer	Aug. 27, '62	
First Lieutenant	Joseph Fitzsimmons	Aug. 27, '62	
Second Lieutenant	Otis S. Favor	Aug. 27, '62	

SCHEDULE G—Continued.

Roster of One Hundred and Fifth Regiment Illinois Volunteers.

Field and Staff.		Rank.	Remarks.
Colonel	Daniel Dustin	Sept. 2, '62	
Lieutenant Colonel	Henry F. Vallette	Sept. 2, '62	
Major	Everett F. Dutton	Sept. 22, '62	
Adjutant	William N. Phillips	Sept. 2, '62	Resigned Dec. 2, '62
"	David D. Chandler	Dec. 2, 62	
Quartermaster	Timothy Wells	Sept. 2, '62	
Surgeon	Horace S. Potter	Sept. 5, '62	
1st Ass't Surgeon	Alfred Waterman	Sept. 2, '62	
2d Ass't Surgeon			
Chaplain	Levi P. Crawford	Sept. 15, '62	Resigned Dec. 24, '61

COMPANY A.

Captain	Henry D. Brown	Sept. 2, '62	
First Lieutenant	George B. Heath	Sept. 2, '62	
Second Lieutenant	Robert D. Lord	Sept. 2, '62	Resigned Dec. 17, '62
"	W. Robert Thomas	Dec. 17, '62	

B.

Captain	Theodore S. Rogers	Sept. 2, '62	
First Lieutenant	Lucius B. Church	Sept. 2, '62	
Second Lieutenant	Willard Scott, jr	Sept. 2, '62	

C.

Captain	Alexander L. Warner	Sept. 2, '62	
First Lieutenant	George W. Field	Sept. 2, '62	
Second Lieutenant	Henry B. Mason	Sept. 2, 62	

D.

Captain	Amos C. Graves	Sept. 2, '62	
First Lieutenant	William H. Jeffers	Sept. 2, '62	
Second Lieutenant	Luther L. Peaslee	Sept. 2, '62	

E.

Captain	Thomas S. Terry	Sept. 2, '62	
First Lieutenant	Martin V. Allen	Sept. 2, '62	
Second Lieutenant	Albert C. Overton	Sept. 2, '62	

F

Captain	Seth F. Daniels	Sept. 2, '62	
First Lieutenant	Samuel Adams	Sept. 2, '62	
Second Lieutenant	Porter Warner	Sept. 2, '62	

G.

Captain	John B. Nash	Sept. 2, '62	
First Lieutenant	Richard R. Woodruff	Sept. 2, '62	Resigned Dec. 24, '62
Second Lieutenant	John M. Smith	Sept. 2, '62	

H.

Captain	Eli L. Hunt	Sept. 2, '62	Resigned Dec. 17, '62
"	James S. Forsythe	Dec. 17, '62	
First Lieutenant	James S. Forsythe	Sept. 2, '62	Promoted
"	Charles G. Culver	Dec. 17, '62	
Second Lieutenant	Charles G. Culver	Sept. 2, '62	Promoted
"	Harvey Potter	Dec. 17, '62	

SCHEDULE G.— Continued.

		Rank.	Remarks.
L.			
Captain	Enos Jones	Sept. 2, '62	Resigned Dec. 17, '62
"	William O. Locke	Dec. 17, '62	
First Lieutenant	William O. Locke	Sept. 2, '62	Promoted
Second Lieutenant	Augustus H. Fisher	Sept. 2, '62	
K.			
Captain	Horace Austin	Sept. 2, '62	Resigned Nov. 26, '62
"	Nathan S. Greenwood	Nov. 26, '62	
First Lieutenant	Nathan S. Greenwood	Sept. 2, '62	Promoted
"	Almon F. Parke	Nov. 26, 62	
Second Lieutenant	Almon F. Parke	Sept. 2, '62	Promoted
"	John Ellis	Nov. 26, '62	

Schedule G — Continued.

Roster of One Hundred and Sixth Regiment Illinois Volunteers.

Field and Staff.		Rank.	Remarks.
Colonel	Robert B. Latham	Sept. 18, '62	
Lieutenant Colonel	George H. Campbell	Sept. 18, '62	
Major	John M. Hurt	Sept. 18, '61	
Adjutant	Charles H. Miller	Sept. 18, '62	
Quartermaster	David Kern	Sept. 13, '62	
Surgeon	Albert H. Lanphier	Nov. 1, '62	
1st Ass't Surgeon	P. Harvey Ellsworth	Dec. 2, '62	
2d Ass't Surgeon			
Chaplain	Thomas K. Hedges	Sept. 18, '62	

Company A.

Captain	Henry Yates, jr.	Sept. 17, '62	
First Lieutenant	George W. Harmon	Sept. 17, '62	
Second Lieutenant	Horace O. Clark	Sept. 17, '62	

B.

Captain	John K. Ashhurst	Sept. 17, '62	
First Lieutenant	Abram F. Risser	Sept. 17, '62	
Second Lieutenant	Richard E. Turley	Sept. 17, '62	

C.

Captain	Benjamin B. Pegram	Sept. 17, '62	
First Lieutenant	Henry Johnson	Sept. 17, '62	
Second Lieutenant	John P. Edds	Sept. 17, '62	

D.

Captain	David Vanhise	Sept. 17, '62	
First Lieutenant	John Everly	Sept. 17, '62	
Second Lieutenant	Monroe Shoup	Sept. 17, '62	

E.

Captain	James Christie	Sept. 17, '62	
First Lieutenant	Francis M. Tuttle	Sept. 17, '62	
Second Lieutenant	Thomas R. Pattison	Sept. 17, '62	

F.

Captain	William Beezley	Sept. 17, '62	
First Lieutenant	James J. Ewing	Sept. 17, '62	
Second Lieutenant	John R. Ash	Sept. 17, '62	

G.

Captain	Benjamin Williams	Sept. 17, '62	
First Lieutenant	Isaac L. Bowman	Sept. 17, '62	
Second Lieutenant	James F. Bell	Sept. 17, '62	

H.

Captain	P. Wilde Harts	Sept. 17, '62	
First Lieutenant	Henry B. Clark	Sept. 17, '62	
Second Lieutenant	William V. Brown	Sept. 17, '62	

SCHEDULE G—Continued.

		Rank.	Remarks.

I.

Captain	John Shockey	Sept. 17, '62.	
First Lieutenant	Culver Staggers	Sept. 17, '62.	
Second Lieutenant	John A. Morris	Sept. 17, '62.	

K.

Captain	Alonzo E. Currier	Sept. 17, '62.	
First Lieutenant	George Collier	Sept. 17, '62.	
Second Lieutenant	John A. Hurt	Sept. 17, '62.	

SCHEDULE G—Continued.

Roster of One Hundred and Seventh Regiment Illinois Volunteers.

Field and Staff.		Rank.	Remarks.
Colonel	Thomas Snell	Sept. 4, '62	Mustered out Dec. 13, '62.
Lieutenant Colonel	Hamilton C. McComas	Sept. 4, '62	
Major	Joseph J. Kelly	Sept. 4, '62	
Adjutant	Silas H. Hubbell	Sept. 4, '62	
Quartermaster	Barzilla Campbell	Aug. 25, '62	
Surgeon	John Wright	Sept. 4, '62	
1st. Ass't. Surgeon	Nelson G. Coffin	Sept. 4, '62	
2d Asst. Surgeon			
Chaplain	Samuel H. Martin	Sept. 28, '62	

COMPANY A.

Captain	James S. Brooks	Sept. 4, '62	
First Lieutenant	John Cuppy	Sept. 4, '62	
Second Lieutenant	Thomas J. Milholand	Sept. 4, '62	

B.

Captain	James R. Turner	Sept. 4, '62	
First Lieutenant	David W. Edminsten	Sept. 4, '62	
Second Lieutenant	Edward Giddings	Sept. 4, '62	

C.

Captain	David J. Ford	Sept. 4, '66	
First Lieutenant	Benjamin F. Cresap	Sept. 4, '62	
Second Lieutenant	William F. McMillen	Sept. 4, '62	

D.

Captain	Samuel McGowan	Sept. 4, '62	
First Lieutenant	Leander S. McGraw	Sept. 4, '62	
Second Lieutenant	William M. Clagg	Sept. 4, '62	

E.

Captain	Frank H. Lowry	Sept. 4, '62	
First Lieutenant	John W. Wood	Sept. 4, '62	
Second Lieutenant	Griffin M. Bruffitt	Sept. 4, '62	

F.

Captain	Henry G. Wismer	Sept. 4, '62	
First Lieutenant	John D. Graham	Sept. 4, '62	
Second Lieutenant	James Parker	Sept. 4, '62	

G.

Captain	Benjamin S. Lewis	Sept. 4, '62	
First Lieutenant	Zadock C. Weidman	Sept. 4, '62	
Second Lieutenant	Israel S. Cope	Sept. 4, '62	

H.

Captain	Alonzo Newton	Sept. 4, '62	
First Lieutenant	Aaron Harshberger	Sept. 4, '62	
Second Lieutenant	Joseph Zeigler	Sept. 4, '62	

SCHEDULE G—Continued.

		Rank.	Remarks.

I.

Captain	Emory L. Waller	Sept. 4, '62	
First Lieutenant	John R. Richards	Sept. 4, '62	
Second Lieutenant	David Lowry	Sept. 4, '62	

K.

Captain	Uriah M. Lawrence	Sept. 4, '62	
First Lieutenant	S. S. Williams	Sept. 4, '62	
Second Lieutenant	Benjamin Brittingham	Sept. 4, '62	

SCHEDULE G—Continued.

Roster of One Hundred and Eighth Regiment Illinois Volunteers.

Field and Staff.		Rank.	Remarks.
Colonel	John Warren	Aug. 28, '62.	
Lieutenant Colonel	Charles Turner	Aug. 28, '62.	
Major	Reuben L. Sidwell	Aug. 28, '62.	
Adjutant	Benjamin T. Foster	Aug. 23, '62.	
Quartermaster	George W. Raney	Aug. 18, '62.	
Surgeon			
1st Ass't Surgeon			
2d Ass't Surgeon	Richard A. Conover	Aug. 28, '62.	
Chaplain	George W. Gue	Aug. 28, '62.	

COMPANY A.

Captain	William R. Lackland	Aug. 28, '62.	
First Lieutenant	Philo W. Hill	Aug. 28, '62.	
Second Lieutenant	John W. Plummer	Aug. 28, '62.	

B.

Captain	Richard B. Howell	Aug. 28, '62.	
First Lieutenant	Garrett G. Ruhaak	Aug. 28, '62.	Resigned Nov. 13, '62
"	Wilber F. Henry	Nov. 13, '62.	
Second Lieutenant	Wilber F. Henry	Aug. 28, '62.	Promoted
"	William Franks	Nov. 13, '62.	

C.

Captain	Sylvester V. Dooley	Aug. 28, '62.	
First Lieutenant	Patrick Moore	Aug. 28, '62.	
Second Lieutenant	Thomas Lynch	Aug. 28, '62.	

D.

Captain	David R. McCutchen	Aug. 28, '62.	
First Lieutenant	William A. Stewart	Aug. 28, '62.	
Second Lieutenant	George H. Megguire	Aug. 28, '62.	

E.

Captain	Winefield M. Bullock	Aug. 28, '62.	
First Lieutenant	Francis F. Briggs	Aug. 28, '62.	
Second Lieutenant	William A. Davidson	Aug. 28, '62.	

F.

Captain	Isaac Sarff	Aug. 28, '62.	
First Lieutenant	James Tippett	Aug. 28, '62.	
Second Lieutenant	John H. Schulte	Aug. 28, '62.	

G.

Captain	George R. Haglitt	Aug. 28, '62.	
First Lieutenant	Samuel B. Hartz	Aug. 28, '62.	
Second Lieutenant	Henry C. Sommers	Aug. 28, '62.	

H.

Captain	William M. Duffy	Aug. 28, '62.	
First Lieutenant	Isaac C. Brown	Aug. 23, '62.	
Second Lieutenant	William W. Nelson	Aug. 28, '62.	

SCHEDULE G — Continued.

		Rank.	Remarks.

I.

Captain	John W. Carroll	Aug. 28, '62.	
First Lieutenant	Richard Scholes	Aug. 23, '62.	
Second Lieutenant	Daniel Dulaney	Aug. 28, '62.	

K.

Captain	Lyman W. Clark	Aug. 28, '62.	
First Lieutenant	James F. Davidson	Aug. 28, '62.	
Second Lieutenant	Philander E. Davis	Aug. 28, '62.	

SCHEDULE G—Continued.

Roster of One Hundred and Ninth Regiment Illinois Volunteers.

Field and Staff.		Rank.	Remarks.
Colonel	Alexander J. Nimmo	Sept. 11, '62.	
Lieutenant Colonel	Elijah A. Willard	Sept. 11, '62.	
Major	Thomas M. Perrine	Sept. 11, '62.	
Adjutant	James Evans	Sept. 11, '62.	
Quartermaster	Calvin B. Dishon	Aug. 29, '62.	
Surgeon	John S. Dewey	Nov. 3, '62.	
1st Ass't Surgeon	John W. Henley	Aug. 21, '62.	
2d Ass't Surgeon	George H. Dewey	Nov. 3, '62.	
Chaplain	Phillip H. Kroh	Sept. 11, '62.	

COMPANY A.

Captain	John C. Hansaker	Sept. 11, '62.	
First Lieutenant	James P. McLane	Sept. 11, '62.	
Second Lieutenant	Moses A. Goodman	Sept. 11, '62.	

B.

Captain	Samuel M. P. McClure	Sept. 11, '62.	
First Lieutenant	Jacob A. Millikin	Sept. 11, '62.	
Second Lieutenant	Thomas T. Robinson	Sept. 11, '62.	

C.

Captain	John M. Rich	Sept. 11, '62.	
First Lieutenant	Benjamin F. Hartline	Sept. 11, '62.	
Second Lieutenant	Daniel Kimmel	Sept. 11, '62.	

D.

Captain	Hugh Andrews	Sept. 11, '62.	
First Lieutenant	Benjamin F. Sullivan	Sept. 11, '62.	
Second Lieutenant	Jasper N. McElhaney	Sept. 11, '62.	

E.

Captain	Thomas Boswell	Sept. 11, '62.	
First Lieutenant	Morgan Stokes	Sept. 11, '62.	
Second Lieutenant	John Stokes	Sept. 11, '62.	

F.

Captain	John J. McIntosh	Sept. 11, '62.	
First Lieutenant	Charles Barringer	Sept. 11, '62.	
Second Lieutenant	Charles Klutts	Sept. 11, '62.	

G.

Captain	George W. Penninger	Sept. 11, '62.	
First Lieutenant	Josiah Toler	Sept. 11, '62.	
Second Lieutenant	Squire Crabtree	Sept. 11, '62.	

H.

Captain	Joseph H. McElhaney	Sept. 11, '62.	
First Lieutenant	James M. Johnson	Sept. 11, '62.	
Second Lieutenant	James D. Kerr	Sept. 11, '62.	

SCHEDULE G—Continued.

		Rank.	Remarks.

I.

Captain	Wilson Misenheimer	Sept. 11, '62.	
First Lieutenant	Abraham L. Misenheimer	Sept. 11, '62.	
Second Lieutenant	Henry Gassaway	Sept. 11, '62.	

K.

Captain	Wilburn M. Boren	Sept. 11, '62.	
First Lieutenant	Samuel O. Lewis	Sept. 11, '62.	
Second Lieutenant	Robert B. Bartleson	Sept. 11, '62.	

Schedule G — Continued.

Roster of One Hundred and Tenth Regiment Illinois Volunteers.

Field and Staff.		Rank.	Remarks.
Colonel	Thomas S. Casey	Sept. 11, '62.	
Lieutenant Colonel	Munroe C. Crawford	Sept. 11, '62.	
Major	Daniel Mooneyham	Sept. 11, '62.	
Adjutant	Oscar A. Taylor	Sept. 11, '62.	
Quartermaster	Thomas H. Hobbs	Aug. 28, '62.	
Surgeon	William C. Pace	Sept. 11, '62.	
1st Ass't Surgeon	Hiram S. Plummer	Sept. 11, '62.	
2d Ass't Surgeon	Zachariah Hickman	Sept. 11, '62.	
Chaplain			

Company A.

Captain	Marion D. Hoge	Sept. 11, '62.	
First Lieutenant	Green M. Contrell	Sept. 11, '62.	
Second Lieutenant	William B. Deming	Sept. 11, '62.	

B.

Captain	Charles H. Maxey	Sept. 11, '62.	
First Lieutenant	Samuel T. Maxey	Sept. 11, '62.	
Second Lieutenant	John H. Dukes	Sept. 11, '62.	

C.

Captain	Francis M. Norman	Sept. 11, '62.	Resigned Nov. 26, '62
"	James L. Parks	Nov. 26, '62.	
First Lieutenant	Richard T. McHaney	Sept. 11, '62.	Resigned Dec. 19, '62
Second Lieutenant	James L. Parks	Sept. 11, '62.	Promoted

D.

Captain	Ebenezer H. Topping	Sept. 11, '62.	
First Lieutenant	Robert A. Cameron	Sept. 11, '62.	
Second Lieutenant	William J. Cameron	Sept. 11, '62.	

E.

Captain	George E. Burnett	Sept. 11, '62.	
First Lieutenant	Willis A. Spiller	Sept. 11, '62.	
Second Lieutenant	Charles Burnett	Sept. 11, '62.	

F.

Captain	Grayson Dellitt	Sept. 11, '62.	
First Lieutenant	Carrol Payne	Sept. 11, '62.	
Second Lieutenant	Jesse G. Payne	Sept. 11, '62.	

G.

Captain	John F. Day	Sept. 11, '62.	
First Lieutenant	Samuel Gibson	Sept. 11, '62.	Resigned
"	Joseph B. Scudmore	Dec. 19, '62.	
Second Lieutenant	Joseph B. Scudmore	Sept. 11, '62.	Promoted

H.

Captain	William K. Murphy	Sept. 11, '62.	
First Lieutenant	Enos D. Hays	Sept. 11, '62.	
Second Lieutenant	James Richie	Sept. 11, '62.	Resigned Dec. 19, '62

SCHEDULE G—Continued.

		Rank.	Remarks.
I.			
Captain	William L. Britton	Sept. 11, '62.	
First Lieutenant	William S. Bales	Sept. 11, '62.	Resigned Nov. 24, '62
Second Lieutenant	William W. McAmie	Sept. 11, '62.	Resigned Dec. 18, '62
K.			
Captain	Mark Harper	Sept. 11, '62.	Resigned Nov. 24, '62
First Lieutenant	James S. Wycough	Sept. 11, '62.	
Second Lieutenant	John T. Barnett	Sept. 11, '62.	Resigned Nov. 26, '62

SCHEDULE G—Continued.

Roster of One Hundred and Eleventh Regiment Illinois Volunteers.

Field and Staff.		Rank.	Remarks.
Colonel	James S. Martin	Sept. 18, '62.	
Lieutenant Colonel	Joseph F. Black	Sept. 18, '62.	
Major	William H. Mabry	Sept. 18, '62.	
Adjutant	William C. Stiles	Sept. 18, '62.	
Quartermaster	Benjamin F. Marshall	Sept. 18, '62.	
Surgeon	James Phillips	Sept. 18, '62.	
1st Ass't Surgeon	John K. Rainey	Sept. 18, '62.	
2d Ass't Surgeon	Thomas S. Hawley	Sept. 18, '62.	
Chaplain	James B. Woolard	Sept. 18, '62.	

COMPANY A.

Captain	Amos A. Clark	Sept. 18, '62.	
First Lieutenant	John K. Morton	Sept. 18, '62.	Deceased
"	Jacob V. Andrews	Sept. 18, '62.	
Second Lieutenant	Jacob V. Andrews	Sept. 18, '62.	Promoted
"	Robert Martin	Oct. 6, '62.	

B.

Captain	Anderson Myers	Sept. 18, '62.	
First Lieutenant	William H. Walker	Sept. 18, '62.	
Second Lieutenant	George C. McCord	Sept. 18, '62.	

C.

Captain	Thomas O. Pierce	Sept. 18, '62.	
First Lieutenant	James M. North	Sept. 18, '62.	
Second Lieutenant	William B. Holleman	Sept. 18, '62.	

D.

Captain	John Foster	Sept. 18, '62.	
First Lieutenant	Robert W. Elder	Sept. 18, '62.	
Second Lieutenant	George W. Smith	Sept. 18, '62.	

E.

Captain	Joseph F. McGuire	Sept. 18, '62.	
First Lieutenant	Lewellyn W. Castellom	Sept. 18, '62.	
Second Lieutenant	William J. Young	Sept. 18, '62.	

F.

Captain	Abner S. Gray	Sept. 18, '62.	
First Lieutenant	William C. Dorris	Sept. 18, '62.	
Second Lieutenant	William H. Carpenter	Sept. 18, '62.	

G.

Captain	Reuben W. Jolliff	Sept. 18, '62.	
First Lieutenant	Henry Simpson	Sept. 18, '62.	
Second Lieutenant	John W. Stover	Sept. 18, '62.	

H.

Captain	George E. Castle	Sept. 18, '62.	
First Lieutenant	Andrew J. Larimer	Sept. 18, '62.	
Second Lieutenant	Robert M. Lovell	Sept. 18, '62.	

Schedule G—Continued.

		Rank.	Remarks.

I.

Captain	Alfred J. Nichols	Sept. 18, '62.	
First Lieutenant	John L. Souter	Sept. 18, '62.	
Second Lieutenant	Franklin W. Kirkham	Sept. 18, '62.	

K.

Captain	Joseph Shultz	Sept. 18, '62.	
First Lieutenant	Isaac H. Berry	Sept. 18, '62.	
Second Lieutenant	James B. Pendleton	Sept. 18, '62.	

SCHEDULE G — Continued.

Roster of One Hundred and Twelfth Regiment Illinois Volunteers.

Field and Staff.		Rank.	Remarks.
Colonel	Thomas J. Henderson	Sept. 22, '62	
Lieutenant Colonel	Emery S. Bond	Sept. 20, '62	
Major	James M. Hosford	Sept. 20, '62	
Adjutant	Henry W Wells	Sept. 22, '62	
Quartermaster	George C. Alden	Sept. 10, '62	
Surgeon	John W. Spalding	Sept. 11, '62	
1st Ass't Surgeon	Luther S. Milliken	Sept. 15, '62	
2d Ass't Surgeon			
Chaplain	Rosnill N. Henderson	Oct. 13, '62	

COMPANY A.

Captain	Triston T. Dow	Sept. 20, '62	
First Lieutenant	Asa A. Lee	Sept. 20, '62	
Second Lieutenant	John L. Dow	Sept. 20, '62	

B.

Captain	James B. Doyle	Sept. 20, '62	
First Lieutenant	Jonathan C. Dickerson	Sept. 20, '62	
Second Lieutenant	John Gudgel	Sept. 20, '62	

C.

Captain	John J. Biggs	Sept. 20, '62	
First Lieutenant	John B. Mitchell	Sept. 20, '61	
Second Lieutenant	Alexander P. Petrie	Sept. 20, '62	

D.

Captain	Augustus A. Dunn	Sept. 20, '62	
First Lieutenant	Henry G. Griffin	Sept. 20, '62	
Second Lieutenant	Samuel L. Patterson	Sept. 20, '62	

E.

Captain	Sylvester F. Otman	Sept. 20, '62	
First Lieutenant	Cranmer W. Brown	Sept. 20, '62	
Second Lieutenant	Elmer A. Sage	Sept. 20, '62	

F.

Captain	William W. Wright	Sept. 20, '62	
First Lieutenant	Jackson Lawrence	Sept. 20, '62	
Second Lieutenant	Robert E. Westfall	Sept. 20, '62	

G.

Captain	Alexander W. Albra	Sept. 20, '62	
First Lieutenant	James McCartney	Sept. 20, '62	
Second Lieutenant	Thomas E. Milchirst	Sept. 20, '62	

H.

Captain	George W. Sroufe	Sept. 20, '62	
First Lieutenant	Thomas T. Davenport	Sept. 20, '62	
Second Lieutenant	Elisha Atwater	Sept. 20, '62	

SCHEDULE G—Continued.

		Rank.	Remarks.
I.			
Captain	James E. Wilkins	Sept. 20, '62.	
First Lieutenant	George W. Lawrence	Sept. 20, '62.	
Second Lieutenant	Henry S. Comstock	Sept. 20, '62.	
K.			
Captain	Joseph Westley	Sept. 20, '62.	
First Lieutenant	Christian G. Gearhart	Sept. 20, '62.	
Second Lieutenant	Edward H. Colcord	Sept. 20, '62.	

Schedule G—Continued.

Roster of One Hundred and Thirteenth Regiment Illinois Volunteers.

Field and Staff.		Rank.	Remarks.
Colonel	George B. Hoge	Oct. 1, '62	
Lieutenant Colonel	John W. Paddock	Oct. 1, '62	
Major	Lucius H. Yates	Oct. 1, '62	
Adjutant	Daniel S. Parker	Oct. 1, '62	
Quartermaster	William A. McLean	Oct. 1, '62	
Surgeon	Joel M. Mack	Oct. 1, '62	
1st Ass't Surgeon	Lucien B. Brown	Oct. 1, '62	
2d Ass't Surgeon	William N. Bailey	Oct. 1, '62	
Chaplain	Adam L. Rankin	Oct. 1, '62	

Company A.

Captain	George R. Clark	Oct. 1, '62	
First Lieutenant	Henry W. B. Hoyt	Oct. 1, '62	
Second Lieutenant	Daniel Ferguson	Oct. 1, '62	

B.

Captain	Cephas Williams	Oct. 1, '62	
First Lieutenant	Andrew Beckett	Oct. 1, '62	
Second Lieutenant	John Jeffcoat	Oct. 1, '62	

C.

Captain	George W. Lyman	Oct. 1, '62	
First Lieutenant	William E. Barry	Oct. 1, '62	
Second Lieutenant	Harvey P. Hosmer	Oct. 1, '62	

D.

Captain	Robert B. Lucas	Oct. 1, '62	
First Lieutenant	David H. Metzger	Oct. 1, '62	
Second Lieutenant	George B. Fickle	Oct. 1, '62	

E.

Captain	Mason Southerland	Oct. 1, '62	
First Lieutenant	U. Rial Burlingham	Oct. 1, '62	
Second Lieutenant	Charles D. Trumbull	Oct. 1, '62	

F.

Captain	William I. Bridges	Oct. 1, '62	
First Lieutenant	Joseph Rogers	Oct. 1, '62	
Second Lieutenant	William German	Oct. 1, '62	

G.

Captain	John G. Woodruff	Oct. 1, '62	
First Lieutenant	Frank Brown	Oct. 1, '62	
Second Lieutenant	James I. Conway	Oct. 1, '62	

H.

Captain	Bliss Sutherland	Oct. 1, '62	
First Lieutenant	Harrison Daniels	Oct. 1, '62	
Second Lieutenant	Aquilla C. Cowgill	Oct. 1, '62	

SCHEDULE G—Continued.

		Rank.	Remarks.
I.			
Captain	George West	Oct. 1, '62	
First Lieutenant	Anderson Tyler	Oct. 1, '62	
Second Lieutenant	Aaron F. Kane	Oct. 1, '62	
K.			
Captain	Silas J. Garrett	Oct. 1, '62	
First Lieutenant	Levi Sargent	Oct. 1, '62	
Second Lieutenant	Charles Squires	Oct. 1, '62	

SCHEDULE G—Continued.

Roster of One Hundred and Fourteenth Regiment Illinois Volunteers.

Field and Staff.		Rank.	Remarks.
Colonel	James W. Judy	Sept. 18, '62.	
Lieutenant Colonel	John F. King	Sept. 18, '62.	
Major	Joseph M. McLane	Sept. 18, '62.	
Adjutant	William H. Latham	Sept. 18, '62.	
Quartermaster	George W. Mourer	Aug. 27, '62.	
Surgeon	James M. Giggins	Oct. 11, '62.	
1st Ass't Surgeon.	John F. Willson	Oct. 17, '62.	
2d Ass't Surgeon.	Henry Van Meter	Sept. 1, '62.	
Chaplain	Caleb P. Baldwin	Sept. 29, '62.	

COMPANY A.

Captain	John M. Johnson	Sept. 18, '62.	
First Lieutenant	Philander Lucas	Sept. 18, '62.	
Second Lieutenant	Joseph A. McClure	Sept. 18, '62.	

B.

Captain	Benjamin H. Ferguson	Sept. 18, '62.	
First Lieutenant	Edward P. Strickland	Sept. 18, '62.	
Second Lieutenant	Joseph Zeigler	Sept. 18, '62.	

C.

Captain	William A. Mallory	Sept. 18, '62.	
First Lieutenant	Oramel H. Abel	Sept. 18, '62.	
Second Lieutenant	Jesse Cantrall	Sept. 18, '62.	

D.

Captain	Benjamin C. Berry	Sept. 18, '62.	
First Lieutenant	Thomas S. Berry	Sept. 18, '62.	
Second Lieutenant	David N. Downing	Sept. 18, '62.	

E.

Captain	Samuel N. Shoup	Sept. 18, '62.	
First Lieutenant	Adam Hively	Sept. 18, '62.	
Second Lieutenant	Lewis R. Hedrick	Sept. 18, '62.	

F.

Captain	Absalom Miller	Sept. 18, '62.	
First Lieutenant	Willet B. Taylor	Sept. 18, '62.	
Second Lieutenant	James T. Workman	Sept. 18, '62.	

G.

Captain	John L. Wilson	Sept. 18, '62.	
First Lieutenant	Henry L. Vanhoff	Sept. 18, '62.	
Second Lieutenant	John S. Caulfield	Sept. 18, '62.	

H.

Captain	George W. Bailey	Sept. 18, '62.	
First Lieutenant	Jerome M. Foster	Sept. 18, '62.	
Second Lieutenant	Charles W. Stanton	Sept. 18, '62.	

SCHEDULE G—Continued.

		Rank.	Remarks.

I.

Captain	John Gibson	Sept. 18, '62.	
First Lieutenant	Egbert O. Mallory	Sept. 18, '62.	
Second Lieutenant	Daniel Bailey	Sept. 18, '62.	

K.

Captain	Samuel Estill	Sept. 18, '62.	
First Lieutenant	Lucian Ferhune	Sept. 18, '62.	
Second Lieutenant	Henry C. Rogge	Sept. 18, '61.	

Schedule G — Continued.

Roster of One Hundred and Fifteenth Regiment Illinois Volunteers.

Field and Staff.		Rank.	Remarks.
Colonel	Jesse H. Moore	Sept. 13, '62.	
Lieutenant Colonel	William Kinman	Sept. 13, '62.	
Major	George A. Poteet	Sept. 13, '62.	
Adjutant	John H. Woods	Sept. 13, '62.	
Qurtermaster	Benjamin F. Farley	Sept. 13, '62.	
Surgeon	Enoch W. Moore	Oct. 4, '62.	
1st Ass't Surgeon	Nelson G. Blalock	Sept. 13, '62.	
2d Ass't Surgeon	James A. Jones	Oct. 3, '62	
Chaplain	Arthur Bradshaw	Sept. 23, '62.	

Company A.

Captain	John W. Lapham	Sept. 13, '62.	
First Lieutenant	Arthur C. Bankson	Sept. 13, '62.	
Second Lieutenant	Jesse Hanon	Sept. 13, '62.	

B.

Captain	Elezer Slocum	Sept. 13, '62.	
First Lieutenant	Eramus D. Stean	Sept. 13, '62	
Second Lieutenant	John Beauchamp	Sept. 13, '62.	

C.

Captain	David Williams	Sept. 13, '62.	
First Lieutenant	Ephraim H. Kingery	Sept. 13, '62.	
Second Lieutenant	Gideon L. Utter	Sept. 13, '62.	

D.

Captain	Stephen M. Huckstep	Sept. 13, '62.	
First Lieutenant	Christian C. Bridgewater	Sept. 13, '62.	
Second Lieutenant	Samuel Hymer	Sept. 13, '62.	

E.

Captain	John M. Lane	Sept. 13, '62.	
First Lieutenant	David S. Moffitt	Sept. 13, '62.	
Second Lieutenant	Adam C. Allison	Sept. 13, '62.	

F.

Captain	Frank L. Hayes	Sept. 13, '62.	
First Lieutenant	James Smith	Sept. 13, '62.	
Second Lieutenant	Matthew Freeman	Sept. 13, '62.	

G.

Captain	S. Barlow Espy	Sept. 13, '62.	
First Lieutenant	John W. Dove	Sept. 13, '62.	
Second Lieutenant	John M. Baker	Sept. 13, '62.	

H.

Captain	Henry Pratt	Sept. 13, '62.	
First Lieutenant	Silas Parker	Sept. 13, '62.	
Second Lieutenant	John Reardon	Sept. 13, '62.	

Schedule G—Continued.

		Rank.	Remarks.

I.

Captain	Simon P. Neuman	Sept. 13, '62.	
First Lieutenant	James S. Samuels	Sept. 13, '62.	
Second Lieutenant	Cyrus L. Kinman	Sept. 13, '62.	

K.

Captain	James Steele	Sept. 13, '62.	
First Lieutenant	Sylvester M. Bailey	Sept. 13, '62.	
Second Lieutenant	Phillip Riley	Sept. 13, '62.	

SCHEDULE G—Continued.

Roster of One Hundred and Sixteenth Regiment Illinois Volunteers.

Field and Staff.		Rank.	Remarks.
Colonel	Nathan W. Tupper	Sept. 30, '62.	
Lieutenant Colonel	James P. Boyd	Sept. 6, '62.	
Major	Anderson Froman	Sept. 30, '62.	
Adjutant	Charles H. Fuller	Sept. 30, '62.	
Quartermaster	Lyman King	Sept. 3, '62.	
Surgeon			
1st Ass't Surgeon.	John A. Heckleman	Sept. 17, '62.	
2d Ass't Surgeon.	Joseph A. W. Hostetter	Oct. 1, '62.	
Chaplain	N. M. Baker	Sept. 30, '62.	

COMPANY A.

Captain	William J. Brown	Sept. 30, '62.	
First Lieutenant	John B. Perdew	Sept. 6, '62.	
Second Lieutenant	Gustin F. Hardy	Sept. 6, '62.	

B.

Captain	Austin McClurg	Sept. 6, '62.	
First Lieutenant	John S. Taylor	Sept. 6, '62.	
Second Lieutenant	Andrew J. Williams	Sept. 6, '62.	

C.

Captain	Thomas White	Sept. 6, '62.	
First Lieutenant	James M. Wallace	Sept. 6, '62.	
Second Lieutenant	Robert M. Foster	Sept. 6, '62.	

D.

Captain	Joseph Lingle	Sept. 6, '62.	
First Lieutenant	James R. Briggs	Sept. 6, '62.	
Second Lieutenant	G. A. Milmine	Sept. 6, '62.	

E.

Captain	Lewis J. Eyman	Sept. 6, '62.	
First Lieutenant	Stephen H. Varney	Sept. 6, '62.	
Second Lieutenant	Washington L. Harris	Sept. 6, '62.	

F.

Captain	L. N. Bishop	Sept. 6, '62.	
First Lieutenant	John B. Tutt	Sept. 6, '62.	
Second Lieutenant	Edwin R. Prall	Sept. 30, '62.	

G.

Captain	Alonzo B. Davis	Sept. 30, '62.	
First Lieutenant	Harvey Mahannah	Sept. 6, '62.	
Second Lieutenant	Lafayette Helm	Sept. 30, '62.	

H.

Captain	James L. Dobson	Sept. 30, '62.	
First Lieutenant	John P. Lamb	Sept. 6, '62.	
Second Lieutenant	Theophilus Short	Sept. 30, '62.	

SCHEDULE G—Continued.

		Rank.	Remarks.

I.

Captain	Uriah P. Forbes	Sept. 30, '62.	
First Lieutenant	J. T. Bishop	Sept. 6, '62.	
Second Lieutenant	Irwin Miller	Sept. 30, '62.	

K.

Captain	John E. Madux	Sept. 30, '62.	
First Lieutenant	John S. Windsor	Sept. 30, '62.	
Second Lieutenant	Nathan W. Wheeler	Sept. 30, '62.	

314

SCHEDULE G—Continued.

Roster of One Hundred and Seventeenth Regiment Illinois Volunteers.

Field and Staff.		Rank.	Remarks.
Colonel	Risdon M. Moore	Sept. 19, '62	
Lieutenant Colonel	Jonathan Merriam	Sept. 19, '62	
Major	Thomas J. Newsham	Sept. 19, '62	
Adjutant	Samuel H. Deneen	Oct. 9, '62	
Quartermaster	Henry C. Fike	Aug. 26, '62	
Surgeon	Martin Wiley	Oct. 9, '62	
1st Ass't Surgeon	Humphrey H. Hood	Nov. 7, '62	
2d Ass't Surgeon	Thomas C. Jennings	Nov. 15, '62	
Chaplain	John D. Gilham	Sept. 26, '62	

COMPANY A.

Captain	Samuel B. Kinsey	Sept. 19, '62	
First Lieutenant	Harrison W. Wood	Sept. 19, '62	
Second Lieutenant	Dennis Kenyon	Sept. 19, '62	

B.

Captain	Robert McWilliams	Sept. 19, '62	
First Lieutenant	Frank H. Gilmore	Oct. 28, '62	
Second Lieutenant	Frank H. Gilmore	Sept. 19, '62	Promoted
"	George W. Potter	Oct. 28, '62	

C.

Captain	George F. Lowe	Sept. 19, '62	
First Lieutenant	William H. Whitaker	Sept. 19, '62	
Second Lieutenant	William Wallis	Sept. 19, '62	

D.

Captain	William P. Olden	Sept. 19, '62	
First Lieutenant	Abraham B. Keagle	Sept. 19, '62	
Second Lieutenant	Benjamin F. Olden	Sept. 19, '62	

E.

Captain	Andrew J. Randall	Sept. 19, '62	
First Lieutenant	Erastus M. Burson	Sept. 19, '62	
Second Lieutenant	John A. B. Apperson	Sept. 19, '62	

F.

Captain	Jacob I. Kinder	Sept. 19, '62	
First Lieutenant	Charles W. Blake	Sept. 19, '62	
Second Lieutenant	Gersham P. Gilham	Sept. 19, '62	

G.

Captain	Curtis Blakeman	Sept. 19, '62	
First Lieutenant	Alexander I. Gregg	Sept. 19, '62	
Second Lieutenant	James G. Elliff	Sept. 19, '62	

H.

Captain	Robert A. Halbert	Sept. 19, '62	
First Lieutenant	James M. Hay	Sept. 19, '62	
Second Lieutenant	David H. Wilderman	Sept. 19, '62	

SCHEDULE G—Continued.

		Rank.	Remarks.

I.

Captain	David McFarland	Sept. 19, '62.	
First Lieutenant	Samuel M. Stiles	Sept. 19, '62.	
Second Lieutenant	John R. Thomas	Sept. 19, '62.	

K.

Captain	Nathan Land	Sept. 19, '62.	
First Lieutenant	John W. Fike	Sept. 19, '62.	
Second Lieutenant	James A. Curtiss	Sept. 19, '62.	

316

SCHEDULE G—Continued.

Roster of One Hundred and Eighteenth Regiment Illinois Volunteers.

Field and Staff.		Rank.	Remarks.
Colonel	John G. Fonda	Nov. 29, '62	
Lieutenant Colonel	John G. Fonda	Nov. 20, '62	Promoted
Major	Robert M. McClaughry	Nov. 8, '62	
Adjutant	John W. Barnes	Oct. 17, '62	
Quartermaster	William K. Davidson	Oct. 13, '62	
Surgeon	Madison Reece	Dec. 15, '62	
1st Ass't Surgeon	John K. Boude	Nov. 27, '62	
2d Ass't Surgeon	Elmer Nichols	Dec. 19, '62	
Chaplain	Thomas M. Walker	Nov. 29, '62	

COMPANY A.

Captain	Thomas I. Campbell	Nov. 7, '62	
First Lieutenant	Alexander W. Geddes	Nov. 7, '62	
Second Lieutenant	Thomas B. White	Nov. 7, '62	

B.

Captain	Robert W. McClaughry	Nov. 7, '62	Promoted Major
"	Morgan Rymer	Nov. 8, '62	
First Lieutenant	William H. Odell	Nov. 7, '62	
Second Lieutenant	Morgan Rymer	Nov. 7, '62	Promoted
"	Alexander Sholl	Nov. 8, '62	

C.

Captain	Arthur W. Marsh	Nov. 7, '62	
First Lieutenant	Ephraim Grubb	Nov. 7, '62	
Second Lieutenant	Abram W. Robinson	Nov. 7, '62	

D.

Captain	John H. Holton	Nov. 7, '62	
First Lieutenant	William I. Brown, jr.	Nov. 29, '62	
Second Lieutenant	William J. Sturr	Nov. 7, '62	

E.

Captain			
First Lieutenant	Jarvis S. Allen	Nov. 7, '62	
Second Lieutenant	Washington L. Lemley	Nov. 7, '62	

F.

Captain	William I. Evans	Nov. 7, '62	
First Lieutenant	Hamilton Young	Nov. 7, '62	
Second Lieutenant	Ira Tyler	Nov. 7, '62	

G.

Captain	Joseph Shaw	Nov. 7, '62	
First Lieutenant	James H. Butler	Nov. 7, '62	
Second Lieutenant	Charles T. Painter	Nov. 7, '62	

H.

Captain	Felix G. Mowring	Nov. 7, '62	
First Lieutenant	Rice C. Williams	Nov. 7, '62	
Second Lieutenant	Calender Rohrbough	Nov. 7, '62	

SCHEDULE G—Continued.

		Rank.	Remarks.
I.			
Captain........	....	....	....
First Lieutenant..	Allen Ellsworth........	Nov. 7, '62..	....
Second Lieutenant	....	....	....
K.			
Captain........	John D. Rosenbrook....	Nov. 29, '62.	....
First Lieutenant..	John D. Rosenbrook....	Nov. 7, '62..	Promoted ....
" ..	John S. Spangler.......	Nov. 29, '62.	....
Second Lieutenant	Edmund Higbie........	Nov. 29, '62.	....

SCHEDULE G — Continued.

Roster of One Hundred and Nineteenth Regiment Illinois Volunteers.

Field and Staff.		Rank.	Remarks.
Colonel	Thomas J. Kinney	Oct. 7, '62	
Lieutenant Colonel	Samuel E. Taylor	Sept. 12, '62	
Major	William H. Watson	Sept. 19, '62	
Adjutant	Harvey S. Buck	Sept. 19, '62	
Quartermaster	Delos Allen	Aug. 25, '62	
Surgeon	Thomas Munroe	Sept. 22, '62	
1st Ass't Surgeon	Reuben Woods	Oct. 10, '62	
2d Ass't Surgeon	George A. Byrns	Nov. 14, '62	
Chaplain	Charles S. Callihan	Oct. 10, '62	

COMPANY A.

Captain	Hugo Hollan	Oct. 7, '62	
First Lieutenant	Sylvester T. Worley	Oct. 7, '62	
Second Lieutenant	Harmon B. Hubbard	Oct. 7, '62	

B.

Captain	George Parker	Oct. 7, '62	
First Lieutenant	Johnston C. Dilworth	Oct. 7, '62	
Second Lieutenant	Ezekiel M. Bradley	Oct. 7, '62	

C.

Captain	Robert L. Greer	Oct. 7, '62	
First Lieutenant	Thomas J. Curry	Oct. 7, '62	
Second Lieutenant	Adam J. Bower	Oct. 7, '62	

D.

Captain	John H. Hambaugh	Oct. 7, '62	
First Lieutenant	Hiram E. Henry	Oct. 7, '62	
Second Lieutenant	William H. Brackenridge	Oct. 7, '62	

E.

Captain	William N. Mumford	Oct. 7, '62	
First Lieutenant	David K. Watson	Oct. 7, '62	
Second Lieutenant	Sylvester D. Nokes	Oct. 7, '62	

F.

Captain	Josiah Slack	Oct. 7, '62	
First Lieutenant	Oliver P. Brumback	Oct. 7, '62	
Second Lieutenant	Lewis Craycraft	Oct. 7, '62	

G.

Captain	Peyton C. Smith	Oct. 7, '62	
First Lieutenant	Edward Corey	Oct. 7, '62	
Second Lieutenant	Livingston S. Dennis	Oct. 7, '62	

H.

Captain	Samuel McConnell	Oct. 7, '62	
First Lieutenant	Henry C. Mullen	Oct. 7, '62	
Second Lieutenant	Jackson Wells	Oct. 7, '62	

SCHEDULE G—Continued.

		Rank.	Remarks.

I.

Captain	John T. May	Oct. 7, '62	
First Lieutenant	Irven W. Anderson	Oct. 7, '62	
Second Lieutenant	Robert H. Ellis	Oct. 7, '62	

K.

Captain	Calvin Johnson	Oct. 7, '62	
First Lieutenant	Erastus P. Julian	Oct. 7, '62	
Second Lieutenant	Jacob A. Bennett	Oct. 7, '62	

SCHEDULE G — Continued.

Roster of One Hundred and Twentieth Regiment Illinois Volunteers.

Field and Staff.		Rank.	Remarks.
Colonel	George W. McKeaig	Oct. 29, '62	
Lieutenant Colonel	John G. Hardy	Oct. 29, '62	
Major	Spencer B. Floyd	Oct. 29, '62	
Adjutant	Bluford Wilson	Oct. 29, '62	
Quartermaster	Larkin H. Simpson	Aug. 27, '62	
Surgeon	Phineas K. Guild	Nov. 19, '62	
1st Ass't Surgeon	Phillip J. Wardner	Nov. 6, '62	
2d Ass't Surgeon	Seely Brownell	Nov. 12, '62	
Chaplain	Lewis J. Simpson	Oct. 29, '62	

COMPANY A.

Captain	John M. Raum	Oct. 29, '62	
First Lieutenant	Henry D. Baker	Oct. 29, '62	
Second Lieutenant	Robert N. Wright	Oct. 29, '62	

B.

Captain	Burton Sexton	Oct. 29, '62	
First Lieutenant	John T. Mozley	Oct. 29, '62	
Second Lieutenant	Samuel W. Scoggins	Oct. 29, '62	

C.

Captain	Uriah Axley	Oct. 29, '62	
First Lieutenant	Joel Dubois	Oct. 29, '62	
Second Lieutenant	Owen H. Clark	Oct. 29, '62	

D.

Captain	Parker B. Pillow	Oct. 29, '62	
First Lieutenant	Washington Kanady	Oct. 29, '62	
Second Lieutenant	Joseph D. Jennings	Oct. 29, '62	

E.

Captain	William S. Hodge	Oct. 29, '62	
First Lieutenant	Thomas J. Carr	Oct. 29, '62	
Second Lieutenant	William J. Mitchell	Oct. 29, '62	

F.

Captain	William Roark	Oct. 29, '62	
First Lieutenant	Benjamin H. Rice	Oct. 29, '62	
Second Lieutenant	Zepheniah Phillips	Oct. 29, '62	

G.

Captain	Mark Whittaker	Oct. 29, '62	
First Lieutenant	James H. McSpavin	Oct. 29, '62	
Second Lieutenant	James H. Ballance	Oct. 29, '62	

H.

Captain	David M. Porter	Oct. 29, '62	
First Lieutenant	William Walters	Oct. 29, '62	
Second Lieutenant	William L. Blackard	Oct. 29, '62	

Schedule G — Continued.

		Rank.	Remarks.
I.			
Captain	James J. Bridges	Oct. 29, '62	
First Lieutenant	James E. Race	Oct. 29, '62	
Second Lieutenant	James B. Gillispie	Oct. 29, '62	
K.			
Captain	Sample G. Parks	Oct. 29, '62	
First Lieutenant	John F. Benson	Oct. 29, '62	
Second Lieutenant	Charles N. Damron	Oct. 29, '62	

Schedule G — Continued.

Roster of One Hundred and Twenty-Second Regiment Illinois Volunteers.

Field and Staff.		Rank.	Remarks.
Colonel	John J. Rinaker	Sept. 4, '62	
Lieutenant Colonel	James F. Drish	Sept. 9, '62	
Major	James F. Chapman	Sept. 4, '62	
Adjutant	Hardin G. Kaplinger	Oct. 14, '62	
Quartermaster	William W. Freeman	Aug. 28, '62	
Surgeon	William A. Knox	Oct. 4, '62	
1st Ass't Surgeon	William A. Knox	Sept. 2, '62	Promoted
"	John P. Mathews	Oct. 4, '62	
2d Ass't Surgeon	Marinus W. Seaman	Sept. 24, '62	
Chaplain	John H. Austin	Sept. 4, '62	

Company A.

Captain	William B. Dugger	Sept. 4, '62	
First Lieutenant	Thomas G. Lofton	Sept. 4, '62	
Second Lieutenant	David B. Haldeman	Sept. 9, '62	

B.

Captain	Manoah Bostick	Sept. 4, '62	
First Lieutenant	John Harding	Sept. 4, '62	
Second Lieutenant	Eli H. Davis	Sept. 4, '62	

C.

Captain	Lucien King	Sept. 4, '62	
First Lieutenant	Jacob L. Pope	Sept. 4, '62	
Second Lieutenant	Samuel L. Chapman	Sept. 4, '62	

D.

Captain	Lewis P. Peebles	Sept. 4, '62	
First Lieutenant	James N. Halt	Sept. 4, '62	
Second Lieutenant	Henry C. Gooding	Sept. 4, '62	

E.

Captain	Baxter Haynes	Sept. 4, '62	
First Lieutenant	Benjamin V. Casey	Sept. 4, '62	
Second Lieutenant	Abraham C. Hulse	Sept. 4, '62	

F.

Captain	Sidney Hall	Sept. 4, '62	
First Lieutenant	James S. Childs	Sept. 4, '62	
Second Lieutenant	Alvis Shass	Sept. 4, '62	

G.

Captain	Balfour Cowen	Sept. 4, '62	
First Lieutenant	William H. Cox	Sept. 4, '62	
Second Lieutenant	Rufus W. Loud	Sept. 4, '62	

H.

Captain	Benjamin Leigh	Sept. 4, '62	
First Lieutenant	James C. McKnight	Sept. 4, '62	
Second Lieutenant	Pleasant L. Bristow	Sept. 4, '62	

SCHEDULE G — Continued.

		Rank.	Remarks.
I.			
Captain	Andrew F. Duncan	Sept. 4, '62	
First Lieutenant	Stephen T Sawyer	Sept. 4, '62	
Second Lieutenant	Augustus M. Sparks	Sept. 4, '62	
K.			
Captain	Josiah Borough	Sept. 4, '62	
First Lieutenant	John S. Colter	Sept. 4, '62	
Second Lieutenant	Thomas Miller	Sept. 4, '62	

SCHEDULE G—Continued.

Roster of One Hundred and Twenty-Third Regiment Illinois Volunteers.

Field and Staff.		Rank.	Remarks.
Colonel	James Monroe	Sept. 6, '62	
Lieutenant Colonel	Jonathan Biggs	Sept. 6, '62	
Major	James N. Conally	Sept. 6, '62	
Adjutant	Leander H. Hamlin	Sept. 6, '62	
Quartermaster		Sept. 6, '62	
Surgeon	Horace R. Allen	Sept. 6, '62	
1st Ass't Surgeon		Sept. 6, '62	
2d Ass't Surgeon	Alvin Ballou	Sept. 6, '62	
Chaplain	John P. Shoe	Sept. 6, '62	

COMPANY A.

Captain	James B. Hill	Sept. 6, '62	
First Lieutenant	Silas M. Shepard	Sept. 6, '62	
Second Lieutenant	Oscar F. Bane	Sept. 6, '62	

B.

Captain	Edward Talbott	Sept. 6, '62	
First Lieutenant	Lemuel Leggett	Sept. 6, '62	
Second Lieutenant	Charles Conzet	Sept. 6, '62	

C.

Captain	Clark C. Starkweather	Sept. 6, '62	
First Lieutenant	James Shewmaker	Sept. 6, '62	
Second Lieutenant	William J. Horner	Sept. 6, '62	

D.

Captain	James L. Hart	Sept. 6, '62	
First Lieutenant	James B. Grant	Sept. 6, '62	
Second Lieutenant	Miles W. Hart	Sept. 6, '62	

E.

Captain	Samuel Coblentz	Sept. 6, '62	Died Nov. 30, '62
"	Norman Comstock	Nov. 30, '62	
First Lieutenant	Norman Comstock	Sept. 6, '62	Promoted
"	Zachariah H. McCubbins	Nov. 30, '62	
Second Lieutenant	Zachariah H. McCubbins	Sept. 6, '62	Promoted
"	Jacob R. Harding	Nov. 30, '62	

F.

Captain	Calvin B. York	Sept. 6, '62	
First Lieutenant	James D. Nicholas	Sept. 6, '62	
Second Lieutenant	James Biggs	Sept. 6, '62	

G.

Captain	Reson L. Lovelace	Sept. 6, '62	
First Lieutenant	George W. Thompson	Sept. 6, '62	
Second Lieutenant	Simon F. Andrews	Sept. 6, '62	

Schedule G—Continued.

		Rank.	Remarks.

H.

Captain	Abram C. Vanbuskirk	Sept. 6, '62	
First Lieutenant	John W. Champ	Sept. 6, '62	
Second Lieutenant	William H. House	Sept. 6, '62	

I.

Captain	William E. Adams	Sept. 6, '62	
First Lieutenant	William E. McDonald	Sept. 6, '62	
Second Lieutenant	Gregory R. Hawkins	Sept. 6, '62	

K.

Captain	Owen Wiley	Sept. 6, '62	
First Lieutenant	John M. Eastin	Sept. 6, '62	
Second Lieutenant	William Bell	Sept. 6, '62	

SCHEDULE G — Continued.

Roster of One Hundred and Twenty-Fourth Regiment Illinois Volunteers.

Field and Staff.		Rank.	Remarks.
Colonel	Thomas J. Sloan	Sept. 20, '62.	
Lieutenant Colonel	John H. Howe	Sept. 10, '62.	
Major	Rufus P. Pattison	Sept. 10, '62.	
Adjutant	William E. Smith	Sept. 2, '62.	
Quartermaster	Alonzo N. Reece	Sept. 1, '62.	
Surgeon	Leland H. Angell	Oct. 4, '62.	
1st Ass't Surgeon	James R. Kay	Oct. 28, '62.	
2d Ass't Surgeon			
Chaplain	Horace B. Foskett	Sept. 10, '62.	

COMPANY A.

Captain	Ralph A. Tenney	Sept. 10, '62.	
First Lieutenant	Julius A. Pratt	Sept. 10, '62.	
Second Lieutenant	Edmund C. Raymond	Sept. 10, '62.	

B.

Captain	Adin Mann	Sept. 10, '62.	
First Lieutenant	Edwin F. Stafford	Sept. 10, '62.	
Second Lieutenant	Fernando C. Vanvlack	Sept. 10, '62.	

C.

Captain	Henry L. Field	Sept. 10, '62.	
First Lieutenant	John W. Terry	Sept. 10, '62.	
Second Lieutenant	James Rickey	Sept. 10, '62.	

D.

Captain	Stephen Brink	Sept. 10, '62.	
First Lieutenant	Asa A. Cowdery	Sept. 10, '62.	
Second Lieutenant	Travis Mellar	Sept. 10, '62.	

E.

Captain	William B. Sigley	Sept. 10, '62.	
First Lieutenant	James H. Blackmore	Sept. 10, '62.	
Second Lieutenant	Osborn Willson	Sept. 10, '62.	

F.

Captain	Matthew B. Potter	Sept. 10, '62.	
First Lieutenant	Norman H. Pratt	Sept. 10, '62.	
Second Lieutenant	Enoch W. Taylor	Sept. 10, '62.	

G.

Captain	Lyman H. Scudder	Sept. 10, '62.	
First Lieutenant	Ezra C. Benedict	Sept. 10, '62.	
Second Lieutenant	Benton Pratt	Sept. 10, '62.	

H.

Captain	John W. Kendall	Sept. 10, '62.	
First Lieutenant	Justus D. Andrews	Sept. 10, '62.	
Second Lieutenant	Theodore Potter	Sept. 10, '62.	

SCHEDULE G—Continued.

		Rank.	Remarks.
\multicolumn{4}{c}{I.}

I.

		Rank.	Remarks.
Captain	Thomas K. Roach	Sept. 10, '62.	
First Lieutenant	Richard L. Howard	Sept. 10, '62.	
Second Lieutenant	Benjamin A. Griffith	Sept. 10, '62.	

K.

		Rank.	Remarks.
Captain	James H. Morgan	Sept. 10, '62.	
First Lieutenant	Thomas J. Willian	Sept. 10, '62.	Died
"	Stephen N. Sanders	Nov. 15, '62.	
Second Lieutenant	Stephen N. Sanders	Sept. 10, '62.	Promoted
"	Hiram H. Hall	Nov. 15, '62.	

SCHEDULE G — Continued.

Roster of One Hundred and Twenty-Fifth Regiment Illinois Volunteers.

Field and Staff.		Rank.	Remarks.
Colonel	Oscar F. Harmon	Sept. 4, '62	
Lieutenant Colonel	James W. Langley	Sept. 4, '62	
Major	John B. Lee	Sept. 4, '62	
Adjutant	William Mann	Sept. 4, '62	
Quartermaster	Alexander M. Ayers	Aug. 29, '62	
Surgeon			
1st Ass't Surgeon	Charles H. Mills	Sept. 4, '62	
2d Ass't Surgeon			
Chaplain			

COMPANY A.

Captain	Clark Ralston	Sept. 4, '62	
First Lieutenant	Charles Jackson	Sept. 4, '62	
Second Lieutenant	Harrison Low	Sept. 4, '62	

B.

Captain	Robert Steward	Sept. 4, '62	Resigned Dec. 18, '62
First Lieutenant	William R. Wilson	Sept. 4, '62	
Second Lieutenant	Stephen D. Conover	Sept. 4, '62	

C.

Captain	William W. Fellows	Sept. 4, '62	
First Lieutenant	Alexander Pollock	Sept. 4, '62	
Second Lieutenant	James D. New	Sept. 4, '62	

D.

Captain	George W. Galloway	Sept. 4, '62	
First Lieutenant	James B. Stevens	Sept. 4, '62	
Second Lieutenant	John L. Jones	Sept. 4, '62	

E.

Captain	Nathan M. Clark	Sept. 4, '62	
First Lieutenant	William G. Isom	Sept. 4, '62	
Second Lieutenant	John Urquhart	Sept. 4, '62	

F.

Captain	Frederick B. Sale	Sept 4, '62	
First Lieutenant	John B. Lester	Sept. 4, '62	
Second Lieutenant	Alfred Johnson	Sept. 4, '62	

G.

Captain	Pleasant M. Parks	Sept. 4, '62	
First Lieutenant	David A. Benton	Sept. 4, '62	
Second Lieutenant	John C. Harbor	Sept. 4, '62	

H.

Captain	John H. Gass	Sept. 4, '62	Resigned Dec. 30, '62
First Lieutenant	Ephraim S. Howell	Sept. 4, '62	
Second Lieutenant	Josiah Lee	Sept. 4, '62	

SCHEDULE G—Continued.

		Rank.	Remarks.

I.

Captain	Levin Vinson	Sept. 4, '62	
First Lieutenant	John E. Vinson	Sept. 4, '62	Resigned Nov. 21, '62
" "	Edward B. Kingsbury	Nov, 25, '62	
Second Lieutenant	Stephen Brothers	Sept. 4, '62	

K.

Captain	George W. Cook	Sept 4., '62	
First Lieutenant	Oliver P. Hunt	Sept. 4, '62	
Second Lieutenant	Joseph F. Crosby	Sept. 4, '62	

Schedule G — Continued.

Roster of One Hundred and Twenty-Sixth Regiment Illinois Volunteers.

Field and Staff.		Rank.	Remarks.
Colonel	Jonathan Richmond	Sept. 4, '62	
Lieutenant Colonel	Ezra M. Beardsley	Sept. 4, '62	
Major	William W. Wilshire	Sept. 4, '62	
Adjutant	Daniel W. Munn	Sept. 4, '62	
Quartermaster	Napoleon B. Stage	Sept. 4, '62	
Surgeon	Charles A. Hunt	Dec. 6, '62	
1st Ass't Surgeon	Erastus W. Mills	Sept. 4, '62	
2d Ass't Surgeon	Thomas D. Washburn	Sept. 4, '62	
Chaplain	Samuel Rosebora	Sept. 4, '62	

Company A.

Captain	Martin N. Van Fleet	Sept. 4, '62	
First Lieutenant	Adley N. Gregory	Sept. 4, '62	
Second Lieutenant	Allen H. Morgan	Sept. 4, '62	

B.

Captain	Henry D. Cline	Sept. 4, '62	
First Lieutenant	John B. Mitchell	Sept. 4, '62	
Second Lieutenant	Isaac D. Cox	Sept. 4, '62	

C.

Captain	Alfred N. Smyser	Sept. 4, '62	
First Lieutenant	James M. Powell	Sept. 4, '62	
Second Lieutenant	George W. Vaughan	Sept. 4, '62	

D.

Captain	Larkin R. Slaughter	Sept. 4, '62	
First Lieutenant	Daniel W. Munn	Sept. 4, '62	
Second Lieutenant	Joseph W. Newbury	Sept. 4, '62	

E.

Captain	Lucius W. Beal	Sept. 4, '62	
First Lieutenant	Emery Hughes	Sept. 4, '62	
Second Lieutenant	Frederick S. Gates	Sept. 4, '62	

F.

Captain	James H. Kabrick	Sept. 4, '62	
First Lieutenant	John J. Wetmore	Sept. 4, '62	
Second Lieutenant	Martin V. Easterday	Sept. 4, '62	

G.

Captain	Edwin H. Johnston	Sept. 4, '62	
First Lieutenant	William H. Schriver	Sept. 4, '62	
Second Lieutenant	Gabriel Armstrong	Sept. 4, '62	

H.

Captain	Thomas Martin	Sept. 4, '62	
First Lieutenant	David E. Evans	Sept. 4, '62	
Second Lieutenant	Christian Koerber	Sept. 4, '62	

Schedule G—Continued.

		Rank.	Remarks.

I.

Captain	John Morris	Sept. 4, '62	
First Lieutenant	Charles M. Knox	Sept. 4, '62	
Second Lieutenant	Brooks R. Hamilton	Sept. 4, '62	

K.

Captain	Alfred Francisca	Sept. 4, '62	
First Lieutenant	Joseph L. Thorp	Sept. 4, '62	
Second Lieutenant	Allen Francisca	Sept. 4, '62	

SCHEDULE G—Continued.

Roster of One Hundred and Twenty-Seventh Regiment Illinois Volunteers.

Field and Staff.		Rank.	Remarks.
Colonel	John VanArman	Sept. 6, '62	
Lieutenant Colonel	Hamilton N. Eldridge	Sept. 6, '62	
Major	Frank S. Curtiss	Sept. 6, '62	
Adjutant	John Van Arman, jr.	Sept. 6, '62	
Quartermaster	Daniel H. Hale	Sept. 6, '62	
Surgeon	Joel R. Gore	Sept. 6, '62	
1st Ass't Surgeon	Anson L. Clark	Sept. 6, '62	
2d Ass't Surgeon	Julius P. Anthony	Sept. 6, '62	
Chaplain	Jonathan C. Stoughton	Sept. 6, '62	

COMPANY A.

Captain	William L. Fowler	Sept. 5, '62	
First Lieutenant	William Walker	Sept. 5, '62	
Second Lieutenant	William S. Bunn	Sept. 5, '62	

B.

Captain	Adoniram J. Burrows	Sept. 5, '62	Discharged Oct. 31, '62
First Lieutenant	John R. Morgan	Sept. 5, '62	
Second Lieutenant	Frank J. Woodward	Sept. 5, '62	

C.

Captain	John S. Riddle	Sept. 5, '62	
First Lieutenant	Thomas Clark	Sept. 5, '62	
Second Lieutenant	William Warner	Sept. 5, '62	

D.

Captain	Thomas W. Chandler	Sept. 5, '62	
First Lieutenant	Edgar W. Pike	Sept. 5, '62	
Second Lieutenant	Charles M. Libby	Sept. 5, '62	

E.

Captain	Frank C. Gillette	Sept. 5, '62	
First Lieutenant	James F. Richmond	Sept. 5, '62	
Second Lieutenant	Frederick Knight	Sept. 5, '62	

F.

Captain	Charles Schryver	Sept. 5, '62	
First Lieutenant	Jeremiah Evarts	Sept. 5, '62	
Second Lieutenant	Alfred Darnell	Sept. 5, '62	

G.

Captain	John S. Williams	Oct. 23, '62	
First Lieutenant	Augustus F. Higgs	Oct. 23, '62	
Second Lieutenant	Thomas Sewell	Oct. 23, '62	

H.

Captain	Lawrence Riley	Sept. 5, '62	
First Lieutenant	Hiram McClintock	Sept. 5, '62	
Second Lieutenant	Joseph S. Berry	Oct. 23, '62	

SCHEDULE G—Continued.

		Rank.	Remarks.

I.

Captain	Frederick A. Raymond	Sept. 5, '62	....
First Lieutenant	Horace Perry	Sept. 5, '62	....
Second Lieutenant	Addison A. Keys	Sept. 5, '62	....

K.

Captain	John H. Lowe	Sept. 5, '62	....
First Lieutenant	John B. Moulton	Sept. 5, '62	....
Second Lieutenant	Edgar Percival	Sept. 5, '62	....

SCHEDULE G—Continued.

Roster of One Hundred and Twenty-Eighth Regiment Illinois Volunteers.

Field and Staff.		Rank.	Remarks.
Colonel	Robert M. Hundley	Dec. 18, '62	
Lieutenant Colonel	James D. Pulley	Nov. 4, '62	
Major	James D. McCown	Nov. 4, '62	
Adjutant	William A. Lemma	Nov. 4, '62	
Quartermaster	George W. Akin	Oct. 11, '62	
Surgeon			
1st. Ass't Surgeon	George W. French	Oct. 7, '62	
2d Ass't Surgeon			
Chaplain	Archibald J. Benker	Dec. 18, '62	

COMPANY A.

Captain	William J. Moyers	Nov. 4, '62	
First Lieutenant	Alexander McRoyall	Nov. 4, '62	
Second Lieutenant	Martin V. B. Dial	Nov. 4, '62	

B.

Captain	William G. Durham	Nov. 4, '62	
First Lieutenant	James V. Moore	Nov. 4, '62	
Second Lieutenant	Josiah M. Dorris	Nov. 4, '62	

C.

Captain	Jefferson J. Allen	Nov. 4, '62	
First Lieutenant	Hubert H. Harris	Nov. 4, '62	
Second Lieutenant	John A. Ensminger	Nov. 4, '62	

D.

Captain	John Brown	Dec. 8, '62	
First Lieutenant	Seaborn A. Walker	Nov. 5, '62	
Second Lieutenant	Jasper V. Crain	Dec. 8, '62	

E.

Captain	Joel H. Swindell	Nov. 4, '62	
First Lieutenant	Zachariah Hudgens	Nov. 4, '62	
Second Lieutenant	Addison Reese	Nov. 4, '62	

F.

Captain	Robert M. Allen	Nov. 4, '62	
First Lieutenant	Iradell W. Williams	Nov. 4, '62	
Second Lieutenant	Martin W. Robertson	Nov. 4, '62	

G.

Captain	William Huffstutler	Dec. 8, '62	
First Lieutenant	Jesse A. McIntosh	Nov. 5, '62	
Second Lieutenant	Noah E. Norris	Dec. 8, '62	

H.

Captain	Aaron A. Bell	Dec. 8, '62	
First Lieutenant	William L. Stilley	Nov. 5, '62	
Second Lieutenant	Joseph B. Fuller	Dec. 8, '62	

Schedule G — Continued.

		Rank.	Remarks.
I.			
Captain	William A. Fry	Dec. 18, '62	
First Lieutenant	William A. Fry	Nov. 4, '62	Promoted
"	William M. Cooper	Dec. 18, '62	
Second Lieutenant	Wylie W. Hall	Dec. 18, '62	
K.			
Captain	Joshua Pemberton	Nov. 4, '62	
First Lieutenant	Samuel R. Upchurch	Nov. 4, '62	
Second Lieutenant	Samuel H. Pemberton	Nov. 4, '62	

SCHEDULE G — Continued.

Roster of One Hundred and Twenty-Ninth Regiment Illinois Volunteers.

Field and Staff.		Rank.	Remarks.
Colonel	George P. Smith	Sept. 8, '62	
Lieutenant Colonel	Henry Case	Sept. 8, '62	
Major	Andrew J. Cropsey	Sept. 8, '62	
Adjutant	Phillip D. Plattenburg	Sept. 8, '62	
Quartermaster	William C. Gwin	Sept. 8, '62	
Surgeon	Harvey C. Johns	Nov. 18, '62	
1st Ass't Surgeon	Darius Johnson	Sept. 8, '62	
2d Ass't Surgeon	William H. Walters	Nov. 10, '62	
Chaplain	Thomas Cotton	Sept. 8, '62	

COMPANY A.

Captain	John A. Hoskins	Sept. 8, '62	
First Lieutenant	Joseph F. Culver	Sept. 8, '62	
Second Lieutenant	John W. Smith	Sept. 8, '62	

B.

Captain	Samuel T. Walkley	Sept. 8, '62	
First Lieutenant	George W. Gilcrist	Sept. 8, '62	
Second Lieutenant	Elihu Chilcott	Sept. 8, '62	

C.

Captain	John B. Perry	Sept. 8, '62	
First Lieutenant	Robert P. Edgington	Sept. 8, '62	
Second Lieutenant	Stephen H. Kyle	Sept. 8, '62	

D.

Captain	Thomas H. Flynn	Sept. 8, '62	
First Lieutenant	William C. Gwin	Sept. 8, '62	Promoted Quartermaster.
Second Lieutenant	William Birch	Sept. 8, '62	

E.

Captain	Cyrus N. Baird	Sept. 8, '62	
First Lieutenant	John F. Blackburn	Sept. 8, '62	
Second Lieutenant	Benjamin F. Fitch	Sept. 8, '62	

F.

Captain	Erastus L. Gillham	Sept. 8, '62	
First Lieutenant	George W. Horton	Sept. 8, '62	
Second Lieutenant	John B. Mayes	Sept. 8, '62	

G.

Captain	Henry B. Reed	Sept. 8, '62	
First Lieutenant	Lemuel Morse	Sept. 8, '62	
Second Lieutenant	John P. McKnight	Sept. 8, '62	

H

Captain	George W. Martin	Sept. 8, 62	
First Lieutenant			
Second Lieutenant			

SCHEDULE G—Continued.

		Rank.	Remarks.

I.

Captain	James Edmundson	Sept. 8, '62	Resigned Dec. 2, '62
First Lieutenant	James F. Crawford	Sept. 8, '62	Resigned Dec. 9, '62
Second Lieutenant	Joseph W. Coppage	Sept. 8, '62	

K.

Captain	Wolf H. Anderson	Sept. 8, '62	
First Lieutenant	James Chapman	Sept. 8, '62	
Second Lieutenant	Albert Lamb	Sept. 8, '62	

Schedule G—Continued.

Roster of One Hundred and Thirtieth Regiment Illinois Volunteers.

Field and Staff.		Rank.	Remarks.
Colonel	Nathaniel Niles	Oct. 25, '62	
Lieutenant Colonel	James H. Matheny	Sept. 18, '62	
Major	John B. Reid	Sept. 18, '62	
Adjutant	John B. Hay	Sept. 18, '62	
Quartermaster	Silas J. Stiles	Oct. 16, '62	
Surgeon	Lewis K. Wilcox	Nov. 19, '62	
1st Ass't Surgeon	David Wilkins	Oct. 18, '62	
2d Ass't Surgeon	Edward L. H. Barry	Oct. 4, '62	
Chaplain	William D. H. Johnson	Oct. 25, '62	

Company A.

Captain	William H. Copp	Oct. 25, '62	
First Lieutenant	William H. Miller	Oct. 25, '62	
Second Lieutenant	Charles T. Mullin	Oct. 25, '62	

B.

Captain	William Prescott	Oct. 25, '62	
First Lieutenant	Francis M. Pickerell	Oct. 25, '62	
Second Lieutenant	Jacob W. Panlon	Oct. 25, '62	

C.

Captain	John H. Robinson	Oct. 25, '62	
First Lieutenant	William C. James	Oct. 25, '62	
Second Lieutenant	Joseph F. Parker	Oct. 25, '62	

D.

Captain	Daniel DeCamp	Oct. 25, '62	
First Lieutenant	Abraham May	Oct. 25, '62	
Second Lieutenant	James B. Hallford	Oct. 25, '62	

E.

Captain	Urbane B. Harris	Oct. 25, '62	
First Lieutenant	William Harlan	Oct. 25, '62	
Second Lieutenant	William C. Harned	Oct. 25, '62	

F.

Captain	William M. Colby	Oct. 25, '62	
First Lieutenant	John D. Donnell	Oct. 25, '62	
Second Lieutenant	Charles Ives	Oct. 25, '62	

G.

Captain	John P. H. Keller	Oct. 25, '62	
First Lieutenant	Daniel A. Crum	Oct. 25, '62	
Second Lieutenant	Duff Leitch	Oct. 25, '62	

H.

Captain	Jesse R. Johnson	Oct. 25, '62	
First Lieutenant	Joel Gardner	Oct. 25, '62	
Second Lieutenant	John Blew	Oct. 25, '62	

SCHEDULE G—Continued.

		Rank.	Remarks.

I.

Captain	John W. Watts	Oct. 25, '62	
First Lieutenant	Richard S. Taylor	Oct. 25, '62	
Second Lieutenant	Wilson I. Niell	Oct. 25, '62	

K.

Captain	Jacob W. Wilkin	Oct. 25, '62	
First Lieutenant	William O. Pool	Oct. 25, '62	
Second Lieutenant	Andrew S. Martin	Oct. 25, '62	

SCHEDULE G—Continued.

Roster of One Hundred and Thirty-First Regiment Illinois Volunteers.

Field and Staff.		Rank.	Remarks.
Colonel	George W. Neeley	Nov. 13, '62 ..	....
Lieutenant Colonel	Richard A. Peter	Nov. 13, '62 ..	....
Major	Joseph L. Purvis	Nov. 13, '62 ..	....
Adjutant	Lafayette Twitchell	Nov. 13, '62 ..	....
Quartermaster ...	Josiah Dayhuff	Sept. 20, '62 ..	....
Surgeon	Joseph Brown	Nov. 13, '62 ..	....
1st Ass't Surgeon.	....	....	....
2d Ass't Surgeon.	....	....	....
Chaplain	Benjamin S. Jwan	Sept. 3, '62 ..	....

COMPANY A.

Captain	Elisha T. Woods	Nov. 13, '62.	....
First Lieutenant..	Thomas N. Stephens	Nov. 13, '62.	....
Second Lieutenant	Charles Barfield	Nov. 13, '62.	....

B.

Captain	James S. Herod	Nov. 13, '62.	....
First Lieutenant..	John A. Carrey	Nov. 13, '62.	....
Second Lieutenant	Daniel W. Herod	Nov. 13, '62.	....

C.

Captain	William D. Purdom	Nov. 13, '62.	....
First Lieutenant..	William H. Field	Nov. 13, '62.	....
Second Lieutenant	Calvin Mason	Nov. 13, '62.	....

D.

Captain	Thomas S. Woodward ...	Nov. 13, '62.	....
First Lieutenant..	Isaac M. Choat	Nov. 13, '62.	....
Second Lieutenant	Abner Mizell	Nov. 13, '62.	....

E.

Captain	Cornelius W. Halley	Nov. 13, '62.	....
First Lieutenant..	Amster B. Pate	Nov. 13, '62.	....
Second Lieutenant	Sidney A. Pinney	Nov. 13, '62.	....

F.

Captain	Wiley Hobbs	Nov. 13, '62.	....
First Lieutenant..	John R. Brown	Nov. 13, '62.	....
Second Lieutenant	Ira McFarlan	Nov. 13, '62.	....

G.

Captain	Edward H. McCaleb	Nov. 13, '62.	....
First Lieutenant..	John Daily	Nov. 13, '62.	....
Second Lieutenant	James A. Peter	Nov. 13, '62.	....

H.

Captain	Thomas N. Pulsifer	Nov. 13, '62.	....
First Lieutenant..	Hallet B. Spooner	Nov. 13, '62.	....
Second Lieutenant	James H. Parker	Nov. 13, '62.	....

SCHEDULE G—Continued.

		Rank.	Remarks.
I.			
Captain	David H. Lasater	Nov. 13, '62.	
First Lieutenant	Lewis L. Moore	Nov. 13, '62.	
Second Lieutenant	James C. Lasater	Nov. 13, '62.	
K.			
Captain	Frederick Sollars	Nov. 13, '62.	
First Lieutenant	Daniel M. Willis	Nov. 13, '62.	
Second Lieutenant	James H. Young	Nov. 13, '62.	

SCHEDULE G—Continued.

Roster of First Cavalry Regiment Illinois Volunteers.

Field and Staff.		Rank.	Remarks.
Colonel	Thomas A. Marshall	July 1, '61	
Lieutenant Colonel	Henry M. Day	July 1, '61	Mustered out June 14, '62; com. Col. 91st inf. Sep. 8, '62
Major	David P. Jenkins	July 1, '61	Resigned June 14, '62
"	Christopher A. Morgan	Sept. 1, '61	
"	Edward Wright	Sept. 7, '61	
Adjutant	William S. Marshall	July 17, '61	Mustered out June 1, '62
" 1st Batt'n	George A. Day	Jan. 1, '62	Mustered out June 16, '62
" 2d Batt'n	Harry S. Smith	Jan. 1, '62	Mustered out June 16, '62
" 3d Batt'n	John Warren	March 20, '62	Promoted Captain Co. C
Quartermaster	James M. Ruggles		Resigned
"	Albert Rayburn	Jan. 1, '62	Mustered out June 1, '62
" 1st Batt'n			
" 2d Batt'n			
" 3d Batt'n			
Commissary			
Surgeon	Henry M. Parker	July 5, '61	
Assistant Surgeon	Theodore J. Bluthardt	July 26, '61	Resigned April 5, '62, with view of promotion to Surgeon of 23d Mo. vol's
Chaplain	Daniel S. Altman	March 27, '62	

COMPANY A.

Captain	John McNulta	May 3, '61	
First Lieutenant	George F. Tannatt	May 3, '61	Mustered out July 6, '62
Second Lieutenant	James B. Dent	July 3, '61	

B.

Captain	James Foster	July 4, '61	Mustered out Dec. 30, '61
"	Samuel L. M. Proctor	Dec. 30, '61	
First Lieutenant	Samuel L. M. Proctor	July 4, '61	Promoted
"	Casper Yost	Dec. 30, '61	
Second Lieutenant	Casper Yost	July 4, '61	Promoted
"	John Yost	Dec. 30, '61	

C.

Captain	Greenville M. Mitchell	July 19, '61	Promoted to 54th
"	John Warren	April 22, '62	
First Lieutenant	Justin C. Smith	July 19, '61	
Second Lieutenant	Camden Knight	July 19, '61	

D.

Captain	Jehiel B. Smith	July 1, '61	
First Lieutenant	Leonard Hollenberg	July 1, '61	Mustered out June 20, '62
Second Lieutenant	William A. Murray	July 1, '61	

E.

Captain	Paul Walters	July 7, '61	
First Lieutenant	Isaac Sekillman	July 7, '61	
Second Lieutenant	Morgan Blair	July 7, '61	

Schedule G—Continued.

		Rank.	Remarks.

F.

Captain	John Burnap	July 3, '61	[cavalry.
First Lieutenant	Garrett Elkin	July 8, '61	Resigned and transf'd 10th
"	Thomas S. Pinckard	Jan. 10, '62	Resigned March 1, '62
"	John Q. A. Floyd	March 1, '62	
Second Lieutenant	John C. Parks	July 8, '61	

G.

Captain	George W. Palmer	July 5, '61	
First Lieutenant	Samuel Douglas	July 5, '61	Resigned June 23, '62
Second Lieutenant	Alexander H. Holt	July 5, '61	

H.

Captain	Robert D. Noleman	June 24, '61	
First Lieutenant	Samuel P. Tufts	June 24, '61	
Second Lieutenant	Wesley B. Casey	June 24, '61	Declared error by Gen.
"	Robert R. Whitlock	June 24, '61	[Halleck.

I.

Captain	Orlando Burrell	July 9, '61	
First Lieutenant	Leonard S. Ross	July 9, 61	
Second Lieutenant	Frank Lindsey	July 9, '61	

K.

Captain	Oscar H. Huntley	Dec. 9, '61	Resigned Dec. 8, '62
First Lieutenant	Thomas A. Stevens	Dec. 9, '61	
Second Lieutenant	William Hebard	Dec. 9, '61	

L.

Captain			
First Lieutenant			
Second Lieutenant			

M.

Captain			
First Lieutenant			
Second Lieutenant			

SCHEDULE G—Continued.

Roster of Second Cavalry Regiment Illinois Volunteers.

Field and Staff.		Rank.	Remarks.
Colonel	Silas Noble	July 24, '61	
Lieutenant Colonel	Harvey Hogg	July 24, '61	Killed in battle at Bolivar,
"	Quincy McNeil	Aug. 30, '62	[Tenn., Aug. 30, '62
Major	Louis H. Waters	July 24, '61	Res. and com. as Colonel of 84th Infantry, Sept. 1, '62
"	Quincy McNeil	Aug. 6, '61	Promoted Lieut. Colonel.
"	Hugh Fullerton	Aug. 30, '62	
"	John J. Mudd	Sept. 23, '61	
"	Daniel B. Bush, jr	Sept. 23, '61	
Adjutant	William Stadden	Aug. 5, '61	Resigned October 18, 1861
"	Henry G. Hicks	Oct. 15, '61	Mustered out June 1, '62
"	James K. Catlin	Sept. 30, '62	
" 1st Batt'n	John R. Howlett	May 17, '62	
" 2d Batt'n	Livander W. Pattison	April 12, '62	
" 3d Batt'n	Joshua Rodgers	April 12, '62	
Quartermaster	Jerome W. Hollenbeck	Aug. 5, '61	Mustered out June 1, '62
"	Edgar Z. Hunt	Sept. 6, '62	
" 1st Batt'n			
" 2d Batt'n			
" 3d Batt'n			
Commissary	Lewis Aubere	Oct. 4, '62	
Surgeon	J. B. Cutts	Sept. 2, '61	
Assistant Surgeon	Andrew J. Crane	Aug. 14, '61	Resigned Sept. 29, 1862
"	Daniel C. Jones	Dec. 17, '62	
Chaplain	James R. Locke	Aug. 6, '61	

COMPANY A.

Captain	John R. Hotaling	Aug. 24, '61	
First Lieutenant	Frank B. Bennett	Aug. 24, '61	Resigned June 3, '62
"	William B. Cummins	June 3, '62	
Second Lieutenant	Albert J. Jackson	Aug. 24, '61	Resigned March 19, '62
"	William B. Cummins	March 18, '62	Promoted
"	Stephen G. Patrick	June 3, '62	Resigned Sept. 13, '62
"	James S. McHenry	Sept. 13, '62	

B.

Captain	Thomas J. Larrison	Aug. 24, '61	
First Lieutenant	Alfred U. Stone	Aug. 24, '61	Mustered out.
"	James Ewert	Aug. 19, '62	
Second Lieutenant	Jerome B. Tenney	Aug. 24, '61	Mustered out.
"	Austin S. Dement	Aug. 19, '62	

C.

Captain	Hugh Fullerton	Aug. 24, '61	Promoted
"	Samuel Whitaker	Oct. 4, '62	
First Lieutenant	Calvin Terry	Aug. 24, '61	Killed at Union City, Aug. [15, '62.
"	John Fallis	Aug. 17, '62	Died Oct. 23, '62
"	George Moore	Oct. 23, '62	
Second Lieutenant	David Solenberger	Aug. 24, '61	Promoted
"	John Goodheart	Dec. 30, '61	Killed in battle Aug. 15, '62
"	George Moore	Aug. 17, '62	Promoted
"	Peter Holt	Oct. 23, '62	

SCHEDULE G—Continued.

		Rank.	Remarks.
D.			
Captain	Franklin B. Moore	Aug. 24, '61	
First Lieutenant	George Lebold	Aug. 24, '61	
Second Lieutenant	Thomas Brown	Aug. 24, '61	Resigned Oct. 1, '62
"	William Munger	Oct. 1, '62	
E.			
Captain	Samuel P. Tipton	Aug. 24, '61	Resigned March 15, '62
First Lieutenant	Edwin F. Babcock	Aug. 24, '61	Resigned Nov. 22, 62
"	David H. Porter	March 15, '62	
"	Augustus Whiting	Nov. 22, '62	
Second Lieutenant	David H. Porter	Aug. 24, '61	Promoted
"	Augustus Whiting	March 15, '62	Promoted
"	Marcus L. Moore	Nov. 22, '62	
F.			
Captain	Reuben Bowman	Aug. 24, '61	Resigned June 17, '62
"	Melville H. Musser	June 17, '62	
First Lieutenant	Melville H. Musser	Aug. 24, '61	Promoted
"	Neil T. Shannon	June 17, '62	Killed in battle Aug. 30, '62
"	Isaiah Stickle	Aug. 30, '62	
Second Lieutenant	Neil T. Shannon	Aug. 24, '61	Promoted
"	Isaiah Stickle	June 17, '62	Promoted
"	Levi H. Leib	Aug. 30, '62	Died of wounds
"	Joseph E. Cox	Sept. 26, '62	
G.			
Captain	Benjamin F. Marsh, jr	Aug. 24, '61	
First Lieutenant	John G. Fonda	Aug. 24, '61	Resigned Dec. 27, 1861
"	Thomas Logan	Dec. 27, '61	Transferr'd to 12th cavalry
"	John J. Weakley	March 12, '62	
Second Lieutenant	Thomas Logan	Aug. 24, '61	Promoted
"	John G. Weakley	Dec. 27, '61	Promoted
"	William H. Williams	March 12, '62	
H.			
Captain	James D. Walker	Aug. 24, '61	Resigned Jan. 17, '62
"	Silas C. Higgins	Jan. 17, '62	
First Lieutenant	Silas C. Higgins	Aug. 24, '61	Promoted
"	Joseph B. Vernard	Jan. 17, '62	
Second Lieutenant	John C. Reynolds	Aug. 24, '61	Resigned to Governor
"	Joseph B. Vernard	Sept. 1, '61	Promoted
"	William Birdwell	Jan. 17, '62	Resigned July 5, '62
"	George W. Naylor	July 5, '62	
I.			
Captain	Charles A. Vieregg	Aug. 24, '61	
First Lieutenant	Henry Bartling	Aug. 24, '61	
Second Lieutenant	John H. Cacy	Aug. 24, '61	Resigned July. 1, '62
"	Albert T. Hall	July 1, '62	
K.			
Captain	Presley G. Athey	Aug. 24, '61	Resigned Jan. 27, '62
"	Thomas W. Jones	Jan. 27, '62	
First Lieutenant	Thomas W. Jones	Aug. 24, '61	Promoted
"	Benjamin F. Garrett	Jan. 27, '62	
Second Lieutenant	Benjamin F. Garrett	Aug. 24, '61	Promoted
"	Franklin Kinman	Jan. 27, '62	

SCHEDULE G—Continued.

		Rank.	Remarks.
L.			
Captain	Sterling P. Delano	Aug. 24, '61	Died April 27, '62
"	Francis T. Moore	May 6, '62	
First Lieutenant	James K. Catlin	Aug. 24, '61	Promoted Adjutant
Second Lieutenant	Joseph L. Sawyer	Aug. 24, '61	Resigned Oct. 25, '61
"	Francis T. Moore	Nov. 15, '61	Promoted
"	John Clayton	May 6, '62	
M.			
Captain	David Sollenbarger	Dec. 30, '61	
First Lieutenant	Henry B. Crawford	Dec. 30, '61	
Second Lieutenant	William A. Mattice	Dec. 30, '61	

Schedule G—Continued.

Roster of Third Cavalry Regiment Illinois Volunteers.

Field and Staff.		Rank.	Remarks.
Colonel	Eugene A. Carr	Aug. 15, '61	Promoted to Brig. General
"	Lafayette McCrellis	March 7, '62	[March 7, 1862
Lieutenant Colonel	Lafayette McCrellis	Aug. 30, '61	Promoted
"	James M. Ruggles	March 7, '62	
Major	Thomas Hamar	Aug. 30, '61	Resigned to Governor
"	Louis D. Hubbard	Oct. 19, '61	
"	James M. Ruggles	Sept. 11, '61	Promoted
"	Thomas W. Macfall	Sept. 26, '62	Resigned to Governor Oct.
"	James H. O'Conner	March 7, '62	[15, 1862
"	John McConnell	Sept. 11, '61	
Adjutant	William O'Connell	Aug. 29, '62	Promoted
"	Thomas W. Sullivan	Oct. 24, '61	Mustered out June 17, '62
"	Norreden Cowen	Sept. 6, '62	Declined
"	William McEvoy	Sept. 6, '62	
" 1st Batt'n	Theodore Leland	Jan. 1, '62	
" 2d Batt'n	James S. Crow	Jan. 1, '62	
" 3d Batt'n	Burr Sanders	Jan. 1, '62	
Quartermaster	Byron O. Carr	Sept. 6, '61	
"	Theodore Leland	Sept. 6, '62	Declined and returned
"	John B. Bierce	Sept. 6, '62	
" 1st Batt'n			
" 2d Batt'n			
" 3d Batt'n			
Commissary	James S. Crow	Sept. 6, '62	Declined and returned
"	Julius Weiss	Sept. 6, '62	
Surgeon	Albert H. Lanphere	Sept. 24, '61	Resigned December 26, '61
"	Asa Bigelow	Jan. 22, '62	Resigned Oct. 1, 1862
"	J. Spafford Hunt	Oct. 1, '62	
Ass't Surgeon	J. Spafford Hunt	Sept. 4, '61	Promoted
"	Charles N. Irwin	Nov. 14, '62	
Chaplain	Horace M. Carr	Sept. 6, '61	

Company A.

Captain	Dwight D. Johnson	Sept. 21, '61	Honor'bly discharged Sept. [11, 1862
"	Richard H. Ballinger	Sept. 11, '62	
First Lieutenant	Andrew J. Taylor	Sept. 21, '61	Resigned Februray 6, 1862
"	Joshua Tuthill	Feb. 6, '62	Resigned August 11, 1862
"	Jesse W. Brice	Aug. 11, '62	
Second Lieutenant	Joshua Tuthill	Sept. 21, '61	Promoted
"	Richard H. Ballinger	Feb. 6, '62	Promoted
"	James W. Kincaid	Sept. 11, '62	

B.

Captain	Joseph S. Maus	Sept. 21, '61	Resigned July 8, 1862
"	John B. Baker	July 8, '62	
First Lieutenant	Joel B. Ketchum	Sept. 21, '61	Resigned March 18, 1862
"	John B. Baker	March 18, '62	Promoted
"	Samuel L. Shellenberger	July 8, '62	
Second Lieutenant	Michael Fisher	Sept. 21, '62	Resigned Dec. 26, '61
"	William E. Dorwin	Dec. 26, '61	Resigned June 18, 1862
"	Charles C. Worth	July 8, '62	

SCHEDULE G—Continued.

		Rank.	Remarks.

C.

Captain	Charles P. Dunbaugh	Sept. 21, '61.	Resigned May 16, 1862...
"	David Black	May 16, '62	
First Lieutenant	David Black	Sept. 21, '61.	Promoted
"	Augustus W. Tilford	May 16, '62.	Resigned Sept. 7, 1862...
"	James B. Black	Sept. 7, '62.	
Second Lieutenant	Augustus W. Tilford	Sept. 21, '62.	Promoted
"	James B. Black	May 16, '62.	Promoted
"	Henry M. Sturtevant	Sept. 7, '62.	

D.

Captain	Thomas M. Davis	Sept. 21, '61.	
First Lieutenant	James K. McLean	Sept. 21, '61.	
Second Lieutenant	Moses Lytaker	Sept. 21, '61.	Resigned Dec. 5, '61
"	Jonathan Kershner	Dec. 5, '61	

E.

Captain	John L. Campbell	Sept. 21, '61.	
First Lieutenant	Charles C. Guard	Sept. 21, '61.	Promoted Surgeon of 29th
"	Thomas B. Vaughn	Sept. 25, '61.	[Infantry
Second Lieutenant	Thomas B. Vaughn	Sept. 21, '61.	Promoted
"	Willis B. Hargrave	Sept. 25, '61.	

F.

Captain	Thomas W. Macfall	Sept. 21, '61.	Resigned June 21, 1862
"	Wellington S. Lee	June 21, '62.	
First Lieutenant	Wellington S. Lee	Sept. 21, '61.	Promoted
"	James W. Lay	June 21, '62.	
Second Lieutenant	John Hendrickson	Dec. 28, '61.	Died January 17, 1862
"	James W. Lay	Jan. 17, '62.	Promoted
"	Frederick W. Dickhut	June 21, '62.	

G.

Captain	James B. Moore	Sept. 21, '61.	Resigned April 8, 1862
"	Enos P. McPhail	April 8, '62.	
First Lieutenant	Enos P. McPhail	Sept. 21, '61.	Promoted
"	Charles N. Clark	April 8, '62.	
Second Lieutenant	Charles L. Raymond	Sept. 21, '61.	Resigned February 10, '62
"	Charles N. Clark	Feb. 10, '62.	Promoted
"	Warren Yaples	April 8, '62.	

H.

Captain	Edward Rutledge	Sept. 21, '61.	Resigned December 31, '61
"	Thomas G. McClelland	Dec. 31, '61.	Died May 11, 1862
"	Andrew B. Kirkbridge	May 12, '62.	
First Lieutenant	Thomas G. McClelland	Sept. 21, '61.	Promoted
"	Andrew B. Kirkbridge	Dec. 31, '61.	Promoted
"	George H. Horton	May 12, '62.	
Second Lieutenant	Andrew B. Kirkbridge	Sept. 21, '61.	Promoted
"	George H. Horton	Dec. 31, '61.	Promoted
"	Wash'n A. Kirkpatrick	May 12, '62.	

SCHEDULE G—Continued.

		Rank.	Remarks.

I.

Captain	James Nicolls	Sept. 21, '61	Resigned July 25, 1862
"	Samuel F. Dolloff	July 25, '62	
First Lieutenant	Samuel F. Dolloff	Sept. 21, '61	Promoted
"	John Duncan	July 25, '62	
Second Lieutenant	Edward O. Rowley	Sept. 21, '61	Resigned January 13, 1862
"	John Paul	Jan. 14, '62	Died August 10, 1862
"	Francis Cullum	Aug. 15, '62	

K.

Captain	Robert H. Carnahan	Sept. 21, '61	
First Lieutenant	Andrew Weider	Sept. 21, '61	
Second Lieutenant	John Zimmerman	Sept. 21, '61	

L.

Captain	David R. Sparks	Sept. 21, '61	
First Lieutenant	Norreden Cowen	Sept. 21, '61	
Second Lieutenant	Aaron Vanhooser	Sept. 21, '61	Resigned April 12, '62
"	Benjamin F. Cowel	May 1, '62	

M.

Captain	George E. Pease	Sept. 21, '61	Resigned December 17, '61
"	James H. O'Conner	Dec. 17, '61	Promoted Major
"	Shuler Vrooman	Dec. 20, '61	
First Lieutenant	Henry M. Condee	Sept. 21, '62	Resigned Nov. 27, 1861
"	James H. O'Conner	Nov. 27, '61	Promoted
"	Shuler Vrooman	Dec. 17, '62	Promoted
"	Charles F. Russell	Dec. 20, '62	
Second Lieutenant	James H. O'Conner	Sept. 21, '61	Promoted
"	Joseph Horseman	Nov. 27, '61	Died—commission in office
"	Shuler Vrooman	Nov. 27, '61	Promoted
"	Charles F. Russell	Dec. 17, '62	Promoted

SCHEDULE G—Continued.

Roster of Fourth Cavalry Regiment Illinois Volunteers.

Field and Staff.		Rank.	Remarks.
Colonel	T. Lyle Dickey	Aug. 6, '61	
Lieutenant Colonel	William McCullough	Oct. 3, '61	Killed in battle Dec. 5, '62
"	Martin R. M. Wallace	Dec. 5, '62	
Major	Charles C. James	Oct. 3, '61	Resigned May 5, '62
"	William McCullough	Aug. 20, '61	Promoted
"	William L. Gibson	May 5, '62	
"	Martin R. M. Wallace	Oct. 4, '61	Promoted Lieut. Colonel.
"	Embury D. Osband	Dec. 5, '62	
"	Samuel M. Bowman	Oct. 5, '61	Resigned June 20, '62
"	Mindret Wemple	July 1, '62	
Adjutant	Harry B. Dox	Oct. 13, '61	Resigned May 3, '62
"	Alexander T. Crego	Aug. 1, '62	
" 1st Batt'n			
" 2d Batt'n	Hezekiah T. Buckley	March 1, '62	
" 3d Batt'n			
Quartermaster	Raymond W. Hanford	Aug. 1, '62	
" 1st Batt'n			
" 2d Batt'n			
" 3d Batt'n			
Commissary	David Jolly	Aug. 1, '62	
Surgeon	Darius A. Dow	Oct. 15, '61	Resigned April 20, '62
"	Hiram C. Luce	May 20, '62	
Ass't Surgeon	Hiram C. Luce	Sept. 29, '61	Promoted May 20, '62
"	William T. Beadles	Oct. 11, '62	
Chaplain	Alfred Eddy	Sept. 16, '61	Resigned, Feb. 1, '62
"	Samuel Hibben	Feb. 10, '62	Died November 9, '62
"	Eben G. Trask	Oct. 27, '62	
COMPANY A.			
Captain	Embury D. Osband	Aug. 23, '61	Promoted Major
"	James Sherlock	Dec. 5, '62	
First Lieutenant	David H. Gile	Aug. 23, '61	
Second Lieutenant	James Sherlock	Aug. 23, '61	Promoted Captain
B.			
Captain	Charles C. James	Aug. 23, '61	Major
"	Garrett L. Collins	Sept. 5, '61	
First Lieutenant	Garrett L. Collins	Aug. 23, '61	Promoted
"	Joseph E. Hitt	Sept. 5, '61	
Second Lieutenant	Alexander T. Crego	Aug. 23, '61	Promoted Adjutant
"	Charlie H. Dickey	Aug. 1, '62	
C.			
Captain	Charles D. Townsend	Aug. 27, '61	
First Lieutenant	George A. Walter	Aug. 23, '61	Resigned Sept. 3, '62
"	Asher B. Hall	May 3, '62	
Second Lieutenant	Asher B. Hall	Sept. 2, '61	Promoted
"	William W. Webber	May 3 '62	
D.			
Captain	John H. Felter	Aug. 27, '61	
First Lieutenant	Edmund Moore	Aug. 23, '61	Resigned Feb. 23, '62
"	Charles H. Chapin	March 1, '62	
Second Lieutenant	Eli C. Sheafer	Aug. 27, '61	Resigned April 24, '62
"	Ira W. Smith	April 24, '62	

SCHEDULE G—Continued.

		Rank.	Remarks.
E.			
Captain	Aaron L. Rockwood	Aug. 26, '61	Resigned Aug. 31, '62
"	William D. Wardlaw	Sept. 1, '62	
First Lieutenant	William D. Wardlaw	Aug. 26, '61	Promoted
"	John F. Wallace	Sept. 1, '62	
Second Lieutenant	John F. Wallace	Aug. 26, '61	Promoted
"	James W. Willis	Sept. 1, '62	
F.			
Captain	Anthony T. Search	Aug. 30, '61	
First Lieutenant	Raymond W. Hanford	Aug. 30, '61	Quartermaster
"	Orrin W. Cartter	Aug. 1, '62	
Second Lieutenant	Alonzo W. Loutzenheiser	Aug. 30, '61	Resigned May 3, '62
"	Orrin W. Cartter	May 3, '62	Promoted
"	Jeremiah B. Cook	Aug. 1, '62	
G.			
Captain	Harry D. Cook	Aug. 27, '61	Resigned March 1, 1862
First Lieutenant	Silas W. Ogden	Aug. 27, '61	Resigned September 3, '62
"	John T. Harper	March 1, '62	
"	Elijah H. Baker	Sept. 3, '62	
Second Lieutenant	John T. Harper	Aug. 27, '61	Promoted
"	Elijah H. Baker	March 1, '62	Promoted
"	Abraham Donica	Sept. 3, '62	
H.			
Captain	Mindret Wemple	Aug. 27, '61	Promoted Major
"	Franklin Fiske	July 1, '62	
First Lieutenant	Franklin Fiske	Aug. 27, '61	Promoted
"	William P. Callon	July 1, '62	
Second Lieutenant	William P. Callon	Aug. 27, '61	Promoted
"	Charles H. Chapin	Oct. 5, '61	Promoted
"	John P. Van Dorstan	July 1, '62	
I.			
Captain	George I. Shepardson	Aug. 27, '61	
First Lieutenant	William E. Hapeman	Aug. 27, '61	Promoted to Co. M
"	Benjamin F. Hyde	May 16, '62	
Second Lieutenant	Benjamin F. Hyde	Aug. 27, '61	Promoted
"	John H. Parker	May 16, '61	
K.			
Captain	Phillip Worcester	Sept. 3, '61	
First Lieutenant	William L. Gibson	Aug. 23, '61	Promoted
"	William M. True	May 5, '62	Resigned Sept. 3, '62
"	Henry C. Dashiell	Sept. 3, '62	
Second Lieutenant	William M. True	Sept. 3, '61	Promoted
"	David Jolly	May 5, '62	Commissary
"	Henry C. Dashiel	Aug. 1, '62	Promoted
"	Henry Sirpless	Sept. 3, '62	
L.			
Captain	John M. Longstreth	Aug. 29, '61	Resigned May 3, '62
"	Harvey H. Merriman	May 3, '62	Promoted
First Lieutenant	Harvey H. Merriman	Aug. 29, '61	Promoted
"	Ruthven W. Pike	May 3, '62	
Second Lieutenant	David Quigg	Aug. 29, '61	Appointed Batt'n Adj't
"	James M. McKinstry	Oct. 5, '61	Resigned Nov. 8, '62
"	Robert D. Taylor	Nov. 8, '62	

SCHEDULE G—Continued.

M.

		Rank.	Remarks.
Captain	George Dodge	Aug. 24, '61	Resigned May 16, '62
"	William E. Hapeman	May 16, '62	
First Lieutenant	Samuel Allshouse	Sept. 5, '61	
Second Lieutenant	Edward H. Daily	Sept. 5, '61	Resigned July 31, '62
"	Charles B. Throop	Sept. 22, '62	

SCHEDULE G — Continued.

Roster of Fifth Cavalry Regiment Illinois Volunteers.

Field and Staff.		Rank.	Remarks.
Colonel	John J. Updegraff	Sept. 9, '61	Dismissed
"	Hall Wilson	Dec. 12, '61	
Lieutenant Colonel	Benjamin L. Wiley	Sept. 9, '61	
Major	Thomas A. Apperson	Sept. 9, '61	
"	Speed Butler	Sept. 1, '61	Promoted in regular army.
"	Abel H. Seley	Sept. 28, '61	
"	James Farnan	July 8, '62	
Adjutant	Daniel M. Turney	Sept. 10, '61	Mustered out
"	Edwin P. Martin	Oct. 1, '62	
" 1st Batt'n	Frederick A. Nichey	Jan. 15, '62	Position declined. Com-
" "	Thomas Howes	March 1, '62	[mission canceled.
" 2d Batt'n	Oscar F. Lindsey	Jan. 15, '62	
" 3d Batt'n	Edward P. Harris	Jan. 15, '62	
Quartermaster	Robert C. Wilson	Jan. 15, '62	Mustered out April 28, '62.
" 1st Batt'n	Charles Nicewanger	Jan. 15, '62	
" 2d Batt'n	William N. Elliott	Jan. 15, '62	
" 3d Batt'n	Calvin A. Mann	Jan. 15, '62	
Commissary	Webster C. Wilkinson	Dec. 10, '62	
Surgeon	Charles W. Higgins	Sept. 27, '61	
Ass't Surgeon	John B. Ensey	Sept. 28, '61	
Chaplain	John W. Wood	Dec. 1, '61	

COMPANY A.

Captain	Edward W. Pierson	Aug. 31, '61	
First Lieutenant	Charles Niscewanger	Aug. 31, '61	Resigned July 27, '62
"	Gordon Webster	July 27, '62	
Second Lieutenant	Gordon Webster	Aug. 31, '61	Promoted
"	Jacob M. Cullers	July 27, '62	

B.

Captain	Thomas McKee	Nov. 8, '61	Resigned July 15, '62
"	Kendall B. Peniwell	Oct. 11, '62	
First Lieutenant	Alfred Thayer	Nov. 8, '61	Resigned April 10, '62
"	Robert C. Wilson	April 20, '62	
Second Lieutenant	Dennis A. Harrison	Nov. 8, '61	Discharged for ill health
"	Kendall B. Peniwell	July 26, '62	Promoted. [Sept. 29, '62.
"	Silas W. Wishard	Oct. 11, '62	

C.

Captain	William P. Withers	Nov. 8, '61	
First Lieutenant	James Depew	Nov. 8, '61	Mustered out April 28, '62.
"	Francis A. Wheelock	April 28, '62	
Second Lieutenant	James A. Lawrence	Nov. 8, '61	

D.

Captain	Henry A. Organ	Dec. 30, '61	
First Lieutenant	Samuel J. R. Wilson	Dec. 30, '61	
Second Lieutenant	Calvin Schell	Dec. 30, '61	

E.

Captain	George W. McConkey	Oct. 22, '61	
First Lieutenant	John J. Adams	Oct. 12, '61	
Second Lieutenant	Madison Glassco	Oct. 22, '61	

Schedule G — Continued.

		Rank.	Remarks.

F.

Captain	Horace P. Mumford	Oct. 15, '61	
First Lieutenant	Francis M. Dorathy	Oct. 15, '61	
Second Lieutenant	William Wagenseller	Oct. 15, '61	

G.

Captain	John A. Harvey	Nov. 8, '61	Resigned Dec. 29, '62
First Lieutenant	William N. Elliott	Nov. 8, '61	
Second Lieutenant	Amos H. Smith	Dec. 8, '61	

H.

Captain	Joseph A. Cox	Dec. 8, '61	
First Lieutenant	Washington F. Crane	Dec. 8, '61	
Second Lieutenant	William G. Nelson	Dec. 8, '61	Mustered out April 28, '62.
"	John Nelson	April 28, '62	

I.

Captain	Bartholomew Jenkins	Nov. 8, '61	Resigned April 28, 1862
"	Benjamin G. Glenn	May 8, '62	Resigned Dec. 4, 1862
"	Edwin S. Norfolk	Dec. 4, '62	
First Lieutenant	Edwin S. Norfolk	Nov. 8, '61	Promoted
Second Lieutenant	John F. Smith	Nov. 8, '61	Resigned Sept. 27, 1862.

K.

Captain	James Farnan	Oct. 20, '61	Major
"	Calvin A. Mann	July 8, '62	
First Lieutenant	Charles J. Childs	Sept. 10, '61	
Second Lieutenant	Calvin A. Mann	Oct. 21, '61	Promoted
"	John P. Mann	July 8, '62	

L.

Captain	Henry D. Caldwell	Dec. 30, '61	
First Lieutenant	Harrison H. Brown	Dec. 30, '61	
Second Lieutenant	William N. Berry	Dec. 30, '61	

M.

Captain	Robert Schell	Dec. 8, '61	Resigned Sept. 4, 1862
"	Alexander Jessup	Sept. 4, '62	
First Lieutenant	Samuel Burrell	Dec. 8, '61	
Second Lieutenant	Albert S. Robinson	Dec. 8, '61	Dismissed for desertion [July 28, 1862.

SCHEDULE G — Continued.

Roster of Sixth Cavalry Regiment Illinois Volunteers.

Field and Staff.		Rank.	Remarks.
Colonel	Thomas H. Cavanaugh	Aug. 28, '61	Resigned March 28, '62
"	Benjamin H. Grierson	March 28, '62	
Lieutenant Colonel	John Olney	Aug. 31, '61	Honorably discharged Nov. 1, '62
Major	William L. Caldwell	Aug. 31, '61	Resigned Oct. 14, '62
"	John J. Ritchey	Oct. 15, '62	
"	Arno Voss	Sept. 4, '61	Resigned to Governor
"	Isaac Gibson	Feb. 13, '62	Resigned June 4, '62
"	James D. Stacy	June 4, '62	Resigned Oct. 23, '62
"	Thomas G. S. Herod	Oct. 23, '62	
"	Benjamin H. Grierson	Aug. 28, '61	Promoted
"	Capt. Reuben Loomis	April 13, '62	
Adjutant	Thomas H. Cavanaugh, jr	Aug. 28, '61	Resigned April 15, '62
"	William H. Beck	Oct. 21, '62	
" 1st Batt'n	Joseph T. Janes	Jan. 9, '62	
" 2d Batt'n	Samuel N. Docker	Jan. 9, '62	Resigned March 4, '62
" "	Nelson B. Newman	March 4, '62	Killed
" 3d Batt'n	Henry C. Jacques	Jan. 9, '62	
Quartermaster	John M. Snyder	Sept. 1, '61	Mustered out June 1, '62.
"	John C. Grierson	Oct. 29, '62	
" 1st Batt'n	James D. Stacy	Jan 9, '62	Mustered out June 1, '62.
" 2d Batt'n	Thomas P. Stacy	Jan. 9, '62	Mustered out June, 1 '62.
" 3d Batt'n	George N. Hubbard	Jan. 9, '62	Mustered out June 1, '62.
Commissary	George T. Redfern	Oct. 21, '62	
Surgeon	John N. Niglas	Oct. 1, '61	
Assistant Surgeon	James S. Whitmire	Oct. 13, '61	Promoted to 56th infantry.
"	Archibald B. Agnew	Sept. 24, '62	
Chaplain	James F. Jaquess	Aug. 28, '61	Promoted to Col. 73d infantry

COMPANY A.

Captain	George W. Peck	Nov. 19, '61	Died
"	Alonzo Pierce	Nov. 22, '62	
First Lieutenant	Thomas Baker	Nov. 19, '61	
Second Lieutenant	Jacob E. Vaughn	Nov. 19, '61	

B.

Captain	James B. Morray	Nov. 17, '61	
First Lieutenant	John C. Fite	Nov. 17, '61	Resigned Nov. 27, '62
Second Lieutenant	Samuel L. Lawrence	Nov. 17, '61	Resigned May 7, '62
"	William B. Peterson	May 7, '62	

C.

Captain	David P. Foster	Nov. 19, '61	
First Lieutenant	William L. Edwards	Nov. 19, '61	Resigned March 14, '62
"	William L. Edwards	April 15, '62	Re-appointed, consent Sec. War
Second Lieutenant	William H. Short	Nov. 19, '61	Resigned April 25, '62
"	Charles H. Hazard	April 25, '62	

SCHEDULE G—Continued.

		Rank.	Remarks.

D.

Captain	Hosea Vise	Jan. 9, '62	
First Lieutenant	William L. Stephens	Jan. 9, '62	Resigned May 7, '62
"	Joseph Coker	May 7, '62	
Second Lieutenant	Joseph Coker	Jan. 9, '62	Promoted
"	James H. Dailey	May 7, '62	

E.

Captain	Isaac Gibson	Oct. 20, '61	Promoted
"	John Lynch	Feb. 13, '62	
First Lieutenant	John Lynch	Nov. 19, '61	Promoted
"	Edward Ball	Feb. 13, '62	
Second Lieutenant	Elijah G. Tarpley	Nov. 19, '61	

F.

Captain	Cressa K. Davis	Jan. 9, '62	
First Lieutenant	William G. Sloan	Jan. 9, '62	
Second Lieutenant	James A. Roark	Jan. 9, '62	Resigned Oct. 23, '62

G.

Captain	John M. Boicourt	Nov. 19, '61	Resigned Oct. 21, '62
"	William D. Glass	Oct. 21, '62	
First Lieutenant	Elijah E. Trovillion	Nov. 19, '61	Resigned May 13, '62
"	Nathaniel B. Cunningham	May 13, '62	Shot by guerrillas Sept. 5, '62
"	William D. Glass	Sept. 5, '62	Promoted
Second Lieutenant	William D. Glass	Nov. 19, '61	Promoted
"	Samuel L. Woodward	Sept. 5, '62	

H.

Captain	John J. Ritchey	Jan. 9, '62	Promoted Major
First Lieutenant	James M. Blades	Jan. 9, '62	Resigned July 18, '62
"	Samuel L. Marshall	July 18, '62	
Second Lieutenant	Samuel L. Marshall	Jan. 9, '62	Promoted
"	Daniel M. Maulding	Sept. 5, '62	

I.

Captain	Reuben Loomis	Nov. 19, '61	Promoted
"	Charles W. Whitsit	April 13, '62	
First Lieutenant	James H. Gordon	Nov. 19, '61	Resigned April 25, '62
"	Charles W. Whitsit	April 25, '62	Promoted
"	Lucius B. Skinner	April 13, '62	
Second Lieutenant	Charles W. Whitsit	Nov. 19, '61	Promoted
"	Lucius B. Skinner	April 25, '62	Promoted
"	Benjamin F. Guiteau	April 13, '62	

K.

Captain	Edward Dawes	Jan. 9, '62	
First Lieutenant	Jesse B. Wilson	Jan. 9, '62	
Second Lieutenant	Cornelius Baker	Jan. 9, '62	

SCHEDULE G—Continued.

		Rank.	Remarks.

L.

Captain	Thomas G. S. Herod	Oct. 15, '61	Promoted Major
"	Matthew L. Starr	Oct. 23, '62	
First Lieutenant	Benedict Crandall	Oct. 15, '61	Resigned May 7, '62
"	Samuel A. Armstrong	May 7, '62	Resigned July 30, '62
"	Matthew L. Starr	July 30, '62	Promoted
"	Firth Charlesworth	Oct. 23, '62	
Second Lieutenant	Henry Stout	Oct. 15, '61	Resigned March 14, '62
"	Samuel A. Armstrong	March 14, '62	Promoted
"	Matthew L. Starr	May 7, '62	Promoted
"	Firth Charlesworth	July 30, '62	Promoted
"	John W. Hughes	Oct. 23, '62	

M.

Captain	Isaiah M. Sperry	Jan. 9, '62	
First Lieutenant	Abraham Cover	Jan. 9, '62	Resigned March 14, '62
Second Lieutenant	Charles A. Rixlebin	Jan. 9, '62	
"	Edgar A. Finch	March 14, '62	

SCHEDULE G—Continued.

Roster of Seventh Cavalry Regiment Illinois Volunteers.

Field and Staff.		Rank.	Remarks.
Colonel	William Pitt Kellogg	Sept. 8, '61	Resigned June 1, 1862
Lieutenant Colonel	Edward Prince	Sept. 8, '61	9, 1862.
Major	Cyrus Hall	Sept. 21, '61	Resigned for promot'n Feb.
"	Henry Case	Feb. 1, '61	Resigned April 24, 1862.
"	Horatio C. Nelson	April 24, '62	
"	Jonas Rawalt	Sept. 21, '61	Resigned June 10, 1862
"	William D. Blackburn	June 10, '62	
"	Zennas Applington	Nov. 13, '61	Killed in battle May. 15,'62
"	Antrim P. Koehler	May 15, '62	
Adjutant	Sidney Stockdale	Jan. 30, '62	Mustered out May 26, 1862
"	George A. Root	Oct. 1, '62	
" 1st Batt'n	Allen W. Heald	Oct. 1, '62	
" 2d Batt'n	George Bestor	Jan. 15, '62	
" 3d Batt'n	Charles Wills	Jan. 15, '62	
Quartermaster	William A. Dickerman	Oct. 25, '61	Mustered out May 26, '62
"	James R. W. Hinchman	Oct. 28, '62	
" 1st Batt'n			
" 2d Batt'n	Josiah T. Noys	Dec. 25, '61	
" 3d Batt'n	John W. Resor	Dec. 25, '61	Mustered out May 26, '62.
Commissary	Henry F. Barker	Oct. 1, '62	
Surgeon	Clark D. Rankin	Oct. 28, '61	Resigned June 1, 1862
"	Daniel Stahl	Sept. 9, '62	
Ass't Surgeon	Thomas J. Riggs	Jan. 1, '62	
Chaplain	Simon G. Minor	Oct. 3, '61	

COMPANY A.

Captain	William D. Blackburn	Aug. 10, '61	Major
"	Charles Hunting	June 10, '62	
First Lieutenant	Charles Hunting	Aug. 10, '61	Promoted
Second Lieutenant	James R. Morrison	Aug. 10, '61	Resigned May 5, 1862
"	Jacob J. LaGrange	May 5, '62	

B.

Captain	Zenas Applington	Aug. 11, '61	Promoted
"	Henry C. Forbes	Nov. 18, '61	
First Lieutenant	Henry C. Forbes	Aug. 11, '61	Promoted
"	William McClausland	Nov. 18, '61	
Second Lieutenant	Oscar F. Sammis	Aug. 11, '61	

C.

Captain	Prescott Bartlett	Aug. 12, '61	
First Lieutenant	John H. Shaw	Aug. 12, '61	
Second Lieutenant	Benjamin F. Berkley	Aug. 12, '61	Resigned Sept. 2, 1862
"	Stephen H. Richardson	Sept. 2, '62	

D.

Captain	Wright Woolsey	Aug. 13, '61	Resigned Jan. 8, 1862
"	Levi Hodge	Jan. 8, '62	Resigned June 1, 1862
"	William H. Reynolds	June 1, '62	
First Lieutenant	William H. Reynolds	Aug. 13, '61	Promoted
"	David W. Bradshaw	June 1, '62	
Second Lieutenant	Levi Hodge	Aug. 13, '61	Promoted
"	William O. Yaryan	Jan. 8, '62	Resigned May 23, 1862
"	David W. Bradshaw	May 23, '62	Promoted
"	James S. McCool	June 1, '62	

SCHEDULE G — Continued.

		Rank.	Remarks.

E.

Captain	John M. Graham	Aug. 14, '61	
First Lieutenant	Daniel Hasty	Aug. 14, '61	Resigned May 28, 1862
"	Miles G. Wiley	May 29, '62	
Second Lieutenant	James M. Caldwell	Aug. 14, '61	

F.

Captain	Antrim P. Koehler	Aug. 15, '61	Promoted
"	Asa W. McDonald	June 29, '62	
First Lieutenant	Charles Lee	Aug. 15, '61	
Second Lieutenant	Jacob Schamb	Aug. 15, '61	Resigned April 15, 1862
"	James Breeze	Jan. 29, '62	

G.

Captain	George W. Trafton	Aug. 16, '61	
First Lieutenant	Richard Harden	Aug. 16, '61	Died
"	James M. Gaston	Dec. 5, '61	
Second Lieutenant	William H. Styles	Aug. 16, '61	

H.

Captain	Milton L. Webster	Aug. 17, '61	From 14th Infantry
First Lieutenant	Isaac V. D. Moore	Aug. 17, '61	Died
"	Jacob C. Miller	April 15, '62	Resigned June 8, '62
"	Henry Voris	June 8, '62	Dismissed Nov. 11, 1862
"	Uriah Brant	Nov. 11, '62	
Second Lieutenant	Jacob C. Miller	Aug. 17, '61	Promoted
"	Uriah Brant	April 9, '62	Promoted
"	Samuel A. Kitch	Nov. 11, '62	

I.

Captain	Arthur J. Gallagher	Aug. 19, '61	Resigned June 20, 1862
"	William Ashmead	June 20, '62	
First Lieutenant	William H. Stratton	Aug. 19, '61	
Second Lieutenant	William Ashmead	Aug. 19, '61	Pomoted
"	Stephen G. Washburn	June 20, '62	

K.

Captain	Horatio C. Nelson	Aug. 20, '61	Promoted
"	Joseph R. Herring	April 24, '62	
First Lieutenant	Joseph R. Herring	Aug. 20, '61	Promoted
"	John W. Maxwell	April 24, '62	
Second Lieutenant	Andrew B. Hulit	Aug. 20, '61	Resigned April 24, 1862
"	Henry Jane	June 7, '62	

L.

Captain	George M. Scott	Aug. 21, '61	Resigned July 3, 1862
"	Squire A. Epperson	July 3, '62	
First Lieutenant	Warren W. Porter	Aug. 21, '61	
Second Lieutenant	Squire A. Epperson	Aug. 21, '61	Promoted
"	Daniel M. Wilt	July 3, '62	

K.

Captain	John P. Ludwig	Aug. 22, '61	Resigned May 28, 1862
"	Bernhard C. Janssen	May 28, '62	Promoted
First Lieutenant	Bernhard C. Janssen	Aug. 22, '61	Promoted
"	Charles Stoll	May 28, '62	
Second Lieutenant	John H. Meyer	Aug. 22, '61	Resigned May 28, 1862
"	Henry Nicholson	May 28, '62	

Schedule G—Continued.

Roster of Eighth Cavalry Regiment Illinois Volunteers.

Field and Staff.		Rank.	Remarks.
Colonel	John F. Farnsworth	Aug. 12, '61	Promoted Brig. Gen. Dec.
"	William Gamble	Dec. 5, '62	[5, '62
Lieutenant Colonel	William Gamble	Sept. 5, '61	Promoted
"	David R. Clendenin	Dec. 5, '62	
Major	David R. Clendenin	Sept. 18, '61	Promoted
"	Elisha S. Kelly	Dec. 5, '62	
"	John L. Beveridge	Sept. 18, '61	
"	William G. Conklin	Sept. 18, '61	Resigned
"	Daniel Dustin	Jan. 8, '62	Resigned Sept. 8, '62
"	William H. Medill	Sept. 10, '62	
Adjutant	Robert T. Sill	Oct. 1, '62	
" 1st Batt'n	Campbell W. Waite	Sept. 18, '61	Resigned Feb. 17, '62
" 2d Batt'n	Edmund Gifford	Sept. 18, '61	Resigned July 6, '62
" 3d Batt'n	John Tifield	Dec. 1, '61	
Quartermaster	James S. VanPatton	Sept. 1, '62	Resigned Oct. 3, '62
" 1st Batt'n			
" 2d Batt'n			
" 3d Batt'n			
Commissary	Bradley L. Chamberlain	Sept. 1, '62	
Surgeon	Abner Hard	Sept. 15, '61	
Ass't Surgeon	Samuel K. Crawford	Sept. 18, '61	
Chaplain	Lucius C. Matlack	Oct. 8, '61	

Company A.

Captain	Patrick G. Jennings	Sept. 18, '61	Resigned Jan. 10, '62
"	George A. Forsyth	Feb 12, '62	
First Lieutenant	Bryant Beach	Sept. 18, '61	
Second Lieutenant	Nelson L. Blanchard	Sept. 18, '61	Resigned Jan. 20, '62
"	Richard Vanblack	Jan. 27, '62	

B.

Captain	Lorenzo H. Whitney	Sept. 18, '61	Resigned July 15, '62
"	John G. Smith	July 17, '62	
First Lieutenant	John G. Smith	Sept. 18, '61	Promoted
"	John A. Kelly	Sept. 10, '62	
Second Lieutenant	Jacob M. Liglen	Sept. 18, '61	Resigned July 15, '62
"	S. Spencer Carr	Sept. 10, '62	

C.

Captain	Alpheus Clark	Sept. 18, '61	
First Lieutenant	Daniel D. Lincoln	Sept. 18, '61	
Second Lieutenant	John C. Mitchell	Sept. 18, '61	

D.

Captain	Jacob S. Gerhart	Sept. 18, '61	
First Lieutenant	Henry I. Hotopp	Sept. 18, '61	
Second Lieutenant	Carlos H. Verbeck	Sept. 18, '61	

E.

Captain	Elisha S. Kelly	Sept. 18, '61	Promoted Major
First Lieutenant	Benjamin L. Flagg	Sept. 18, '61	Resigned July 15, '62
Second Lieutenant	Woodbury M. Taylor	Sept. 18, '61	

F

Captain	Reuben Cleveland	Sept. 18, '61	Resigned July 31, '62
First Lieutenant	Edward S. Smith	Sept. 18, '61	
Second Lieutenant	Alvin P. Granger	Sept. 18, '61	

Schedule G — Continued.

		Rank.	Remarks.
G.			
Captain	William H. Medill	Sept. 18, '61.	Major
"	Dennis J. Hynes	Sept. 10, '62.	
First Lieutenant	George A. Forsyth	Sept. 18, '61.	Promoted to A
"	Dennis J. Hynes	Feb. 12, '62	Promoted
"	Malcomb H. Wing	Sept. 10, '62.	
Second Lieutenant	Dennis J. Hynes	Sept. ,18 '61.	Promoted
"	Malcomb H. Wing	Feb. 12, '62.	Promoted
"	George F. Warner	Sept. 10, '62.	
H.			
Captain	Rufus M. Hooker	Sept. 18, '61.	Died Aug. 1, 1862
First Lieutenant	Charles Harrison	Sept. 18, '61.	
Second Lieutenant	John M. Southworth	Sept. 18, '61.	
I.			
Captain	Hiram L. Rapelge	Sept. 18, '61.	Resigned August 29, '62
First Lieutenant	William H. Sheldon	Sept. 18, '61.	
Second Lieutenant	John Cool	Sept. 18, '61.	
K.			
Captain	Elon J. Farnsworth	Dec. 24, '61.	
First Lieutenant	George W. Flagg	Sept. 18, '61.	Resigned Jan. 24, '62
"	Darius Sullivan	Jan. 28, '62.	
Second Lieutenant	Darius Sullivan	Sept. 18, '61.	Promoted
"	I. Wayland Trask	Jan. 28, '62.	
L.			
Captain	Daniel Dustin	Sept. 18, '61.	Promoted
"	Amasa E. Dana	Jan. 8, '62.	Resigned July 15, '62
"	John M. Waite	July 17, '62.	
First Lieutenant	Amasa E. Dana	Sept. 18, '61.	Promoted
"	John M. Waite	Jan. 8, '62.	Promoted
Second Lieutenant	John M. Waite	Sept. 18, '61.	Promoted
"	Austin C. Lowry	Jan. 8, '62.	Resigned July 15, '62
M.			
Captain	John Austin	Sept. 18, '61.	
First Lieutenant	Andrew J. Martin	Sept. 18, '61.	Resigned Oct. 24, '62
Second Lieutenant	John F. Austin	Sept. 18, '61.	

Schedule G—Continued.

Roster of Ninth Cavalry Regiment Illinois Volunteers.

Field and Staff.		Rank.	Remarks.
Colonel	Albert G. Brackett	Sept. 1, '61	
Lieutenant Colonel	Solomon A. Paddock	Dec. 2, '61	Died
"	Hiram F. Sickles	Feb. 18, '62	
Major	Rossell M. Hough	Sept. 10, '61	Resigned April 23, '62
"	Henry B. Burgh	Aug. 16, '62	
"	Hiram F. Sickles	Sept. 24, '61	Promoted Lieut. Colonel
"	William J. Wallis	Feb. 18, '62	
"	Hector J. Humphrey	Sept. 25, '61	
Adjutant	Joseph H. Knox	Sept. 18, '61	
"	Thomas W. Stevenson	Dec. 2, '61	Mustered out April 11, '62
"	John H. Carpenter	Oct. 1, '62	
" 1st Batt'n	Charles M. Waterbury	Jan. 1, '62	Mustered out
" 2nd Batt'n	Samuel Rockwood	Jan. 1, '62	Resigned April 10, '62
" "	William C. Blackburn	April 10, '62	Promoted Captain Co. A
" 3d Batt'n	Frank Cantella	Jan. 1, '62	Mustered out
Quartermaster	Samuel H. Price	Sept. 14, '61	Mustered out April 7, '62
"	Samuel H. Price	Oct. 1, '62	
" 1st Batt'n	Joseph W. Brackett	Jan. 1, '62	Mustered out April 7, '62
" 2nd Batt'n	Thomas E. Morrison	Jan. 1, '62	Mustered out April 7, '62
" 3d Batt'n	Frank Sheffield	Jan. 1, '62	Mustered out April 7, '62
Commissary	Joseph W. Brackett	Oct. 1, '62	
Surgeon	Charles Brackett	Feb. 15, '62	
Assistant Surgeon	James W. Brackett	Sept. 10, '61	
Chaplain	O. Winsor Briggs	Sept. 25, '61	

Company A.

Captain	Henry B. Burgh	Sept. 18, '61	Promoted Major
"	William C. Blackburn	Aug. 16, '62	
First Lieutenant	William C. Blackburn	Sept. 18, '61	Promoted
"	William M. Benton	April 10, '62	
Second Lieutenant	William M. Benton	Sept. 18, '61	Promoted
"	David Hillier	April 10, '62	

B.

Captain	Hector J. Humphrey	Sept. 19, '61	Promoted Major
"	Thaddeus W. O. Broffett	Sept. 25, '61	
First Lieutenant	Thaddeus W. O. Broffett	Sept. 19, '61	Promoted
"	Ransom Harrington	Sept. 25, '61	
Second Lieutenant	Ransom Harrington	Sept. 19, '61	Promoted
"	Arthur M. Kinzie	Sept. 25, '61	

C.

Captain	John S. Buckle	Sept. 19, '61	Resigned April 2, '62
"	Charles W. Blakemore	April 2, '62	Resigned Sept. 27, '62
"	Francis H. McArthur	Sept. 27, '62	
First Lieutenant	Charles W. Blakemore	Sept. 19, '61	Promoted
"	Joseph W. Brackett	April 8, '62	Promoted Commissary
"	Anthony R. Mock	Oct. 1, '62	
Second Lieutenant	Francis H. McArthur	Sept. 19, '61	Promoted
"	Charles M. Marshall	Oct. 1, '62	

D.

Captain	William J. Wallis	Sept. 26, '61	Promoted Major
"	Lewellyn Cowen	March 1, '62	

SCHEDULE G—Continued.

		Rank.	Remarks.
First Lieutenant..	Lewellyn Cowen.......	Sept. 26, '61.	Promoted ....
" "	John H. McMahon.....	March 1, '62.	....
Second Lieutenant	John H. McMahon.....	Sept. 26, '61.	Promoted ....
" "	George W. Conn	March 1, '62.	Resigned Oct. 18, '62.....
" "	Patrick Kelly.........	Oct. 18, '62..	....

E.

Captain	Ira R. Gifford..........	Oct. 3, '61...	....
First Lieutenant..	Richard D. Ellsworth....	Oct. 3, '61...	Resigned April 7, '62.....
Second Lieutenant	Benjamin O. Wilkinson..	Oct. 3, '61...	Died at Helena Aug. 23, '62
" "	Thomas E. Morrison	April 8, '62..	....
" "	Spencer T. Weirick.....	Aug. 24, '62..	....

F.

Captain	Bernard A. Stampoffski.	Oct. 7, '61...	Mustered out May 29, '62..
" "	Marland L. Perkins.....	May 29, '62..	....
First Lieutenant..	Marland L. Perkins	Oct. 7, '61...	Promoted ....
" "	Erastus G. Butler.......	May 29, '62..	....
Second Lieutenant	Dwight S. Heald......	Oct. 7, '61...	Resigned Nov. 7, '61.....
" "	Erastus G. Butler.	Nov. 7, '61...	Promoted ....
" "	James Smith...........	May 29, '62..	Resigned Sept. 4, '62.....
" "	George H. Boone.......	Sept. 4, '62 ..	....

G

Captain	Henry M. Buell.........	Oct. 9, '61...	Dismissed for desertion,
First Lieutenant..	John E. Warner........	Oct. 9, '61...	[Sept. 9, '62
" "	Sidney O. Roberts......	Nov. 25, '62 .	Transferred to U. S. Army
Second Lieutenant	Henry A. Huntington...	Oct. 9, '61...	Resigned Oct. 21, '62.....
" "	Arza F. Brown.........	Nov. 9, '61...	Promoted ....
" "	Sidney O. Roberts......	Oct. 21, '62..	....
" "	Ennis Van Dolson......	Nov. 25, '62 .	....

H.

Captain	Linns D. Bishop........	Oct. 17, '61..	....
First Lieutenant..	Edwin W. Luce	Oct. 17, '61..	Resigned April 2, '62.....
" "	Thomas W. Stevenson..	April 8, '62..	Resigned Oct. 1, '62.....
" "	Alexander H. McClure ..	Oct. 1, '62...	....
Second Lieutenant	Henry Prather.........	Oct. 17, '61..	Resigned Nov. 10, '61....
" "	Walter B. Anderson	Nov. 10, '61 .	Resigned May 26, '62.....
" "	Anthony R. Mock	June 1, '62 ..	Promoted to Co. C.......
" "	Edward Cunningham....	Oct. 1, '62...	....

I.

Captain	William M. Chidister....	Nov. 17, '61..	Hon. discharged Oct. 3, '62
" "	Joseph W. Harper......	Oct. 3, '62...	....
First Lieutenant..	William M. Chidister....	Oct. 23, '61..	Promoted ....
" "	Joseph W. Harper......	Nov. 17, '61..	Promoted ....
" "	Leander L. Shattuck....	Oct. 3, '62...	....
Second Lieutenant	Joseph W. Harper......	Oct. 23, '61..	Promoted ....
" "	Leander L. Shattuck....	Nov. 17, '61..	Promoted ....
" "	Abner H. Westbrook....	Oct. 3, '62...	....

K.

Captain	Solomon A. Paddock....	Oct. 26, '61..	Promoted Lieut. Colonel..
" "	Charles S. Cameron.....	Dec. 2, '61...	....
First Lieutenant..	Charles S. Cameron.....	Oct. 26, '61..	Promoted ....
" "	Joseph K. Knox........	Dec. 2, '61...	Resigned April 5, '62.....
" "	Samuel H. Price........	April 8, '62..	Promoted Quartermaster.
" "	William McMannis	Oct. 1, '62...	....
Second Lieutenant	William McMannis	Oct. 26, '61..	Promoted ....
" "	Atherton Clark.........	Oct. 1, '62...	....

SCHEDULE G — Continued.

		Rank.	Remarks.
L.			
Captain	Louis F. Booth	Nov. 11, '61	
First Lieutenant	Charles T. Scammon	Nov. 11, '61	
Second Lieutenant	William E. Bayley	Nov. 11, '61	
M.			
Captain	Eliphalet R. Knight	Nov. 30, '61	
First Lieutenant	Jacob C. Shear	Nov. 30, '61	
Second Lieutenant	Jacob Riner	Nov. 30, '61	Resigned March 27, '62
"	Frank Sheffield	April 8, '62	Resigned Oct. 18, '62
"	John H. Avery	Oct. 18, '62	

SCHEDULE G — Continued.

Roster of Tenth Cavalry Regiment Illinois Volunteers.

Field and Staff.		Rank.	Remarks.
Colonel	James A. Barrett	Nov. 25, '61	Resigned May 15, 1862
"	Dudley Wickersham	May 15, '62	
Lieutenant Colonel	Dudley Wickersham	Nov. 25, '61	Promoted
"	James Stuart	May 15, '62	
Major	Elvis P. Shaw	Dec. 5, '61	
"	Joseph S. Smith	Nov. 25, '61	
"	Marshal L. Stephenson	Nov. 25, '61	
Adjutant	James Stuart	Nov. 25, '61	Mustered out April 4, 1862
"	Gideon Brainard	Oct. 1, '62	
" 1st Batt'n	Eli H. Hosea	Nov. 25, '61	
" 2d Batt'n	Thomas D. Vredenburg	April 8, '62	
" 3d Batt'n	Henry Turney	Nov. 25, '61	
Quartermaster	John H. Barrett	Nov. 25, '61	
" 1st Batt'n	Daniel L. Canfield	Nov. 25, '61	Mustered out April 4, 1862
" 2d Batt'n	John P. Cavanaugh	Nov. 25, '61	Mustered out April 4, 1862
" 3d Batt'n			
Commissary	Edwin R. Neal	Oct. 1, '62	
Surgeon			
Assistant Surgeon	William E. Wilson	Jan. 23, '62	
Chaplain	Francis Springer	Sept. 30, '61	

COMPANY A.

Captain	Garrett Elkin	Nov. 25, '61	Resigned August 2, 1862
"	Christopher H. Anderson	Aug. 2, '62	
First Lieutenant	Alfred A. North	Nov. 25, '61	
Second Lieutenant	Christopher H. Anderson	Nov. 25, '61	Promoted
"	Thomas O'Conner	Aug. 2, '62	

B.

Captain	Samuel N. Hitt	Nov. 25, '61	
First Lieutenant	Augustus A. Shutt	Nov. 25, '61	
Second Lieutenant	Joseph S. McCartney	Feb. 14, '62	Promoted to Co. H
"	Byron L. Crouch	Oct. 29, '62	

C.

Captain	Hiram E. Barstow	Nov. 28, '61	
First Lieutenant	Hiram C. Walker	Nov. 28, '61	
Second Lieutenant	Seth Ingalsbe	Nov. 28, '61	Dis., ill health Nov. 27, '62

D.

Captain	Ephriam Bortle	Nov. 25, '61	Resigned April 12, 1862
"	William Sands	May 1, '62	Resigned October 14, 1862
"	Richard C. Keiley	Oct. 14, '62	
First Lieutenant	Hiram Cady	Nov. 25, '61	Resigned April 12, 1862
"	Richard C. Keiley	May 1, '62	Promoted
"	Thomas D. Vredenberg	Oct. 14, '62	
Second Lieutenant	William Bennett	Nov. 25, '61	Resigned September 4, '62
"	Robert J. Belomy	Sept. 4, '62	

Schedule G — Continued.

		Rank.	Remarks.
E.			
Captain	Henry Reily	Nov. 25, '61	.. ..
First Lieutenant	Columbus Cross	Nov. 25, '61	Resigned April 4, 1862....
" "	William H. Eart	April 4, '62	Resigned July 7, 1862....
" "	Samuel J. Boyd	Sept. 5, '62	....
Second Lieutenant	John Mabee	Nov. 25, '61	Dismissed, ill health, April
" "	Edwin B. Neal	May 31, '62	.............[12, 1862
F.			
Captain	Isaac H. Ferguson	Dec. 31, '61	Resigned June 23, 1862..
" "	William A. Chapin	June 23, '62	....
First Lieutenant	William A. Chapin	Dec. 31, '61	Promoted ....
" "	Felix Droll	June 23, '62	....
Second Lieutenant	Felix Droll	Dec. 31, '61	Promoted ....
" "	William Schwerdsfeger	June 23, '61	....
G.			
Captain	William S. Hunter	Nov. 25, '61	Resigned October 20, 1862
" "	Zimri B. Bates	Oct. 20, '62	....
First Lieutenant	Zimri B. Bates	Nov. 25, '61	Promoted ....
" "	William A. Montgomery	Oct. 20, '62	....
Second Lieutenant	William W. Stinnett	Nov. 25, '61	Resigned October 18, 1862
" "	Alexander Rucker	Oct. 18, '62	....
H.			
Captain	Thomas S. Crafton	Nov. 25, '61	Resigned April 4, 1862....
" "	James Stewart	April 4, '62	Major....................
" "	Joseph S. McCartney	Oct. 29, '62	....
First Lieutenant	Herman B. Hoffman	Nov. 25, '61	....
Second Lieutenant	John W. Crafton	Nov. 25, '61	Resigned March 25, 1862..
" "	Barton W. Fox	March 25, '62	....
I.			
Captain	James Butterfield	Dec. 6, '61	Resigned July 9, 1862....
" "	George Snelling	July 9, '62	....
First Lieutenant	James S. Freeman	Dec. 6, '61	Resigned April 4, 1862....
" "	Daniel L. Canfield	April 4, '62	....
Second Lieutenant	John F. Black	Dec. 6, '61	Resigned October 24, 1862
K.			
Captain	Cavil K. Wilson	Nov. 25, '61	....
First Lieutenant	David H. Wilson	Nov. 25, '61	....
Second Lieutenant	George W. Curry	Nov. 25, '61	....
L.			
Captain	Thomas V. Wilson	Dec. 30, '61	Disch'd ill h'th Sept. 29, '62
First Lieutenant	John G. Roberts	Dec. 30, '61	....
Second Lieutenant	Thomas D. Vredenburg	Dec. 30, '61	Promoted ....
" "	Gardner A. Bruce	April 8, '62	....

Schedule G—Continued.

		Rank.	Remarks.
M.			
Captain	William S. Moore	Dec. 30, '61	Resigned July 7, 1862
"	Elhanen J. Searle	July 7, '62	
First Lieutenant	Elhanen J. Searle	Dec. 30, '61	Promoted
"	Joseph A. McClure	July 17, '62	
Second Lieutenant	William H. Watson	Dec. 30, '61	Dismissed
"	Joseph A. McClure	April 6, '62	Promoted
"	Silas W. Hickox	Sept. 13, '62	

Schedule G—Continued.

Roster of Eleventh Cavalry Regiment Illinois Volunteers.

Field and Staff.		Rank.	Remarks.
Colonel	Robert G. Ingersoll	Oct. 22, '61	
Lieutenant Colonel	Bazil D. Meek	Oct. 22, '61	
Major	Sabine D. Puterbaugh	Oct. 22, '61	Resigned Nov. 1, '62
"	Otto Funke	Nov. 1, '62	
"	David J. Waggoner	Oct. 25, '61	
"	James F Johnson	Oct. 25, '61	Died
"	Lucien H. Kerr	May 25, '62	
Adjutant	David T. N. Sanderson	Sept. 6, '62	Mustered out
" 1st Batt'n	George P. Chappell	Dec. 20, '61	Died
" "	Maurice Dee	May 25, '62	
" 2d Batt'n	Thomas Bracken	Dec. 20, '61	
" 3d Batt'n	Lucien H. Kerr	Dec. 20, '61	Promoted Major
Quartermaster	William Currie	Oct. 22, '61	Mustered out March 23, '62
"	William Currie	Sept. 1, '62	[and mustered in Second
" 1st Batt'n			[Lieut. Co. F.
" 2d Batt'n			
" 3d Batt'n			
Commissary	Maurice Dee	Aug. 29, '62	
Surgeon	Z. James McMaster	Jan. 22, '62	Resigned May 3, '62
"	Robert F. Stratton	July 1, '62	
Assistant Surgeon	Robert F. Stratton	Jan. 23, '62	Promoted
Chaplain	George W. Pilcher	Sept. 9, '62	

Company A.

Captain	Otto Funke	Dec. 20, '61	Major
"	Anthony Roehrig	Nov. 1, '62	
First Lieutenant	Anthony Roehrig	Dec. 20, '61	Promoted
"	Theophilus Schaerer	Nov. 1, '62	
Second Lieutenant	Theophilus Schaerer	Dec. 20, '61	Promoted
"	Herman Herald	Nov. 1, '62	

B.

Captain	Simon C. Burbridge	Dec. 20, '61	
First Lieutenant	Frank C. Worden	Dec. 20, '61	Resigned May 23, '62
"	Charles Bancroft	May 23, '62	
Second Lieutenant	Charles L. Bancroft	Dec. 20, '61	Promoted
"	George W. Hunter	May 23, '62	

C.

Captain	George W. Freeman	Dec. 20, '61	Resigned Jan. 20, '62
"	Charles E. Johnson	March 20, '62	
First Lieutenant	Charles E. Johnson	Dec. 20, '61	Promoted
"	David T. N. Sanderson	March 20, '62	Adjutant
"	Moses T. Lewman	Sept. 6, '62	
Second Lieutenant	Moses T. Lewman	Dec. 20, '61	Promoted
"	George W. Greenwood	Sept. 6, '62	

D.

Captain	Louis H. Armstrong	Dec. 20, '61	
First Lieutenant	George W. Odell	Dec. 20, '61	Resigned Nov. 5, 1862
Second Lieutenant	William P. Armstrong	Dec. 20, '61	Resigned Aug. 31, '62

Schedule G—Continued.

		Rank.	Remarks.

E.

Captain	John R. Zeigler	Dec. 20, '61	
First Lieutenant	Phillip F. Elliott	Dec. 20, '61	
Second Lieutenant	Samuel Craig	Dec. 20, '61	Resigned June 20, '62
"	Charles S. Beardsley	June 20, '62	

F.

Captain	William Olmstead	Dec. 20, '61	Resigned April 18, 62
"	Dennis S. Shepherd	April 20, '62	
First Lieutenant	Richard Burns	Dec. 20, '61	Killed in Shiloh battle
"	David M. Cummings	April 10, '62	
Second Lieutenant	William Donovan	Dec. 20, '61	Resigned March 22, '62
"	William Corrie	March 24, '62	Quartermaster
"	Bernard Wagner	Sept. 1, '62	

G.

Captain	John R. Coykendall	Dec. 20, '61	
First Lieutenant	Lot Sabine Willard	Dec. 20, '61	
Second Lieutenant	Stephen S. Tripp	Dec. 20, '61	Resigned Sept. 3, '62

H.

Captain	John C. Knowlton	Dec. 20, '61	Resigned Sept. 3, 1862
"	Aquilla I. Davis	Sept. 3, '62	
First Lieutenant	Francis Leclair	Dec. 20, '61	Resigned, June 6, '62
"	Henry M. Cornell	July 3, '62	
Second Lieutenant	Aquilla I. Davis	Dec. 20, '61	Promoted
"	Andrew T. Linbarger	Sept. 3, '62	

I.

Captain	John J. Worden	Dec. 20, '61	Resigned April 18, '62
"	Harvey T. Gregg	April 18, '62	Resigned, Sept. 23, '62
"	William R. Hays	Sept. 23, '62	
First Lieutenant	Harvey T. Gregg	Dec. 20, '61	Promoted
"	William R. Hays	April 18, '62	Promoted
"	David S. Scott	Sept. 23, '62	
Second Lieutenant	William R. Hays	Dec. 20, '61	Promoted
"	David S. Scott	April 18, '62	Promoted
"	John H. Hays	Sept. 23, '62	

K.

Captain	Henry C. Woods	Dec. 20, '61	
First Lieutenant	Richard A. Howk	Dec. 20, '61	Resigned July 8, 1862
"	John McFarland	July 9, '62	Promoted
Second Lieutenant	John McFarland	Dec. 20, '61	

L.

Captain	James Rote	Dec. 20, '61	
First Lieutenant	Thomas O'Harra	Dec. 20, '61	
Second Lieutenant	William D. Slater	Dec. 20, '61	

M.

Captain	Adam Stuber	Dec. 20, '61	Resigned November 18, '62
"	Hugh C. Moffitt	Nov. 18, '62	Promoted
First Lieutenant	Hugh C. Moffitt	Dec. 20, '61	
"	George A. Quin	Nov. 18, '62	Promoted
Second Lieutenant	George A. Quin	Dec. 20, '61	
"	John A. Gray	Nov. 18, '62	

Schedule G—Continued.

Roster of Twelfth Cavalry Regiment Illinois Volunteers.

Field and Staff.		Rank.	Remarks.
Colonel	Arno Voss	Feb. 1, '62	
Lieutenant Colonel	Hasbruck Davis	Feb. 1, '62	
Major	Francis T. Sherman	March 8, '62	Mustered out for promotion
"	Thomas W. Grosvenor	Sept. 4, '62	[Colonel 88th Infant'y
"	John G. Fonda	March 8, '62	Mustered out for promotion
"	Stephen Bronson	Nov. 17, '62	[Col. 118th Infantry
Adjutant	James Daley	Dec. 15, '62	
" 1st Batt'n	Jonathan Slade	March 8, '62	
" 2d Batt'n	Alexander Stewart	March 8, '62	
" 3d Batt'n			
Quartermaster	Lawrence J. J. Nissen	Dec. 6, '61	Transferred to First Lieut.
"	Lawrence J. J. Nissen	Dec. 15, '62	[of Co. E
" 1st Batt'n			
" 2d Batt'n			
" 3d Batt'n			
Commissary	Moses Shields	Dec. 15, '62	
Surgeon	John Higgins	Feb. 10, '62	
Assistant Surgeon	John McCarthy	March 1, '62	
Chaplain	Abraham J. Warner	June 1, '62	

Company A.

Captain	Thomas W. Grosvenor	Feb. 28, '62	Promoted
"	Phillip E. Fisher	Sept. 4, '62	
First Lieutenant	Phillip E. Fisher	Feb. 28, '62	Promoted
"	William M. Luff	Sept. 4, '62	
Second Lieutenant	William M. Luff	Feb. 28, '62	Promoted
"	Frederick Blaisdell	Sept. 4, '62	

B.

Captain	Andrew H. Langholz	Feb. 28, '62	Coward—dism'd Oct. 8, '62
First Lieutenant	Henry Jansen	Feb. 12, '62	
Second Lieutenant	Charles Grimm	Feb. 28, '62	

C.

Captain	Stephen Bronson	Feb. 28, '62	Promoted Major
"	William J. Steel	Nov. 17, '62	
First Lieutenant	William J. Steel	Jan. 1, '62	Promoted
"	George F Ward	Nov. 17, '62	
Second Lieutenant	George F. Ward	Feb. 28, '62	
"	Charles Coombs	Nov. 17, '62	

D.

Captain	Richard N. Hayden	Feb. 24, '62	
First Lieutenant	Charles Roden	Feb. 24, '62	
Second Lieutenant	Nathan J. Kidder	Feb. 24, '62	Dismissed Sept. 18, 1862
"	Gustavus Marsh	Dec. 18, '62	

E.

Captain	John P. Harvey	Feb. 28, '62	Died at Camp Butler April
"	Cephas Strong	April 26, '62	[25, 1862
First Lieutenant	Cephas Strong	Feb. 12, '62	Promoted

SCHEDULE G—Continued.

		Rank.	Remarks.
First Lieutenant..	Lawrence J. J. Nissen....	April 26, '62..	Promoted Quartermaster.
"	Edward Vasseur......	Dec. 15, '62..	....
Second Lieutenant	Edward Vasseur........	Feb. 28, '62..	Promoted ....
"	Alexander Stewart......	Dec. 15, '62..	....

F.

Captain	Ephriam M. Gilmore....	Dec. 31, '61..	Resigned June 28, 1862...
"	Henly L. Reans.........	June 28, '62..	Withheld ....
First Lieutenant..	Henly L. Reans.........	Dec. 31, '61..	....
Second Lieutenant	Dennis Palmer	Dec. 31, '61..	Resigned May 27, 1862...
"	Jackson Drennan.......	May 27, '62..	....

G.

Captain	Thomas Logan.........	March 21, '62	Mustered out for promot'n
"	John H. Clyburn.......	Nov. 15, '62..	........[Nov. 17, 1862
First Lieutenant..	John H. Clyburn.......	Feb. 24, '62..	Promoted ....
"	Joseph Logan..........	Nov. 15, '62..	....
Second Lieutenant	Joseph Logan..........	March 21, '62	Promoted ....
"	Charles E. Overrocker...	Nov. 15, '62..	....

H.

Captain	Franklin T. Gilbert	Sept. 14, '61..	....
"	George W. Shears......	Nov. 1, '61...	....
First Lieutenant..	Charles O'Connell	Sept. 14, '61..	....
"	George S. Phelps	Nov. 1, '61...	Resigned July 14, 1862...
"	Earl H. Chapman.......	July 14, '62..	....
Second Lieutenant	Theodore G. Knox......	Sept. 14, '61..	....
"	Oliver M. Pugh	Nov. 1, '61...	Resigned Nov. 24, 1862 ..
"	Isaac Conroe	Nov. 24, '62..	....

This Company transferred to the Fifteenth Cavalry.

I.

Captain	David C. Brown........	Nov. 1, '61...	....
First Lieutenant..	Edwin A. Webber......	Nov. 1, '61...	....
Second Lieutenant	George H. Sitts	Nov. 1, '61...	Resigned May 3, 1862....
"	Frederick W. Mitchell ..	Nov. 9, '62...	....

K.

Captain			
First Lieutenant..			
Second Lieutenant			

L.

Captain			
First Lieutenant..			
Second Lieutenant			

M.

Captain			
First Lieutenant..			
Second Lieutenant			

Schedule G—Continued.

Roster of Thirteenth Cavalry Regiment Illinois Volunteers.

Field and Staff.		Rank.	Remarks.
Colonel	Joseph W. Bell	Dec. 7, '61	Dismissed Nov. 24, '62
Lieutenant Colonel	Theobald Hartman	Dec. 31, '61	
Major	Lothar Lippert	Jan. 27, '62	
"	Charles A. Dell	Feb. 26, '62	
"			
Adjutant	Thaddeus S. Clarkson	Dec. 31, '61	M. O. April 16, '62; M. I. as 2d Lieut. Co. A, April 19, '62
" 1st Batt'n	William Werther	Dec. 31, '62	Resigned July 20, '62
" 2d Batt'n			
" 3d Batt'n			
Quartermaster	Emil Newbarger	Dec. 31, '61	Mustered out April 16, '62
"	Emil Newbarger	Oct. 1, '62	
" 1st Batt'n			
" 2d Batt'n			
" 3d Batt'n			
Commissary	Hall P. Talbot	Oct. 25, '62	
Surgeon	Charles Storch	March 3, '62	
Assistant Surgeon	Leonard L. Lake	Dec. 31, '61	Resigned Feb. 19, '62; disability removed Oct. 9,'62
"	Jacob Bockee	Feb. 19, '62	Promoted
"	Horace Austin	May 28, '62	
Chaplain	Abner W. Henderson	Oct. 1, '62	

Company A.

Captain			
First Lieutenant	Julius Grossenheider	Dec. 31, '61	Resigned Feb. 12, '62
"	Friedrich Behlendorff	Feb. 13, '62	
Second Lieutenant	John Stuber	Dec. 31, '61	Promoted to Co. C
"	Friedrich Behlendorff	Jan. 1, '62	Promoted
"	Henry Kymer	May 19, '62	

B.

Captain	Henry M. Peters	Dec. 31, '61	
First Lieutenant	William Werther	Dec. 31, '61	Adjutant 1st Battalion
"	Emil Newbarger	May 29, '62	Quartermaster
"	Felix C. Marx	Oct. 1, '62	
Second Lieutenant	Carl Wm. Krueger	Dec. 31, '61	Resigned May 3, '62
"	Felix C. Marx	June 7, '62	Promoted
"	John Douch	Oct. 1, '62	

C.

Captain	John E. Kimberly	Dec. 31, '61	Discharged, ill health, Nov. 27, '62
"	Adam Sachs	May 4, '62	
First Lieutenant	Ernst Riedel	Dec. 31, '61	Resigned May 3, '62
"	John Stuber	May 4, '62	
Second Lieutenant	Adam Sachs	Dec. 31, '61	Promoted
"	George Wolf	Oct. 1, '62	

Schedule G—Continued.

		Rank.	Remarks.

D.

Captain	William W. Bell	Feb. 28, '62	Discharged, ill health, Oct. 3, '62
"	Robert G. Dyhrenfurth	Oct. 3, '62	
First Lieutenant	Robert G. Dyhrenfurth	Feb. 20, '62	Promoted
Second Lieutenant	S. Chester Hall	April 18, '62	Resigned Dec. 10, '62

E.

Captain			
First Lieutenant			
Second Lieutenant			

F.

Captain	Willis Danforth	Dec. 31, '61	
First Lieutenant	Ira D. Swain	Dec. 31, '61	
Second Lieutenant	G. Allen May	Jan. 1, '62	

G.

Captain	Charles H. Roland	Dec. 31, '61	Dismissed Aug. 9, '62
First Lieutenant	Albert Erskine	Dec. 31, '61	
Second Lieutenant	William K. Trabue	Dec. 31, '61	M. O. as Capt. Aug. 9, '62

H.

Captain	Robert H. Flemming	Dec. 31, '61	
First Lieutenant	Dick A. McOmber	Dec. 31, '61	
Second Lieutenant	Joseph H. Graham	Dec. 31, '61	

I.

Captain			
First Lieutenant			
Second Lieutenant			

K.

Captain			
First Lieutenant			
Second Lieutenant			

L.

Captain			
First Lieutenant			
Second Lieutenant			

M.

Captain			
First Lieutenant			
Second Lieutenant			

Schedule G—Continued.

Roster of Fifteenth Cavalry Regiment Illinois Volunteers.

Field and Staff.		Rank.	Remarks.
Colonel	Warren Stewart	Dec. 25, '62	
Lieutenant Colonel	George A. Bacon	Dec. 25, '62	
Major	Warren Stewart	Feb. 1, '62	Promoted Colonel
"	Franklin T. Gilbert	Dec. 25, '62	
"	James Grant Wilson	Dec. 25, '62	
Adjutant	T. L. Morris	Dec. 25, '62	
Quartermaster	Samuel B. Stewart	Oct. 25, '62	
Commissary	Louis Souther	Dec. 25, '62	
Surgeon			
Assistant Surgeon			
Chaplain			

Company A.

Captain	Warren Stewart	Aug. 10, '61	Promoted Major
"	Ezra King	Feb. 1, '62	
First Lieutenant	Ezra King	Aug. 10, '61	Promoted
"	Esau Brown	Feb. 1, '62	
Second Lieutenant	Esau Brown	Aug. 10, '61	Promoted
"	Cyrus M. Eversall	Feb. 1, '62	

B.

Captain	Eagleton Carmichael	Aug. 7, '61	
First Lieutenant	Robert H. Leek	Aug. 7, '61	
Second Lieutenant	Wilmot C. Munson	Aug. 7, '61	

C.

Captain	James J. Dollins	Sept. 8, '61	Promoted Col. 81st Inf'try
"	Montreville Fitts	Aug. 26, '62	
First Lieutenant	Montreville Fitts	Sept. 8, '61	Promoted
"	Joseph M. Weir	Aug. 26, '62	
Second Lieutenant	Oliver C. Martin	Sept. 8, '61	Resigned May 8, 1862
"	Joseph M. Weir	May 8, '62	Promoted
"	John H. Hogan	Aug. 26, '62	

D.

Captain	Morrison J. O'Harnett	Sept. 1, '61	
First Lieutenant	John J. Richards	Sept. 1, '61	
Second Lieutenant	Francis W. Webster	Sept. 1, '61	

E.

Captain	William D. Hutchins	March 1, '62	
First Lieutenant	William B. Ford	March 1, '62	
Second Lieutenant	Samuel P. Jones	March 1, '62	

F.

Captain	Joseph Adams	Dec. 25, '62	
First Lieutenant	George Hubbard	Dec. 25, '62	
Second Lieutenant			

G.

Captain	Franklin T. Gilbert	Sept. 14, '61	
First Lieutenant	Charles O'Connell	Sept. 14, '61	
Second Lieutenant	Theodore G. Knox	Sept. 14, '61	

Schedule G — Continued.

		Rank.	Remarks.

H.

Captain	Christian B. Dodson	Aug. 7, '61	Resigned Aug. 10, '62
"	William C. Wilder	Aug. 10, '62	
First Lieutenant	William C. Wilder	Aug. 7, '61	Promoted
"	Thomas J. Beebe	Aug. 10, '62	
Second Lieutenant	John C. Bundy	Aug. 7, '61	Pro. Lieut. Col. in Ark. Reg
"	Ebenezer C. Litherland	Aug. 10, '62	

I.

Captain	Albert Jenks	Aug. 20, '61	Pro. Lt. Col. 36th Inf'try.
"	George A. Willis	Sept. 18, '62	
First Lieutenant	Samuel B. Sherer	Aug. 20, '61	Promoted
"	George A. Willis	July 9, '62	Promoted
"	Azariah C. Ferrie	Sept. 18, '62	
Second Lieutenant	Azariah C. Ferrie	Aug. 20, '61	Promoted
"	George A. Willis	Aug. 20, '61	Promoted
"	Albert Collins	Sept. 18, '62	

K.

Captain	Henry A. Smith	Aug. 20, '61	Cashiered
"	Samuel B. Sherer	July 9, '62	
First Lieutenant	Samuel Chapman	Aug. 20, '61	Resigned April 1, 1862
"	Francis E. Reynolds	April 1, '62	
Second Lieutenant	John S. Durand	Aug. 20, '61	Resigned March 28, 1862
"	Henry C. Pa-Delford	March 28, '62	Resigned July 14, 1862
"	Edward M. Barnard	July 14, '62	

L.

Captain	William Ford	Dec. 1, '61	
First Lieutenant	John F. Mariner	Dec. 1, '61	Resigned July 8, 1862
"	John King	July 8, '62	
Second Lieutenant	John King	Dec. 1, '61	Promoted
"	Miciah F. Fairfield	July 8, '62	

M.

Captain	Oscar H. Huntley	Dec. 9, '61	Resigned Dec. 8, 1862
First Lieutenant	Thomas A. Stevens	Dec. 9, '61	
Second Lieutenant	William Hebard	Dec. 9, '61	

Schedule G—Continued.

"Thielman's Battalion" Illinois Cavalry.

Officers.		Rank.	Remarks.
Company A.			
Captain	Berthold Marschuer	Nov. 1, '61	
First Lieutenant	James W. Lavigne	Nov. 1, '61	
Second Lieutenant	Irving L. L. Ponds	Nov. 1, '61	Resigned March 15, 1862.
"	William H. Dorchester	March 15, '62	
B.			
Captain	Matthew Marx	Nov. 1, '61	Resigned Jan. 25, 1862.
"	Milo Thielman	Jan. 25, '62	
First Lieutenant	Milo Thielman	Nov. 1, '61	Promoted
"	George Hamilton	Jan. 25, '62	
Second Lieutenant	George Hamilton	Nov. 1, '61	Promoted
"	William S. Kelly	Jan. 25, '62	

"Schambeck's Battalion" Illinois Cavalry.

Officers.		Rank.	Remarks.
Captain	Frederick Schambeck	July 6, '61	
First Lieutenant	John G. Rolli	July 6, '61	Resigned Dec. 15, 1862.
Second Lieutenant	Julius Jaehe	July 6, '61	

Schedule G—Continued.

Roster of First Regiment Illinois Light Artillery.

Field and Staff.		Rank.	Remarks.
Colonel.........	Joseph D. Webster.....	Feb. 1, '62...	
Lieutenant Colonel	Charles H. Adams......	Oct. 23, '61..	
Major........	Ezra Taylor............	Oct. 23, '61..	
"	Charles C. Campbell....	Oct. 23, '61..	
"	Charles M. Willard.....	March 1, '62..	
Adjutant.........			
Quartermaster...	John Dismant, jr......	Feb. 8, '62...	
Surgeon.........	Edmund Andrews......	April 3, '62..	
1st Ass't Surgeon.	John M. Woodworth...	May 15, '62..	
2d Ass't Surgeon.	William T. Kirk.......	Sept. 23, '62..	
Chaplain.........	Jeremiah Porter........	Feb. 1, '62...	

Company A.

Captain.........	Charles M. Willard.....	Sept. 27, '61.	Promoted Major.........
"	Francis Morgan........	March 1, '62.	Mustered out May 24, '62.
"	Peter P. Wood.........	May 24, '62..	
Sen. First Lieut.	Francis Morgan........	Sept. 27, '61.	Promoted...............
" "	Peter P. Wood.........	March 1, '62.	Promoted
" "	John W. Rumsey.......	May 24, '62..	
Jun. "	Peter P. Wood.........	Sept. 27, '61.	Promoted
" "	John W. Rumsey......	March 1, '62.	Promoted
" "	George McCagg	May 24, '62..	
Sen. Second Lieut.	Edgar P. Tobey........	Sept. 27, '61.	Resigned Feb. 3, 1862....
" "	John W. Rumsey.......	Feb. 3, '62...	Promoted
" "	George McCagg........	March 1, '62.	Promoted............
" "	Frederick W. Young...	May 24, '62..	
Jun. "	John W. Rumsey.......	Sept. 27, '61.	Promoted
" "	George McCagg........	Feb. 3, 62...	Promoted
" "	Frederick W. Young....	March 1, '62.	Promoted
" "	Hixie L Huffman	May 24, '62..	

B.

Captain.........	Ezra Taylor............	May 15, '61..	Promoted Major.........
"	Samuel E. Barrett......	Oct. 23, '61..	
Sen. First Lieut..	Samuel E. Barrett......	May 15, '61..	Promoted
" "	Levi W. Hart..........	Oct. 23, '61..	
Jun. "	Levi W. Hart..........	May 15, '61..	Promoted
" "	Patrick H. White......	Oct. 23, '61..	
Sen. Second Lieut.	Patrick H. White	May 15, '61..	Promoted
" "	Israel P. Rumsey......	Oct. 23, '61..	
Jun. "	Israel P. Rumsey.....	May 15, '61..	Promoted
" "	Theodore P. Roberts....	March 1, '62.	

C.

Captain.........	Charles Houghtaling....	April 18, '61.	
Sen. First Lieut..	Edward M. Wright	Aug. 1, '61..	
Jun. "	Mark H. Prescott.......	Aug. 1, '61 ..	
Sen. Second Lieut.	John J. VanDyke	Aug. 1, '61...	Resigned April 15, 1862...
Jun. "	John M. Hunter........	Aug 1, '61...	
" "	Joseph R. Channel......	April 15, '62.	

D.

Captain.........	Edward McAlister......	May 15, '61..	Resigned May 5, 1862....
"	Henry A. Rogers.......	May 5, '62 ..	Resigned June 1, 1862....
Sen. First Lieut..	George J. Wood........	Sept. 23, '62.	

SCHEDULE G — Continued.

		Rank.	Remarks.
Jun. First Lieut..	Mathew W. Borland....	Aug. 1, '61..	Resigned April 24, 1862..
" "	James A. Borland......	April 24, '62..	....
Sen. Second Lieut.	Uzziel P. Smith........	Aug. 16, '61..	Resigned March 4, 1862..
" "	James A. Borland......	March 4, '62.	Promoted...............
" "	Edgar H. Cooper.......	April 24, '62.	....
Jun. "	Edgar H. Cooper	March 4, '62.	Promoted ....
" "	Emmit F. Hill	April 24, '62.	....

E.

Captain.........	Allen C. Waterhouse....	Dec. 19, '61..	....
Sen. First Lieut..	Abial R. Abbott........	Dec. 19, '61..	....
Jun. " ..	John A. Fitch	Dec. 19, '61..	....
Sen. Second Lieut.	William Chandler	Dec. 19, '61..	....
Jun. "	Alfred W. Woodard	Dec. 19, '61..	....

F.

Captain.........	John T. Cheney........	Feb. 25, '62..	....
Sen. First Lieut..	Josiah H. Burton.......	Feb. 25, '62..	....
Jun. " ..	Henry L. Benn.........	Feb. 25, '62..	Resigned Sept. 2, 1862...
" "	Samuel S. Smith	Sept. 2, '62..	....
Sen. Second Lieut.	Samuel S. Smith	Feb. 25, '62.	Promoted ....
" "	Jefferson F. Whaley	Sept. 2, '62..	....
Jun. "	John W. Risley........	July 21, '62..	....

G.

Captain.........	Arthur O'Leary	Feb. 1, '62..	Discharged Aug. 21, 1862.
Sen. First Lieut..	Raphael G. Rombauer ..	Feb. 1, '62..	....
Jun. " .	Donald Campbell.......	Feb. 1, '62..	Discharged Aug. 21, 1862.
Sen. Second Lieut.	Henry E. Jones	Feb. 1, '62..	....
Jun. "	....		

H.

Captain.........	Axel Silfversparre......	Dec. 26, '61..	....
Sen. First Lieut..	Lewis B. Mitchell	Feb. 1, '62..	....
Jun. " ..	George G. Knox........	March 6, '62.	Honorably discharged Nov-
Sen. Second Lieut.	Francis DeGress	Jan. 1, '62...	.............[1, '62.
Jun. "	Edward Adams	Feb. 1, '62..	Hon'ably disch'd Nov.1,'62

I.

Captain.........	Edward Bouton........	Feb. 10, '62..	....
Sen. First Lieut..	Henry A. Rogers.......	Feb. 1, '62..	Promoted to Battery 'D'..
" " ..	Albert Cudney	May 5, '62..	....
Jun. "	Albert Cudney........	Feb. 1, '62..	Promoted ....
" " ..	William N. Lansing.....	May 5, '62..	....
Sen. Second Lieut.	William N. Lansing.....	Feb. 1, '62..	Promoted ....
" "	John C. Neely.........	May 5, '62..	....
Jun. "	John C. Neely.........	Feb. 1, '62..	Promoted ....
" "	Robert Cowden........	May 5, '62..	....

K.

Captain.........	Angrean Franklin......	Jan. 9, '62...	Resigned March 31, 1862.
"	Jason B. Smith.........	April 1, '62..	....
Sen. First Lieut..	Jason B. Smith.........	Jan. 9, '62...	Promoted ....
" " ..	Isaac W. Curtis........	April 1, '62..	....
Jun. " "	Joseph P. Shelton..,...	March 24, '62	....
Sen. Second Lieut.	William O. Stephenson..	Jan. 9, '62...	....
Jun. "	James G. Helm........	Aug. 15, '62..	....

SCHEDULE G—Continued.

		Rank.	Remarks.

L.

Captain	John Rourke	Feb. 22, '62	
Sen. First Lieut.	John McAfee	Feb. 1, '62	
Jun. "	Charles Bagley	Feb. 1, '62	
Sen. Second Lieut.			
Jun. "			

H.

Captain	John. B. Miller	Aug. 12, '62	
Sen. First Lieut.	George W. Spencer	Aug. 12, '62	
Jun. "	John H. Colvin	June 12, '62	
Sen. Second Lieut.	Thomas Burton	Aug. 25, '62	
Jun. "	Bela H. Flusky	Sept. 23, '62	

SCHEDULE G—Continued.

Roster of Second Regiment Illinois Light Artillery.

Field and Staff.		Rank.	Remarks.
Colonel	Thomas S Mather	Feb. 2, '62	
Lieutenant Colonel	William L. Duff	Jan. 11, '62	
Major	Charles J. Stolbrand	Dec. 31, '61	
"	Frederick A. Starring	Jan. 30, '62	Pro. Colonel 72d Infantry.
"	Edwin H. Smith	Aug. 21, '62	
"	Andolph Schwartz	Feb. 1, '62	
Adjutant	Isaac N. Higgins	Nov. 27, '61	Resigned March 13, '62
Quartermaster	John Pyatt	Nov. 27, '61	Transferred to Battery K.
Surgeon	Hezekiah Williams	Feb. 5, '62	
1st Ass't Surgeon	Giles P. Ransom	March 18, '62	
2d Ass't Surgeon			
Chaplain	William M. Reynolds	Jan. 30, '62	Resigned Aug. 31, '62
"	William C. Merritt	Sept. 22, '62	Hon. disch'd Dec. 6, '62

COMPANY A.

Captain	Peter Davidson	May 14, '61	
Sen. First Lieut.	Herman Borris	May 14, '61	
Jun. "	J. Corwin Hansel	Jan. 25, '62	
Sen. Second Lieut.	Frank B. Fenton	May 14, '61	
Jun. "	Abraham B. Batterson	Jan. 25, '62	Died
" "	Matthew C. Goodenow	Dec. 5, '62	

B.

Captain	Relly Madison	Aug. 26, '61	
Sen. First Lieut.	Thomas Dawson	Aug. 26, '61	Resigned
" "	Fletcher H. Chapman	March 18, '62	
Jun. "	William Gard	Aug. 26, '61	Mustered out March 25, '62
Sen. Second Lieut.	Jeremiah Crane	Aug. 26, '61	Mustered out March 25, '62
" "	Augustus Hoyer	March 18, '62	
Jun. "	Richard Gard	Aug. 26, '61	Resigned Jan. 21, '62
" "	Frank Allaire	Jan. 27, '62	

C.

Captain	Caleb Hopkins	April 22, '61	Resigned April 20, '62
"	James P. Flood	April 20, '62	
Sen. First Lieut.	James P. Flood	Aug. 5, '61	Promoted
" "	Elijah V. Moore	April 20, '62	
Jun. "	Amos H. Fletcher	Aug. 5, '61	Resigned Jan. 3, '62
" "	Frank B. Smith	April 28, '62	
Sen. Second Lieut.	Alexander Busby	Aug. 5, '61	Resigned March 17, '62
" "	Horatio N. Towner	March 1, '62	
Jun. "	John G. Loy	Aug. 5, '61	Resigned Feb. 25, '62
" "	Thomas McIntyre	Feb. 25, '62	

D.

Captain	Jasper M. Dresser	Aug. 28, '61	Mustered out for promotion March 28, '62
"	James P. Timmony	March 28, '62	Resigned April 17, '62
"	Fritz Anneke	May 1, '62	Mustered out for promotion Dec. 18, '62
Sen. First Lieut.	James P. Timmony	Aug. 28, '61	Promoted
" "	Harrison C. Barger	March 28, '62	
Jun. "	James D. W. Whitall	March 28, '62	
Sen. Second Lieut.	Charles S. Cooper	March 28, '62	
Jun. "	George A. Dunlap	Feb. 1, '62	Resigned April 18, '62
" "	Walter Scates	Sept. 23, '62	

SCHEDULE G—Continued.

			Rank.	Remarks.
E.				
Captain		Conrad Gumbart	Feb. 1, '62	
Sen. First Lieut.		Morris Ball	Feb. 1, '62	Resigned March 14, '62
"	"	George L. Nispell	March 14, '62	
Jun.	"	George L. Nispell	Feb. 1, '62	Promoted
"	"	Emil Steger	March 14, '62	
Sen. Second Lieut.		Joseph Hanger	Feb. 1, '62	Died
"	"	William Denzel	March 14, '62	
Jun.	"	Emil Steger	Feb. 1, '62	Promoted
"	"	Julian Carter	March 14, '62	
F.				
Captain		John W. Powell	Dec. 11, '61	
Sen. First Lieut.		Michael Dittlinger	Dec. 11, '61	Resigned March 26, '62
"	"	Joseph W. Mitchell	March 26, '62	
Jun.	"	Christian D. Bless	Dec. 11, '61	Mustered out May 22, '62
"	"	Henry R. Henning	May 22, '62	
Sen. Second Lieut.		Gustavus A. Tirmenstein	Dec. 11, '61	Resigned April 15, '62
"	"	Henry R. Henning	April 15, '62	Promoted
"	"	Walter H. Powell	May 22, '62	
Jun.	"	Joseph W. Mitchell	Dec. 11, '61	Promoted
"	"	Israel H. Eldridge	Nov. 26, '62	
G.				
Captain		Charles J. Stolbrand	Oct. 5, '61	Promoted Major
		Frederick Sparrestrom	Dec. 31, '61	
Sen. First Lieut.		Frederick Sparrestrom	Sept. 16, '61	Promoted
"	"	John W. Lowell	Dec. 31, '61	
Jun.	"	John W. Lowell	Oct. 5, '61	Promoted
"	"	William C. Whitney	Dec. 31, '61	
Sen. Second Lieut.		William C. Whitney	Oct. 5, '61	Promoted
"	"	Nott Smith	Dec. 31, '61	
Jun.	"	Nott Smith	Oct. 5, '61	Promoted
"	"	Samuel T. Durkee	Dec. 31, '61	
H.				
Captain		Andrew Stenbeck	Dec. 31, '61	Promoted Major
Sen. First Lieut.		Edwin H. Smith	Dec. 31, '61	
"	"	Henry C. Whittemore	Aug. 21, '62	Promoted
Jun.	"	Henry C. Whittemore	Dec. 31, '61	
"	"	Lothar Becker	Aug. 21, '62	Transferred to Co. C
Sen. Second Lieut.		Horatio N. Towner	Feb. 22, '62	
"	"	Lothar Becker	March 17, '62	Promoted
"	"	Jonas Eckdall	Aug. 21, '62	
Jun.	"	Jonas Eckdall	Jan. 1, '62	Promoted
"	"	Harvy Gordon	Aug. 21, '62	
I.				
Captain		Charles W. Keith	Dec. 31, '61	Resigned April 7, '62
"		Charles M. Barnett	April 7, '62	
Sen. First Lieut.		Charles M. Barnett	Dec. 31, '61	Promoted
"	"	Henry B. Plant	April 7, '62	
Jun.	"	Henry B. Plant	Dec. 31, '61	Promoted
"	"	Alonzo W. Coe	April 7, '62	
Sen. Second Lieut.		Alonzo W. Coe	Dec. 31, '61	Promoted
"	"	W. Eugene Hayward	April 7, '62	
Jun.	"	W. Eugene Hayward	Feb. 3, '62	Promoted
"	"	Charles D. Haight	June 6, '62	

Schedule G—Continued.

		Rank.	Remarks.

K.

Captain	Benjamin F. Rodgers	Dec. 31, '61	
Sen. First Lieut.	Francis M. Ross	Dec. 31, '61	
Jun. "	Abel S. Gale	Dec. 31, '61	
Sen. Second Lieut.	Wesley Pratt	Feb. 3, '62	
Jun. "	John Pyatt	May 31, '62	

L.

Captain	William H. Bolton	Feb. 28, '62	
Sen. First Lieut.	Jabez H. Moore	March 17, '62	
Jun. "	Edward A. James	Feb. 1, '62	Died Nov. 2, '62
Sen. Second Lieut.	Simon P. Tracy	Feb. 28, '62	
Jun. "	Julius D. Roberts	April 10, '62	Resigned Sept. 18, '62

M.

Captain	John C. Phillips	June 6, '62	
Sen. First Lieut.	Edward G. Hillier	June 6, '62	Hon. dis. Nov. 19, '62
Jun. "	George W. Reed	June 6, '62	
Sen. Second Lieut.	W. C. G. L. Stevenson	June 6, '62	
Jun. "			

Schedule G—Continued.

Chicago Board of Trade Battery—Illinois Light Artillery.

Officers.		Rank.	Remarks.
Captain	James S. Stokes	July 31, '62.	
Sen. First Lieut.	George J. Robinson	July 31, '62.	
Jun. First Lieut.	Albert F. Baxter	July 31, '62.	Resigned Nov. 18 '62.
"	Sylvanus H. Stevens	Nov. 18, '62.	
Sen. Second Lieut.	Trumbull D. Griffin	July 31, '62.	
Jun. Second Lieut.	Henry Bennett	July 31, '62.	

Chicago Mercantile Battery—Illinois Light Artillery.

Officers.		Rank.	Remarks.
Captain	Charles G. Cooley	Aug. 29, '62.	
Sen. First Lieut.	Frank C. Wilson	Aug. 29, '62.	
Jun. First Lieut.	James H. Swan	Aug. 29, '62.	
Sen. Second Lieut.	David R. Crego	Aug. 29, '62.	
Jun. Second Lieut.	Frederick B. Bickford	Aug. 29, '62.	

Springfield Light Artillery—Illinois Volunteers.

Officers.		Rank.	Remarks.
Captain	Thomas F. Vaughn	Aug. 21, '62.	
Sen. First Lieut.	Edward B. Stillings	Aug. 21, '62.	
Jun. First Lieut.	Henry D. Colby	Aug. 21, '62.	
Sen. Second Lieut.	Charles W. Thomas	Aug. 21, '62.	
Jun. Second Lieut.	Louis D. Rosette	Aug. 21, '62.	

Battery of Light Artillery attached to the Fifty-Third Illinois Infantry.

Officers.		Rank.	Remarks.
Captain	William Cogswell	Sept. 23, '61.	
Sen. First Lieut.	Henry G. Eddy	Nov. 12, '61.	
Jun. First Lieut.	Hamilton S. McClary	Nov. 12, '61.	
Sen. Second Lieut.	Asa Williams	Nov. 12, '61.	
Jun. Second Lieut.	Hiram S. Prescott	Nov. 12, '61.	Resigned March 26, '62.
"	William R. Elting	March 26, '62.	

Elgin Battery—Illinois Light Artillery.

Officers.		Rank.	Remarks.
Captain	George W. Renwick	Nov. 15, '62	
Sen. First Lieut.	Andrew M. Wood	Nov. 15, '62.	
Jun. First Lieut.	Caleb Rich	Nov. 15, '62.	
Sen. Second Lieut.	Lorin G. Jeffers	Nov. 15, '62.	
Jun. Second Lieut.	Waldo W. Paine	Nov. 15, '62.	

Henshaw's Battery—Illinois Light Artillery.

Officers.		Rank.	Remarks.
Captain	Edward C. Henshaw	Dec. 23, '62.	
Sen. First Lieut.	Azro C. Putnam	Dec. 3, '62.	
Jun. First Lieut.	Aven Pearson	Dec. 3, '62.	
Sen. Second Lieut.			
Jun. Second Lieut.			

SURNAME INDEX

ABBEY, 155
ABBOTT, 124 125 146 225 240 378
ABELL, 308
ABERCROMBIE, 248
ACHENBACH, 275
ACKEN, 106
ADAIR, 170
ADAM, 98
ADAMS, 37 84 86 89 90 94 116 124 126 147 151 153 177 194 199 200 210-212 241 248 258 290 353 374 377 378
AGNEW, 355
AKENS, 193
AKIN, 334
AKINS, 237
ALBIN, 238
ALBRA, 304
ALCOKE, 156
ALDEN, 156 201 304
ALDRICH, 162
ALEXANDER, 103 122-124 204 212
ALGUR, 146
ALLAIRE, 380
ALLARD, 119
ALLEN, 55 60 70 95 104 108 124 125 134 144 147 173 184 185 214 219 220 236

ALLEN (Continued) 240 290 316 318 334
ALLISON, 186 310
ALLSHOUSE, 352
ALLSOP, 226
ALMON, 143
ALTMAN, 230 342
ALVORD, 122
AMESLEY, 287
AMSDEN, 280
ANDBERG, 166
ANDERSON, 117 142 154 163 167 176 177 180 195 200 205 236 254 319 337 363 365
ANDREA, 232
ANDRESS, 191
ANDREWS, 110 130 165 174 175 228 240 298 302 326 377
ANDRUS, 92 102
ANGASON, 191
ANGEL, 184
ANGELL, 326
ANKENY, 172
ANNEKE, 380
ANTES, 146
ANTHONY, 198 332
APERN, 95
APPERSON, 176 314 353
APPLEGATE, 204

APPLETON, 163
APPLINGTON, 358
ARCHDEACON, 120
ARCHER, 133 275
ARMAN, 56 61 74
ARMMTROUT, 175
ARMSTRONG, 89 99 123 162 186 192 202 242 284 330 357 368
ARNO, 172
ARNOLD, 172
ASH, 89 154 292
ASHBAUGH, 266
ASHBROOK, 189
ASHHURST, 292
ASHMEAD, 359
ASHMORE, 88 96 130
ASKEW, 142
ASKINS, 204
ATCHISON, 274 284
ATHEY, 345
ATKINS, 55 61 71 92 102 264
ATKINSON, 155
ATWATER, 164 183 304
ATWELL, 192
ATWOOD, 187
AUBERE, 344
AUGUSTINE, 190
AUSTIN, 120 123 153 291 322 361 372
AVERY, 93 115 270 364
AXLEY, 320
AYERS, 143 232 328
BABB, 174
BABBETT, 144
BABBITT, 145 196
BABCOCK, 56 61 72 87 94 232 286 345
BACHELDER, 252
BACON, 93 105 163 224 228 280 374
BAGLEY, 238 379

BAGSLEY, 138
BAILEY, 56 60 71 120 121 126 184 189 278 286 306 308 309 311
BAILHACHE, 118 156
BAIRD, 116 336
BAKER, 110 158 174 192 200 209 218 229 240 274 310 312 320 347 351 355 356
BALCH, 188
BALDWIN, 27 29 55 60 68 114 133 152 194 308
BALES, 301
BALFOUR, 171
BALL, 150 248 257 356 381
BALLANCE, 234 320
BALLARD, 173 210
BALLEN, 101
BALLINGER, 347
BALLOU, 202
BANCROFT, 368
BANDY, 154 155
BANE, 25 55 60 67 180
BANGER, 170
BANGS, 118
BANKSON, 310
BANNISTER, 230
BANTA, 277
BARBER, 110
BARFIELD, 340
BARGER, 226 227 380
BARKER, 21 22 27 184 192 228 273 358
BARKLEY, 188 189
BARLOW, 230
BARNARD, 97 257 269 375
BARNES, 111 117 154 165 200 224 225 276 316
BARNETT, 284 301 381
BARNHILL, 160
BARNUM, 194
BARR, 173 194

BARRELL, 134
BARRETT, 26 29 57 63 75 84 96 181 261 365 377
BARRICK, 226
BARRICKMAN, 204
BARRINGER, 298
BARRY, 104 152 195 306 338
BARSTOW, 365
BARTHOLEMEW, 112
BARTLESON, 56 60 71 120 243 280 299
BARTLETT, 152 280 358
BARTLING, 345
BARTO, 185
BARTON, 117
BARTRAM, 91
BASSELL, 238
BASSETT, 186
BATES, 108 182 270 366
BATEY, 268
BATSON, 142
BATTERSON, 380
BATTEY, 195
BAUGH, 161
BAXTER, 383
BAYLEY, 364
BAYNE, 272
BEACH, 199 360
BEADLES, 350
BEAL, 330
BEALL, 177
BEALS, 202
BEAN, 252
BEAR, 217
BEARDSLEY, 106 135 218 330 369
BEATTY, 118
BEAUCHAMP, 310
BEAUMONT, 105
BEAVER, 149
BECHDOLDT, 136
BECHSTEIN, 244

BECK, 355
BECKER, 128 265 381
BECKETT, 306
BECKIER, 89 98
BECKLEY, 270
BEDFORD, 116 176
BEEBE, 252 375
BEELER, 148
BEERS, 224 236
BEEZLEY, 292
BEHLENDORFF, 372
BELCHER, 159
BELFORD, 136 139
BELKNAP, 188
BELL, 26 29 57 63 75 119 148 155 162 208 292 334 372 373
BELLOWS, 182
BELOMY, 365
BELSER, 84
BELT, 282
BELTS, 228
BENEDICT, 326
BENKER, 334
BENN, 378
BENNER, 111
BENNESON, 60
BENNETT, 218 226 230 319 344 365 383
BENNISON, 55 70 236
BENSON, 93 201 321
BENTON, 328 362
BERGK, 244
BERGLEND, 194
BERKELY, 177
BERKLEY, 358
BERNARD, 88
BERNIER, 120
BERRY, 106 123 138 144 214 303 308 332 354
BEST, 160
BESTOR, 358

BESWICK, 115 284
BEVERIDGE, 360
BEVIS, 163
BEWLEY, 197
BEYLES, 220
BEYLS, 238
BEZ, 280
BICKFORD, 383
BIDDOLPH, 153
BIERCE, 347
BIERER, 135
BIGELOW, 154 239 256 347
BIGGS, 114 304
BILLING, 185
BILLINGALE, 260
BILLINGS, 210
BILLS, 220
BINGHAM, 212 224
BIRCH, 336
BIRCHARD, 180
BIRD, 92 190
BIRDWELL, 345
BIRGE, 20
BISER, 174
BISHOP, 97 119 144 216 258 286 312 313 363
BISSELL, 180
BITTER, 129
BLACK, 114 154 155 191 220 222 236 250 272 302 348 366
BLACKARD, 320
BLACKBURN, 117 123 236 336 358 362
BLACKLIDGE, 161
BLACKMORE, 326
BLACKSTONE, 103 163
BLADES, 232 356
BLAIN, 211
BLAIR, 206 342
BLAISDELL, 228 370

BLAKE, 118 158 170 216 259 314
BLAKELY, 228
BLAKEMAN, 314
BLAKEMORE, 362
BLALOCK, 310
BLANCHARD, 101 107 250 360
BLANDEN, 270
BLANDER, 264
BLANDIN, 236
BLANKE, 128 129
BLANKENBAKER, 188
BLATHEMICK, 183
BLEAN, 230
BLESS, 381
BLEW, 338
BLISS, 111
BLOCK, 128
BLODGETT, 154 228 230 272
BLOOD, 174 194
BLOOMFIELD, 133
BLOSSER, 226
BLOUNEY, 272
BLOUNT, 130
BLUTHARDT, 342
BOAL, 256
BOAS, 121
BOATMAN, 189
BOCKEE, 372
BOGARDUS, 216 252
BOHN, 110 264
BOICOURT, 356
BOLLEN, 98
BOLLINGER, 264
BOLT, 274
BOLTON, 29 58 62 76 382
BOND, 126 246 304
BONHAM, 175 198
BONNELL, 285
BONYER, 143

BOOMER, 165
BOONE, 118 363
BOOTH, 364
BOOTHE, 160
BORAH, 254
BORCHERS, 172
BOREN, 299
BORLAND, 378
BORNEMANN, 125 129
BORNMAN, 98
BOROUGH, 144 323
BORRIS, 380
BORTLE, 365
BOSTICK, 322
BOSTWICK, 102
BOSWELL, 138 200 298
BOSWORTH, 148
BOUDE, 316
BOUGHAN, 206
BOURQUINN, 108
BOUTON, 29 57 76 256 378
BOVELL, 212
BOWEN, 174 184 226 280
BOWER, 318
BOWLBY, 269
BOWMAN, 122 134 143 185 250 292 345 350
BOWSER, 105
BOWTON, 62
BOWYER, 143
BOYCE, 103 171
BOYD, 115 182 184 210 212 287 312 366
BOYDEN, 131
BOYER, 121
BOYINGTON, 246
BOYLE, 100
BOZARTH, 135
BOZMAN, 138 139
BRACKEN, 368
BRACKENRIDGE, 318

BRACKETT, 24 29 57 63 75 362
BRADDOCK, 239
BRADLEY, 110 120 175 182 210 318
BRADSBY, 162
BRADSHAW, 172 238 310 358
BRAINARD, 49 182 184 365
BRANDEN, 105
BRANT, 359
BRASHER, 198
BRASLETON, 188
BRASSFIELD, 175
BRAUNS, 97
BRAXTON, 220
BRAYMAN, 138
BRAZEE, 228
BRAZELTON, 130
BREASLEY, 252
BREESE, 220
BREEZE, 201 359
BREMER, 118
BRENDEL, 244
BRENNAN, 126
BREWER, 165 195
BREWSAUGH, 137
BRIAN, 131
BRICE, 264 347
BRIDGEFORD, 284
BRIDGES, 119 142 201 204 306 321
BRIDGEWATER, 137 310
BRIDGFORD, 171
BRIGGS, 153 207 296 312 362
BRIGHTMAN, 212
BRILL, 139
BRINGHURST, 136
BRINK, 326
BRINKERHOFF, 106
BRISCOE, 268
BRISTOL, 148

BRISTOW, 322
BRITT, 98
BRITTINGHAM, 295
BRITTON, 301
BROAD, 174
BROADUS, 112
BROCK, 134 234
BROCKETT, 255
BRODDUS, 236
BROFFETT, 362
BRONSON, 370
BROOK, 122
BROOKINGS, 93
BROOKS, 84 135 271 294
BROSS, 256
BROSSEAU, 232
BROTHERS, 329
BROTT, 246
BROWN, 63 94 96 97 106 116
    124 130 131 163 164 175
    180-182 184 185 191 192
    210 212 216 222 252 256
    262 266 268 282 284 287
    290 292 296 304 306 312
    316 334 340 345 354 363
    371 374
BROWNE, 136
BROWNELL, 110 320
BROWNING, 134
BRUCE, 88 96 282 366
BRUCKER, 158
BRUFFITT, 294
BRUHN, 244
BRUINGTON, 115
BRUMBACK, 318
BRUMLAY, 221
BRUNER, 115 133
BRUNING, 244
BRUNNER, 192
BRUSH, 116 117 186 288
BRYAN, 49 81 135
BRYANT, 108 146 164

BRYNER, 24 55 60 67 174
BUCHANAN, 125 132 134 274
BUCK, 107 110 115 152 214
    286 318
BUCKHALTER, 252
BUCKINGHAM, 41
BUCKLE, 362
BUCKLES, 268
BUCKLEY, 187 350
BUCKMASTER, 132
BUCKNER, 131 238
BUDLONG, 171
BUELL, 186 363
BUFFINGTON, 203
BUFORD, 25 54 59 65 134
BULER, 126
BULL, 187
BULLARD, 256
BULLOCK, 162 173 296
BUNCE, 198
BUNDY, 176 375
BUNN, 192 332
BURBRIDGE, 368
BURCH, 269
BURDETT, 234
BURDICK, 256
BURGESS, 115 116 121
BURGH, 362
BURKE, 55 60 212
BURKS, 69
BURLINGHAM, 306
BURNAP, 22 343
BURNETT, 90 139 144 300
BURNETTE, 272
BURNHAM, 146 180
BURNS, 170 369
BURNSIDE, 111 222
BURR, 136 268
BURRELL, 21 280 343 354
BURRILL, 158
BURROUGHS, 226
BURROWS, 220 332

BURSON, 314
BURT, 131 196
BURTON, 113 378 379
BUSBY, 380
BUSEY, 232
BUSH, 114 171 218 270 344
BUSHNELL, 106
BUSSE, 128 195
BUSWELL, 266
BUTLER, 88 136 163 316 353 363
BUTTERFIELD, 159 366
BUTTOLPH, 228
BUTTON, 120
BUTTS, 165
BUZARD, 86
BYRNE, 170
BYRNS, 318
CACY, 345
CADY, 104 365
CAHILL, 112
CAIN, 142 208
CAINE, 208
CALAWAY, 122
CALDWELL, 97 214 354 355 359
CALHOUN, 118
CALL, 138
CALLICOTT, 138
CALLIHAN, 318
CALLON, 351
CALLOWAY, 122
CALLSEN, 115
CAM, 108 109
CAMERON, 7 12 19 24 25 27 31 55 60 69 204 208 210 300 363
CAMP, 153
CAMPBELL, 13 90 93 105 117 119 142 144 152 162 173 193 201 212 242 275 292 294 316 348 377 378

CAMPION, 260
CANFIELD, 86 365 366
CANNON, 236
CANTELLA, 362
CANTRALL, 308
CAPEHART, 142 143
CAPRON, 37 57 63 75
CAREY, 197
CARLE, 162 172
CARLIN, 25 54 59 66 156
CARLTON, 268
CARMICHAEL, 63 139 374
CARMIKEL, 26
CARNAHAN, 349
CARPENTER, 49 100 101 106 160 223 254 286 302 362
CARPER, 195
CARR, 13 25 57 63 74 90 100 101 110 240 320 347 360
CARREY, 340
CARRICO, 202
CARROLL, 297
CARTER, 92 103 225 381
CARTTER, 351
CARTWRIGHT, 206 236
CARWITH, 134
CASE, 109 218 336 358
CASEY, 56 61 72 142 246 260 300 322 343
CASS, 152
CASSELL, 133 282
CASTELLOM, 302
CASTLE, 302
CASWELL, 248
CATHERWOOD, 163
CATLIN, 282 344 346
CAULFIELD, 308
CAVANAUGH, 25 57 63 75 355 365
CAVENDER, 149
CELLER, 244
CHADBURN, 195 256

CHADWICK, 176
CHAFER, 108
CHALLENER, 125
CHAMBERLAIN, 360
CHAMBERS, 49 174 206
CHAMPION, 56 61 71 120 206 272
CHANDLER, 119 150 190 256 290 332 378
CHANNEL, 377
CHAPIN, 134 135 350 351 366
CHAPMAN, 91 112 157 188 322 337 371 375 380
CHAPPELL, 152 368
CHAPPLE, 174
CHARLESWORTH, 357
CHARTER, 115
CHASE, 15
CHATFIELD, 134 250
CHEANEY, 138
CHEENEY, 29
CHENEY, 57 62 76 193 378
CHENOWETH, 150
CHESLEY, 104
CHESTER, 224 256
CHETLAIN, 93 104
CHICKERING, 256
CHIDISTER, 363
CHILCOTT, 336
CHILDS, 322 354
CHIMLEY, 146
CHIPMAN, 236
CHISM, 202 254
CHOAT, 340
CHOISSER, 139 200
CHRISTIANSON, 196
CHRISTIE, 292
CHRISTOPHER, 55 60 71 258
CHRISTY, 144
CHURCH, 56 61 71 94 164 270 290
CHURCHILL, 102 157

CLAGG, 294
CLAPP, 174
CLARK, 88 94-96 105 110 115 122 130 152 154 158 164 175 197 220 234 238 246 258 267 272 292 297 302 306 320 328 332 348 360 363
CLARKSON, 372
CLARRY, 250
CLAY, 191 284
CLAYTON, 346
CLEGHORN, 120
CLEMENS, 202
CLEMENTS, 99
CLENDENIN, 360
CLENDENNING, 272
CLEVELAND, 148 186 360
CLIFF, 124
CLIFFE, 276
CLIFFORD, 138 170
CLIFT, 124
CLINE, 330
CLINGMAN, 172
CLISE, 151
CLOUGH, 115
CLOWSE, 112
CLUB, 221
CLYBORNE, 13 14
CLYBURN, 371
COAKLEY, 219
COATES, 102 103 262
COATSWORTH, 124 256
COCHENNOUR, 201
COCHRAN, 192
COCKEREL, 274
COE, 109 172 182 183 381
COFFEE, 127
COFFEY, 216
COFFIN, 294
COFFMAN, 282
COGGSWELL, 29 58 62 77

COGSWELL, 383
COHREN, 250
COKER, 356
COLBY, 118 224 230 338 383
COLCORD, 305
COLE, 107 156 183 214 256
COLEMAN, 162 200
COLER, 24 54 59 65 130
COLHOUR, 265
COLLIER, 114 270 293
COLLINS, 100 124 126 139
    197 222 263 288 350 375
COLLMER, 96
COLT, 226
COLTER, 323
COLTRIN, 216
COLVIN, 278 379
COLYER, 157
COMBS, 252
COMINGS, 220
COMPTON, 184 204
COMRIE, 177
COMSTOCK, 181 259 305
CONANT, 118
CONDEE, 349
CONE, 192
CONELLY, 158
CONGER, 208
CONGERS, 113
CONGON, 285
CONKEY, 194
CONKLIN, 120 162 212 360
CONN, 363
CONNER, 117
CONNOR, 170
CONOVER, 136 296 328
CONRAD, 89
CONROE, 371
CONTRELL, 300
CONVERSE, 181
CONWAY, 260 306
COOK, 16 54 59 64 86 94 104

COOK (Continued)
    161 195 270 276 329 351
COOL, 361
COOLEY, 36 37 58 61 62 77
    383
COOMBS, 370
COOPER, 117 181 192 232
    246 254 276 279 335 378
    380
COPE, 294
COPELAND, 108
COPLEY, 258
COPP, 338
COPPAGE, 337
CORBUS, 230
CORCRAN, 260
COREY, 318
CORMICK, 116
CORNELEY, 163
CORNELL, 369
CORNMAN, 108
CORNWELL, 271 284
CORRIE, 369
CORWIN, 181
COSGROVE, 126
COSPER, 228
COTTEL, 110
COTTEN, 196
COTTON, 246 336
COULSON, 248
COULTER, 112
COURTNEY, 282
COVER, 97 357
COWAN, 100 242
COWDEN, 378
COWDERY, 326
COWEL, 349
COWEN, 170 234 322 347 349
    362 363
COWGILL, 99 306
COX, 89 108 123 163 248 264
    276 322 330 345 354

COXE, 122
COYKENDALL, 222 369
CRABTREE, 298
CRACKEL, 161
CRAFTON, 366
CRAIG, 98 100 116 207 369
CRAIN, 334
CRAMER, 180
CRANDALL, 146 234 278 357
CRANE, 214 242 278 344 354 380
CRAWFORD, 116 186 196 290 300 337 346 360
CRAYCRAFT, 318
CREBS, 254
CREED, 223
CREGO, 350 383
CRESAP, 294
CREWDSON, 112
CREWS, 116 117 280
CRINGLE, 218
CRISKY, 217
CRITZER, 100
CROMWELL, 174
CRONEMILLER, 229
CROOKER, 191
CROOKS, 204
CROPSEY, 336
CROSBY, 176 329
CROSS, 116 366
CROSSLEY, 194
CROUCH, 200 365
CROW, 347
CROWELL, 264
CROWLEY, 145
CROZIER, 158
CRUM, 338
CUDNEY, 378
CULLERS, 353
CULLUM, 349
CULVER, 202 263 290 336
CUMMING, 55 60 67 182

CUMMINGS, 27 28 86 95 145 182 250 369
CUMMINS, 344
CUNIFFE, 107
CUNNINGHAM, 118 127 240 261 356 363
CUPPY, 294
CUREN, 270
CURLESS, 250
CURRIE, 198 368
CURRIER, 293
CURRY, 143 318 366
CURTIS, 110 118 139 154 165 224 238 378
CURTISS, 315 332
CUSHING, 256
CUSHMAN, 27 28 55 60 68 186
CUSICK, 133 180
CUSTER, 133
CUTLER, 158 195 246
CUTTS, 344
CYRUS, 180
DABNEY, 278
DAILEY, 126 356
DAILY, 177 340 352
DALEY, 370
DALGAR, 274
DALLAM, 90 100
DAMRON, 321
DANA, 361
DANFORTH, 373
DANIELS, 290 306
DANISON, 162
DARNELL, 332
DASHIELL, 351
DAVENPORT, 304
DAVEY, 216
DAVIDSON, 23 58 62 76 86 144 161 185 200 212 226 260 288 296 297 316 380
DAVIS, 25 29 49 55 60 67 89

DAVIS (Continued)
  94 102 112 113 115-117 122
  132 142 162 163 172 182
  185 200 206 207 213 216
  226 232 239 241 248 260
  267 274 297 312 322 348
  356 369 370
DAWES, 203 356
DAWSEY, 258
DAWSON, 264 272 380
DAY, 55 61 71 96 139 154 262
  300 342
DAYHUFF, 340
DEAN, 102 252
DEANE, 102
DEANGUERA, 182
DECAMP, 338
DECKER, 148 166 167
DEE, 368
DEGRESS, 378
DELABAR, 113
DELANO, 346
DELLITT, 300
DEMENT, 106 344
DEMING, 300
DEMOTTE, 157 216
DEMPSEY, 192 220
DENCHFIELD, 175
DENEEN, 314
DENGLER, 166
DENINGER, 10
DENISON, 96
DENNESS, 137
DENNING, 116 153
DENNIS, 263 264 318
DENNISON, 88 97 268
DENOMAN, 274
DENT, 342
DENTON, 263
DENZEL, 381
DEPEW, 353
DEPUY, 172

DERICKS, 159
DERRICK, 84
DESELMS, 266
DESHON, 176
DETRICH, 125
DEVOLL, 106
DEWEY, 186 288 298
DEWITT, 138
DEWOLF, 175
DEXTER, 148
DIAL, 334
DICK, 92
DICKERMAN, 286 358
DICKERSON, 304
DICKEY, 24 57 63 74 102 172
  350
DICKHUT, 348
DICKINSON, 154
DICKSON, 93 104 105 131
DIEDRICH, 212
DIETZ, 150
DILL, 207 258
DILLE, 232
DILLER, 210
DILLON, 116 133 156 193
DILLS, 90
DILWORTH, 250 318
DIMICK, 258
DIMOCK, 93
DINSMORE, 278
DISHON, 298
DISMANT, 377
DITTLINGER, 381
DIX, 120
DIXON, 137 190
DOANE, 92 102
DOBBS, 151
DOBSON, 312
DOCKER, 355
DOCKSTATER, 214
DODDS, 114 174 200
DODGE, 155 352

DODSON, 26 63 375
DOGETT, 195
DOLAN, 117
DOLLINS, 26 55 60 63 70 242 374
DOLLOFF, 349
DONALD, 220 235
DONALDSON, 112
DONICA, 351
DONNELL, 338
DONOVAN, 369
DOOLEY, 296
DOOLITTLE, 199
DORAN, 208
DORATHY, 354
DORCHESTER, 376
DORNBLASER, 172
DORR, 266
DORRENCE, 286
DORRIS, 302 334
DORWIN, 347
DOTY, 155 185 288
DOUCH, 372
DOUGHERTY, 20 54 59 65 124
DOUGLAS, 152 228 343
DOVE, 264 310
DOW, 270 304 350
DOWLEY, 247
DOWNING, 308
DOX, 350
DOYLE, 204 304
DRAKE, 105 145
DRENNAN, 371
DRESSER, 58 62 76 380
DRISH, 144 322
DROLL, 366
DRUCKENBRODT, 166 167
DRUM, 119
DUBOIS, 232 320
DUCAT, 93 104
DUER, 170

DUFF, 380
DUFFENBECKER, 250
DUFFY, 260 296
DUFOE, 164
DUGGER, 132 322
DUGUID, 210
DUKES, 300
DULANEY, 297
DUNBAUGH, 348
DUNCAN, 103 145 323 349
DUNCKLEE, 146
DUNHAM, 264
DUNLAP, 138 160 181 232 380
DUNN, 185 217 304
DUNNING, 122
DURAND, 375
DURELL, 137
DURFEE, 96
DURHAM, 224 232 334
DURKEE, 381
DUSTIN, 56 61 72 196 290 360 361
DUTCHER, 228
DUTTON, 107 146 278 290
DYER, 121 185 214 242 266 288
DYHRENFURTH, 373
DYKE, 153
DYSART, 148
EADS, 182 212
EAMES, 145
EARL, 185 186 236
EARLY, 109 181
EART, 366
EASLEY, 123
EASTERDAY, 330
EASTHAM, 108
EATON, 116 122 155
EBEY, 136
ECKDALL, 381
EDDS, 292

EDDY, 138 146 270 350 383
EDGAR, 144
EDGINGTON, 336
EDMISTEN, 294
EDMONSTON, 120
EDMUNDSON, 337
EDSON, 90
EDVALL, 166
EDWARDS, 116 117 160 193 235 242 278 355
EELS, 230
EGE, 148
EHRHARD, 166
ELA, 147
ELBERT, 147
ELDER, 268 302
ELDRIDGE, 332 381
ELKIN, 343 365
ELLAS, 145
ELLEDGE, 278
ELLIFF, 314
ELLINGTON, 130
ELLINWOOD, 228
ELLIOTT, 146 153 160 181 232 238 250 284 353 354 369
ELLIS, 85 94 110 212 258 291 319
ELLISON, 214
ELLSWORTH, 292 317 363
ELMORE, 142
ELTING, 383
ELTON, 92
ELWOOD, 187 280
EM, 235
EMERSON, 254
EMERY, 160 254
ENGEL, 166
ENGELMANN, 166
ENGLISH, 144
ENLOW, 254
ENOCH, 214

ENSEY, 353
ENSMINGER, 334
EPPERSON, 359
ERBE, 129
EROST, 230
ERSKINE, 373
ERVIN, 136 248
ERWIN, 120 121 274
ESPY, 310
ESTABROOK, 86 94 95
ESTILL, 137 309
EVANS, 121 200 204 272 298 316 330
EVARTS, 332
EVEREST, 107
EVERLY, 292
EVERSALL, 374
EVERTS, 184 218
EWELL, 185
EWEN, 280
EWER, 210
EWERT, 344
EWING, 292
EXTER, 167
EYMAN, 150 312
FACKNEY, 254
FAHNESTOCK, 253
FAIRBANKS, 88
FAIRFIELD, 375
FAIRMAN, 155
FALLIS, 344
FANNING, 282
FARLEY, 310
FARMER, 242
FARNAM, 270
FARNAN, 353 354
FARNSWORTH, 24 57 63 75 360 361
FARR, 105
FARRAR, 176
FARRELL, 176
FARRIS, 104 105 177

FARWELL, 136
FAULKNER, 118 252
FAUNTLEROY, 120
FAUST, 172
FAVOR, 289
FEE, 181 278
FEENEY, 260
FELLOWS, 120 159 328
FELT, 243
FELTER, 350
FENTON, 380
FERGUS, 95
FERGUSON, 94 164 268 306
   308 366
FERHUNE, 309
FERREE, 98
FERRELL, 138
FERRIE, 375
FERRILL, 138
FERRIMAN, 157
FERRIS, 93
FESTER, 342
FETZER, 109
FICK, 117
FICKLE, 306
FIELD, 102 192 290 326 340
FIELDCAMP, 166
FIELDS, 92 160
FIFE, 231
FIFER, 146
FIGG, 161
FIKE, 314 315
FILES, 193
FILGER, 234
FILKINS, 118
FILLER, 92 204
FILLERS, 102
FILLMORE, 191
FINCH, 357
FISH, 152 184
FISHER, 93 95 104 105 188
   204 210 228 266 267 291

FISHER (Continued)
   347 370
FISK, 170
FISKE, 351
FITCH, 164 336 378
FITE, 355
FITHIAN, 155
FITTS, 374
FITZER, 124
FITZGERALD, 127
FITZSIMMONS, 289
FLAGG, 360 361
FLANNIGAN, 192
FLANSBURY, 194 195
FLEMING, 98 189
FLEMMING, 373
FLESHBEIN, 220
FLETCHER, 57 380
FLICKINGER, 159
FLOOD, 91 276 380
FLORENCE, 167
FLOWER, 232
FLOYD, 180 193 210 320 343
FLUSKY, 379
FLYNN, 130 131 133 260 336
FOGARTY, 200
FOGGY, 142
FOLEY, 153 205
FOLKS, 133
FONDA, 56 61 73 316 345 370
FONDEY, 116
FOOT, 92
FOOTE, 157
FORBES, 313 358
FORD, 37 63 124 130 131 204
   232 294 374 375
FORSEE, 194
FORSYTH, 148 360 361
FORSYTHE, 290
FORT, 103
FORTH, 302
FOSHA, 262

FOSKETT, 326
FOSTER, 21 22 165 240 254 276 277 296 302 308 312 355
FOUKE, 25 54 59 66
FOUNTAIN, 174 252
FOUTCH, 132
FOWLER, 332
FOX, 56 61 72 150 220 222 282 366
FRANCIS, 94 95
FRANCISCA, 331
FRANK, 244
FRANKLIN, 57 62 76 268 378
FRANKS, 296
FRASIER, 182
FRAZIER, 93 198
FREDERICK, 163 198
FREELAND, 122
FREEMAN, 159 288 310 322 366 368
FREMONT, 22-24 26
FRENCH, 125 224 253 334
FREY, 128 244
FRICK, 155 167
FRIDAY, 101
FRIEDRICH, 128
FRINKEN, 113
FRISBIE, 121 154 155
FRITES, 214
FRITSCH, 128
FRITZ, 113 166
FRITZE, 129
FRIZELL, 201
FROHLICH, 125
FROHOCK, 170
FROMAN, 312
FROST, 248
FRY, 29 55 60 68 202 335
FUCHS, 129 245
FUESS, 167

FULLER, 41 48 53 81 84 149 172 197 211 222 248 312 334
FULLERTON, 208 344
FUNKE, 368
FUNKHOUSER, 56 60 71 132 276
GADD, 276
GAINES, 180
GALBRAITH, 177
GALE, 382
GALION, 100 149
GALLAGHER, 359
GALLAHER, 224
GALLOWAY, 124 328
GALRAITH, 177
GALVIN, 161
GAMBALL, 246
GAMBLE, 360
GAPIN, 137
GARD, 380
GARDNER, 107 182 281 286 338
GARLAND, 136
GARLOCK, 165
GARRETSON, 204
GARRETT, 247 307 345
GARRIOTT, 119
GARTERNICHT, 137 248
GARWOOD, 105
GASH, 112
GASS, 328
GASSAWAY, 299
GASTON, 359
GATES, 193 330
GEARHART, 305
GEDDES, 316
GENTRY, 138 284
GEORGE, 117 123 160 210
GERHARDI, 128
GERHARDT, 129

GERHARDY, 129
GERHART, 360
GERMAN, 306
GERRIDE, 89
GETTMAN, 165
GIBBONS, 208
GIBBS, 111
GIBON, 93
GIBSON, 92 124 158 201 256 300 309 350 351 355 356
GIDDINGS, 294
GIDEON, 135
GIFFORD, 360 363
GIGGINS, 308
GILBERT, 31 37 55 60 69 206 222 371 374
GILCRIST, 336
GILE, 350
GILES, 230
GILHAM, 282 314
GILL, 88 146
GILLELAND, 279
GILLESPIE, 101 109 162 216
GILLETT, 191 230
GILLETTE, 332
GILLHAM, 336
GILLILAND, 142
GILLISPIE, 321
GILLITT, 172
GILLMAN, 136
GILLMORE, 99
GILLUM, 137
GILMAN, 106 126
GILMER, 91 144 156
GILMORE, 132 314 371
GILSON, 246
GIRNT, 101
GISHWILLER, 264
GLADDING, 225
GLASS, 88 356
GLASSCO, 353
GLASSNER, 196

GLAZE, 206
GLEESON, 126
GLENN, 135 144 180 181 354
GLOSSBRENNER, 207
GOBLE, 157
GODDARD, 142 143 201 266 280
GOLD, 84
GOLDEN, 157
GOODBRAKE, 120
GOODE, 122
GOODELL, 274
GOODENOW, 380
GOODHEART, 344
GOODING, 180 198 322
GOODMAN, 88 298
GOODRICH, 234
GOODSPEED, 202 203
GOODWIN, 120 160 218 242 256
GORDON, 93 175 356 381
GORE, 332
GORGAS, 106
GORMAN, 268
GOSLIN, 176 177
GOSSETT, 139
GOTTLOB, 98 244
GOVE, 146
GRAHAM, 160 236 254 255 294 359 373
GRAMMAR, 242
GRANGER, 165 360
GRANT, 6 20 46 54 59 65 104 122 262
GRASS, 88 203 262
GRATTON, 193
GRAVE, 252
GRAVES, 125 184 290
GRAY, 146 158 162 171 175 200 206 260 267 279 302 369
GRAYSON, 206

GREATHOUSE, 176
GREATON, 278
GREEN, 49 51 100 116 138 163 171 272
GREENE, 236
GREENHUT, 245
GREENLEE, 143
GREENWOOD, 149 183 291 368
GREER, 318
GREGG, 126 197 314 369
GREGORY, 124 252 330
GREUSEL, 24 54 60 66 86 94 152
GREVE, 155
GREWELL, 248
GRIER, 55 61 70 234
GRIERSON, 355
GRIFFIN, 136 153 171 196 304 383
GRIFFITH, 249 250 327
GRIGGS, 192
GRIMES, 176 177 184
GRIMM, 167 370
GRISWOLD, 186 193 266
GROSSENHEIDER, 372
GROSVENOR, 370
GROVER, 208
GROW, 135
GRUBB, 316
GRUNDY, 130
GRUTH, 252
GUARD, 138 348
GUDGEL, 304
GUE, 296
GUENTHER, 128 129
GUILD, 184 320
GUILICK, 98
GUINNIP, 55 60 70 238
GUITEAU, 356
GULLICH, 256
GUMBART, 381

GUMBERT, 58 76
GUNTHER, 128
GUTHRIE, 118 119
GUY, 283
GWIN, 336
GWINN, 156
HACKETT, 204
HACKNEY, 198 263
HADLEY, 222
HADSELL, 137
HAGER, 170
HAGERTY, 266
HAGGARD, 202
HAGLITT, 296
HAHN, 194
HAIGH, 152
HAIGHT, 381
HAILES, 200
HAINES, 113
HAKES, 93
HALBERT, 314
HALDEMAN, 158 322
HALE, 93 104 143 214 219 231 259 287 332
HALL, 105 108 130 148 160 163 182 192 193 198 206 214 216 252 258 322 327 335 345 350 358 373
HALLECK, 31
HALLEY, 340
HALLFORD, 338
HALLIGAN, 190
HALT, 322
HALTEMAN, 110
HAMAR, 347
HAMBAUGH, 318
HAMER, 248
HAMILTON, 94 98 108 119 124 194 202 216 284 288 330 376
HAMMAKER, 161
HAMMERICH, 129

HAMMERS, 234
HAMMICK, 246
HAMMOCK, 242
HAMMOND, 150 153 280
HAN, 151
HANAH, 188
HANBACK, 135
HANCE, 258
HAND, 129
HANDBERRY, 97
HANDY, 238
HANEY, 112 190 288
HANFORD, 256 350 351
HANGER, 381
HANNA, 88 97 180 262
HANNAH, 205
HANNIFIN, 230
HANON, 310
HANSAKER, 298
HANSEL, 380
HANSON, 164 245
HAPEMAN, 103 288 351 352
HARBERTS, 172
HARBISON, 180
HARBOR, 328
HARD, 360
HARDEN, 359
HARDIN, 186 282
HARDING, 13 14 22 55 60 70 115 118 210 246 284 322
HARDY, 163 312 320
HARGRAVE, 348
HARKEY, 188
HARKNESS, 171 235 259
HARLAN, 123 220 338
HARLAND, 117
HARMAN, 60
HARMER, 240
HARMON, 56 73 292 328
HARNED, 338
HARNEY, 12
HARNNI, 167

HARPER, 301 351 363
HARRINGTON, 134 159 232 260 362
HARRIS, 14 27 55 60 68 91 132 138 150 157 181 186 188 195 206 248 312 334 338 353
HARRISON, 94 216 353 361
HARROLD, 163
HARSHBERGER, 294
HART, 124 134 138 377
HARTLINE, 298
HARTMAN, 26 129 222 372
HARTS, 292
HARTSOCK, 156 238
HARTSOUGH, 266
HARTZ, 296
HARTZELL, 212
HARVEY, 88 97 225 354 370
HARWOOD, 280
HASE, 193
HASKELL, 214
HASSEMAN, 92
HASTINGS, 131 272
HASTY, 359
HATCH, 113 228
HATFIELD, 182 187
HATHAWAY, 110 172
HAWES, 89 98 154
HAWK, 264
HAWKINS, 201 236
HAWKS, 175
HAWLEY, 13 98 150 152 171 302
HAWS, 226
HAWTHORNE, 37
HAY, 89 241 314 338
HAYDEN, 13 14 118 370
HAYES, 269 310
HAYNES, 117 322
HAYNIE, 25 55 60 67 176
HAYS, 112 213 300 369

HAYWARD, 381
HAYWOOD, 110
HAZARD, 355
HAZEN, 174
HAZLEHURST, 153
HAZLEWOOD, 180
HEALD, 358 363
HEALY, 126 127 196
HEARD, 160
HEART, 189
HEARTLEY, 109
HEATH, 116 117 290
HEBARD, 343 375
HECKER, 24 54 55 59 61 65 70 128 244
HECKLEMAN, 312
HEDERICK, 113
HEDGER, 113
HEDGES, 292
HEDRICK, 308
HEELAN, 197
HEFFELFINGER, 149
HEFFERNAN, 191
HEFFINGTON, 222
HEIFFMAN, 270
HEILIG, 214
HEINRICHS, 128
HEINZ, 282
HEINZMANN, 244
HEISE, 102 280
HELM, 132 264 312 378
HENDERSON, 56 61 72 106 158 175 198 283 304 372
HENDRICKS, 195
HENDRICKSON, 348
HENDRIX, 238
HENLY, 298
HENNING, 381
HENRY, 109 111 236 296 318
HENSHAW, 37 58 62 77 383
HENSTEIN, 165
HERALD, 368

HERBERT, 113 218
HERITAGE, 158
HERNDON, 236
HEROD, 340 355 357
HERRELSON, 160
HERRICK, 148 149 288
HERRING, 359
HERRINGTON, 185
HESLET, 288
HESS, 200
HESSER, 202
HEWITT, 111 135 148
HIBBEN, 350
HICE, 110
HICKEY, 127
HICKMAN, 131 162 300
HICKOX, 232 367
HICKS, 24 54 59 66 155 160 222 266 272 344
HIGBIE, 317
HIGBY, 106
HIGGINS, 113 126 147 210 246 248 345 353 370 380
HIGGS, 332
HIGHT, 200
HIGHTOWER, 242
HILDEBRAND, 121
HILL, 88 118 176 213 230 296 378
HILLBORG, 245
HILLER, 149
HILLIARD, 214
HILLIER, 362 382
HILLMAN, 15
HINCHMAN, 358
HINCKLEY, 260
HINDMAN, 149
HINES, 126
HINMAN, 220
HINMON, 107
HINZ, 129
HIPOLITE, 116

HITCHCOCK, 145 252
HITT, 134 186 350 365
HIVELY, 308
HOADLEY, 228
HOAG, 122
HOBBS, 152 259 276 300 340
HOBSON, 107
HODGE, 116 241 252 320 358
HODGES, 232
HODSDUN, 254
HOENNY, 167
HOERING, 166 167
HOFF, 262
HOFFMAN, 159 276 366
HOGAN, 374
HOGDEN, 278
HOGE, 56 61 73 300 306
HOGG, 344
HOLBROOK, 224
HOLCOMB, 171
HOLDEN, 87 95 153 256
HOLE, 115
HOLLAN, 318
HOLLEMAN, 302
HOLLENBECK, 230 344
HOLLENBERG, 342
HOLLIS, 149
HOLMES, 177
HOLSTEAD, 251
HOLT, 176 343 344
HOLTON, 208 316
HOOD, 125 173 314
HOOKER, 158 361
HOOPER, 160
HOOTON, 252
HOOVER, 143
HOPKINS, 23 58 62 76 91 92
    117 161 266 268 380
HOPPE, 244
HOPPER, 258
HORN, 104 180
HORR, 150

HORSEMAN, 349
HORTEN, 274
HORTON, 336 348
HOSEA, 365
HOSFORD, 304
HOSKINS, 120 336
HOSKINSON, 161
HOSMER, 306
HOSTETTER, 139 148 149
    312
HOTALING, 344
HOTCHKISS, 92 234 258
HOTOPP, 360
HOTTENSTEIN, 164
HOUGH, 31 32 55 60 69 114
    214 234 362
HOUGHTALING, 13 23 57 62
    76 90 377
HOUGHTON, 250
HOUSELMAN, 207
HOUSTIN, 188
HOUSTON, 131 182 186
HOUTS, 124
HOVE, 220
HOVEY, 24 54 60 66 146 237
HOWARD, 85 119 138 197 223
    275 280 327
HOWDEN, 236
HOWE, 123 133 288 326
HOWELL, 97 173 258 269 296
    328
HOWES, 353
HOWK, 369
HOWLAND, 182
HOWLETT, 344
HOYER, 380
HOYLE, 232
HOYT, 176 184 306
HUBBARD, 84 121 124 256
    278 318 347 355 374
HUBBELL, 294
HUCKSTEP, 310

HUDGENS, 334
HUDSON, 126 186 221
HUFFMAN, 377
HUFFNER, 163
HUFFSTUTLER, 334
HUGHES, 99 173 232 330 357
HUGUNIN, 93 104 105
HULBERT, 201
HULBURD, 126
HULBUT, 192
HULIT, 359
HULL, 214 278
HULSE, 322
HUME, 236
HUMESTON, 154
HUMPHREY, 184 236 270 362
HUMPHRIES, 161
HUNDLEY, 56 61 74 334
HUNGERFORD, 136
HUNT, 102 156 171 182 231 290 329 330 344 347
HUNTER, 87 95 117 118 123 143 144 206 218 239 366 368 377
HUNTING, 358
HUNTINGTON, 363
HUNTLEY, 23 37 154 222 343 375
HUNTOON, 232
HURD, 184
HURLBURT, 194
HURLBUT, 102
HURLESS, 231
HURT, 97 137 292 293
HUTCHENS, 26 63
HUTCHINS, 374
HUYETT, 266
HYDE, 186 351
HYMER, 310
HYNES, 361
ICE, 116
IHRIE, 202

IJAMIS, 216
ING, 161
INGALSBE, 365
INGERSOLL, 24 57 63 75 102 161 232 368
INGRAHAM, 173 280
INGRAM, 161 200 204
INNESS, 118
IRELAND, 92
IRONS, 55 60 70 252
IRVIN, 229 232 253
IRVINE, 230
IRWIN, 133 218 234 347
ISAMINGER, 206
ISBELL, 174
ISHMEL, 181
ISLAND, 234
ISOM, 131 328
IVES, 338
JACKMAN, 175
JACKSON, 14 105 107 118 125 154 259 284 328 344
JACOBI, 128 129
JACOBS, 238 254
JACQUES, 355
JAEHE, 376
JAMES, 189 224 262 272 338 350 382
JAMISON, 122 138 222
JANE, 359
JANES, 355
JANSEN, 134 370
JANSSEN, 359
JAQUESS, 55 61 69 226 355
JAQUIS, 132
JEFFCOAT, 306
JEFFERS, 272 290 383
JEHUE, 102
JEMISON, 175
JENKINS, 216 234 342 354
JENKS, 63 86 107 144 152 375
JENNINGS, 151 314 320 360

JESSUP, 354
JEWELL, 92
JOBE, 104
JOBES, 276
JOHNS, 206 254 276 336
JOHNSON, 25 49 51 54 59 65
  81 83 84 95 104 108 109
  113 124 136 142 148 154
  158 165 171 173 183 189
  190 194 198 246 266 276
  279 286 292 298 308 319
  328 336 338 347 368
JOHNSTON, 176 268 330
JOINER, 193
JOLLIFF, 302
JOLLY, 350 351
JONAS, 181
JONES, 90 92 96 97 104 110
  111 114-116 122 135 138
  142 151 154 172 188 190
  210 213 217 226 232 238
  240 246 254 262 276 291
  310 328 344 345 374 378
JORDAN, 154 219 236
JORDON, 204
JOSEPH, 236
JOSLYN, 86 106 110 152 153
JUDD, 202
JUDY, 56 61 73 95 202 308
JULIAN, 319
JWAN, 340
KABRICK, 330
KAFKA, 244
KAGAY, 151
KALFALURY, 128 129
KANADY, 138 320
KANE, 197 307
KANEN, 162
KAPLINGER, 322
KAUFMAN, 129
KAY, 326
KAYS, 234

KEAGLE, 314
KEAL, 180
KEASEY, 208
KEE, 210
KEEDY, 234
KEEFNER, 98
KEELER, 118 270
KEEN, 206
KEENER, 132
KEFFER, 193
KEILEY, 365
KEISER, 150
KEITH, 29 58 62 76 88 182
  381
KELLER, 144 338
KELLEY, 116 260 277 281
KELLOGG, 25 57 63 75 93 114
  126 146 358
KELLY, 110 117 133 161 163
  189 202 242 286 294 360
  363 376
KELSER, 184
KELSON, 116
KEMPER, 136
KENDALL, 180 326
KENDRICK, 191 249
KENNARD, 120 121
KENNEDY, 210 250
KENNICOTT, 155 159
KENT, 138
KENYAN, 103 194
KENYON, 111 314
KERCHEVAL, 84 86
KERLIN, 132
KERN, 292
KERR, 112 214 228 270 298
  368
KERSHNER, 348
KERSTING, 108
KETCHUM, 347
KEYES, 190
KEYMER, 166

KEYS, 150 333
KHRUMNE, 172
KIDDER, 258 370
KIECHER, 85
KIERSEY, 241
KILGOUR, 106 230 231
KILLION, 116
KILLPATRICK, 136
KIMBALL, 94 114 115 218
KIMBER, 282
KIMBERLY, 372
KIMBLE, 189
KIMMEL, 298
KINCAID, 347
KINCHELOE, 236
KINDER, 314
KING, 90 97 112 120 121 132 181 216 285 287 308 312 322 374 375
KINGERY, 310
KINGMAN, 252
KINGSBURY, 114 329
KINGSLEY, 252
KINMAN, 279 310 311 345
KINNEAR, 174
KINNEY, 56 61 73 147 185 266 318
KINSEY, 314
KINSLOE, 186
KINZIE, 362
KIPP, 210
KIRCHNER, 244
KIRK, 24 54 60 66 148 377
KIRKBRIDGE, 348
KIRKHAM, 27 55 60 68 109 192 303
KIRKLAND, 93
KIRKMAN, 122
KIRKPATRICK, 277 348
KITCH, 359
KITCHELL, 89 276
KITCHEN, 181

KITTEL, 196
KITTELL, 196
KITTOE, 170
KLEEKNER, 266
KLEIN, 57
KLINE, 188
KLOCK, 98
KLOKKE, 128
KLUTSCH, 245
KLUTTS, 298
KNAPP, 131 133 158 184 202
KNICKERBOCKER, 209
KNIFFIN, 200
KNIGHT, 123 198 266 332 342 364
KNOBELSDORF, 24
KNOBELSDORFF, 54 67
KNOBLESDORFF, 59
KNOWLES, 211
KNOWLTON, 95 369
KNOX, 106 322 330 362 363 371 374 378
KNUTSON, 166
KOCHLEIN, 89
KOEHLER, 104 358 359
KOERBER, 330
KOERCHA, 89
KOLBN, 240
KORGLE, 105
KORN, 98
KOTHE, 196
KOVATS, 129
KOWALD, 13
KREBS, 98
KROEGER, 166 167
KROH, 298
KRUEGER, 372
KUHN, 98 175
KUME, 126
KUNE, 128
KURTH, 196
KUYKENDALL, 142

KYLE, 248 336
KYMER, 372
LABAUGH, 111
LABOYTAUX, 144
LACKEY, 104 216 276
LACKLAND, 296
LACRONE, 276
LACY, 92 220 239 276
LAFFERTY, 222
LAGOU, 123
LAGRANGE, 358
LAIMBEER, 154
LAKE, 110 131 258 372
LAKIN, 229 262
LAMB, 238 282 312 337
LAMBERSON, 119
LAMBERT, 116
LANCASTER, 227
LAND, 254 315
LANE, 127 161 172 240 256 310
LANG, 128
LANGEFELD, 129
LANGELFELD, 129
LANGHOLZ, 370
LANGLEY, 328
LANGSTON, 250
LANIGAN, 127
LANPHERE, 347
LANPHIER, 216 292
LANSING, 378
LANZENDORFER, 244
LAPHAM, 150 310
LARIMER, 302
LARKIN, 194 261
LARRIMORE, 216
LARRISON, 344
LASALLE, 244
LASATER, 223 341
LASH, 218
LATHAM, 56 61 72 292 308
LATHROP, 132

LATIMER, 188 247
LATTIMER, 222
LAUGHLIN, 227 268 272
LAVIGNE, 376
LAW, 106 174
LAWLER, 20 54 59 65 116
LAWRENCE, 117 171 190 203 268 295 304 305 353 355
LAWS, 206 276
LAWTON, 147
LAWVER, 264
LAWYER, 86 94
LAY, 348
LAYCOCK, 194
LEAHEY, 187
LEAMON, 207
LEAVITT, 148
LEBOLD, 345
LECLAIR, 369
LEDBETTER, 188
LEDERGERBER, 89
LEDLIE, 278
LEDYARD, 224
LEE, 144 151 162 185 188 253 266 304 328 348 359
LEEK, 374
LEEPER, 96
LEFFINGWELL, 228
LEIB, 345
LEIBER, 89 98
LEIGH, 322
LEIGHTON, 288
LEISER, 128
LEISHMAN, 125
LEITCH, 338
LELAND, 347
LEMLEY, 316
LEMMA, 334
LEMON, 159 206 212
LENDER, 244
LEONARD, 155 260
LEROY, 262

LESAGE, 282
LESTER, 182 328
LETTMAN, 164
LETTON, 180
LETTS, 280
LEVANWAY, 148
LEWIS, 125 142 146 151 163
    172 206 220 248 264 274
    294 299
LEWMAN, 368
LIBBY, 332
LIDACK, 212
LIDDLE, 260
LIEB, 96
LIGHT, 24 54 60 66 158
LIGHTFOOT, 283
LIGHTON, 164
LIGLEN, 360
LIKELY, 284
LIKES, 137
LINBARGER, 369
LINCOLN, 360
LINDLEY, 186
LINDROTH, 167
LINDSAY, 177
LINDSEY, 343 353
LINDSLEY, 288
LINGENFELTER, 161
LINGLE, 312
LININGER, 238
LINK, 122
LINSLEY, 132
LINTON, 158 194
LIPPERT, 128 372
LIPPINCOTT, 146 147 242
LITHERLAND, 375
LITTLEFIELD, 109
LITTLER, 211
LIVELL, 100
LIVINGSTON, 125
LOCKE, 291 344
LOCKER, 103

LOCKWOOD, 146 266
LODGE, 187 206
LOFTON, 322
LOGAN, 25 29 54 59 60 66 142
    144 188 345 371
LOHMANN, 128
LONERGAN, 197
LONG, 102 118 162 163 262
LONGCER, 110
LONGHORN, 119
LONGLEY, 90 100
LONGSTRETH, 212 351
LONGWORTH, 153
LOOMIS, 25 54 59 65 84 132
    355 356
LOONEY, 142
LOOP, 270
LORD, 158 172 194 290
LORIMER, 115
LORING, 107
LOTT, 91
LOUD, 322
LOUTZENHEISER, 351
LOVE, 122 135
LOVELL, 165 302
LOW, 99 238 328
LOWE, 26 99 112 175 314 333
LOWELL, 381
LOWREY, 266
LOWRY, 88 294 295 361
LOY, 223 380
LOYD, 267
LUCAS, 174 306 308
LUCE, 350 363
LUDDINGTON, 150
LUDINGTON, 288
LUDWIG, 359
LUFF, 370
LUKE, 111
LUND, 113
LURTON, 274
LUSK, 101 212

LUTTRELL, 282
LYDICK, 177
LYMAN, 170 306
LYNCH, 27 28 29 55 60 68 88 196 197 296 356
LYNN, 218
LYON, 147 152
LYTAKER, 348
LYTLE, 134 135 182
MAAGER, 196
MABEE, 366
MABIE, 218
MABRY, 88 151 302
MACFALL, 347 348
MACK, 55 60 69 184 232 306
MACKEY, 190
MACREADING, 158
MADDOX, 198
MADDUX, 220
MADISON, 23 58 62 76 119 380
MADUX, 313
MAFFATT, 185
MAGARITY, 252
MAGEE, 182 204 252
MAGNER, 105
MAGOFFIN, 14
MAHANNAH, 312
MAHER, 123
MAHLHORN, 124
MAJOR, 252
MALLORY, 210 250 308 309
MALMBORG, 190
MALONEY, 214
MALTBY, 170
MANIER, 176
MANLOVE, 113
MANN, 101 158 202 240 269 326 328 353 354
MANNING, 202 208 210
MANNON, 284
MANSKER, 116

MANSUR, 119
MANZER, 194 270
MAPES, 211
MARBLE, 172 251
MARINER, 375
MARION, 95
MARIS, 206
MARKS, 116 117
MARQUIS, 276
MARRAH, 262
MARSCHNER, 57 63
MARSCHUER, 376
MARSH, 20 54 55 59 61 65 69 94 113 120 172 228 316 345 370
MARSHALL, 57 63 74 88 119 158 203 222 248 264 302 342 356 362
MARSHNER, 26
MARTIN, 56 61 72 88 130 138 149 160 194 196 220 239 254 272 274 276 294 302 330 336 339 353 361 374
MARX, 26 57 63 244 372 376
MASON, 87 100 104 109 146 222 264 290 340
MASSEY, 160 193
MASSIE, 278
MASTERS, 217
MATHENY, 338
MATHER, 84 380
MATHEWS, 114 322
MATHIE, 95
MATLACK, 360
MATLESON, 286
MATTERN, 203
MATTESON, 126 208
MATTHEWS, 278
MATTICE, 346
MAUFF, 128
MAULDING, 356
MAUM, 93

MAUNS, 128
MAUS, 347
MAUSS, 166
MAXEY, 201 300
MAXON, 150
MAXWELL, 250 359
MAY, 146 181 186 201 208 282 319 338 373
MAYA, 107
MAYER, 128
MAYERS, 264
MAYES, 336
MAYFIELD, 87 176
MAYNARD, 139
MAYO, 254
MAZELL, 154
MCADAMS, 124
MCAFEE, 379
MCALISTER, 91 377
MCALLISTER, 13 23 57 62 76 112 113 238
MCAMIE, 301
MCARTHUR, 16 49 51 54 59 64 93 104 105 362
MCASSEY, 260
MCATEE, 101
MCAULEY, 190
MCBEAN, 286
MCCAGG, 377
MCCALEB, 234 340
MCCANDLESS, 237
MCCARTHY, 260 370
MCCARTNEY, 114 304 365 366
MCCARTY, 124
MCCLANAHAN, 92 115 186 187 246
MCCLARY, 383
MCCLAUGHRY, 280 316
MCCLAUSLAND, 358
MCCLEARY, 99
MCCLEAVE, 204

MCCLEAVY, 260
MCCLELLAN, 22 218
MCCLELLAND, 130 250 348
MCCLERNAND, 57
MCCLERNANDS, 26
MCCLINTOCK, 332
MCCLUNG, 97
MCCLURE, 126 206 242 298 308 363 367
MCCLURG, 256 312
MCCOMAS, 294
MCCONKEY, 353
MCCONNELL, 151 204 281 318 347
MCCOOK, 142 143 162 163
MCCOOL, 166 358
MCCORD, 212 302
MCCORMACK, 125 226 240
MCCORMICK, 134
MCCOWN, 206 334
MCCOY, 206
MCCRACKEN, 172 173 276
MCCRANER, 88
MCCRELLIS, 347
MCCULLOCK, 234
MCCULLOUGH, 350
MCCUTCHEN, 296
MCDERMOTT, 126
MCDILL, 240 248
MCDONALD, 200 211 257 260 266 278 280 359
MCDOUGALL, 202
MCEATHORN, 111
MCELHANEY, 298
MCENALLY, 100
MCEVOY, 95 347
MCFADDEN, 86 162 164
MCFARLAN, 340
MCFARLAND, 114 268 315 369
MCGAW, 249
MCGILLICUDDY, 181

MCGLAUGHRY, 316
MCGOWAN, 117 162 294
MCGRATH, 100 185
MCGRAW, 294
MCGREW, 204
MCGUIRE, 94 302
MCHANEY, 300
MCHENRY, 151 255 344
MCHUGH, 84 251
MCILWAIN, 150
MCINTIRE, 139 236
MCINTOSH, 159 190 298 334
MCINTYRE, 380
MCKAIG, 228
MCKEAIG, 56 61 320
MCKEAN, 121
MCKEE, 102 201 282 353
MCKEEN, 123
MCKENZIE, 124 138 147
MCKERNAN, 288
MCKIBBIN, 130
MCKIBBON, 173
MCKIM, 110
MCKINNEY, 100 189 204 206 234 262
MCKINSTRY, 156 351
MCKINZIE, 192
MCKNIGHT, 108 216 322 336
MCKOWN, 126
MCKRAIG, 73
MCLAIN, 205
MCLANE, 194 298 308
MCLEAN, 104 160 306 348
MCLENNAN, 144
MCLURE, 174
MCMAHON, 363
MCMAKEN, 122
MCMANNIS, 363
MCMANUS, 284
MCMASTER, 368
MCMASTERS, 134
MCMILLEN, 294

MCMILLIAN, 144
MCMOORE, 230
MCMURRAY, 126
MCMURTRY, 56 72
MCMURTY, 61 256 284
MCNABB, 226
MCNAIR, 85
MCNEAL, 152 278
MCNEIL, 148 344
MCNEILL, 93 242 250
MCNIEL, 106
MCNULTA, 22 268 342
MCOMBER, 373
MCPHAIL, 348
MCPHERSON, 136 282
MCROYALL, 334
MCSPAVIN, 320
MCVICKAR, 214
MCVICKER, 252
MCWILLIAMS, 88 182 314
MCWYLDER, 202
MEACHAM, 109 280 282
MEAD, 109 136 156
MEADOR, 254
MEATYARD, 135
MEDILL, 360 361
MEDLEY, 287
MEEK, 368
MEEKER, 204
MEGGUIRE, 296
MELLAR, 326
MELLOR, 286
MENDELL, 87 95
MENNET, 198
MERCER, 97 236
MERCHANT, 136
MERRIAM, 314
MERRICK, 183
MERRIFIELD, 196
MERRILL, 135 153 190
MERRIMAN, 105 133 351
MERRITT, 160 270 285 380

MERSEY, 89 98
MERTZ, 205
MERWIN, 252
MESLER, 210
MESSER, 155
MESSINGER, 106
METCALF, 94
METZGER, 306
MEYER, 167 359
MIHALOTZY, 13 128
MILCHIRST, 304
MILES, 114 134 135 150 174
MILHOLAND, 294
MILLER, 36 57 62 76 84 86
    104 106 117 118 136 142
    143 149 152 157 170 188
    200 201 210 211 241 254
    257 274 292 308 313 323
    338 359 379
MILLIKEN, 214 304
MILLIKIN, 298
MILLINGTON, 139
MILLITZER, 166
MILLS, 93 105 249 328 330
MILLSPAUGH, 139
MILMINE, 312
MINEAR, 130
MINER, 282
MINESSINGER, 274
MINNICK, 243
MINOR, 358
MINTER, 90
MISENHEIMER, 299
MISNER, 288
MITCHEL, 144
MITCHELL, 22 90 101 115
    130 139 152 188 200 212
    232 238 278 280 304 320
    330 342 360 371 378 381
MIZELL, 340
MOBERLY, 117
MOCK, 362 363

MOFFITT, 87 277 310 369
MOHR, 13
MONROE, 56 73 86 94 96 188
MONTAGUE, 125
MONTANDON, 182
MONTGOMERY, 165 210 226
    272 287 366
MOODY, 123 180 183
MOONEYHAM, 143 300
MOORE, 55 56 60 61 70 72 73
    102 109 112 114 115 126
    134 142-145 147 151 156
    161 170 200 208 216 222
    246 250 268 273 283 288
    296 310 314 334 341 344-
    346 348 350 359 367 380
    382
MORA, 55 60 68 206
MOREY, 92 154
MORGAN, 54 59 64 90 100
    124 146 148 246 327 330
    332 342 377
MORIARTY, 126
MORLAN, 161
MORO, 27
MORRAY, 355
MORRILL, 208
MORRIS, 108 109 143 171 216
    246 266 286 293 331 374
MORRISON, 25 29 31 37 55
    60 67 132 133 358 362 363
MORSE, 154 194 336
MORTON, 126 144 248 302
MOSES, 137
MOSIER, 117
MOSS, 196 200 236 282
MOSSMANS, 198
MOTHERSPAW, 226
MOULTON, 175 333
MOURER, 308
MOUTRAY, 276
MOWRING, 316

MOWRY, 224
MOXOM, 196 197
MOYERS, 334
MOZLEY, 320
MUDD, 344
MUELLER, 244
MUHLEMAN, 108
MULLEN, 156 318
MULLETT, 92
MULLIGAN, 24 28 31 54 59 65 126
MULLIN, 338
MUMFORD, 318 354
MUNGER, 345
MUNGERS, 280
MUNN, 86 89 94 158 330
MUNROE, 60 318
MUNSON, 101 374
MUNZ, 122
MURCHISON, 118
MURPHY, 125 126 132 134 142 154 160 181 196 197 223 260 300
MURRAY, 103 126 224 260 342
MUSGRAVE, 221
MUSSER, 172 345
MYERS, 87 170 302
NABB, 204
NAIRN, 274
NALE, 162
NANCE, 160
NAPIER, 107
NASE, 110 111
NASH, 290
NAUGHTON, 26 63
NAY, 84
NAYLOR, 345
NAZRA, 132
NEAL, 250 365 366
NEBLECK, 222
NEEDHAM, 243

NEELEY, 56 61 74 340
NEELY, 378
NEFF, 106
NEIGHMEYER, 101
NELSON, 142 248 249 280 296 354 358 359
NESBIT, 160
NEUMAN, 311
NEUSSEL, 244
NEVILL, 125
NEVILLE, 240
NEVIUS, 92 102
NEW, 328
NEWBARGER, 372
NEWBURY, 330
NEWCOMB, 132
NEWCOMER, 92
NEWLAN, 196
NEWLANDS, 111
NEWMAN, 120 263 282 355
NEWSHAM, 89 98 314
NEWTON, 137 155 184 294
NICESWANGER, 353
NICHEY, 353
NICHOLS, 232 303 316
NICHOLSON, 159 192 193 359
NICKLAUS, 196
NICOLET, 286
NICOLLS, 349
NIELL, 339
NIEMAN, 154
NIGLAS, 355
NILES, 56 61 74 84 338
NIMMO, 56 61 72 298
NISH, 271
NISPELL, 381
NISSEN, 370 371
NIXON, 147 284
NOBLE, 24 57 63 74 106 344
NODINE, 130
NOKES, 318

NOLEMAN, 21 343
NOLTE, 108
NOONAN, 136
NORFOLK, 354
NORMAN, 300
NORRIS, 334
NORTH, 120 365
NORTHCUTT, 226
NORTHROP, 164
NORTON, 109 114 146 164 186
NORVELL, 162
NOURSE, 190
NOYES, 93
NOYS, 358
NUGENT, 126
NULTON, 203
NYE, 228
O'BRIEN, 111
O'BRINE, 260
O'CANE, 126
O'CONNELL, 371 374
O'CONNER, 260 347 349 365
O'DEAR, 188
O'HARNETT, 26 63 374
O'HARRA, 369
O'KEAN, 156
O'LEARY, 57 62 76 261 378
O'MARAH, 260
O'MEARA, 55 61 71 260
O'NEAL, 193
O'REAR, 283
OAKLEY, 214
OAKS, 262
OATES, 99
ODELL, 316 368
OGDEN, 351
OGLESBY, 16 54 59 64 88 96 162 163
OHR, 202
OKESON, 268
OLDEN, 314

OLIN, 121
OLIVER, 150
OLMSTEAD, 369
OLNEY, 91 116 117 355
OLSEN, 153
OLSON, 153
OPITZ, 108
OPPENDICK, 166
ORGAN, 353
ORME, 56 60 71 268
ORMSBY, 116
OSBAND, 350
OSBORN, 130 142 158
OSBURN, 142
OSGOOD, 234 280
OSMAN, 288
OTIS, 194
OTMAN, 304
OVERMIRE, 204
OVERROCKER, 371
OVERSTREET, 170
OVERTON, 290
OWEN, 268
PACE, 240 300
PACK, 262
PADDOCK, 84 93 105 111 131 306 362 363
PADELFORD, 375
PADEN, 99
PAGE, 120 194 195
PAINE, 16 54 59 64 89 98 198 383
PAINTER, 316
PALMER, 20 22 54 59 64 108 162 171 232 246 289 343 371
PANLON, 338
PANN, 128
PANSE, 244
PARCEL, 205
PARISH, 139 163
PARK, 210 212 232

PARKE, 134 278 291
PARKER, 130 152 177 197 202 207 216 222 230 264 294 306 310 318 338 340 342 351
PARKHURST, 153
PARKS, 92 106 107 114 190 300 321 328 343
PARMETER, 234
PARROTT, 113 148
PARSONS, 237 246
PARTRIDGE, 95 106 272
PASHLEY, 182
PATE, 340
PATRICK, 112 148 344
PATTEN, 238
PATTERSON, 98 106 111 113 280 304
PATTISON, 86 123 292 326 344
PATTON, 238
PAUL, 349
PAVEY, 240
PAYNE, 100 154 187 208 209 242 266 300
PEACE, 132
PEAKE, 150
PEARCE, 262
PEARSE, 96
PEARSON, 136 142 248 383
PEASE, 126 349
PEASLEE, 290
PEATS, 114
PECK, 122 123 154 355
PEDAN, 109
PEEBLES, 322
PEET, 253
PEETZ, 166
PEGRAM, 95 292
PEMBERTON, 335
PENDERGAST, 139
PENDLETON, 303
PENFIELD, 131
PENIWELL, 353
PENNELL, 239
PENNEMAN, 114
PENNINGER, 298
PENY, 219
PEPOON, 273
PEPPER, 248
PERCE, 220
PERCIVAL, 333
PERDEW, 312
PERKINS, 224 363
PERRIN, 94
PERRINE, 99 298
PERRY, 15 184 333 336
PETER, 340
PETERS, 238 252 372
PETERSON, 286 355
PETRIE, 112 113 304
PETTS, 182
PFEIF, 196
PHARRES, 120
PHELPS, 144 184 259 371
PHILIPS, 89
PHILLIP, 29
PHILLIPS, 32 58 62 76 89 98 124 126 144 159 165 167 194 198 206 222 230 262 290 302 320 382
PHIPPS, 96 160
PICKERELL, 338
PICKETT, 180 218
PICQUET, 145
PIERCE, 144 152 174 234 242 246 250 271 302 355
PIERSOL, 266
PIERSON, 102 353
PIGGOTT, 212
PIKE, 173 332 351
PILCHER, 368
PILLOW, 320
PINCKARD, 98 343

PINCKLEY, 112
PINNEY, 340
PIPE, 212
PIPER, 212
PITMAN, 284
PITTMAN, 222
PLANT, 381
PLANTZ, 172
PLATTENBURG, 336
PLUMMER, 106 232 296 300
PLUNCKETT, 250
PLUNKETT, 156
POGUE, 212
POINDEXTER, 192 254
POLK, 132
POLLARD, 157
POLLOCK, 236 272 328
POLSGROVE, 170
POMEROY, 224
POMROY, 254
POND, 226
PONDS, 376
POOL, 272 339
POOLE, 94 174
POOR, 99
POPE, 12 146 322
PORTER, 106 134 288 320 345 359 377
POSEY, 202
POST, 55 60 68 88 96 139 198 242 286
POTEET, 108 310
POTHOFF, 84
POTTER, 117 146 186 290 314 326
POTTHOFF, 166
POTTS, 202
POULL, 128
POWELL, 58 62 76 109 121 164 224 228 276 280 330 381
POWERS, 154
PRALL, 312
PRATHER, 363
PRATT, 111 146 148 226 310 326 382
PRENTISS, 14-16 43 59 90
PRESCOTT, 176 252 288 338 377 383
PRESSON, 137 190 226
PRESTON, 164 264 276
PRICE, 231 238 254 362 363
PRIDE, 172 173
PRINCE, 358
PRIOR, 224
PRITCHARD, 107
PROBST, 124
PROCTOR, 289 342
PROEBESTING, 88
PRUNTY, 254
PUGH, 24 54 59 67 88 162 371
PULLEN, 120
PULLEY, 142 334
PULSIFER, 340
PURCELL, 226
PURDOM, 340
PURINTON, 188
PURONNET, 102
PURPLE, 214
PURVIANCE, 99
PURVIS, 340
PUTERBAUGH, 111 174 368
PUTNAM, 56 61 71 132 210 266 383
PYATT, 100 170 380 382
PYLE, 243
QUACKENBUSH, 148
QUIGG, 351
QUIN, 369
QUINTON, 119
QUIRK, 126 127
RACE, 101 321
RAE, 127
RAFFEN, 118

RAGAINS, 201
RAILSBACK, 96
RAINEY, 302
RAITH, 25 54 60 67 166
RALSTON, 112 136 137 328
RAMMING, 128
RANDALL, 180 224 226 270 314
RANDOLPH, 105 176 288
RANEY, 165 296
RANK, 177
RANKIN, 156 157 192 210 256 306 358
RANNY, 164
RANSOM, 92 102 224 254 380
RANY, 110 111
RAPELGE, 361
RAPP, 242
RATHBUN, 187
RATTERAY, 195
RAUM, 192 320
RAVENOT, 164
RAWALT, 358
RAWLINGS, 149
RAY, 274
RAYBURN, 342
RAYMON, 250
RAYMOND, 85 94 95 182 326 333 348
READ, 214 238
REAL, 261
REANS, 371
REARDEN, 54 138 218
REARDON, 25 59 66 232 310
REAVIS, 193
REDDIN, 176
REDDING, 188
REDDISH, 202
REDFERN, 355
REDFIELD, 116
REECE, 220 316 326
REED, 117 120 122 129 132 150 156 246 266 336 382
REEDER, 100
REES, 142 243
REESE, 142 242 334
REEVES, 31 32 55 60 69 220
REICHARDT, 129
REICHMAN, 136
REID, 111 171 208 225 338
REILLEY, 170
REILY, 366
REINER, 109
REITZELL, 172
REMINGTON, 228 230
RENBART, 262
RENWICK, 37 58 62 77 94 383
RESOR, 358
REX, 146
REYNOLDS, 114 177 209 216 237 247 345 358 375 380
RHOADS, 96 97
RHODES, 88 96 136 137 200
RHOR, 184
RICE, 144 256 258 284 320
RICH, 226 298 383
RICHARDS, 84 120 131 164 278 295 374
RICHARDSON, 206 254 272 358
RICHERSON, 158
RICHHELM, 244
RICHIE, 300
RICHMOND, 56 61 74 137 330 332
RICKARD, 276
RICKART, 180
RICKETTS, 207
RICKEY, 326
RIDDER, 113
RIDDLE, 332
RIDEOUT, 238

RIDER, 145 160 251 262
RIDGELY, 93 105
RIDGEWAY, 232
RIEDEL, 372
RIEGERT, 244
RIELING, 138
RIGBY, 143
RIGGS, 358
RILEY, 143 148 232 311 332
RINAKER, 56 61 73 322
RINER, 364
RING, 95 200
RIPLEY, 144
RIPPSTEIN, 109
RISLEY, 145 378
RISSER, 292
RITCHEY, 112 113 355 356
RITTER, 133 136
RIVES, 238
RIXLEBIN, 357
ROACH, 327
ROARK, 320 356
ROBARDS, 96
ROBB, 246
ROBBERDS, 143
ROBBINS, 114 188 195
ROBERTS, 88 94 137 146 164 190 231 248 250 282 363 366 377 382
ROBERTSON, 211 334
ROBINSON, 89 99 117 146 175 185 204 218 220 250 258 298 316 338 354 383
ROBSON, 114
ROCKWOOD, 92 351 362
RODECKER, 108
RODEEN, 194
RODEN, 370
RODGERS, 180 240 285 344 382
RODING, 156
RODRIG, 189

ROE, 146 210 248
ROEHRIG, 368
ROESSLER, 189
ROGERS, 29 58 62 76 85 101 110 111 240 242 252 290 306 377 378
ROGERSON, 101
ROGGE, 309
ROGUE, 118
ROHLSHAUSEN, 129
ROHRBOUGH, 316
ROLAND, 373
ROLER, 164 190
ROLLI, 376
ROLLINS, 171
ROLLMAN, 98
ROLSHANSON, 244
ROMAN, 89
ROMBAUER, 378
ROOD, 95
ROODHOUSE, 262
ROOT, 272 358
ROOTS, 242
ROPER, 139 193
ROSCOTTON, 49
ROSE, 93 114 167 183 273
ROSEBORA, 330
ROSENBROOK, 317
ROSENTHAL, 195
ROSETTE, 383
ROSS, 20 54 59 65 114 115 120 144 180 268 278 343 382
ROTE, 369
ROTH, 105 184
ROUNDS, 126
ROURKE, 31 57 62 76 379
ROUSE, 170 234 280
ROUSH, 172
ROUTT, 268
ROWAN, 272
ROWE, 112

ROWELL, 115 258
ROWETT, 87 94 95
ROWLAND, 90 93 100 119
ROWLEY, 170 349
ROY, 160
RUCKER, 145 366
RUCKSTAHL, 274
RUDD, 159
RUDDELL, 236
RUGAR, 284
RUGER, 232
RUGGLES, 342 347
RUHAAK, 296
RUMSEY, 377
RUSS, 128
RUSSELL, 135 139 147 206 242 247 248 266 349
RUST, 93 134 135 154
RUTGER, 105
RUTHERFORD, 56 61 71 90 274
RUTISHAUSER, 196
RUTISHOWSER, 196
RUTLEDGE, 108 202 348
RYAN, 49 55 61 69 114 127 138 188 230 262
RYDER, 214
RYMER, 316
RYNEARSON, 235 288
SACHS, 372
SACKER, 167
SACKETT, 163
SAGE, 106 220 304
SAINTCLAIR, 151
SAINTJOHN, 216
SALE, 328
SALIBURY, 272
SALLIE, 130
SALTER, 194
SAMIS, 264
SAMMIS, 358
SAMPLE, 112 282

SAMPSON, 259
SAMUELS, 311
SANBORN, 105
SANDERS, 115 142 242 327 347
SANDERSON, 368
SANDS, 86 365
SANFORD, 93 176 230
SANGER, 190
SAPP, 267
SARFF, 296
SARGEANT, 262
SARGENT, 262 307
SATTERFIELD, 270
SAUNDERS, 115
SAVAGE, 159
SAVOIL, 232
SAWIN, 196
SAWYER, 323 346
SAXTON, 172
SAYER, 88
SAYERS, 96
SCAGGAN, 248
SCAMMON, 364
SCANLAN, 214
SCANLAND, 116
SCARBOROUGH, 189
SCARITT, 100
SCATES, 380
SCHAERER, 368
SCHAMBECK, 21 57 63 76 376
SCHAUMB, 359
SCHEEL, 98
SCHEINMINGER, 89
SCHEITTEIN, 89
SCHELL, 353 354
SCHELLENGER, 271
SCHEMERHORN, 218
SCHENERMANN, 125
SCHERMERHORN, 264
SCHEVE, 98

SCHIFFERSTEIN, 145
SCHILLING, 194
SCHIMMINGER, 166
SCHLAG, 97
SCHLOETZER, 244
SCHLOSSER, 96
SCHLUND, 218
SCHMITT, 134 167
SCHNEBLY, 234
SCHOLES, 297
SCHOMMAKER, 111
SCHONDER, 244
SCHOONMAKER, 281
SCHRIVER, 330
SCHRYVER, 332
SCHULTE, 296
SCHWARTZ, 62 380
SCHWEINFURTH, 128 129
SCHWERDSFEGER, 366
SCIBIRD, 220
SCOGGINS, 320
SCOTT, 15 19 109 118 131 157
    161 165 193 197 248-250
    274 290 359 369
SCOVILLE, 265
SCRIBNER, 218
SCUDDER, 326
SCUDMORE, 240 300
SEAMAN, 104 322
SEARCH, 351
SEARIGHT, 144
SEARING, 159
SEARLE, 367
SEARS, 111 120 134
SEARY, 159
SEATON, 124
SECORD, 234
SEDWICK, 284
SEELBACH, 191
SEELBACK, 262
SEELEY, 122
SEELY, 171

SEGUIN, 232
SEIBEL, 57
SEKILLMAN, 342
SELEY, 353
SELLAN, 105
SELLAR, 105
SELLARDS, 158
SELLERS, 153 177 276
SELLON, 136
SEVER, 279
SEWARD, 220
SEWELL, 332
SEXTON, 214 224 320
SEYMOUR, 171 282
SHAFER, 283
SHANE, 181
SHANLY, 127
SHANNON, 345
SHAPLEY, 110
SHARP, 214 239
SHASS, 322
SHATTUCK, 363
SHAW, 92 97 102 153 173 190
    230 262 278 284 316 358
    365
SHEAFER, 350
SHEAR, 364
SHEARER, 27 37
SHEARS, 63 371
SHEDD, 284
SHEELEY, 90
SHEETS, 264
SHEETZ, 88 97
SHEFFIELD, 272 362 364
SHEILDS, 250
SHELDON, 134 135 361
SHELEY, 100
SHELLENBERGER, 347
SHELTON, 282 378
SHEPARDSON, 351
SHEPHERD, 369
SHEPLEY, 119

SHERER, 375
SHERIDAN, 255 256 260
SHERIFF, 200
SHERLOCK, 350
SHERMAN, 55 60 70 110 131 152 205 256 370
SHIBLEY, 109
SHIELDS, 121 234 370
SHINN, 226 284
SHIPLEY, 134
SHIRLEY, 161
SHLEICH, 190
SHOAFF, 150
SHOCKEY, 293
SHOLL, 316
SHOOP, 247
SHORT, 90 142 162 200 251 312 355
SHOUP, 292 308
SHULTZ, 303
SHUMWAY, 109
SHUTT, 365
SICKLES, 362
SIDES, 134
SIDWELL, 296
SIEZICK, 172
SIGLEY, 326
SILFVERSPARRE, 378
SILL, 360
SILLS, 194
SILVERSPARRE, 29 57 62 76
SIMISON, 126
SIMMONS, 90 109 236
SIMMS, 272
SIMONS, 183
SIMPKINS, 212
SIMPSON, 109 187 288 302 320
SINKS, 150
SIPPLE, 143
SIRPLESS, 351
SISK, 143

SISNEY, 242
SISSON, 156
SITTON, 97 278
SITTS, 371
SKEELS, 130
SKILLMAN, 262
SKINNER, 92 186 264 356
SLACK, 318
SLADE, 370
SLATER, 369
SLATON, 275
SLATTERY, 186 191
SLAUGHTER, 149 159 330
SLAVENS, 226
SLENGER, 192
SLOAN, 56 61 73 228 326 356
SLOCUM, 310
SMALL, 225
SMART, 130
SMEDLEY, 222
SMEIDELL, 122
SMITH, 13 15 20 22-24 26 29 54 56 59-61 63 64 66 67 74 90 94 95 97 100 107-115 117 123 125 128 138 139 144 147 149 150-154 160 164 170 171 173 176 180 186 190 196 202 208 212 213 218 224 226 230 232 234 240 242 246 256 258 262 265 270 272 274 278 284 286 287 290 302 310 318 326 336 342 350 354 360 363 365 375 378 380 381
SMYSER, 330
SMYTH, 151
SNEDAKER, 288
SNEED, 176
SNELL, 56 61 72 294
SNELLING, 366
SNOOKS, 150

SNOW, 108
SNOWDEN, 158
SNYDER, 143 173 181 185 199 220 222 246 282 355
SOLENBERGER, 344
SOLLARS, 341
SOLLENBARGER, 346
SOLOMON, 244
SOMERVILLE, 143
SOMMERS, 296
SOMMERVILLE, 113
SONGER, 123
SOUTER, 303
SOUTH, 130
SOUTHARD, 174
SOUTHER, 374
SOUTHERLAND, 306
SOUTHWARD, 135
SOUTHWORTH, 86 271 361
SPALDING, 120 184 257 304
SPANGLER, 317
SPARKS, 266 323 349
SPARRESTROM, 381
SPARSTROM, 29
SPAULDING, 104 275
SPEAR, 264
SPENCER, 258 278 379
SPERRY, 357
SPICER, 120
SPILLER, 300
SPINK, 84 258
SPOENEMANN, 244
SPONABLE, 270
SPOONER, 340
SPORRE, 244
SPRAGUE, 139
SPRING, 132 254
SPRINGER, 136 365
SPROUSE, 160
SQUIRE, 109 228
SQUIRES, 307
SROUFE, 304

STAATS, 151
STACY, 355
STADDEN, 344
STAFFORD, 326
STAGE, 330
STAGGERS, 293
STAHL, 90 100 358
STALEY, 117
STAMPOFFSKI, 363
STANBAUGH, 231
STANDAN, 128 129
STANFORD, 206
STANSIFER, 124
STANTON, 31 46 308
STANWAY, 284
STARK, 184
STARKEY, 198 207
STARKLOFF, 166
STARLING, 195
STARR, 187 357
STARRING, 55 60 69 172 224 380
STARTSMAN, 88 96
STAUFFER, 196
STEAN, 310
STEARNS, 124 234 248 286
STEEL, 370
STEELE, 122 132 162 311
STEEN, 163
STEERE, 268
STEFFENS, 129
STEFFERS, 129
STEGER, 381
STEGNER, 229
STEINBECK, 58
STEINSCKE, 240
STEN, 128
STENBECK, 381
STEPHANI, 166 167
STEPHENS, 340 356
STEPHENSON, 93 104 108 176 246 264 365 378

STERRETT, 180
STEVENS, 121 124 173 234 288 328 343 375 383
STEVENSON, 122 145 164 226 362 363 382
STEWARD, 328
STEWART, 26 37 57 63 113 118 139 156 173 174 176 208 210 242 254 270 280 296 366 370 371 374
STICKLE, 345
STICKNEY, 224
STIENBECK, 29 62 76
STIERLIN, 124
STILES, 302 315 338
STILLEY, 334
STILLINGS, 383
STIMSON, 173
STINGER, 204
STINNETT, 366
STINSON, 126 201
STIPP, 49 208
STOBIE, 136 278
STOCK, 128
STOCKDALE, 115 286 358
STOCKTON, 224
STOKES, 36 37 58 62 77 176 201 298 383
STOLBRAND, 58 62 76 380 381
STOLL, 359
STONAX, 153
STONE, 138 146 344
STONER, 234
STOOKEY, 198
STORCH, 372
STORCK, 167
STOUFFER, 264
STOUGHTON, 332
STOUT, 134 138 216 224
STOVER, 222 302
STRAIT, 162

STRASSINGER, 166
STRATTON, 240 359 368
STRAUN, 288
STRAWN, 288
STRICKLAND, 308
STRICKLIN, 143
STRONG, 109 228 370
STRUISBIG, 167
STUART, 24 31 55 60 68 69 75 160 161 164 190 202 216 260 365
STUBER, 369 372
STUEVEN, 244
STUFF, 164
STULL, 200
STURGESS, 88 96 97
STURR, 316
STURTEVANT, 348
STYLES, 359
SUITER, 270
SULLIVAN, 95 284 298 347 361
SUMME, 220
SUMMERS, 130 160 222
SUMMERVILLE, 112
SUMNER, 135
SURBER, 151
SUTHERLAND, 153 156 306
SUTTON, 188 226
SUYDAM, 286
SWAIN, 93 105 165 373
SWAN, 104 194 383
SWANWICK, 124 125
SWARINGUIN, 137
SWARTHOUT, 180
SWARTOUT, 164
SWARTS, 191
SWARTZ, 162
SWEENEY, 182 184
SWEENY, 94
SWEET, 111
SWIFT, 13 14 23 111 228

SWINDELL, 334
SWORTZCOPE, 142
SYKES, 246
SYLLA, 101
TABLER, 150 206
TAGGART, 103 266
TAGGERT, 130
TAIT, 100
TALBOT, 372
TANGUARY, 192
TANNATT, 342
TANNEY, 210
TARPLEY, 273 356
TASSEL, 149
TAYLOR, 23 57 62 76 96 112
    113 120-122 126 132 160
    163 203 213 216 228 236
    239 272 300 308 312 318
    326 339 347 351 360 377
TAZEWELL, 190
TEAHON, 261
TEDEMAN, 98
TEED, 156 172
TEFFT, 218
TEMPLE, 119
TENNEY, 250 326 344
TERRY, 290 326 344
TEWKSBURY, 288
THAYER, 122 353
THIELEMAN, 37 76
THIELMAN, 26 376
THOMAS, 19 30 103 111 128
    150 184 224 252 255 256
    284 290 315 383
THOMPSON, 106 108 117 120
    130 136 152 160 173 185
    192 208 228 231
THORP, 117 331
THRASH, 200
THROOP, 352
THRUSH, 174
THURTSON, 190

TICE, 222
TICHNER, 156
TIDBALL, 150
TIEDEMAN, 89
TIFFANY, 120 211
TIFIELD, 360
TILFORD, 348
TILLSON, 90 100
TILTON, 182 226
TIMMONS, 150
TIMMONY, 380
TIMMS, 264
TINKHAM, 132 133
TIPPETT, 296
TIPTON, 95 286 345
TIRMENSTEIN, 381
TISDALE, 175
TITSWORTH, 256
TITUS, 274
TOBEY, 175 210 377
TOBIAS, 121
TOBIEN, 166
TOBIN, 197
TODD, 218 232
TOLER, 27 55 60 68 200 298
TOMPKINS, 114
TOPLIFF, 278
TOPPING, 300
TORRENT, 277
TOURTILLOTT, 230
TOUSLEY, 219 248
TOWLE, 116
TOWNE, 102
TOWNER, 104 158 222 380
    381
TOWNES, 143
TOWNSEND, 144 164 170 174
    273 350
TRABUE, 373
TRACY, 382
TRAFTON, 359
TRASK, 350 361

TREGO, 284
TRIBLE, 274
TRIMBLE, 204 205
TRIPP, 369
TROUTNER, 136
TROVILLION, 356
TROWBRIDGE, 96
TRUAX, 151
TRUE, 27 55 60 68 84 86 156
    162 188 204 216 351
TRUMBULL, 272 306
TRYON, 270
TUCKER, 31 32 55 60 69 84
    89 132 175 218 257
TUFTS, 343
TULLIS, 284
TUNISON, 150
TUNNISON, 121
TUPPER, 56 61 73 162 312
TURCHIN, 20 54 59 65 118
TURLEY, 292
TURNBULL, 152 246
TURNER, 20 54 59 64 110 276
    294 296
TURNEY, 163 353 365
TURPIN, 227
TUTHILL, 117 347
TUTT, 312
TUTTEN, 99
TUTTLE, 138 258 292
TWITCHELL, 340
TYLER, 307 316
TYNER, 156
ULLRICH, 212
ULM, 99 145 160
UNDERWOOD, 224 226
UPCHURCH, 335
UPDEGRAFF, 26 57 63 74 133
    353
URQUHART, 328
USREY, 150
UTLEY, 230

UTTER, 310
VAIL, 174
VALENTINE, 214
VALLETTE, 290
VALZAH, 110
VANANTWERP, 262
VANARMAN, 196 332
VANBLACK, 360
VANBRUNT, 286
VANBUREN, 218
VANBUSKIRK, 264
VANCE, 123 238
VANCLEVE, 89
VANDENBURG, 88
VANDENBURGH, 196
VANDERANDER, 286
VANDEREN, 131
VANDERIN, 238
VANDEWATER, 144
VANDEWORT, 170
VANDOLSON, 363
VANDORSTAN, 351
VANDYKE, 377
VANFLEET, 330
VANGUNDY, 268
VANHISE, 292
VANHOFF, 308
VANHOOSER, 349
VANHORN, 128 129
VANKENDLE, 240
VANMETER, 308
VANOSDEL, 199
VANPATTON, 360
VANPELT, 152
VANSTA, 268
VANSTEINBURG, 194
VANTUYL, 100
VANVECKTEN, 214
VANVLACK, 326
VANVLECK, 236
VANWINKLE, 144
VARDAN, 164

VARGES, 218
VARNER, 130
VARNEY, 312
VASSEUR, 371
VAUGHAN, 330
VAUGHN, 36 37 58 61 62 77 185 186 348 355 383
VAUGHT, 255
VEATCH, 198
VEDDER, 202
VERBECK, 360
VERE, 102
VERNARD, 345
VERNAY, 102
VERNON, 237
VEST, 132
VIEREGG, 345
VIFQUAIN, 274
VINCENT, 170 218 272
VINSON, 329
VIRDEN, 218
VISE, 356
VOCKE, 128
VOELLINGER, 134
VOGEL, 212 214
VOGELER, 98
VORHIS, 264
VORIS, 156 359
VORREY, 230
VORTREES, 276
VOSS, 26 27 57 63 75 153 355 370
VREDENBERG, 365
VREDENBURG, 365 366
VROOMAN, 95 349
WADDELL, 92 102
WADE, 277
WADLEIGH, 289
WADSWORTH, 107 121
WAGENFUCHER, 166
WAGENSELLER, 354
WAGER, 105

WAGGONER, 368
WAGNER, 128 149 369
WAGONER, 235
WAIT, 181
WAITE, 93 105 360 361
WAKEFIELD, 139 173
WAKEMAN, 152
WALBRIGHT, 192
WALDEN, 268
WALDOCK, 110 111
WALKER, 84 94 115 136 148 152 153 158 176 200 250 270 302 316 332 334 345 365
WALKLEY, 336
WALL, 130
WALLACE, 16 54 59 64 92 102 106 126 227 312 350 351
WALLER, 94 159 295
WALLIS, 314 362
WALROD, 103
WALSER, 121 206
WALSH, 114 124 286
WALTER, 350
WALTERS, 22 320 336 342
WALTHER, 166
WALWORTH, 164
WARD, 93 94 105 109 148 184 229 242 370
WARDLAW, 351
WARDNER, 104 320
WARE, 121
WARMOTH, 162
WARNER, 56 61 72 120 158 162 187 204 244 290 332 361 363 370
WARNING, 150
WARRELL, 174
WARREN, 163 296 342
WARRINGTON, 226
WARROLL, 236
WARWICK, 163

WASHBURN, 330 359
WASSON, 254
WATERBURY, 362
WATERHOUSE, 29 57 62 76 378
WATERMAN, 182 280 290
WATERS, 55 60 70 101 136 248 344
WATKINS, 105 258
WATSON, 112 113 116 125 149 161 230 276 318 367
WATTS, 143 256 276 339
WAY, 164
WAYNE, 110
WEAKLEY, 181 345
WEAVER, 116 147 170 222
WEBB, 24 54 60 67 89 98 164 234
WEBBER, 116 193 244 289 350 371
WEBER, 113
WEBSTER, 108 353 359 374 377
WEDGEWOOD, 270
WEEK, 239
WEEKS, 182
WEENS, 177
WEID, 245
WEIDER, 349
WEIDMAN, 294
WEIGEL, 244
WEIGLE, 122
WEIR, 374
WEIRICK, 195 363
WEISS, 347
WEIYRICK, 98
WELCH, 195 274
WELD, 148
WELDON, 191
WELLMAN, 177
WELLS, 112 156 184 185 258 290 304 318

WELSH, 186 192
WELSIE, 284
WEMPLE, 350 351
WENDT, 128
WENT, 107
WENTZ, 183
WENZELL, 278
WERTHER, 372
WERTZ, 133
WESCOTT, 148 156 182
WEST, 130 136 198 217 307
WESTBROOK, 363
WESTERFIELD, 88
WESTERMAN, 89
WESTERMANN, 167
WESTFALL, 112 250 304
WESTLEY, 305
WETHERELL, 118
WETMORE, 104 270 330
WETZEL, 88 97
WHALEN, 96
WHALEY, 378
WHALLON, 230
WHARTON, 118
WHEATON, 97
WHEELER, 94 115 159 186 238 242 313
WHEELOCK, 111 353
WHETMORE, 93
WHIPPLE, 158 191
WHITAKER, 314 344
WHITALL, 380
WHITE, 24 54 60 66 112 134 142 154 156 181 184 188 235 258 260 312 316 377
WHITEHILL, 132
WHITEHURST, 156
WHITEMAN, 216
WHITESIDE, 138
WHITING, 55 60 70 121 138 254 256 258 345
WHITLOCK, 343

WHITMIRE, 192 355
WHITMORE, 120
WHITMYER, 228
WHITNELL, 142
WHITNEY, 173 272 360 381
WHITSIT, 356
WHITSON, 183
WHITTAKER, 320
WHITTEMORE, 381
WHITTLE, 224
WICKERSHAM, 365
WICKS, 280
WICKSTRUM, 194
WIDMER, 103 288
WIGGS, 200
WIGHTMAN, 158
WIKE, 172
WILBANKS, 200
WILBER, 163
WILCOX, 102 184 185 338
WILD, 128
WILDER, 37 159 172 375
WILDERBOOR, 221
WILDERMAN, 314
WILEY, 150 198 204 314 353 359
WILHELMI, 129 196
WILKIN, 339
WILKINS, 114 122 175 188 305 338
WILKINSON, 266 353 363
WILLARD, 23 57 62 76 239 274 276 298 369 377
WILLENTZKI, 210
WILLETT, 259
WILLETTE, 156
WILLIAMS, 27 29 55 60 68 93 97 102 104 107 108 115 117 119 121 130 131 134 147 150 159 165 170 176 188 192 208 224 228 230 232 238 240 252 258 276 280

WILLIAMS (Continued) 292 295 306 310 312 316 332 334 345 380 383
WILLIAMSON, 142
WILLIAN, 327
WILLIFORD, 98
WILLIGE, 218
WILLIS, 37 142 152 176 285 341 351 375
WILLISON, 115 286
WILLS, 286 358
WILLSON, 155 172 196 308 326
WILMARTH, 185
WILMERTH, 158
WILSHIRE, 330
WILSO, 116
WILSON, 24 29 55 60 67 90 96 97 100 101 112 113 123 125 134 153 163 184 204 205 210 212 218 220 240 262 280 285 308 320 328 353 356 365 366 374 383
WILT, 359
WINANS, 130
WINCHESTER, 184 226
WINDSOR, 313
WINEGARDNER, 163
WINER, 126
WING, 49 81 361
WINNE, 190
WINNIE, 234
WINSHIP, 146
WINSITT, 101
WINSLOW, 197
WINSTON, 264
WINTERS, 198
WISDOM, 248
WISE, 132
WISEMAN, 100 124
WISHARD, 353
WISHHARD, 220

WISMER, 294
WISNER, 274
WISWELL, 262
WITHERS, 353
WOLCOTT, 101
WOLF, 181 282 372
WOLFE, 120
WOLFORD, 155
WOLSHIMER, 122
WOLZ, 166
WOOD, 90 91 100 114 115 118 119 148 201 210 270 274 276 288 294 314 353 377 383
WOODALL, 113
WOODARD, 378
WOODBURY, 172
WOODCOCK, 265
WOODRUFF, 159 188 234 280 290 306
WOODS, 228 240 310 318 340 369
WOODSON, 287
WOODWARD, 124 132 158 163 170 238 270 332 340 356
WOODWORTH, 238 377
WOOLARD, 302
WOOLLARD, 133
WOOLSEY, 358
WORCESTER, 351
WORDEN, 368 369
WORKMAN, 308
WORLEY, 286 318
WORTH, 347
WORTHANHAM, 281
WORTHEN, 135

WORTHINGTON, 86
WRIGHT, 90 108 114 126 130 145 146 186 190 224 240 250 254 268 282 286 294 304 320 342 377
WUERPLE, 167
WUNDT, 204
WYATT, 86 205 282
WYCKOFF, 286
WYCOFF, 284
WYCOUGH, 301
WYLIE, 175
WYMAN, 20 54 59 64 84 106
YAPLES, 348
YARNELL, 115
YARYAN, 358
YATES, 3 7 12 13 15 19 24 25 30 31 40 46 47 251 292 306
YEAGER, 95
YELTON, 157
YOHO, 150
YONSON, 266
YORK, 145 188 265
YOST, 342
YOUNG, 118 125 152 156 173 176 184 210 238 276 302 316 341 377
YOUNGBLOOD, 142
ZEARING, 194
ZEIDLER, 97
ZEIGLER, 294 308 369
ZEIS, 240
ZICK, 96
ZIMMERMAN, 149 349
ZINSER, 252
ZOLMAN, 181

www.ingramcontent.com/pod-product-compliance
Lightning Source LLC
Chambersburg PA
CBHW060937230426
43665CB00015B/1970